BUSINESS HISTORY OF GENERAL TRADING COMPANIES

BUSINESS

The International Conference on Business History 13

HISTORY

Proceedings of the Fuji Conference

OF GENERAL

edited by SHIN'ICHI YONEKAWA   HIDEKI YOSHIHARA

TRADING

COMPANIES

HD
2756
.I58
1987

UNIVERSITY OF TOKYO PRESS

The Fuji International Conference on Business History has been held annually since 1974, with the third series beginning in 1984. We would like to express our deepest gratitude to the Taniguchi Foundation for their continuing sponsorship of the Conference.

Published by University of Tokyo Press
Printed in Japan

ISBN 4–13–047033–7 (UTP 47337)
ISBN 0–86008–408–6

Contents

Notes on Style and Usage

1. Japanese personal names appearing in this volume are given
in the order customary in Japan: family name followed by given
name. The exceptions are the names of the editors and contributors,
which are given in Western order to avoid confusion for librarians
and bibliographers.

2. Macrons have been used to indicate elongated vowel sounds
in transliterated Japanese terms, personal names, and names of
organizations. They have not been used, however, in names of
places, e.g. Osaka or Kyushu.

3. Transliterated titles of Japanese language books with no
English translation are given with only the initial word capitalized;
English-language book titles have all important words capitalized.

Introduction

Shin'ichi Yonekawa
Hitotsubashi University

I

The purpose of this conference was to place general trading companies—particularly those of Japan—in comparative and historical perspective.

The definition of general trading companies has so far differed from one scholar to another: economists have emphasized their financing and organizing functions, while historians have thought a wider definition more useful, and have defined the general trading company as "a firm that trades all kinds of goods with all nations of the world," as Hideki Yoshihara has done in his paper. We use the latter definition here because it makes comparative study more fruitful.

Japan's huge trading companies, the *sōgō shōsha*, are impressive, and therefore well known internationally. Today's general trading companies, however, have not descended unchanged from their formative period. The majority of them remained specialty merchant firms for a long time, later diversifying into mature general trading companies. In the process they passed through several phases:

(1) exporting and importing to and from an area or a country;
(2) multiplying the commodities to be handled in an area or a country;
(3) exporting and importing a variety of commodities to several areas or countries;
(4) dealing with a variety of commodities on a global scale.

As they pass through these phases, the mature general trading companies set about financing and organizing businesses, coming to own a large number of subsidiaries. In due course trading companies diversify into other services.

This is not meant to be a treatise on chronological development from specialty trading firms to general trading companies. What I want to point out is that a wide gray area exists between the two kinds of companies. The uniqueness of Japanese general trading companies in terms of the scale and range of their business activities is undeniable, if we limit our consideration to the present world. Most scholars have assumed that general trading companies are peculiar to Japan. However, if we can develop a theory as to why a specialty merchant firm grew into a general trading company in Japan, such a theory has to be applicable to a company in the West as well.

Even if general trading companies do not now exist in other countries, this does not necessarily mean that they will not in the future. The governments of many countries are keen on fostering general trading companies by means of the enactment of laws, and it is useful to examine these fledgling general trading companies from a historical point of view.

In comparison with manufacturing companies, we have been little interested in the history of trading companies in the West. *Times 1000: The World's Top Companies* lists a number of international trading companies, but many of them are privately owned, so their business records are difficult to investigate. Philippe Chalmin's paper, which outlines their history and present status, is invaluable in this regard. Is there any possibility that these firms will grow into general trading companies? Can the *sōgō shōsha* keep their leading role in Japan's economy in the future? Participants shared their interest in these contemporary problems in the discussion sessions, although the majority of papers treat the period prior to the Second World War.

II

Information on contemporary general trading companies is fairly well diffused among foreign scholars, in particular those studying Japanese businesses and Japan's economy. When we place trading companies in a historical and comparative context, however, we have to pay attention to a few aspects which have tended to escape our notice in the present-day world. It will be of some service to us to clarify these aspects at the start.

When we trace the histories of large companies back to the time of the First World War, the most remarkable characteristic is the speed with which trading companies emerged and disappeared compared with industrial companies. To be engaged in foreign trade at the time, Japanese had to get over a number of hurdles, among them what scholars have called an information gap. Such business groups as Kuhara and Furukawa failed to make a success of their trading companies even in the booming years of the First World War. The commodities most traded at that time were primary goods that tended to be subject to wide price fluctuations. Decisions had to be made quickly, sometimes without the permission of headquarters.

The consequence is that the success of general trading companies depends to a considerable extent on an effective common account and internal auditing system, which is closely associated with modern organization-building. Educated salaried managers (including middle-management employees) are essential, because it is such people who can expand the companies they are serving into general trading companies. Hiroaki Yamazaki has mentioned these factors in his paper. A modern managerial enterprise, to use A. D. Chandler, Jr.'s terminology, is a prerequisite for establishment as a general trading company.

Compared with industrial companies, traditional merchant firms have a far more difficult time converting to modern enterprises. Family businesses in the industrial sector have often been forced to introduce technological innovations in order to survive, with the result that they have had to raise money on the stock exchange, and the family's controlling power has been weakened. In contrast, the impact of technological innovation is not direct in the case of trading firms, so that they tend to change less, sticking to dealing with commodities with which they have experience. The consequence was that in the West industrial enterprises took the lead over trading companies in modernization, and the integration of manufacturing companies raised barriers against trading companies' diversification of their businesses.

Industrial firms integrated their functions to the equivalent of general trading companies, to use the terminology in H. Yoshihara's paper. These processes are described in the papers by W. J. Reader and W. Feldenkirchen. In the West, therefore, where manufacturing companies started integrating earlier than those in Japan, foreign trade firms declined or lost the opportunity for diversification.

Japan was obliged to open the door to foreign merchants in the 1860s. Beginning foreign trade at the government's suggestion, Japanese traders had to import such soft technologies as accounting techniques, foreign exchange procedures, and insurance, in the same way industrial companies were importing hard technologies. In fact, Japanese firms for foreign trade had to be newly created. Here was an opportunity to found a modern trading company entirely free from the business tradition of the Tokugawa period, and this was the case with Mitsui Bussan. It was a closed company until 1942, but in fact salaried managers had controlled management since its foundation. Mitsui Bussan was an exception with its success in building a modern organization. Cotton importers and textile exporters like Itō Chū and Marubeni were slow in developing such organizations, which is one of the major reasons why they could grow into full-fledged general trading companies only after the Second world war.

The relationship of general trading companies to the business groups or *zaibatsu* is also important. It has often been maintained that the two were so closely related that the existence of a business group was a prerequisite for the successful establishment of a trading company. This is not always correct. A general trading company can be placed in one of two categories, depending on whether it came into being after the business group was founded or constituted a core company of a business group, actively participating in forming the group. Mitsui Bussan is of the latter type. It is true that banks have taken a leading role in the amalgamation of trading companies, especially in the postwar period. It is, however, also true that they did not participate much in the process of reconstructing Mitsui Bussan and Mitsubishi Shōji after their postwar dissolution: the small-scale trading companies founded by ex-employees of both companies were not necessarily associated with a bank, as had been the case before the Second World War. Trading firms specializing in textile goods were closely allied with specific banks long before they grew into general trading companies in the years following the Second World War. Financial support by a bank is not a sufficient condition for the emergence of mature general trading companies.

The last but not least important elements are the extent of the economy's dependence on foreign trade and of government support for general trading companies. Japan's dependence on foreign trade was not until recently very large compared with Western countries, but trade has always been of strategic importance. The Japanese government was eager to foster general trading companies, and the national consensus that foreign trade was worthwhile enabled the new companies to recruit able, educated staffs. As Glen Porter's paper properly points out, there have been few opportunities for the formation of general trading companies in countries like the U.S.A., where wholesale merchants have had ample chance for domestic investment (in organizing retailing businesses, for example) and industrial companies early started integrating their sales functions, and where the economy's dependence on foreign trade has been negligible.

Economic circumstances, however, should be considered a necessary, but not a sufficient, condition in explaining why general trading companies emerged in some countries and not in others. Some scholars emphasize the entry barriers Japan faced as a latecomer. This is stimulating but leaves unexplained why even in Japan some companies succeeded in diversifying while others remained specialty trading companies until the years following the Second World War. This is one reason we should focus our attention on the companies' internal organization and management policy.

Selected Bibliography and Criticism

A great number of writings on general trading companies have appeared, although most are not academic works. Furthermore, many historical works refer to general trading companies only as constituent parts of business groups, not describing in detail their internal managerial problems, organizational working, and financing arrangements (13, 22). The few studies that focus on specific companies often rely extensively on interviews and other oral materials.

It is during the past couple of decades that works on the business history of general trading companies have begun to come out (24). A major contribution has been the publication of voluminous company histories by companies themselves. Historians have in some cases participated in their compiling and writing. In particular, the publication of a history of Mitsui Bussan in 1977 contributed greatly to historical understanding (15). Almost all the general trading companies have published company histories. Mitsubishi Shōji has just published its company history of two volumes (12). The latest contribution, by a general trading company originally in the textile business, is Marubeni's history (9). Small-scale general trading companies like Itōman have also compiled company histories (3). However, only Mitsui Bussan has a short history in English (14).

There are even some works dating from the prewar period. Itō Chū published a booklet in 1937, which outlined its business activities at the time (2). The history of the bankruptcy of Suzuki Shōten, which competed with Mitsui Bussan during the First World War, has been discussed in a business history conference volume (6). The history of Takata Shōkai, however, which was mainly engaged in importing machinery and was dissolved in 1925, is still to be written.

Business historians have not been slow to work on the history of general trading companies. The eighth annual meeting of Japan's Business History Society, held in 1972, focused on their origin and development (8, 16). The work so far, however, has concentrated on the prewar period. As a result, dialogue between historians and economists on general trading companies has not been lively. While historians' attention has been focused on the companies' origins, economists have concentrated on their current and changing functions (5, 10, 34). This unfortunate situation makes it almost impossible to outline their history as a whole from a comparative point of view. Stress should be put again on the facts that Mitsui Bussan had a strong influence as the model general trading company and that, in spite of this, the majority of present full-fledged companies attained their diversification in the postwar period.

The volume (in Japanese) based on papers presented at the 1972 Business History Society meeting mentioned above is comprehensive and well balanced except that it includes just one paper concerning trading company development in the postwar period (16). Umezu has written two books—one, which outlines their development, aimed at general readers, and one that treats mainly their recent business activities (25, 26). Two volumes on specific *zaibatsu* outline the histories of Mitsui Bussan and Mitsubishi Shōji (11, 29). In English, Yoshihara Kunio's *Sogo Shosha: The Vanguard of the Japanese Economy* focuses mainly on the development of general trading companies in both the pre- and postwar periods; his arguments on the growth of general trading companies in Japan are persuasive, although he does not take a comparative perspective (33). He emphasizes a "cultural gap" peculiar to Meiji Japan which necessitated the emergence of general trading companies that were independent of manufacturing companies.

In English, *The Sōgō Shōsha: Japan's Multinational Trading Companies* by Young aimed to analyze contemporary problems these companies are facing, presenting a number of useful tables of their activities. His historical description, however, is not always exact (35). Yamamura analyzed the growth of general trading companies from the point of view of transaction cost of modern economics. His work is most stimulating, but one-sided in the sense that he does not explain why his analysis is not applicable to companies in the West (27). Yamazawa's work aims to demonstrate, using the regression method, that the replacement of foreign merchant houses by native trading companies contributed to the remarkable increase of Japan's foreign trade (30). Haber wrote *L'Empire du Commerce Levant* for general readers; in it he speaks highly of Japanese general trading companies as contributors to high economic growth (4).

Nakagawa's *Organized Entrepreneurship* was a pioneering work from the comparative point of view (19). My 1985 article aimed at being a comparative study, looking for reasons why general trading companies became important in Japan but not in Western countries (31).

A number of works on important functions of general trading companies have come out in Japanese or English. Mitsubishi Shōji's prewar activities in the U.S.A. were detailed by Kawabe (7). Two articles described in detail Mitsui Bussan's business in collusion with military forces in Manchuria and China in the 1930s (20, 21). Some agent contracts in the prewar period have been analyzed (28, 32). Morikawa first paid attention to the creation of an organization and the common account system in Mitsui Bussan (17). He also attached importance to human resources as a major reason for the growth of general trading companies (18). Their investment policy in the postwar period was the focus of two articles in English (1, 23). Debates on why general trading companies were created in Japan have attracted scholars' particular interest, as is mentioned in Hideki Yoshihara's paper presented at this conference.

NOTES*

1. Emori, M., Japanese General Trading companies: Their Functions and Roles, in P. Uri, ed., *Trade and Investment Policies for the Seventies*, New York, 1971.
2. Itō Chū Ltd., *An Outline of C. Itoh., Ltd.*, 1937.
3. Itoman Ltd., *Itoman Hyakunen Shi* (An Centenary History of Itoman and Co. Ltd.), 1983.
4. Haber, D., *L'Empire du commerce Levant*, Paris, 1974.
5. Heiwa Keizai Keikaku Kaigi, ed., *Sōgō Shōsha—Softoka e no Taiou* (General Trading Companies—Responses to Softening), 1984. This is one of the latest book that has focussed on current problems general trading companies are facing.
6. Katsura, Y., The Role of One Sogo Shosha in Japanese Industrialization: Suzuki & Co., 1877–1927, H. Krooss ed., *Proceedings of the Business History Conference*, 2nd Ser., Vol. 3, Indiana Univ., 1975.
7. Kawabe, N., Japanese Business in the United States before World War II: The Case of Mitsubishi Shōji Kaisha, the San Francisco and Seattle Branch, Ph.D. thesis, The Ohio State University, 1980.
8. Keiei Shi Gaku, Dai 8 Kai Taikai Tokushu Go (Special Issue on the History of General Trading Companies) *Keiei Shi Gaku*, Vol. 8, No. 1, 1973.
9. Marubeni Ltd., *Marubeni Zenshi* (Pre-history of Marubeni Corporation), 1977; *Marubeni Honshi* (The History of Marubeni Corporation), 1984.
10. Matsui, K., *Boeki Shōsha Ron* (Treaties on Trading Companies), 1952.
11. Mishima, Y. ed., *Mitsubishi Zaibatsu*, 1981.

---

* Unless otherwise stated the place of publication in Tokyo.

12. Mitsubishi Shōji Ltd., Mitsubishi Shōji Shashi (The History of Mitsubishi Corporation), 2 vols., 1986. The same, *Mitsubishi Shōji Nijugonen no Ayumi* (25 Years of Mitsubishi Corporation), 1980. This special issue of Ryowa (the company magazine) was the sole work associated with its history before the recent publication of the company history.

13. Mitsui Bunko ed., Mitsui Jigyo Shi (A History of Mjtsui Businesses), 7 vols., 1971–80.

14. Mitsui Bussan Ltd., *The 100 Years of Mitsui & Co., Ltd.: 1876–1976*, 1977.

15. Mitsui Bussan Ltd., *Kohon Mitsui Bussan Kabushiki Gaisha Hyakunen Shi* (A Centennial History of the Mitsui & Co., Ltd.—A Draft), 2 vols., 1978. This books are only privately circulated.

16. Miyamoto, M. and et al. ed., *Sogo Shosha no Keiei Shi* (A History of General Trading Companies), 1976. This is an extended version of papers presented at the 8th Annual Meeting of Japan Business History Society.

17. Morikawa, H., Meijiki Mitsui Bussan no Keiei Soshiki (Management Structure of Mitsui Bussan in the Meiji Era), *Keiei Shirin*, Vol. 9, No. 1, 1972.

18. Morikawa, H., Sōgō Shōsha no Seiritsu to Ronri (The Growth and Logic of General Trading Companies) in (16).

19. K. Nakagawa, Organized Entrepreneurship in the Course of Industrialization of Pre-World War-II Japan, in H. Nagamine and et al., Nation Building and Regional Development: The Japanese Experience, United Nations Centre for Regional Development, 1981.

20. Sakamoto, M., Mitsui Bussan to 'Manshu.' Chugoku Shijyo (Mitsui and Co. in Manchuria and China Markets) in A. Fujiwara and Y. Nozawa ed., *Nippon Facism to Higashi Asia* (Japanese Militalism in East Asia), 1977.

21. Sakamoto, M., Meiji Matsu-ki no Tai-chugoku Shakkan to Mitsui Bussan (Loans for China and Mitsui Bussan in the late Meiji Era) in Hara, R., ed., *Kindai Nippon no Seiji to Keizai* (The politics and Economy in Modern Japan), 1986.

22. Shibagaki, K., *Nippon Kinyū Shihon Bunseki* (An Analysis on Finance Capital in Japan), 1965.

23. Shioda, N., The Sogo Shosha and its Functions in Direct Foreign Investment, *Developing Economies*, Vol. 14, No. 4, 1976.

24. Togai, Y., *Mitsui Bussan Gaisha no Keieishi-teki Kenkyu* (A Business

History of Mitsui & Co.), 1964.

25. Umezu, K., *Nippon Shōsha Shi*, (A History of Japanese Trading Companies), 1976.

26. Umezu, K., *Nippon's Bōeki Shōsha* (Japanese Trading Companies), 1967.

27. Yamamura, K., General Trading Companies in Japan: Their Origins and Growth, in H. Patrick ed., *Japanese Industrialization and its Social Consequences*, Berkeley, 1976.

28. Yamashita, N., Keisei-ki Nippon Shihonshugi ni okeru Rinsun Kogyo to Mitsui Bussan (Mitsui Bussan and The Match Manufacturing in the Formative Years of Japanese Capitalism), *Mitsui Bunko Ronsō*, No. 6, 1972.

29. Yasuoka, S. ed., *Mitsui Zaibatsu*, 1982.

30. Yamazawa, I. and Kohama, H., Trading Companies and Expansion of Japan's Foreign Trade, in Papers and Proceedings of the Conference on Japan's Historical Development Experience and the Contemporary Developing Countries, International Development Centre of Japan, 1978.

31. Yonekawa, S., The Formation of General Trading Companies: A Comparative Study, K. Nakagawa and H. Morikawa ed., *Japanese Year Book on Business History: 1985;* 1985. This is an enlarged version of *General Trading Companies: A Comparative and Historical Study*, Working Paper, The United Nations University, 1983.

32. Yonekura, S., The Emergence of the Prototype of Enterprise Group Capitalism: A Case of Mitsui, *Hitotsubashi Journal of Commerce and Management*, Vol. 20, No. 1, 1985.

33. Yoshihara, K., *Sogo Shosha: The Vanguard of the Japanese Economy*, Oxford, 1982.

34. M. Y. Yoshino and T. B. Lifson, The Invisible Link: Japan's Sogo Shosha and Organization of Trade. Cambridge, Mass., 1986.

35. Young, A. K., *The Sogo Shosha: Japan's Multinational Trading Companies*, Boulder, 1979.

Some Questions on Japan's Sōgō Shōsha

Hideki Yoshihara
Kobe University

I. The Purpose of the Conference

Foreign trade played an important role in the industrialization of Japan, Europe, and the United States. Interestingly, the kinds of organization which engaged in foreign trade varied from nation to nation. Their patterns of development also differed. The pattern in Japan was extraordinary in that a majority of the nation's export and import was undertaken by a handful of *sōgō shōsha* (general trading companies).

Why and how did the sōgō shōsha develop in Japan? And, conversely, why haven't similar trading firms developed in the United States and the countries of Europe? In the United States and Europe, what kinds of trading organizations performed the foreign trade function assumed by the sōgō shōsha in Japan? Did specialty trading firms perform the function? Or did manufacturing firms export their own products? These questions are the topics of this conference. We will address ourselves to the development of the sōgō shōsha in Japan, in comparison with the development of functionally equivalent trading organizations in Europe and the United States.

The sōgō shōsha, as exemplified by Mitsui Bussan (Mitsui & Co.) and Mitsubishi Shōji (Mitsubishi Corp.), is a firm which is engaged in foreign trade and which has the following characteristics: (1) it handles a wide variety of goods; (2) its trading area is global; (3) it performs such functions as domestic trade, manufacturing, resource development, and financing; (4) its scale of operation is vast.[1] In simple terms, the sōgō shōsha may be defined as a firm that trades all kinds of goods with all nations of the world. Since industrial enterprises played a major role in the industrialization of Japan, Europe, and America, the export of the products of industrial enter-

1

prises will be the main theme of this conference. The export function of the sōgō shōsha will be a focal point of discussion.

Functional equivalent, a concept borrowed from sociology, is a key concept at this conference.[2] Various social entities perform a great variety of functions for the maintenance and development of society. A specific function may be performed by more than a single organization or institution. It is not unusual for different types of organizations or institutions to perform identical functions in different societies or nations. When two different organizations perform the same function, they are defined as functional equivalents.

The sōgō shōsha of Japan import products of foreign manufacturers and raw materials and export Japan's industrial and nonindustrial products. Needless to say, these import and export functions can be performed just as well by specialty trading firms. Manufacturers themselves can perform these functions. In fact, in pre-World War II Japan a number of specialty trading companies engaged in the export and import of their specialty items, and a few of the manufacturers exported their own products. Nonetheless, the weight of Japan's foreign trade was borne by the sōgō shōsha. Questions for us to address, then, are, What functional equivalents (organizations or institutions) of Japan's sōgō shōsha have been handling exports and imports in the advanced industrial countries of Europe and the United States?; Why and how have those functional equivalents developed?

Each country has developed its own foreign trade organizations in response to its unique socio-economic-historical conditions. So to understand the how and why of the development of each country's foreign trade organizations, we should think about such contingency variables as the country's date of commencement of industrialization, its industrial structure, its economic dependence on foreign trade, the size of its domestic market, and the government's trade policy. In considering these variables, we should take a comparative approach.

It is natural for us to focus our attention on our own country, but it may not be wise to stop there. Comparisons with other countries will facilitate our understanding of our own. Since this conference is an international conference, an international comparison should be our common concern.

This conference will hopefully add some new knowledge to the subject of foreign trade organizations. Specifically, the following three contributions are expected from our discussion. First, it should enrich our empirical knowledge of the historical development of Japan's foreign trade organizations. As the study of the subject has long been left undeveloped, this contribution alone will justify this conference. Second, we hope to make a big step toward the construction of a common theoretical framework for the subject. Types of foreign trade organization and their development patterns differ from nation to nation, but the differences may be mostly attributable to each country's contingency variables. A common logic may underlie the seemingly different foreign trade organizations of each country. The search for such a common logic is our second task at this conference. Third, with progress in those two areas, we will hopefully be able to have a better understanding of why sōgō shōsha developed in Japan.

II. The Development of Sōgō Shōsha in Japan

As already mentioned, the sōgō shōsha is a large-scale trading company which is diversified in its trading goods, trading areas, and functions. This concept of the sōgō shōsha neatly applies to two trading companies, Mitsui Bussan and Mitsubishi Shōji. Mitsui Bussan, Japan's first sōgō shōsha, was established in 1876. With the backing of the Mitsui zaibatsu, it grew rapidly, and became a sōgō shōsha in 30 years. In 1907 it had nearly 40 foreign branches and offices not only in Asia but also in Europe and traded more than 120 kinds of goods. Its trading operations included domestic trade (18%), exports (35%), and imports (44%). It handled 18.6% of Japan's exports and 20.7% of its imports.[3]

Mitsubishi Shōji practically started its life when Mitsubishi Gōshi Kaisha established its marketing department in 1894. It grew, first be selling Mitsubishi's coal and copper, and then by extending its line of goods to handle the diverse products of member companies of the Mitsubishi zaibatsu. By 1921, when Mitsubishi Shōji had become a sōgō shōsha,[4] it traded coal, metals, machinery, agricultural products, fats, fertilizer, fishery products, textiles, chemicals, and miscellaneous goods. It had nearly 25 foreign branches and offices in Asia, Europe, the United States, and Oceania. Mitsubishi Shōji's share of Japan's total exports and imports was smaller than Mitsui Bussan's share, but still substantial. In the period 1937–42 Mitsubishi Shōji accounted for 10.3% of Japan's total foreign trade.[5]

Suzuki Shōten (Suzuki & Co.) of the period 1915–27 could also be called a sōgō shōsha.[6] It was founded around 1877 by Suzuki Iwajiro and grew rapidly under the leadership of Kaneko Naokichi. In 1917 it surpassed Mitsui Bussan in its total sales and became Japan's largest trading company, trading a vast variety of goods with almost all nations of the world. A noteworthy feature of Suzuki Shōten was its heavy commitment to production activities. It once owned and controlled nearly 100 industrial enterprises. However, Suzuki Shōten was short-lived and went into bankruptcy in 1927.

There is no question that these three trading companies were sōgō shōsha in prewar Japan. Were there other trading companies worthy of being called sōgō shōsha in the prewar period?

There were a substantial number of other large-scale trading companies: Marubeni Shōten, Itō Chū Shōji, Nihon Menka, Tōyō Menka, Gōshō, Kanematsu Shōten, Ataka Shōkai, Iwai Shōten, Ōkura Shōji, and Asano Bussan. Marubeni was essentially a domestic wholesaler; Itō Chū, Nihon Menka, Tōyō Menka, Gōshō, and Kanematsu were textile traders. They were specialty trading companies. On the other hand, Ataka, Iwai, Ōkura, and Asano Bussan did not concentrate on any particular goods.

The diversified trading companies were much smaller than the three sōgō shōsha mentioned earlier. Iwai, the largest, accounted for only 2.1% of Japan's foreign trade in the period 1937–42. Mitsui Bussan, in comparison, accounted for 18.3%, and Mitsubishi Shōji for 10.3%. This smaller size makes some scholars hesitate to regard these trading companies as sōgō shōsha.[7] However, it should be noted that these companies were never small or medium-sized companies. They were big companies in prewar Japan.

We will probably find substantial differences between the three truly large diversified trading companies and the smaller diversified ones. Yet the latter group of companies met the requirements of being sōgō shōsha. They handled a wide variety of goods and traded with many nations. The size of their operations was substantial and they performed, in addition to their main functions of trade, diverse functions such as manufacturing, technology importing, and financing. Thus, these trading companies could reasonably be called sōgō shōsha.

There are at present nine sōgō shōsha. They are Mitsubishi Shōji, Mitsui Bussan, Itō Chū Shōji, Marubeni Shōten, Sumitomo Shōji, Nissho Iwai, Tōmen, Nichimen Jitsugyō, and Kanematsu Gōshō. Ataka Sangyō, which was a sōgō shōsha, went into bankruptcy and its main portion was acquired by Itō Chū Shōji in 1977.

Mitsubishi Shōji and Mitsui Bussan were each dissolved into more than 100 small companies by order of the general headquarters of the Supreme Commander for the Allied Powers in 1947. But in less than 10 years they reemerged as sōgō shōsha.

Itō Chū, Marubeni, Tōmen, Nichimen, Gōshō, and Kanematsu (the latter two companies merged to become Kanematsu Gōshō) were textile traders in the prewar period. These companies all diversified into nontextile fields, such as foodstuffs, chemicals, metals, and machinery. In entering these new fields they often resorted to merger and acquisition of existing specialty trading companies.

Ataka, Iwai, and Nissho (the latter two companies merged to become Nissho Iwai) were strong in the steel business in the prewar period. Even in the early 1950s they were often called steel traders. In the 1950s and 1960s they concentrated their efforts on strengthening other product categories, such as energy, chemicals, and machinery.

The Sumitomo zaibatsu did not have its own sōgō shōsha in the prewar period. Sumitomo Shōji was established in 1952 as a trading company of the Sumitomo group. It attained spectacular growth in the 1950s and 1960s, and now occupies the fourth position among the nine sōgō shōsha.

Do these sōgō shōsha represent trading companies in Japan? Or are they exceptional even in Japan? In the prewar period there were only two major sōgō shōsha, Mitsui Bussan and Mitsubishi Shōji (three, if Suzuki Shōten is included). So it may seem that the sōgō shōsha were rare and did not represent trading companies in

Japan. However, we could argue that the sōgō shōsha have represented trading companies in Japan since the Meiji era (1868–1912)
for the following reasons.

First, as we have already seen, even in the prewar period there
were several sōgō shōsha in addition to Mitsui Bussan, Mitsubishi
Shōji, and Suzuki Shōten. The total number of sōgō shōsha was near
10. They were not rare exceptions. Second, these sōgō shōsha controlled more than half of Japan's total foreign trade. The importance
of sōgō shōsha among all the trading companies of Japan is unques-
tionable. Third, specialty trading companies made efforts to diversify
their operations.[8] For example, Nihon Menka, which was established
as an importer of raw cotton, later diversified into exporting cotton
textiles. Itō Chū started as a domestic textile wholesaler, diversified
into the foreign trade of cotton textiles, and then broadened its line
of goods. It seems that genuine specialty trading companies were
rare in Japan. Fourth, in the postwar period several specialty
trading companies have diversified and become sōgō shōsha. It seems
that since the Meiji era there has been a tendency for companies to
develop into sōgō shōsha and that these newcomers realized their
development in the 1950s and 1960s.[9] Thus, the tendency to become
sōgō shōsha seems to represent a basic development pattern of trading companies in Japan.

III. Foreign Trade Organizations in Europe and the United States

The United Kingdom has a long history of foreign trade. Until
the 17th century general merchants played a major role in foreign
trade. But as industrialization made progress, specialty trading
companies emerged and took the leading place among the foreign
trade organizations.[10] The cotton industry developed in Lancashire
and consumed a vast amount of raw cotton, which was mostly imported from the United States. This import of raw cotton was
undertaken by a lot of specialty trading companies. They were highly
specialized in the sense that their operations were limited to the
import of raw cotton from the United States. They did not handle
any other goods or import raw cotton from any other countries.
Similar specialization was observed in many fields. For example, in
the wool industry some trading companies exported only wool

textiles only to Portugal. Why did these specialty trading companies develop in the United Kingdom? What happened to the earlier general merchants? Did they successfully transform themselves into the specialty trading companies?

The United Kingdom developed another unique organization for foreign trade, the colonial trading company. Examples are Jardine, Matheson; Inchcape; Dalgety; Harrisons & Crosfield; Guthrie; and Antony Gibbs. These colonial trading companies traded diverse goods.[11]

One, Harrisons & Crosfield, was established in Liverpool in 1844 as a wholesaler of tea and coffee. In the 1890s it started diversification in goods, areas, and functions, extending the line of traded goods to include widely diverse agricultural products and manufactured goods. It set up foreign branches and offices in Colombo, Calcutta, New York, Montreal, Kuala Lumpur, Sumatra, Melbourne, Wellington, Batavia, Quilon, Shanghai, and Kobe. It entered agricultural production and manufacturing itself.[12]

Could we call Harrisons & Crosfield a sōgō shōsha? What are the differences between Japan's sōgō shōsha and the colonial trading companies of the United Kingdom? There is an argument that specialty trading companies dominated the foreign trade of the United Kingdom. Didn't the colonial trading companies occupy an important position in some particular goods or regions?

In domestic distribution in the United States, the dominant players changed from general merchants to specialized jobbers, and then to manufacturers.[13] In the 18th century foreign trade was dominated by general merchants. But in the late 19th century manufacturers started direct export.

The Singer Manufacturing Co. began production of sewing machines in 1850, and in the early 1860s established a nationwide sales network in the United States. It had a policy of "from plants to users directly." This policy was first pursued in the domestic market, and then practiced in foreign markets. Singer established sales subsidiaries and branches in many countries: the United Kingdom, Germany, Denmark, Greece, Japan, China, Malaysia, Peru, and South Africa, to name some. In Japan, Singer controlled 800 stores and sold 100,000 sewing machines in 1937.[14]

This type of direct export marketing was widely practiced by American manufacturers. They first practiced direct marketing (manufacturers bypassed intermediary trading companies and had direct access to customers or retailers) in the domestic market, and then transferred it to foreign countries. Why could American manufacturers practice direct export marketing so successfully? And, conversely, why didn't the general merchants of the 18th century develop into general trading companies like Japan's sōgō shōsha?

We have quickly examined the development of foreign trade organizations in the United Kingdom and the United States. Now we are inclined to ask two questions of the Japanese case. The first question is on the development of specialty trading companies. Didn't specialty trading companies develop in Japan? Did n't they occupy an important position in relation to some specific goods or countries?

The second question is on the direct export marketing of Japanese manufacturers. In 1930 there were at least eight manufacturing companies which were directly involved in export business. They were Dai Nippon Sugar Manufacturing, Katakura Industry, Asahi Glass, Asano Cement, Showa Seikosho, Kokusan Kōgyō, Ajinomoto, and Matsushita Electric Industrial.[15] Why did these eight manufacturers attempt direct export marketing? Did they have some features in common? Were there other manufacturers which practiced direct export marketing?

IV. Theoretical Explanations of Sōgō Shōsha

The first attempt at a theoretical explanation of Japan's sōgō shōsha probably was made by Nakagawa Keiichirō. He argues that the sōgō shōsha is an example of organized entrepreneurship, an argument influenced by Gerschenkron's theory of economic development.[16]

With the change from the Edo period to the Meiji era (1868), Japan entered the international market. No Japanese merchants of the day had experience in foreign trade, since Japan had been closed to the outside world for nearly 200 years. Japanese goods were exported through the hands of foreign merchants. The terms of trade were often disadvantageous to Japanese parties. To remedy the situation, Japanese government officials and business people made an organized effort to develop Japan's own foreign trade organizations.

To compete successfully in the international market, these artificially (not naturally) developed foreign trade organizations were necessarily large in scale. To maintain the scale, they were not allowed to concentrate on any specific products; they were destined from the start to handle diverse goods and trade with many countries. Thus the sōgō shōsha was born in Japan.

Nakagawa's explanation is appealing, but we could ask some questions. Why did sōgō shōsha develop only in Japan? Germany was also a latecomer in foreign trade, but did not have sōgō shōsha. Why not? The organized effort of Japanese government officials and business people produced two important foreign trade organizations, Naigaimen and Nihon Menka. But they were textile traders and never developed into sōgō shōsha. Doesn't this fact contradict Nakagawa's explanation? In Osaka and its vicinity there were many trading companies which were actively engaged in foreign trade but did not have connections with the government. They developed into trading companies naturally. Doesn't Nakagawa put too much emphasis on organized cooperation between government and business?

The Japan of the Meiji era was an underdeveloped country. After 200 years of isolationism, experts who knew how to conduct foreign trade were scarce resources. Some trading companies hired these experts in large numbers. In the early 1880s Mitsui Bussan began annual regular recruitment from the Tokyo Commercial College (now Hitotsubashi University). In 1914 the company had 731 employees who had graduated from colleges or universities.[17] Since these experts were expensive, Morikawa Hidemasa argues that it was necessary to fully use them. To do that, it was often necessary to diversify in goods, areas, and functions, in other words, to become a sōgō shōsha.[18]

We could ask questions regarding Morikawa's explanation. Latecomer industrial countries like Germany, Italy, and the United States seemed to face similar problems when they entered foreign trade. Experts were scarce. But sōgō shōsha did not develop in these countries. Why not? Full use of scarce resources does not necessarily induce diversification if opportunities are abundant in the existing line of business. In the prewar period weren't opportunities abundant in many fields of foreign trade?

Yamamura Kōzō uses economic theory to explain why sōgō shōsha develop. A sōgō shōsha, by trading many kinds of goods with many countries, can distribute risk among these diverse trades and thus reduce risk. Because of its diversification in goods and areas, it can increase the size of its operations and thus benefit from the economies of scale. Economies of scale are important when manpower resources are scarce and information networks are worldwide, since both involve fixed capital. With risk reduction and economies of scale, the sōgō shōsha can effectively utilize its capital. This gives it a competitive advantage over other foreign trade organizations.[19]

Yamamura's explanation of the development of the sōgō shōsha can be seen as an explanation of the advantages of sōgō shōsha over specialty trading companies. His explanation is based on the assumption that not specialization but diversification realizes risk reduction and economies of scale. Is this assumption always true? Unless we could assume the transferability of trade know-how, this basic assumption could be wrong. Cotton traders are efficient in cotton trade. Could they be as efficient in steel trade as steel traders? If cotton traders were not efficient in steel trade, then diversification into steel trade could increase risk and not realize economies of scale. In fact, even in Japan there have been many specialty trading companies enjoying a competitive advantage over sōgō shōsha in their specialized fields. Probably Yamamura's explanation is too general. He needs to be specific about conditions under which diversification leads to risk reduction and economies of scale.

Yoshihara Kunio, in his book *Sogo Shosha*, argues that the inability of manufacturers to handle foreign trade was one major reason for the emergence of sōgō shōsha in Japan. Japanese manufacturers faced great difficulties in trading with foreign countries. One major problem was language. Another problem was that foreign trade

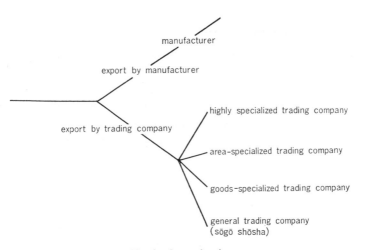

FIG. 1.   Types of Foreign Trade Organization.

required skills in various business practices not common to domestic trade. Also, knowledge of the laws, politics, economies, and cultures of each country was indispensable in foreign trade. As manufacturers lacked these skills and knowledge, they had to rely on foreign trading companies.[20]

European manufacturers did not depend much on foreign trading companies when trading with other European countries and the United States, since there was no large market gap. Trade with Asian countries was quite different. Having little knowledge of Asian languages, customs, and business practices, manufacturers had to trade through trading companies. Such trading companies as Jardine, Matheson; Guthrie; Sime Darby; and Borneo Sumatra acted as intermediaries for European manufacturers in their Asian trade.

Yoshihara's theory of market separation is appealing as an explanation of why country- or area-specialized trading companies develop. They handle diverse goods, but are specialized in some countries or areas. But Japanese sōgō shōsha are diversified not only in goods but also in trading areas. We ask a question: Didn't country- or area-specialized trading companies develop in prewar Japan? If not, why not?

V. Externalization and Synergy

In order to explain why sōgō shōsha developed in Japan, we
need to answer two basic questions. First we need answer the question,
Why did trading companies export for manufacturers? As Figure 1
shows, manufacturers themselves could export. Such direct export
was widely practiced by American manufacturers. But in Japan
manufacturers did not practice direct export, and exported through
trading companies. Why?

The second question is, Why did sōgō shōsha handle exports for
manufacturers? Figure 1 differentiates four types of trading companies. The first type is the highly specialized trading company,
which is specialized in both goods and areas. The specialty trading
companies of the United Kingdom correspond to this type. The
second type is the trading company which is specialized in area but
handles diverse kinds of goods. The colonial trading companies
are this second type. The third type is the trading company which is
specialized in goods but often trades with many countries. Japan's
specialty trading companies, Naigaimen and Nihon Menka, for
example, are this third type. The fourth type is the sōgō shōsha,
which is diversified both in goods and areas. Among these four types
of trading companies, why have sōgō shōsha dominated Japan's
foreign trade?

What are relevant theoretical concepts for these two basic questions? In answering the first question, the concept of externalization
(reversal of the concept of internalization) seems relevant. That
trading companies export for manufacturers means that the export
function of the manufacturers is externalized from the manufacturers.
In other words, manufacturers do not internalize their export function. The search for reasons and conditions of this externalization
may lead us to an answer to the first question. And in this search the
theory of the economics of internal organization may provide us with
useful clues.[21]

The second question could be rephrased as, Why are sōgō shōsha
more efficient than specialty trading companies? An essential feature
of the sōgō shōsha is that it executes plural operations (goods, areas,
and functions). When we address ourselves to finding out why execution of plural operations by one trading company is more efficient

than execution of each different operation by a different trading company, the concept of synergy found in diversification theory may be useful.[22]

NOTES

1. See Miyamoto Mataji, Togai Yoshio, and Mishima Yashuo, eds., *Sōgō shōsha no keiei shi* (The business history of general trading companies), Tokyo, Tōyō Keizai Shimpō Sha, 1976.
2. Robert E. Cole, "Functional Alternatives and Economic Development: An Empirical Example of Permanent Employment in Japan," *American Sociological Review*, August 1973.
3. Togai Yoshio, "Saisho ni shutsugen shita sōgō shōsha: Mitsui Bussan" (The first general trading company: Mitsui Bussan), in Miyamoto et al., eds., *Sōgō shōsha no keiei shi*.
4. Mishima Yasuo, "Sekitan yushutsu shōsha kara sōgō shōsha e: Mitsubishi Shōji" (From coal-exporting company to general trading company: Mitsubishi Shōji), in Miyamoto et al., eds., *Sōgō shōsha no keiei shi*.
5. Yoshihara Kunio, *Sōgō shōsha*, Oxford University Press, 1982, p. 88.
6. Katsura Yoshio, "Sangyō kigyō no ikusei to shōsha: Suzuki Shōten" (The development of industrial companies and general trading companies: Suzuki Shōten), in Miyamoto et al., eds., *Sōgō shōsha no keiei shi*.
7. Yoshihara Kunio, *Sōgō shōsha*, p. 88.
8. Maeda Kazutoshi, "Sōgō shōsha: Sono rekishi-teki kentō" (General trading companies: A historical analysis), Paper of the research project Sōgō Shōsha and Technology Transfer of the United Nations University, 1982, pp. 9–12.
9. See Nakagawa Keiichirō's argument in the panel discussion of the annual conference of the Japan Business History Society, *Japan Business History Review*, Vol. 8, No. 1, 1973, pp. 126–34.
10. Nakagawa Keiichirō, "Nippon no kōgyōka katei ni okeru 'soshiki sareta kigyōsha katsudō'" ("Organized entrepreneurship" in the industrialization of Japan), *Keiei shigaku*, Vol. 2, No. 3, 1967, p. 29.
11. Yonekawa Shin'ichi, "Sōgō shōsha keisei no ronri to zittai" (Logic and reality in the development of general trading companies), *Hitotsubashi ronsō*, Vol. 90, No. 3, 1983.
12. Saruwatari Keiko, "Igirisu shokuminchi shōsha no takakuteki seichō:

Harrisons & Crosfield Sha no zirei, 1844–1982" (The diversified development of British colonial trading companies: The case of Harrisons & Crosfield Ltd., 1844–1982), *Hitotsubashi ronsō*, Vol. 90, No. 3, 1983, p. 19.

13. Glenn Porter and Harold C. Livesay, *Merchants and Manufacturers: Studies in the Changing Structure of Nineteenth-Century Marketing*, The Johns Hopkins University Press, 1971.

14. Nakagawa Keiichirō, "Beikoku no dai kigyō ni okeru kaigai shijō katsudō no hatten" (The development of overseas marketing in large American corporations), in Nippon Keiei Gakkai, ed., *Bōeki ziyūka to keiei no sho-mondai*, Daiyamondo Sha, 1962.

15. I am indebted Suzuki Yoshitaka of Tōhoku University for supplying data.

16. Nakagawa, "Nippon no kōgyō-ka katei."

17. Yonekawa, "Sōgō shōsha keisei."

18. Morikawa Hidemasa, "Sōgō shōsha no seiritsu to ronri" (The development and logic of general trading companies), in Miyamoto et al., eds., *Sōgō shōsha no keiei shi.*

19. Yamamura Kōzō, "Sōgō shōsha ron: Kindai keizaigaku-teki riron yori no ichi shiron" (The theory of general trading companies: An attempt based on economic theory), *Keiei shigaku*, Vol. 8, No. 1, 1973.

20. Yoshihara Kunio, *Sōgō shōsha*, p. 187.

21. Imai Ken'ichi, Itami Hiroyuki, and Koike Kazuo, *Naibu-soshiki no keizai-gaku* (The economics of internal organization), Tōyō Keizai Shimpō Sha, 1982.

22. Yoshihara Hideki, "Research on Japan's General Trading Firms: An Overview," *Japanese Economic Studies*, Vol. 9, No. 3, Spring 1981.

Comment

Harold C. Livesay
Virginia Polytechnic and State University

In calling for the development of a "common logic" that can support "a common theoretical framework" that explains the seemingly different foreign trade organizations of each country, Professor Yoshihara evokes the fine tradition of the Fuji Conference. Indeed, if I understand correctly, the belief that such common logics existed, that they could be discovered, and that international harmony depended upon a mutual awareness and understanding of them motivated the sponsors of this conference to support its creation and continuation.

As historians, we should be more comfortable than most people with the idea of common logic and the concept of "functional equivalents" on which it depends. Professor Yoshihara points out quite correctly that comparative history must rest on functional equivalents if it is to have validity; I would add that all history involves comparison, explicit or implicit, and that all historians a priori accept this principle, for without the use of functional equivalents history can be little more than a chronicle of events. Professor Yoshihara, nevertheless, rightly urges us to think beyond the national experiences we know best, because however much historians believe in the theoretical validity of common logic and functional equivalents, we tend to embody not only the prejudices associated with being national rather than international individuals but also the attitudes nourished by the day-to-day practice of our craft. For most of us this means thinking most of the time in terms of specific individuals, particular institutions, or single national entities and artificially bounding them with discrete time periods, "watersheds," "turning points," and other such practical apparatus.

As business historians, we all realize that successful large-volume businesses depend upon the insistence of several common logics without which the techniques of mass production and distribution must fail. Multinational businesses supply salient demonstrations of these principles. For global traders who deal in generic commodities, the logic may involve nothing more complicated than the fact that wheat is wheat, wool is wool, and almost everybody needs them. Indeed, such generic commodities formed the original stock in trade of most of the examples of general trading companies offered here.

Manufacturing, however, presents a more complicated case, involving the imperatives of technological content in the product, its manufacture, or both. Not only does this necessitate massive capital to achieve scale economies but it also imposes requirements for customer finance, parts, service, and sales techniques tailored to local customer attitudes. It also requires machines that can turn out products that, however much they may have embodied common principles, could appear to have a particular national identity.

For a long period, multinational manufacturers by and large operated on the assumption that, for example, a Chevrolet must be an Opel in Germany, a Vauxhall in Britain, a Holden in Australia— identities that had nothing to do with manufacturing and everything to do with marketing. Since the 1960s this notion has faded steadily, and Japanese manufacturers have led the way. At the Fuji Conference of 1980, the participants discovered that the automobile industry had globally accepted a common logic based in fact on two principles:

1. Producing vehicles with national identities costs more than global competition can bear.
2. Consumers all over the world had come full circle to arrive at the view that automobiles were themselves functional equivalents (ironically in much the same terms that Henry Ford had defined them).

From this discussion we emerged with a common theoretical framework that, we felt, explained the industry's behavior and permitted a prediction summarized in one word, *convergence.* All of us then present have lived to see the accuracy of this forecast. I have no doubt that examination of general trading companies will expose similar common threads.

Obviously the tasks performed by the general trading company had to be performed everywhere, so functional equivalents had to exist. For Japan we have several explanations for the *sōgō shōsha*, although I suspect an economist might argue that Professors Nakagawa, Morikawa, and Yamamura are, with the lack of theoretical rigor economists profess to find in historians, simply describing different parts of Adam Smith's elephant.

In the other national cases we have explanations for the collapse or nondevelopment of such firms, or the demonstration of the rare exception. I would suggest the basic explanation of the emergence of apparently dissimilar agencies performing the same business most often lies in cultural, social, and political realities. The national differences in these may be declining, as many multinational manufacturers now assume.

Finally, Professor Alfred Chandler, from whom Glenn Porter and I learned business history, argued that the common logic found in human experience was resistance to change. In business this manifested itself in the persistence of structures, which by and large changed only when forced to change by some external variable. The origins of any institution reflect the economic, cultural, social, political, and economic realities prevalent at its birth. This we can see in many of the papers presented here. The survival of a structure presents a fascinating phenomenon that challenges understanding. For our task here, then, I think the key to greater understanding of the general questions may lie in discovering how the *sōgō shōsha* has not only survived but played such an important role in the economic tour de force of contemporary Japan.

Comment

Matao Miyamoto
Osaka University

Professor Yoshihara, the organizer of this conference, has done a signal service to us all by indicating the focal points of the conference and by offering some theoretical hypotheses to explain the emergence of *sōgō shōsha*, the general trading companies of Japan. His paper is very useful as a clue to the problems of why and how different types of foreign trade organization have developed from nation to nation. A key concept in his paper, *functional equivalent*, also seems very effective and relevant for the international comparison of trading companies.

Although there are many interesting statements in his paper, I think the most important and the most interesting parts are the fourth and fifth sections, which develop theoretical explanations of sōgō shōsha. I would like to concentrate my comments on these points.

Professor Yoshihara suggested in the last section of his paper that the concepts of externalization and synergy are useful for understanding why the sōgō shōsha developed in Japan. I would like to ask for some additional explanations in this regard.

1. It is my impression that externalization and synergy are factors too general to account for why sōgō shōsha developed especially in Japan. His explanation is based on the assumption that the externalization, rather than the internalization, of the export function would bring about certain advantages to the manufacturers and that the execution of plural operations by sōgō shōsha, that is, diversification not only in terms of variety of commodities handled and multinationality of activities but also in terms of function, would be more efficient than specialization. If this is generally true, then externalization and synergy should be effective in all countries. Why then did sōgō shōsha not develop in other countries? It seems to

me that the effects of externalization and synergy are only realized under specific conditions. I would like to ask Professor Yoshihara for his opinion in this regard.

2. I could not quite understand the examples of the effects of externalization and synergy in the Japanese sōgō shōsha. For instance, the major part of commodity transactions in the Japanese sōgō shōsha has not been trade on its own account but commission business. This means that the manufacturers have not been able to shift (to externalize) perfectly to the sōgō shōsha the risks involved in foreign trade. When Professor Yoshihara refers to externalization, what kinds of function does he think are externalized? I believe that his argument regarding externalization and synergy would be more persuasive if he would show us some examples of Japanese sōgō shōsha which illustrate these effects.

Professor Yoshihara argues that the sōgō shōsha have been representative of the trading companies in Japan since the Meiji era and that the tendency to become a sōgō shōsha seems to represent a basic development pattern of the trading company in Japan. On the other hand, Professor Yamazaki, one of the contributors to this conference, asserted in his paper that sōgō shōsha have not necessarily been representative of Japanese trading companies and that two types of large trading companies, namely sōgō shōsha and specialty trading companies, coexisted in prewar Japan. I expect that this will be one of the controversial issues at this conference. In this connection, it is probably very important to ask whether or not the conditions, both micro- and macro-economic, under which the sōgō shōsha emerged existed from the very beginning of Japan's industrialization. To put this another way, are the factors which brought forth the Japanese sōgō shōsha attributable to the initial conditions under which Japan entered the international market after the 200 years of seclusion or to the subsequent conditions which appeared in the course of Japan's industrialization? It is my impression that Professors Nakagawa and Morikawa, to whom Professor Yoshihara referred, [emphasized the initial condition, while Professor Yamazaki attached importance to the subsequent condition. I would appreciate it greatly if Professor Yoshihara would tell us his view concerning this point.

The Logic of the Formation of General Trading Companies in Japan

Hiroaki Yamazaki
University of Tokyo
</br>

I. Introduction

Most Japanese business historians have assumed that the general trading company (*sōgō shōsha*) was peculiar to Japan, and explained the logic of its formation with Mitsui Bussan in mind.[1] On the other hand, Yonekawa Shin'ichi argues that the general trading company was not peculiar to Japan and that several such companies appeared in England.[2] Some papers submitted to this conference will introduce cases of this type of trading company in foreign countries; this paper will focus on the Japanese case.

While it is true that Mitsui Bussan was the model general trading company in Japan before World War II, it is not true that most trading companies were general trading companies at that time. As shown in this paper, Mitsui Bussan far exceeded other trading companies not only in scale but also in performance. There were many trading companies which specialized either in textile trade or in trade between Japan and specific countries and which were not yet fully developed as general trading companies.

The first object of this paper is to consider the extent to which each of the important trading companies was "generalized" in the light of a definition of the general trading company. In the process, we will be able to get a bird's-eye view of Japanese trading companies in the mid-1920s. Second, we will consider the factors which enabled Mitsui Bussan to develop into a general trading company by looking at its history. We will also consider briefly the reason why other trading companies which have been regarded as general trading companies fell far behind Mitsui Bussan in their development into general trading companies.

21

TABLE 1   Japanese Trading Companies Ranked in Terms of Paid-up Capital and Total Assets in 1926.

Ranking	Name of company	Paid-up capital (¥1,000)	Ranking	Name of company	Total assets (¥1,000)
1	Mitsui Bussan	100,000	1	Mitsui Bussan	392,873
2	Suzuki Shōten	50,000	2	Suzuki Shōten[2]	167,912
3	Nihon Menka	26,000	3	Nihon Menka	124,665
4	Gōshō	20,000	4	Mitsubishi Shōji	92,284
5	Tōyō Menka	15,000	5	Tōyō Menka	77,810
	Mitsubishi Shōji	15,000	6	Gōshō	60,520
7	Ōkura Shōji	8,000	7	Nihon Kiito	24,785
8	Itō Chū Shōji	7,000	8	Iwai Shōten	21,913
	Iwai Shōten	7,000	9	Ōkura Shōji	15,485
10	Marubeni Shōten	5,000	10	Itō Chū Shōji	15,328
	Itō Man Shōten	5,000	11	Marubeni Shōten	15,163
	Kanematsu Shōten	5,000	12	Kanematsu Shōten	10,539
	Nihon Shōgyō[1]	5,000	13	Itō Man Shōten	9,164
14	Ataka Shōkai	3,000	14	Ataka Shōkai	7,127
	Maruei Shōten[1]	3,000	15	Daidō Bōeki	5,993
	Yagi Shōten[1]	3,000	16	Asano Bussan	5,842
	Nihon Kiito	3,000	17	Takashimaya Iida	5,706
18	Takashimaya Iida	2,000	18	Asahi Silk	4,144
19	Morioka Shōten[1]	1,200			
20	Asano Bussan	1,000			
	Asahi Silk	1,000			
	Toyoshima Shōten	1,000			
	Daidō Bōeki	1,000			

Notes: 1. Total assets unknown.
2. March 1927 figure.

Sources: Tōkyō Kōshinjo (Tokyo Commercial Inquiry Agency), *Ginkō kaisha yōroku* (Directory of banks and companies), 31st ed., 1926; *Ōsaka Mainichi*, April 1, 1927.

TABLE 2   The Main Japanese Exports and the Main Companies Trading in

Main items of export	Export value (¥1,000)	Main trading			
Raw silk	643,673	*Mitsui Bussan*	Nihon Kiito	Hara Gōmei	Nihon Menka
Cotton yarn	101,306	Itō Chū Shōji	Nihon Shōgyō	Maruei Shōten	Mata Ichi
Shirting	54,800	*Tōyō Menka*	Nihon Menka	Itō Shū	Itō Chū Shōji
Sheeting	46,794	Gōshō	*Tōyō Menka*	Nihon Menka	Ozu Burin
Habutae	45,921	*Mitsui Bussan*	Mitsubishi Shōji	Horikoshi Gōmei	Taka-shimaya Iida
Pongee & Fuji silk	35,610	Horikoshi Gōmei	Okabe Shōten	Yamato Shōkai	
Pottery	35,235	Imoto Shōten	Morimura Shōji	Nagoya Seitōjyo	Asai Takegorō Shōten
Jeans	34,589	Nihon Menka	*Tōyō Menka*	Gōshō	Takemura Mengyō
Coal	27,693	*Mitsui Bussan*	Mitsubishi Shōji	Kaijima Shōgyō	Yamashita Kisen
Cotton drills	25,919	*Tōyō Menka*	Nihon Menka	Gōshō	Takemura Mengyō
Refined sugar	22,150	*Mitsui Bussan*	Mitsubishi Shōji	Suzuki Shōten	Fukuwa Yūgō
Sateen	19,933	*Tōyō Menka*	Nihon Menka	Ozu Burin	Itō Chū Shōji
Cotton knit, undershirts	18,581				
Waste silk	16,130	*Mitsui Bussan*	Nihon Kiito	Hara Gōmei	Nihon Menka
Striped cotton tissue	14,335				
Kabeori & crepe	13,436	*Mitsui Bussan*	Horikoshi Gōmei	Takashimaya Iida	
T cloths	12,435	Nihon Menka	*Tōyō Menka*	Gōshō	
Matches	12,080	Tōyō Match	Kichijyō Konsu	Dōfutai	Chiri Konsu

Them, 1921–1925.

companies and merchants

Gōshō	Asahi Silk				
Teikoku Menka	Handa Menkō	Iwai Shōten	Nichizui Bōeki	Toyoshima Shōten	Ozu Burin

C.G.
Caesar
Iwai
Shōten

Harrisons
Davis

Tashiro Shōten	Taiyō Shōkō	Miyabe Suetaka Gōmei	Nagai Abe Shōten	Hachiya Kyōdai Shōkai	Sesaka Gōshi

Itō Chū
Shōji
Suzuki
Shōten
Itō Chū
Shōji
Takatsu
Shōji
Gōshō

Gōshō	Asahi Silk	A. Cameron

Mitsui Bussan

TABLE 2   (Continued)

Main items of export	Export value (¥1,000)				Main trading
Prints	11,455	*Tōyō Menka*	Itō Chū Shōji	Nihon Menka	
Bleached shirting	10,094	*Tōyō Menka*	Itō Chū Shōji	Nihon Menka	Mata Ichi

Notes: The items whose average export value exceeded ¥10 million between 1921 and 1925 are listed here.
Mitsui Bussan and Tōyō Menka (which is wholly owned by Mitsui Bussan) are in italics.
Habutae is a kind of silk fabric and *kabeori* is a kind of cotton fabric.

II. The "Generality" of Trading Companies in Japan before World War II

According to Yonekawa, a general trading company is "basically a company which deals in a variety of commodities on a global scale, in the import and export trades. As a logical consequence of this activity, such a company may open a number of overseas branches with their own staff."[3] Two important criteria exist: that is, diversification in commodities handled and multinational presence in terms of the region where the company acts. Nevertheless, when we consider why Japanese general trading companies are of interest to scholars throughout the world, we cannot neglect the important position which they occupied in Japan's economy or its foreign trade. In addition to the criteria of diversity and multinationality, each trading company will therefore be considered with regard to its position in foreign trade.

For Japanese trading companies whose paid-up capital amounted to more than ¥1 million in 1926, Table 1 gives a ranking in terms of paid-up capital and total assets. Total assets are estimated by adding the figures in the asset account listed in the source book. The estimated figures are not exactly equal to the total assets listed on the balance sheets of the companies published earlier, but are nearly equal. With the estimates we can get a rough ranking for the companies and classify them into the following four groups:

companies and merchants

Miyazaki
Shōten

Source: Kokusanshinkōkai (The Association for Promoting Domestic Products), *Kokusan daichō jyō kan* (A ledger of domestic production), Vol. 1, 1928.

Group 1   total assets amount to more than ¥100 million
           Mitsui Bussan, Suzuki Shōten, Nihon Menka
Group 2   total assets are between ¥50 million and ¥100 million
           Mitsubishi Shōji, Tōyō Menka, Gōshō
Group 3   total assets are between ¥10 million and ¥50 million
           Nihon Kiito, Iwai Shōten, Ōkura Shōji, Itō Chū Shōji, Marubeni Shōten, Kanematsu Shōten
Group 4   total assets are under ¥10 million
           Itō Man Shōten, Ataka Shōkai, Daidō Bōeki, Asano Bussan, Takashimaya Iida, Asahi Silk

Although Suzuki Shōten and Nihon Menka belonged to Group 1 together with Mitsui Bussan, Mitsui Bussan was far larger than either. Its total assets were about 2.3 times as much as Suzuki Shōten's and about 3.2 times as much as Nihon Menka's. Mitsui Bussan's total assets were greater than the combined assets of the next three largest trading companies.

Table 2 and Table 3 list the important commodities which were exported from or imported to Japan during the first half of the 1920s and the trading companies which dealt in each commodity. When we glance at these tables, we notice two types of trading company in Japan, one specializing in textiles and the other, the so-called general trading company, which dealt in many commodities.

TABLE 3   The Main Japanese Imports and the Main Companies Trading

Main items of import	Import value (¥1,000)	Main trading			
Cotton	581,563	Nihon Menka	*Tōyō Menka*	Gōshō	Nihon Shōgyō
Beans	91,372	*Mitsui Bussan*	Suzuki Shōten		
Steel sheets	76,266	*Mitsui Bussan*	Mitsubishi Shōji	Asano Bussan	Tamura Shōten
Wool	75,339	Kanematsu Shōten	*Mitsui Bussan*	Mitsubishi Shōji	Taka-shimaya Iida
Wood	75,290	Mitsubishi Shōji	*Mitsui Bussan*	Suzuki Shōten	McMiller Export
Sugar	65,066	*Mitsui Bussan*	Mitsubishi Shōji	Suzuki Shōten	
Rice	62,434	*Mitsui Bussan*	Mitsubishi Shōji	Iwai Shōten	Kongō Shōten
Wheat	56,461	*Mitsui Bussan*	Suzuki Shōten	Mitsubishi Shōji	Asano Bussan
Woolen yarn	51,500	*Mitsui Bussan*	Taka-shimaya Iida	Mitsubishi Shōji	Iwai Shōten
Woolen cloth & serge	44,843	Shibakawa Shōten	Iwai Shōten	Usami Shōten	Marubeni Shōten
Soybeans	36,813	*Mitsui Bussan*	Mitsubishi Shōji	Nisshin Seiyu	Suzuki Shōten
Coal	25,791	*Bujuntan Hanbai*	Kaiheitan Hanbai	Mantetsu	
Steel, bars & rods	23,634	*Mitsui Bussan*	Mitsubishi Shōji	Okaya Gōshi	Iwai Shōten
Sulphate of ammonium	21,685	*Mitsui Bussan*	Kuhara Shōjibu	Masudaya	Suzuka Shōten
India rubber	20,664	*Mitsui Bussan*	Mitsubishi Shōji	Mitsuhiki Shōji	Katō Shōji
Spinning machines	20,445	*Mitsui Bussan*	Asano Bussan	Takada Shōkai	Mitsubishi Shōji
Pig iron	18,662	*Mitsui Bussan*	Mitsubishi Shōji	Suzuki Shōten	Iwai Shōten

in Them, 1921–1925.

companies or merchants

Teikoku Menka	Tata				
Suzuki Shōten					
Ōkura Shōji	Nihon Menka				
American Trading	National Trading	S.L. Jones	Nagashima Shōten	Handa Shōkai	Tamura Shōkai
Yuasa Shōten	Katō Shōten	Yamada Shōkai	Suzuki Benzō Shōten	Dobashi Shōten	Suzuki Shōten
Kanematsu Shōten	Nihon Satō Bōeki				
Marubeni Shōten	Kanematsu Shōten	Suzuki Shōten	Ataka Shōkai	Shibakawa Shōten	Nichizui Bōeki
Takaoka Shōten	Konishi Shōten	Fujii Shōten	Shihatsu Shōten	*Mitsui Bussan*	
Kishimoto Shōten	Suzuki Shōten				
Asano Bussan	Mitsubishi Shōji	Siber Hegner	Suzuki Shoten	H. Ahrens	Brunner Mond (Japan)
Kishimoto Shōten	Ataka Shōkai	Nichiin Tsūshō			

TABLE 3   (Continued)

Main items of import	Import value (¥1,000)	Main trading			
Eggs	16,154	Naigai Keiran	Uematsu Shōkai		
Hemp, jute & manila hemp	14,261	Ogura Bōeki	*Mitsui Bussan*	Daidō Bōeki	Menasa Tsūshō
Electrical machinery (dynamos)	13,081	*Mitsui Bussan*	Mitsubishi Shōji	Nihon Westinghouse	Ōkura Shōji
(transformers)		*Mitsui Bussan*	Mitsubishi Shōji	Nihon Westinghouse	Nichizui Bōeki
Petroleum benzine	12,996	Rising Sun	Asano Bussan	Texas Sekiyu	Yanase Shōji
Coal-tar dyes	10,656	I.G. Farben	du Pont	National Anilin	Yakuhin
Lead	10,532	*Mitsui Bussan*	Mitsubishi Shōji	Furukawa Kōgyō	Suzuki Shōten
Pulp for paper making	10,493	Tōyō Shōkai	Tomoe Bōeki	Samuel & Samuel	A. Cameron
Zinc	10,467				
Rails	10,075	*Mitsui Bussan*	Mitsubishi Shōji	Nihon Rail	Suzuki Shōten

Notes: Same as Table 1. Bujuntan Hanbai is in italics because it was owned by Mitsui Bussan. It was also owned by Mitsubishi Shōji.

Nihon Menka, Tōyō Menka, Gōshō, Nihon Kiito, Itō Chū Shōji, Marubeni Shōten, Kanematsu Shōten, Itō Man Shōten, Takashimaya Iida, and Asahi Silk were the former type, and Mitsui Bussan, Suzuki Shōten, Mitsubishi Shōji, Iwai Shōten, Ōkura Shōji, Ataka Shōkai, Daidō Bōeki, and Asano Bussan belonged to the latter group. The textile trading companies usually specialized in given items. Nihon Menka, Tōyō Menka, and Gōshō specialized in raw cotton and cotton yarn import and cotton cloth export, Nihon Kiito and Asahi Silk specialized in raw silk, waste silk, and silk fabric export; and Kanematsu Shōten and Takashimaya Iida specialized in wool and woolen yarn import. Of course, these companies

companies or merchants

Iwai Shōten	Nihon Menka		
Fuji Denki	Gadelius	Nichizui Bōeki	Suzuki Shōten

Standard Sekiyu			
Taishō Bōeki	*Mitsui Bussan*		
Iwai Shōten	Brunner Mond (Japan)	A. Cameron	
Shimada Shōkai	Ataka Shōkai	Nagata Shōten	

Iwai
Shōten

Source: Kokusanshinkōkai (The Association for Promoting Domestic Products), *Kokusan daichō jō kan* (A ledger of domestic production), Vol. 2, 1928.

diversified into other businesses to some extent. Nihon Menka dealt not only in cotton goods, such as raw cotton, cotton yarn, and cotton fabrics, but also in raw silk and waste silk. But basically there was a division of business among textile traders. They became big trading companies because textiles were the main items of foreign trade in Japan until the 1920s.

Table 4 shows the degree of diversification of each of the general trading companies. If we look at the 20 main items of export and import, it is clear that (1) Mitsui Bussan, Mitsubishi Shōji, and Suzuki Shōten were far more widely diversified than other trading companies, (2) Mitsui Bussan was far more widely diversified than

TABLE 4 The Number of Commodity Items among the Top 20 Items Exported and Imported in 1921–1925 Traded by Japanese General Trading Companies.

Company	Ranking	Number of export items			Number of import items			Grand total
		1–10	11–20	Total	1–10	11–20	Total	
Mitsui Bussan		8	8	16	10	9	19	35
Mitsubishi Shōji		2	1	3	6	7	13	16
Suzuki Shōten		1	1	2	7	5	12	14
Iwai Shōten		1	—	1	3	3	6	7
Asano Bussan		—	—	—	2	2	4	4
Ōkura Shōji		—	—	—	1	1	2	2
Ataka Shōkai		—	—	—	1	1	2	2
Daidō Bōeki		—	1	1	—	—	—	1

Note: This table is based on Tables 2 and 3.

TABLE 5   The Number of Overseas Branches of the Main Trading Companies, 1926.

Mitsui Bussan*	27
Nihon Menka	20
Mitsubishi Shōji	16
Ōkura Shōji	11
Suzuki Shōten**	7
Tōyō Menka	6
Gōshō	5
Iwai Shōten	4
Itō Chū Shōji	4
Takashimaya Iida	3
Asano Bussan	3
Nihon Kiito	2
Daidō Bōeki	2
Kanematsu Shōten	1
Ataka Shōkai	1
Asahi Silk	1

*   Besides branches and subbranches, Mitsui Bussan had local subsidiary companies in Germany and France.

**   Besides branches, Suzuki Shōten had 42 *shūtchō ten* (outlets), which were probably smaller than subbranches.

Source: Tōkyō Kōshinjo (Tokyo Commercial Inquiry Agency), *Ginkō kaisha yōroku* (Directory of banks and companies), 31st ed., 1926.

the other two large companies, and (3) Iwai Shōten was fourth in degree of diversification because it dealt not only in important import goods but also in an important export good, while Asano Bussan, Ōkura Shōji, Ataka Shōkai, and Daidō Bōeki dealt only in a few important import goods.

When we consider the degree of multinationality of trading companies, we should take into account not only the number of overseas branches (including subbranches) of each company but also their location. Table 5 shows the number of overseas branches of the main Japanese trading companies. Taking the structure of Japan's foreign trade and the structure of Japan's foreign exchange transactions by region, we see that New York, London, Bombay, and Shanghai were the most important locations for branches. The overseas branches of the main Japanese trading companies were situated as follows:

	New York	London	Bombay	Shanghai
Mitsui Bussan	○	○	○	○
Nihon Menka	○	○	○	○
Mitsubishi Shōji	○	○		○
Suzuki Shōten	○	○		○
Iwai Shōten	○	○		○
Ōkura Shōji	○	○		○
Takashimaya Iida	○	○		○
Tōyō Menka			○	○
Gōshō			○	○
Nihon Kiito	○			
Asano Bussan	○			
Asahi Silk	○			
Ataka Shōkai	○			
Itō Chū				○

Mitsui Bussan stands out in the number of overseas branches and their location in important cities, followed by Nihon Menka, Mitsubishi Shōji, Suzuki Shōten, Ōkura Shōji, and Iwai Shōten. Among the general trading companies, Ataka Shōkai had an overseas branch only in London and Asano Bussan had branches only in the United States (in New York, San Francisco, and Seattle); it follows that Ataka Shōkai specialized in trade between Japan and England and Asano Bussan in the trade between Japan and the United States.

In summary, we can say that Mitsui Bussan, Mitsubishi Shōji, and Suzuki Shōten meet our criteria for a general trading company. Iwai Shōten and Ōkura Shōji meet all the criteria too, except that Ōkura Shōji did not deal in the main export items. Broadly speaking, the latter two can be considered general trading companies. Mitsui Bussan was the prototypal general trading company in Japan, at least until the middle of the 1920s.

At the same time, trading companies specializing in textile trade occupied an important position in the ranking of trading companies in Japan in the 1920s. As shown in Table 1, Nihon Menka stood between Suzuki Shōten and Mitsubishi Shōji, and Tōyō Menka and Gōshō followed Mitsubishi Shōji. Nihon Kiito, Itō Chū Shōji, and Marubeni Shōten were abreast of Iwai Shōten and Ōkura Shōji. This means that there were two ways for Japanese trading companies to realize ecomonies of scale: one was through diversifying into many lines of commodities and the other was through expanding business in one line of commodity. Japanese trading companies which specialized in textiles could grow without aggressively diversifying because Japanese textile-manufacturing industries grew rapidly, at least until the 1920s.

III. Factors Which Enabled Mitsui Bussan to Develop as a General Trading Company

Mitsui Bussan, a general trading company, was the paramount trading company in Japan. We may find factors which enabled trading companies to develop as general trading companies by observing its developmental process and drawing out factors which helped it open and maintain overseas branches, diversify into transactions of many important goods in foreign trade, and become a trading company which occupied the dominant position in Japanese foreign trade.

Mitsui Bussan was established by the House of Mitsui in 1876, but it had two forerunners, the Mitsui Gumi Kokusangata (Mitsui Office for Domestic Trade) and the Senshū Kaisha. The Mitsui Gumi Kokusangata was established in 1874 by the House of Mitsui to deal in and transport goods produced in the area where the House of Mitsui had 27 branch offices in connection with its function as a government treasury agent. The major products handled were processed marine products, wood, and textiles from the seven islands of Izu, imported cotton yarn, and wool textiles, rice, raw silk, and tea. The Senshū Kaisha was established in 1874 by Inoue Kaoru, who resigned from the government to promote export trade. The company earned a stable commission through importing woolen cloth, blankets, and weapons for the Ministry of the Army; dealing in rice which Yamaguchi Prefecture received as public tax; and handling coal and tea. But when Inoue returned to the government at the end of 1875, the company decided to close. The House of Mitsui took over its business and established a new company named Mitsui Bussan. The Mitsui Gumi Kokusangata was handed over to Mitsui Bussan in 1876.

Mitsui Bussan was owned by Mitsui Yōnosuke and Mitsui Takenosuke, who were neither heads of the family nor eldest sons

TABLE 6 The Percentage of Japanese Foreign Trade Handled by Japanese Merchants and by Mitsui Bussan.

	Percentage handled by Japanese merchants			Percentage handled by Mitsui Bussan			Percentage of Japanese merchants' trade handled by Mitsui Bussan		
	Export	Import	Total	Export	Import	Total	Export	Import	Total
1874	0.6	0.3	0.4						
77	3.6	1.6	2.5						
80	13.4	2.6	7.3						
83	14.2	4.9	10.1						
86	11.7	8.2	10.3						
89	9.7	14.6	12.1						
90	10.8	23.9	18.5	8.6	5.2	6.6	79.6	21.8	35.7
91	11.0	19.4	14.7						
94	18.4	29.2	23.9						
97	27.8	36.7	32.8	6.4	15.3	11.5	23.0	41.7	35.1
1900	37.1	39.4	38.5	10.8	15.8	13.7	29.1	40.1	35.6
1901	24.8	37.0	31.0	8.3	14.5	11.4	33.5	39.2	36.8
06	36.5	46.6	41.6	16.9	17.8	17.3	46.3	38.2	41.6
14				27.3	23.9	25.6			
16	51.5	63.8	56.5	22.8	22.6	22.7	44.3	35.4	40.2

Note: The percentage handled by Japanese merchants is based on the figures for the whole country from 1874 to 1900, but the percentages for 1901, 1906, and 1916 are derived from figures for the port of Kobe alone.

Percentage of Japanese merchants' trade handled by Mitsui Bussan = $\dfrac{\text{Percentage handled by Mitsui Bussan}}{\text{Percentage handled by Japanese merchants}}$

Sources: Kiyoshi Matsui, ed., *Kindai Nihon bōeki shi dai ni kan* (The history of modern Japan's foreign trade), Vol. 2, 1961, p. 135; Asahi Shimbun Sha, *Nihon keizai tōkei sōkan* (A collection of Japanese economic statistics), 1928, p. 236.

and who supplied no capital stock from the family. The House of Mitsui permitted Mitsui Bank to lend no more than ¥50,000 to Mitsui Bussan. The real management of Mitsui Bussan was entrusted to Masuda Takashi, who had undertaken the management of the Senshū Sha; he became president of Mitsui Bussan. The company's business was mainly composed of *seifu goyō shōbai* (business for the government) in the early stage of its development; it constituted 64.6% of its total sales during the period from July to December in 1876. The supply of rice to the Ministry of Finance and the import of woolen cloth for the army were the major goyō shōbai.

The composition of Mitsui Bussan's business changed gradually. "Around 1890 seifu goyō shōbai, which was predominant in the early stage of its development, greatly decreased, and business for the private sector came to the fore. . . . Concurrently, the proportion of domestic trade decreased, and foreign trade became the major part of its business."[4] The relationship between Mitsui Bussan and the House of Mitsui also changed. When Mitsui Bussan was reorganized to become an unlimited partnership with capital of ¥1 million in July 1893, it became a first-rank subsidiary of the Mitsui zaibatsu. In October 1909 it was reorganized again to become a stock company with capital amounting to ¥20 million. At the same time, Mitsui Bank became a stock company with the same amount of capital, and in November 1909 Dōzokukai Kanribu (The Control Department of the Mitsui Family Council) was reorganized to become an unlimited partnership with capital of ¥50 million. In December 1911 Mitsui Mining was reorganized to become a stock company with capital totaling ¥20 million. In this way the Mitsui zaibatsu became a *Konzern* (combination), and Mitsui Bussan, Mitsui Bank, and Mitsui Mining became its first-rank subsidiaries.[5]

Japanese foreign trade was almost completely controlled by foreign merchants at the beginning, as Table 6 shows. The share handled by Japanese merchants was almost negligible in 1874 and under 10% even around 1880. But their share rose gradually and reached 38.5% in 1900. Although we have no national data which show the share handled by Japanese merchants after that time, we do have data for Kobe port after 1900. According to these data, it is clear that the

same trend continued after 1900, the Japanese merchants' share
reaching 56.5% in 1916.

Mitsui Bussan led this trend. Its share in Japanese foreign trade
(the total of export and import) was only 6.6% in 1890. After that,
its share increased steadily, reaching 25.6% in 1914. Its share in
foreign trade undertaken by Japanese merchants was 35.6% in 1900
and 40.2% in 1916.[6] Mitsui Bussan consistently handled over 30%
of the foreign trade undertaken by Japanese merchants, making it
a main pillar of the Japanese foreign trading community.

How could Mitsui Bussan expand its share in foreign trade when
foreign merchants dominated Japanese foreign trade almost completely? One answer to this question may be that Mitsui Bussan
succeeded in introducing an innovation into foreign trade transactions; in other words, it became a general trading company. But
one has to pay more costs and bear more risks when one tries to
multinationalize and diversify. Employees have to learn a foreign
language and foreign customs before they go abroad. They have to
become accustomed to life in the foreign country, accumulate
knowledge about each new commodity in which the company
wants to deal, and find new transaction channels for commodities
before the company can open and succeed in maintaining its overseas branches and before it can succeed in diversifying into the new
business. The factors which enabled Mitsui Bussan to minimize
costs and risks when it attempted to establish overseas branches and
to deal in many lines of commodities must be identified.

1. Masuda Takashi

Masuda Takashi, who became the first president of Mitsui Bussan,
was once a captain in a *bakufu* (shogunate) cavalry division, and he
moved to Yokohama after the Meiji Restoration of 1868. He studied
English, which enabled him to obtain work as a clerk in a foreign
trading house in Yokohama. He learned the business of foreign trade
there and came to be acquainted with an American merchant
named Robert Walker Irwin, who was a director of the trading
house's branch office in Nagasaki. Irwin was employed as an adviser
by Mitsui Bussan when it was established, and went to London to

undertake the company's export and import business in 1877. He laid the foundation for the establishment of the London branch in 1880. Masuda also became acquainted with a Swiss merchant, a fellow clerk, who went to Shanghai to do business independently. Mitsui Bussan opened a branch in Shanghai in 1877 after entrusting its agency business to him for some time.[7]

Because Masuda himself could speak English well and had sufficient experience in the foreign trade business, and because in addition, he was acquainted with a few capable foreign merchants through his work in a foreign trade house, he was able to help Mitsui Bussan minimize the above-mentioned costs and risks.

We must add one thing to the role played by Masuda. His brother-in-law, Yano Jirō, was the first schoolmaster of Furitsu Shōhō Kōshūjo (a commercial school established by the government of Tokyo), a forerunner of today's Hitotsubashi University.[8] Many students who received a modern business education at this school entered Mitsui Bussan after graduation.

2. *Business for the Government*

Business for the government, or seifu goyō syōbai, accounted for the dominant share of Mitsui Bussan's total sales at the beginning of its development. Representative activities were the supply of rice to the Finance Ministry, the export of rice controlled by the government, and the import of woolen cloth to the army.[9] Mitsui Bussan also played a role as a foreign exchange bank, utilizing government funds from 1877 to 1880, when the Yokohama Specie Bank was established. Under this system, Mitsui Bussan lent money at a rate of under 10% per annum to merchants who exported goods directly to European countries and drafted bills as documents to itself. The government lent the necessary sums of money to Mitsui Bussan free up to ¥300,000 per annum and at a rate of 5% per annum over that sum. After selling goods in European countries, merchants repaid the borrowed money (including interest) to Mitsui Bussan and the latter also repaid it to the consul there in foreign currencies.[10] This seifu goyō shobai was done on a commission basis, and Mitsui Bussan could earn a steady profit with which to build its business.

This connection with the government also enabled Mitsui Bussan to undertake much business during the Satsuma Rebellion in 1877 and to earn a large profits, amounting to ¥200,000.[11]

Business for the government played a further important role in opening and maintaining overseas branches. The London branch mainly bought woolen cloth and blankets for the army and sold rice controlled by the government. The commission procured through the latter was 35.7% of the profit which the London branch earned from September 1, 1879, to December 31, 1882. It was 73.0%, 75.0%, 5.8%, 41.7% and 37.9% in 1883, 1884, 1885, 1888, and 1889 respectively.

The Paris branch was also established with the help of government business. This branch was opened to deal in foreign exchange and to sell the raw silk manufactured by the government-operated silk-reeling mill in Tomioka. The interest and commission for this business helped Mitsui Bussan maintain the Paris branch. Other branches, in Shanghai, Hong Kong, and Singapore, were opened to promote the export of coal mined by the government-operated Miike Mine to China and Singapore in 1877, 1886, and 1891 respectively.[12] It is clear that business for the government decreased the risks which the overseas branches might have incurred in their infant days and laid the foundation for the company's development afterward. Moreover, these branches enabled Mitsui Bussan to diversify into dealing in new goods which Japan needed to import and export with fewer costs and risks than those which might have had to be incurred if those branches had not existed.

The existence of the London branch in particular played an important part in Mitsui Bussan's diversifying into cotton-spinning machines, raw cotton, cotton yarn, and cotton cloth. In 1882 Mitsui Bussan imported cotton-spinning machines manufactured by Platt & Co. for the Osaka Cotton Spinning Co.,[13] the first modern cotton-spinning mill in Japan. After that, Mitsui Bussan often dealt in Platt products and made a sole-agency contract with the company in 1886.[14] The existence of the London branch probably enabled Mitsui Bussan to get an order for cotton-spinning machines from the Osaka Cotton Spinning Co., just as the import of cotton-spinning machines enabled it to get an order of raw cotton from the cotton-spinning companies,[15] and furthermore led to the export of cotton yarn and cotton cloth which they manufactured. This relationship was very important because cotton-spinning machines and machines for processing raw cotton and producing cotton goods were later among the five largest transaction items for Mitsui Bussan.

3. *Risk Management and Anticipatory Transactions*

As stated earlier, Mitsui Bussan's commodity transactions centered around business for the government on a commission basis at first, and later they centered around business for private companies and the export and import of goods. Of course, the later business involved business on commission, but to expand business more quickly, trading companies had to enter into anticipatory transactions, in which they oversold or overbought commodities and bore some risks with respect to the items oversold or overbought. Risks were highest in dealing in commodities whose prices fluctuated sharply, and those were the main commodities in Japanese foreign trading.[16] Foreign trading companies could not succeed in transacting in such commodities without forming systems for managing the risks.

Originally, Mitsui Bussan only did business on commission, but employees often took some risks to expand business. Especially in 1894, when the Sino-Japanese War broke out, anticipatory transactions increased in a large way. In 1895 the headquarters let branches submit reports on the volume of overselling or overbuying for evaluation. Later the headquarters prohibited anticipatory transactions in many agricultural and marine products which it considered speculative during war time. On the other hand, it permitted anticipatory transactions with respect to the import of foreign rice, soybeans, soybean cake, Chinese and Indian raw cotton, tin, oil, accessories for cotton-spinning machines, and matches. After that, the number of commodities for which anticipatory transactions were permitted and the limits on anticipatory transactions increased. While all anticipatory transactions were temporarily prohibited in August 1900 and July 1908 during economic crises, the headquarters permitted anticipatory transactions in an increasing number of commodities: coal, cotton yarn, and cotton cloth in 1896; sugar, wool, raw silk, materials for making passenger cars

TABLE 7   The Main Commodities Dealt in by Mitsui Bussan, 1890–1914.

Ranking	1890		1894	
	Commodity	%	Commodity	%
1	Rice	25.8	Raw cotton	18.7
2	Fertilizer and marine products	14.3	Rice	14.7
3	Coal	12.6	Coal	11.7
4	Raw cotton	11.0	Fertilizer and marine products	10.1
5	Machines }	7.8	Machines	8.7
6	Metals }		Metals	4.2
7	Raw silk	3.0	Raw silk	3.9

Note: The percentage shows the ratio of sales in each commodity to total sales for all commodities.

and freight cars, and rails and cross ties in 1897; lead, oil for machines, rape oil, and cottonseed oil in 1898; chemical fertilizer, paper, cement, flour, soybean products at Yukow, woolen yarn, and muslin and other goods in 1899.

In 1908 headquarters permitted anticipatory transactions in 40 types of merchandise, a large part of the 48 important items in which Mitsui Bussan dealt. The amount by which branches could oversell or overbuy each commodity was raised seven times; in 1920 it was as much as 10 times that in 1900. The proportion of this limit to the proceeds of a sale also increased between 1900 and 1921, from ¦3.6% to 6.8% for overselling and from 2.0% to 2.5% for overbuying.

According to Suzuki Kunio, who made a detailed survey of Mitsui Bussan's overselling and overbuying activities, the anticipatory business of Mitsui Bussan came into existence around 1895 and had been firmly established by 1920. The limits on overselling or overbuying were decided by the board of directors of Mitsui Bussan. In 1914 the managing directors were empowered—with certain restrictions—to decide the limits on the amount, and this amount gradually increased.[17]

Mitsui Bussan formed a parallel system for computing overall income and expenditures for a given commodity. Establishment of the supervisory branch for raw cotton in the Osaka branch in 1893

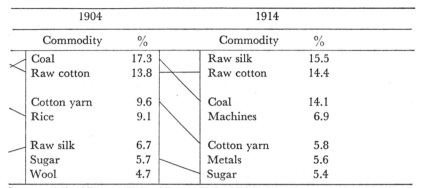

1904		1914	
Commodity	%	Commodity	%
Coal	17.3	Raw silk	15.5
Raw cotton	13.8	Raw cotton	14.4
Cotton yarn	9.6	Coal	14.1
Rice	9.1	Machines	6.9
Raw silk	6.7	Cotton yarn	5.8
Sugar	5.7	Metals	5.6
Wool	4.7	Sugar	5.4

Source: Mitsui Bussan, "Mitsui Bussan Kabushiki Kaisha 100 nen shi jō" (A 100-year history of Mitsui Bussan), Vol. 1, 1978, pp. 84, 92, 222, 346.

represented the beginning of this system. In July 1898 a regulation for overall income and expenditure computation was established, and an overall computation system was introduced for raw silk, raw cotton, cotton yarn and cloth for export, soybeans, soybean cake, rice for export, coal, matches, and fertilizer. In February 1900 this regulation was abolished and a provision which stated the principle of overall computations was inserted in section eight of the company rule book. Detailed regulations based on this provision were introduced with respect to many important commodities. In July 1911 a rule for dealing in special kinds of goods was introduced, and the supervisory branch was subdivided into the supervisory branch and the main dealing branches. The commodities assigned to the supervisory branch were machines, raw cotton, coal, wood, and sugar. The main dealing branches were responsible for rice for export and import, chemical fertilizer, and cement. Under this system the supervisory branch efficiently coordinated buying and selling activities and the use of funds in the branches.[18]

Thus, Mitsui Bussan established two systems to control its commodity transactions; one established control by the board of directors and the managing directors through their establishment of limits on overselling and overbuying, and the other established control by the supervisory branch. It is clear that the former enabled Mitsui Bussan to manage risks incurred in engaging in anticipatory transactions.

Under the latter, buying and selling activities in many branches which dealt in the same commodity were coordinated by the supervisory branch, which was controlled by the managing directors. So it also constituted a part of the risk-management system of the company.

Table 7 shows the change in Mitsui Bussan's commodity dealings between 1890 and 1914. The rankings and the weights of raw silk, raw cotton, cotton yarn, metal, and sugar rose rapidly from 1890 to 1914. The prices of these commodities, which occupied an important place in Japanese foreign trade, fluctuated sharply. Mitsui Bussan succeeded in diversifying into these commodities because it established an effective risk-management system before entering this kind of business aggressively. Furthermore, it became a large trading company which dealt in most of the important export and import goods because it succeeded in this type of diversification.

4.   The Mitsui Zaibatsu and Trade

As shown in Table 7, raw silk, raw cotton, coal, machines, cotton yarn, metals, and sugar occupied an important position in Mitsui Bussan's commodity dealings in 1914. Among them, raw silk, raw cotton, cotton yarn, coal, machines, and sugar were produced by enterprises which belonged to the Mitsui zaibatsu or were financially supported by Mitsui Bank, so Mitsui Bussan could occupy an important position in dealing in each commodity.

Coal: In 1888 the Mitsui zaibatsu bought the Miike Mine from the government and established Miike Tankō Sha (Miike Mine Co.). The next year Mitsui Bussan made a contract to become the sole agency for this company. In 1892 the company was reorganized as Mitsui Kōzan Gōshi Kaisha (Mitsui Mining & Co.), which became the leading coal-mining company in Japan.[19] In 1913 it seized the rights for the management of Hokkaido Tankō Kisen Kaisha (Hokkaido Colliery and Steamship Co.), which was the third-largest coal-mining company in Japan at that time, and entered into a special contract as sole agency for the company outside Hokkaido.[20] In 1911 Mitsui Mining accounted for 20.5% of the coal production in Japan, and the Hokkaido Colliery and Steamship Co. accounted for 6.2%. Together they accounted for 26.7%, far exceeding the

TABLE 8   Mitsui Bank and Mitsui Bussan Loans to Collieries.

(Unit: Yen)

Colliery	Mitsui Bank	Mitsui Bussan	Total
Hōkoku Tankō	582,409	322,207	904,616
Hondō Tankō	125,000		125,000
Kaijima Tasuke	382,500		382,500
Asō Takichi	221,880		221,880
Kaijima Kōgyō	557,907	499,185	1,057,092
Tajima Nobuo		50,000	50,000
Yoshi no Ya Tankō		99,000	99,000
Fukui Tankō		4,000	4,000
Okada Tankō		17,888	17,888
Ōjō Tankō		17,156	17,156
Sasahara Tankō		16,600	16,600
Kansai Saitan		8,945	8,945
Total	1,869,696	1,034,981	2,904,677

Source: Mitsui Bunko (The Mitsui Library), *Mitsui jigyōshi shiryōhen 3* (The history of Mitsui's business: A volume of materials 3), 1974, p. 474.

14.3% of the next-largest coal producer, Mitsubishi Gōshi.[21] It is clear that Mitsui Bussan could occupy an advantageous position in the market by securing coal through sole-agency status for these companies belonging to the Mitsui zaibatsu. Moreover, in 1898 Mitsui Bussan began to buy coal mined by other large companies, and this amounted to more than half of the coal it handled after 1900.[22] As shown in Table 8, Mitsui Bussan lent money to these companies in cooperation with Mitsui Bank, which induced them to sell coal in large quantities to Mitsui Bussan. Mitsui Bussan exported from 70% to 80% of Japanese coal between 1905 to 1912. Its share of the domestic market in 1904 or 1906 was as follows: in Kobe, from 65% to 70%; in Osaka, 36%; in Nagoya, 53%; and in Tokyo, 14%.[23]

Raw Cotton, Cotton Yarn: In 1886 cotton merchants in Tokyo established a company named Tokyo Men Shōsha (Tokyo Cotton Trading Co.) which dealt in raw cotton. Two years later it was renamed Kanegafuchi Bōseki (Kanegafuchi Cotton Spinning Co., later, Kanebō) and set up to produce and sell cotton yarn. But its performance was bad, and in 1890 Mitsui Bank lent money to the company to relieve its financial problems. In addition, the bank assigned Nakamigawa Hikojirō and Asabuki Eiji to its board of directors and became the largest shareholder in 1892. After that, the company actively merged with many cotton-spinning companies and expanded rapidly, becoming the largest cotton-spinning company in Japan.[24]

During this process, the company became a second-rank subsidiary of the Mitsui zaibatsu. For example, in the first half of 1898 Mitsui Takayasu, who was president of Mitsui Bank, owned 24,282 shares in Kanebō, which was 48.6% of its total shares. After 1902, when the Mitsui zaibatsu changed its policy of aiming to control promising manufacturing companies, Mitsui Bank gradually sold its shares. As a result, Mitsui Takayasu held only 1.8% of Kanebō's shares in the latter half of 1909, but holders belonging to the Mitsui zaibatsu owned 8.3% of its total shares. This is far ahead of the 3.6% which Yasuda Zenzaburō, who was the largest individual shareholder, held at that time.[25]

Thus, Kanebō, the largest cotton-spinning company in Japan, continued to be a second-rank subsidiary of the Mitsui zaibatsu. Through the latter connection, Mitsui Bussan could continue to be the largest raw cotton supplier to Kanebō and the largest cotton yarn exporter, although Mitsui Bussan could not obtain sole-agency rights for this company. In 1903 and 1904 Mitsui Bussan had a 61% to 85% share of the raw cotton which Kanebō bought from trading companies, and from the latter half of 1907 to the latter half of 1911, its share was about 45% on the average.[26] Mitsui Bussan was the most important cotton yarn exporter for Kanebō.[27] It controlled 26.0% of the market for raw cotton imported to Japan and ranked first or second during 1904–12, abreast of Nihon Menka. Similarly it controlled an average 35.7% of the cotton yarn exports during 1904–13 and ranked first.[28]

Sugar: After Japan colonized Taiwan, its governor general asked the Mitsui zaibatsu to establish a sugar-manufacturing company there. In 1900 the Mitsui zaibatsu assisted with the establishment of Taiwan Seitō (Formosa Sugar Manufacturing Co.), controlling about 20% of its stock shares. Mitsui Bussan was contracted as the sole agency for selling Taiwan Seitō's products in Japan proper in

1902.[29] Taiwan Seitō had 29.6% of the total production capacity of sugar in Taiwan in 1913–14 and ranked first. Moreover, it ranked with Dai Nippon Seitō (Dai Nippon Sugar Manufacturing Co.) and Meiji Seitō (Meiji Sugar Manufacturing Co.), which were the two largest sugar-manufacturing companies in Japan in terms of profits before World War I.[30]

Machines: Cotton-spinning and weaving machines and electrical machines composed the two largest categories of machines in which Mitsui Bussan dealt immediately before World War I. A large share of the machines in which the company dealt were imported from abroad, and it contracted as the sole agency for the cotton-spinning and weaving machines of Platt Brothers & Co. and for the electrical machines of General Electric Co.[31] These ties with famous foreign manufacturers were sources of the competitive position of the company.

At the same time, the Mitsui zaibatsu had connections with domestic machine manufacturers. Mitsui Bussan established Toyoda Shiki Shokki (Toyoda-Style Cotton Weaving Machine Manufacturing Co.) in cooperation with Toyoda Sakichi, who invented the Toyoda-style cotton-weaving machines in 1907. Toyoda Sakichi and Mitsui Hachirōjirō, who was president of Mitsui Bussan, each owned 5% of this company's shares and ranked first among 145 shareholders.[32] As for electrical machines, in 1893 Mitsui Bank received Tanaka Seizōsho (Tanaka Machine Manufacturing Mill), which had been producing machines for industries as the collateral for the money which the bank lent to it and which it could not repay, and renamed the mill Shibaura Seisakusho (Shibaura Machine Manufacturing Mill). This mill was tranferred from Mitsui Bank to Mitsui Mining in 1898 and separated from it to become a stock company in 1904. Mitsui Gōmei owned a majority of the shares of this company, and General Electric Co. owned a quarter after the company tied up with GE in 1909.[33] Both Toyoda Shiki Shokki and Shibaura Seisakusho were representative of domestic machine manufacturers in their respective fields, and Mitsui Bussan became an outstanding trader in machines even in domestic markets through maintaining sole agency contracts with them.

Raw Silk: The case for raw silk was somewhat different from the above-mentioned cases. The Mitsui zaibatsu did not have any large silk reelers under its control, and the quantities of raw silk in which Mitsui Bussan dealt increased rapidly after it adopted the policy under which it bought or sold raw silk in advance or anticipatory purchases from silk merchants who collected raw silk from silk reelers and sold it to exporters. As shown in Table 7, the ranking of raw silk in Mitsui Bussan's commodity transactions rose rapidly after 1904. This trend almost paralleled the trend of the policy toward anticipatory transactions. Nevertheless, there was a previous history of success for Mitsui Bussan's silk business.

In 1894, when a reform was carried out to promote the development of the Mitsui zaibatsu's manufacturing businesses, Mitsui bought the government-operated silk-reeling mill in Tomioka, received the mill in Osaka as the result of foreclosing on a mortgage, and established two mills in Nagoya and Mie. The number of boilers in these four mills totaled 1,630, exceeding the 778 boilers of Katakura Gumi Co., which had been the largest. Two years later Mitsui Bussan reestablished a New York branch and promoted the shop in Yokohama from *toriatsukaijo* (an office which only delivers goods) to a formal branch to deal in the raw silk manufactured by these mills belonging to the zaibatsu. This business did not perform well, and Mitsui Bussan sold the four silk-reeling mills to Hara & Co. in 1902. As mentioned above, Mitsui Bussan's silk business increased rapidly in another direction, that is, in buying raw silk from silk merchants in Yokahama and exporting it directly to the United States in anticipatory fashion.[34] But it was necessary for Mitsui Bussan to have experience in transactions in raw silk and to reestablish branches in New York and Yokohama through exporting the raw silk manufactured by these mills before it could succeed in the silk business.

Because Mitsui Bussan was a trading company belonging to the Mitsui zaibatsu and the Mitsui zaibatsu was the largest zaibatsu in Japan, Mitsui Bussan had the following two characteristics. First, Mitsui Bussan diversified into many goods which occupied an important position in Japan's foreign trade, and second, in most cases it occupied an advantageous position in the transactions in these goods because it secured sole-agency status with the companies which dominated each industry. Even if it did not secure sole-agency status, it transacted for a large share of the raw materials and machines which the companies bought and sold. Moreover, the money lending of Mitsui Bank to the companies which competed with companies belonging to the Mitsui zaibatsu in each market further strengthened the competitive position of Mitsui Bussan in each commodity market.

IV. Other General Trading Companies—Mitsubishi Shōji, Suzuki Shōten, Ōkura Shōji, and Iwai Shōten

Some companies became general trading companies along with Mitsui Bussan before the national crisis in the early 1930s: Mitsubishi Shōji, Suzuki Shōten, Ōkura Shōji, and Iwai Shōten. The aim of this paper is, while considering factors related to Mitsui Bussan's development, to observe briefly the factors which, on the one hand, enabled these companies to develop as general trading companies and which, on the other hand, placed them in disadvantageous position compared to Mitsui Bussan.

Mitsubishi Shōji: Mitsubishi Shōji was spun off from Mitsubishi Gōshi in 1918 and made into a stock company. Mitsubishi established its branches as stock companies during 1917–20, becoming a zaibatsu combination in the process. It owned all shares of the subsidiary companies, which included Mitsubishi Zōsen (shipbuilding), Mitsubishi Seitetsu (iron manufacturing), Mitsubishi Sōko (warehousing), Mitsubishi Shōji (foreign trading), Mitsubishi Kōgyō (mining), Mitsubishi Ginkō (banking), Mitsubishi Nainenki-seizō (internal-combustion-engine manufacturing), and Mitsubishi Denki (electrical machine manufacturing).[35] Mitsubishi had firmly established an advantageous position in shipbuilding, mining, and banking by this time and was entering iron and electrical machine manufacturing, which meant that Mitsubishi Shōji was established after Mitsubishi was firmly established as a zaibatsu. Mitsubishi Shōji occupied an advantageous position in transactions in commodities which were dealt with in large quantities through gaining sole-agency status for the various oligopolistic enterprises belonging to the zaibatsu. Moreover, it overcame the difficulties it experienced in the early stage of its development with the backing of the zaibatsu's capital resources.

Suzuki Shōten: Suzuki Shōten was only a middle-class sugar merchant in Kobe when its first president, Suzuki Iwajirō, died in
1894. After that, Kaneko Naokichi, its leading clerk, took over the
management and adopted an aggressive business strategy. He
became acquainted with Gotō Shimpei, who was a director of the
Public Welfare Bureau of the governor general of Taiwan, and
undertook business for this government. Suzuki Shōten developed
quickly through close-to-monopolistic dealings in camphor, which
was a government monopoly, and sugar, which was a specialty of
the island. Suzuki Shōten gradually expanded into foreign trading
and mainland business, and in 1907 it earned a large profit through
selling a sugar-manufacturing mill at Dairi in the northern part of
Kyushu to Dai Nippon Seitō. With this profit, Suzuki Shōten
refurbished a plant of Kōbe Seikōsho (steel mill), which it had
bought in 1905, and prepared to receive orders from the navy.

While Kaneko endeavored to expand business with the government, he had other overlapping policies. He wanted Suzuki Shōten
to become a general trading company, and he wanted it to diversify
into promising manufacturing businesses. This strategy was pursued
most aggressively during World War I, and heavily depended upon
the Formosa (Taiwan) Bank for financial support; it was pursued,
even in the 1920s when the company fell into financial difficulties.[36]

Suzuki Shōten's volume of business amounted to ¥1,540 million
in 1917 and ¥540 million in 1926.[37] Mitsui Bussan's volume amounted to ¥1,095 million in 1917 and ¥1,180 million in 1926.[38] Suzuki
Shōten surpassed Mitsui Bussan temporarily during World War I
and maintained half the volume of business of Mitsui Bussan even
in 1926. It dealt mainly in sugar, flour, metal, lumber, raw cotton,
wool, fertilizer, machines, and miscellaneous goods. Sugar was
especially important in sales value, and Suzuki Shōten was one of
the largest Java sugar merchants in the world. In metal, it was the
sole importer for Tata and Bengal pig iron, and dealt in large
quantities of imported steel materials and steel materials manufactured by Kawasaki Shipbuilding Co. It was a sole agent for Nihon
Seifun (flour milling), which was the largest flour-milling company
in Japan. In fertilizer, especially in ammonium sulphate, it competed
with Mitsui Bussan for the top position.[39]

Suzuki Shōten controlled 65 companies, and the amount of their paid-up capital totaled ¥356 million in 1927. Among the many promising companies belonging to Suzuki Shōten were Kōbe Seikōsho (steel manufacturing), Teikoku Jinzō Kenshi (synthetic-fiber manufacturing), Nihon Seifun (flour milling), Hōnen Seiyu (vegetable oil manufacturing), Dai Nippon Celluloid, Asahi Sekiyu (oil refining), Nihon Yakin (metallurgy), and others.[40] In comparison, the amount of paid-up capital of the companies belonging to the Mitsui zaibatsu totaled ¥446 million in 1928.[41] Suzuki Shōten reached about 80% of the size of the Mitsui zaibatsu, the largest zaibatsu in Japan. It developed into a general trading company, becoming a zaibatsu at the same time; indeed, its development as a general trading company was promoted by its development as a zaibatsu.

Ōkura Shōji: In 1918 Ōkura Doboku (civil engineering) and Ōkura Kōgyō (mining) were separated from Kabushiki Kaisha Ōkura Gumi, a stock company which was renamed Ōkura Shōji (Ōkura Foreign Trading Co.). This was the first time a trading company became independent of the Ōkura zaibatsu headquarters. But the history of Ōkura's trading section goes back to the time of the Meiji Restoration of 1868. Ōkura Kihachirō, a founder of the Ōkura zaibatsu, was born in Niigata and went up to Edo (later Tokyo), becoming an apprentice in a dried bonito shop immediately before the Meiji Restoration. After achieving independence as a food-shop owner, he changed his business and earned an enormous amount of profit through gun transactions. He established Ōkura Gumi Shōkai (Ōkura Gumi Co.) in 1873 and opened a branch in London which was the first overseas branch established by a Japanese merchant. After that, his business grew fast, mainly through transactions for the government. Ōkura Gumi Shōkai supplied food and needed supplies to the army, imported weapons and machines for the government, and acquired concessions in China during the Sino-Japanese War (1894–95). It played an active part in the import and transaction of war supplies and acquired concessions in Manchuria during the Russo-Japanese War (1904–5). In 1893 when the Commercial Law went into effect, Ōkura Gumi Shōkai was reorganized as an unlimited partnership. By this time, Ōkura Gumi

TABLE 9   Gross Sales of the Tokyo Headquarters and the Osaka Branch of
K.K. Ōkura Gumi by Section in the Latter Half of 1913.

(Unit: Yen, %)

Sections	Tokyo headquarters	Osaka branch	Total
	(22.5)	(20.5)	(21.6)
Electrical machines	1,662,776	1,230,324	2,893,100
	(23.6)	(19.0)	(21.6)
Machines	1,744,142	1,142,617	2,886,759
	(9.4)	(7.3)	(8.4)
Iron products	693,094	436,674	1,129,768
	(17.8)	(9.8)	(14.2)
Materials	1,311,931	586,920	1,898,851
	(2.2)		(1.2)
Export	164,465		164,465
	(0.3)	(3.4)	(1.7)
Domestic trade	21,086	204,229	225,315
	(6.8)		(3.8)
Rice and sugar	504,101		504,101
	(17.3)	(40.1)	(27.5)
Trade with China	1,275,678	2,411,134	3,686,812
	(100.0)	(100.0)	(100.0)
Total	7,377,273	6,011,896	13,389,171

Source: Kabushiki Kaisha Ōkura Gumi, "*Kessan meisaisho hohyō*" (Detailed statement
of accounts, a supplemental table), 1913.

Shōkai had diversified into civil engineering and mining, so the new
Gōmei Kaisha Ōkura Gumi had three divisions: trading, civil
engineering, and mining. In 1911 Gōmei Kaisha Ōkura Gumi
established itself as a stock company, Kabushiki Kaisha Ōkura
Gumi, which received three divisions from Gōmei Kaisha Ōkura
Gumi. As mentioned above, two divisions were separated from
K.K. Ōkura Gumi in 1917. Thus, Ōkura Shōji started as a merchant
engaging in foreign trade, diversified into civil engineering and
mining, and finally became a zaibatsu engaged mainly in foreign
trade.[42]

The development of the Ōkura zaibatsu's trading division during
the Meiji era (1868–1912) is not clear because of the lack of
data. It is generally accepted that the company depended heavily
on business for the government. Moreover, according to "Kessan

meisaisho hohyō" (Detailed statement of accounts, a supplemental table) for K.K. Ōkura Gumi for the latter half of 1913, it is clear that government business accounted for at least 39.4% of the gross sales of the Tokyo headquarters of the company at that time. The Tokyo headquarters was the largest among the branches in terms of gross sales, there are no data which show gross sales by customer except for the Tokyo headquarters.

Table 9 shows the gross sales for both the Tokyo headquarters and the Osaka branch by section. Electrical machines; machines; materials to be manufactured, such as woolen cloth, leather, and linen; goods for export to China, such as coal, wood, and marine products; and iron products manufactured by the government-operated iron mill and imported from overseas were the main commoditities which K.K. Ōkura Gumi handled. Electrical machines were most important,[43] and the company was the sole agent for AEG for this kind of machines. It developed as a general trading company in terms of the varieties of commodities handled, and its characteristic feature was that it mainly transacted with governmental sectors and dealt in electrical machines, especially AEG's.[44]

Ōkura Gumi had branches or semibranches not only in London but also in Shanghai, Hong Kong, Tientsin, and Dairen, in a process much the same as establishing branches for Seoul, Taipei, Mukden, New York, Sydney, and Hamburg after the Russo-Japanese War.[45] It is safe to say that it could open overseas branches and maintain them through business for the government and that the existence of overseas branches helped the company to transact in commodities which its customers required.

Among the main customers of the Tokyo headquarters were enterprises belonging to the Ōkura zaibatsu: Honkeiko Baitetsu Konsu (an iron-manufacturing company in China), Nihon Hikaku (leather manufacturing), Dai Nippon Beer, and others.[46] Ōkura Shōji increased the variety of commodities which it handled and strengthened its competitive position in the market by handling their products.

Iwai Shōten: In 1896 Iwai Katsujirō, a founder of Iwai Shōten, became independent of his father-in-law, a merchant who bought foreign goods from foreign merchant houses in Kobe and sold them to retailers in Osaka. He began to import goods directly from foreign countries after making an agency contract with William Duff & Co. Ltd. in London. He imported mainly metal, woolen cloth, woolen yarn, and chemicals.

Iwai thought that he could not become a big merchant if he dealt in the same commodities as other merchants did and acted only as an intermediary. Thinking that he could secure a solid basis for trade by starting manufacturing industries himself, he established many manufacturing companies from 1907 to 1921, among them Shirogane Meriyasu Kōjō (knitting mill), Nihon Celluloid Jinzō Kenshi (celluloid and rayon manufacturing), Aen Mekki (zinc plating)—which was later renamed Ōsaka Teppan (iron plate manufacturing), Ōsaka Sen'i Kōgyō (textile manufacturing), Nihon Sōda Kōgyō (soda manufacturing), Kansai Paint, Nihon Kyōryō (bridge building), and Chuō Keito Bōseki (woolen yarn spinning).

Meanwhile, he established Gōshi Kaisha Iwai Honten (Iwai & Co. Ltd.) as a holding company of the affiliated companies listed above. Iwai Honten's capital was ¥3 million in 1916, and in 1918 it was ¥10 million and the amount of its investment in affiliated companies amounted to over ¥12 million.

Iwai Shōten was a general agent for Kansai Paint until 1922 and for Chuō Keito Bōseki until 1938, and it was the sole supplier of essential steel materials to Ōsaka Kyōryō.[47] It is natural that the company was both a large supplier of materials and a large buyer of products for affiliated companies even after the general-agency contracts expired or when there were no such contracts. In Iwai Shōten's case, too, becoming a zaibatsu promoted its development as a general trading company.

We can conclude that the formation of a general trading company was closely related to the existence or the formation of zaibatsu in all four cases discussed above, and that the formation of a general trading company was assisted by heavy reliance on business for the government in two cases, Suzuki Shōten's and Ōkura Shōji's. But why did these companies stand in disadvantageous positions as general trading companies in comparison to Mitsui Bussan?

One answer to this question is the relative backwardness of their start as foreign trading companies. Mitsui Bussan was established in

1876, while Mitsubishi Shōji and Iwai Shōten were established in 1918 and 1896, and Suzuki Shōten was not a foreign trading company until 1894, when Kaneko Naokichi took charge. Only Ōkura Shōji, which traces its beginnings to the establishment of Ōkura Gumi Shōkai in 1873, was on a par with Mitsui Bussan in this respect.

But Ōkura Shōji stood far behind Mitsui Bussan in the 1920s. Moreover, the gap between Mitsui Bussan and the other three companies in the degree to which they developed into general trading companies does not seem to be explained sufficiently by their belated start. It is necessary for us to consider to what extent the first and third factors which enabled Mitsui Bussan to develop as a general trading company were applicable to these companies.

The first factor was the role played by Masuda Takashi. It is true that a founder or quasi founder—Kaneko Naokichi, Ōkura Kihachirō, and Iwai Yūjirō—played an important role in the development of the three companies. But from the standpoint of their contributions to the development of a general trading company, their roles were somewhat different from Masuda's. Masuda could speak English well, had experienced the practical business of foreign trade, and had become acquainted with foreign merchants during his work in a foreign merchant house. Masuda's familiarity with foreign merchants enabled Mitsui Bussan to minimize the risks which occur when trading companies establish overseas branches for the first time. None of the other founders, Kaneko, Ōkura, or Iwai, had these characteristics, although all of them were talented merchants.

As for the third factor, organizing for risk management, it is regrettable that we don't have data as detailed as that for Mitsui Bussan, but some data which are available are partly related to risk taking.

Mitsubishi Shōji: When Mitsubishi Shōji was established as a stock company in 1918, its main business was coal and copper, and transactions in general merchandise were still a small part of its business in spite of the rich variety of the goods it dealt in. In 1918 it established four subsections, for textiles, grains and fertilizer, machines, and timber, and the next year these four subsections were reorganized as four sections, for the cotton industry, oils and fats, machines, and timber. This meant diversification into commodities whose prices fluctuated violently. In 1921 the company had to abolish the sections for the cotton industry and timber because of their bad business records. Nor could the company pay dividends to the shareholders for six half-year periods from November 1919 to November 1922.[48] Furthermore, it could not handle raw silk within itself before 1936, although it had entered the raw silk business through a subsidiary company since 1918 when it established a mutual sole-agency contract with one of the five largest silk merchants in Yokohama, Ono Shōten.[49] Mitsubishi Shōji seems not to have been able to easily establish a risk-management system in anticipatory transactions during the early stage of its development.

Suzuki Shōten: Suzuki Shōten overtook Mitsui Bussan very rapidly during World War I, but its policy in foreign trade was too speculative, and its policy in diversifying into manufacturing industries was too risky. Its records show that business became worse after World War I and that it overcame financial difficulties only by increasing reliance on the Formosa Bank. It went bankrupt in 1927 when a financial crisis occurred. Kaneko Naokichi, dictatorial leader of Suzuki Shōten, himself said, "Then [at the end of World War I] I thought that we should change business policy drastically and began to prepare for the retreat. I told my intentions to the members of the company but unexpectedly they did not act as I wanted to. . . . Viewing it from the perspective of that time, Suzuki completely lost controlling power over the management of the company." Kaneko pointed out another case in which the members of the company did not follow his instructions to buy import bills as fast as possible and to sell export bills as slow as possible when the rate of foreign exchange continued to drop from the end of 1923 to 1924.[50] These episodes suggest that Suzuki Shōten lacked the risk-management system especially necessary for speculative policy.

In addition to these factors, we should add the following facts, which help explain Ōkura's and Iwai's backwardness in developing into general trading companies.

Ōkura Shōji: The characteristic feature of Ōkura Shōji's commodity dealings was its heavy reliance on business for the government and its sole-agency status for AEG for electrical machines. After World War I, the ratio of domestic products to total products consumed in Japan gradually increased, in the case not only of electrical machines but also of machines in general. Ōkura Shōji could adapt to this trend only slowly because it mainly handled imported machines and did not have large machine-manufacturing enterprises under its control. Moreover, the shock of the armaments reduction after World War I was larger to this company than to other companies because of its heavy reliance on army and navy business. In Table 10 it is clear that the net profit of Ōkura Shōji decreased steadily from ¥2.25 million in 1922 to ¥799,000 in 1929, whereas the net profit of Mitsui Bussan increased from ¥11.12 million in 1922 to ¥17.56 million in 1929, while it fluctuated between ¥10.16 million and ¥20.77 million in 1926.

Iwai Shōten: Iwai Shōten imported goods from overseas agents and did not establish branches in foreign countries until World War I. It opened its first overseas subbranch in New York in 1915 and established branches and subbranches in London, Shanghai, Hankow, and San Francisco between 1917 to 1919.[51] Its backwardness in opening overseas branches contributed to its backwardness in developing as a general trading company. The overseas branches accounted for only 9.0% of the company's total dealings even in 1936.[52]

In sum, then, all four companies which we compared to Mitsui Bussan lacked anyone to play the role played by Mitsui Bussan's Masuda Takashi. Mitsubishi Shōji, at the early stage of its development, and Suzuki Shōten, through its whole history, seemed not to be able to form an adequate risk-management system to succeed in anticipatory transactions. Regrettably we have no data on Ōkura Shōji and Iwai Shōten concerning this point, but we can point to Ōkura Shōji's heavy reliance on machine imports and business for the government and to Iwai Shōten's backwardness in establishing overseas branches to explain their inferiority to Mitsui Bussan.

TABLE 10   Net Profit of Major Japanese Foreign Trading Companies.

(Unit: 1,000 Yen)

	(1) Mitsui Bussan	Ōkura Shōji	Iwai Shōten	Mitsubishi Shōji	Nihon Menka	(2) Tōyō Menka	(3) (1)+(2)
1911	5,838	432			478		
12	5,361	347			626		
13	5,218	369	197		431		
14	3,960	397	124		455		
15	7,055	1,215	570		609		
16	19,182	1,132	1,266		1,593		
17	32,187	2,262	1,347	4,755	4,350		
18	36,464	1,990	2,471	876	7,856		
19	19,864	2,430	396		6,543		
20	16,395	1,169	△1,991	964	29,468	1,138	17,533
21	6,718	1,421	△ 210	△1,629	224	△1,047	5,671
22	11,121	2,250	923	1,791	3,868	2,373	13,494
23	10,164	1,562	△ 359	1,963	1,614	2,488	12,652
24	14,177	1,298	837	1,988	4,928	2,997	17,174
25	16,226	1,090	329	952	5,144	3,482	19,708
26	20,766	1,273	97	1,230	2,451	2,976	23,742
27	15,573	1,297	426	1,836	4,412	2,000	17,573
28	17,651	1,137	516	2,923	3,616	797	18,448
29	17,558	799	139	387	2,976	1,442	19,000
An Average of 1911–14	5,094	386	161		498		
1915–19	22,950	1,806	1,210	2,816	4,190		
1920–21	11,557	1,295	△1,101	△ 333	14,846	46	11,602
1922–29	15,405	1,338	364	1,634	3,626	2,319	17,724

Notes: Tōyō Menka was wholly-owned by Mitsui Bussan. Column (3) shows the total of Mitsui Bussan and Tōyō Menka.

Sources: Mitsui Bussan, Jigyō Hōkoku-sho (Report on Business) various issues; Seishi Nakamura et al., "Ōkura Zaibatsu no Kenkyū (4)" (A Study of Ōkura Zaibatsu). *Tokyo keidai gakkaishi* (The Journal of Tokyo Keizai University) Vol. 102, pp. 120, 121; Iwai Sangyō, *Iwai hyakunenshi* (100 Year History of Iwai), p. 557; Mitsubishi Shōji, *Ritsugyō bōeki roku* (A Documental History of Mitsubishi Shōji)", pp. 946, 947; Nichimen Jitsugyō, *Nihon Menka kabushiki gaisha gojūnenshi* (50 Year History of Nihon Menka), 1943, pp. 243, 244; Tōyō Menka, *Tōmen yonjūnenshi* (40 Year History of Tōyō Menka), p. 444.

V. Conclusion

In this paper we have observed the following:

1. There were two types of large trading company in Japan before World War II. One was the general trading company and the other was the trading company dealing mainly in textiles.

2. Among general trading companies, Mitsui Bussan surpassed other companies in scale, the extent of diversification, and the establishment of overseas branches.

3. The factors which enabled Mitsui Bussan to develop as a general trading company were

    a. the special abilities or the specific individuality of its founder;

    b. its reliance on business for the government in its early stage of development;

    c. its success in forming a risk-management system in anticipatory transactions; and

    d. its relationship with a zaibatsu.

4. The other companies we looked at had both business for the government and a zaibatsu relationship, which enabled them to develop into general trading companies, but stood in an inferior position to Mitsui Bussan in lacking an exceptional founder or well-organized risk-taking system. The backwardness of their start as foreign trading companies (Mitsubishi Shōji, Suzuki Shōten, and Iwai Shōten), their backwardness in establishing overseas branches (Iwai Shōten), and their heavy reliance on the machine import business and business for the goverment (Ōkura Shōji) also account for their inferior position.

In Table 10 it is clear that Mitsui Bussan far surpassed other trading companies, and the trading companies specializing in textiles, such as Nihon Menka and Tōyō Menka, surpassed the general trading companies, except for Mitsui Bussan, in average net profit during 1922–29. It is important to recognize that there were two types of trading company and that among general trading companies the business performance of Mitsui Bussan and other companies was very different before World War II. It was during and after World War II that the trading companies specializing in textiles diversified into fields outside textiles and became general trading companies and that the gap between Mitsui Bussan and other general trading companies narrowed. The system composed of the 10 largest general trading companies was thus established and based on "the system of business groups composed of the enterprises which relied heavily on specific banks financially" after World War II.

NOTES

1. Nakagawa Keiichirō, "Nippon no kōgyōka katei ni okeru soshiki sareta kigyōsha katsudō" (Organized entrepreneurship in the industrialization of Japan), *Keiei shigaku*, Vol. 2, No. 3, 1967; Morikawa Hidemasa, "Sōgō shōsha no seiritsu to ronri" (The development and logic of general trading companies), in Miyamoto Mataji, Togai Yoshio, and Mishima Yoshio, eds., *Sōgō shōsha no keiei shi*, Tokyo, Tōyō Keizai Shimpōsha, 1976; Yamamura Kōzō, "General Trading Companies in Japan—Their Origins and Growth," in Hugh Patrick, ed., *Japanese Industrialization and Its Social Consequences*, Berkeley, University of California Press, 1976; Yonekawa Shin'ichi, "The Formation of General Trading Companies; A Comparative Study," *Japanese Yearbook on Business History: 1985*, Vol. 2.
2. Yonekawa, *op. cit.*, pp. 6–17.
3. *Ibid.*, pp. 2–3.
4. Mitsui Bussan, *Kōhon Mitsui Bussan Kabushiki Kaisha 100 nen shi jō* (A manuscript on the 100-year history of Mitsui Bussan Co., Ltd.), Vol. 1, 1978, p. 92.
5. *Ibid.* The description of the development process of Mitsui Bussan is based on pp. 16–93, 176, 302–7.
6. The percentage after 1900 is estimated by assuming that the ratio of sales handled by Japanese merchants in Japan's total foreign trade is equal to the same ratio for Kobe port alone.
7. Mitsui Bussan, *op cit.*, pp. 30–31, 106, 118–19.
8. *Ibid.*, p. 60.
9. *Ibid.*, pp. 78–81.
10. *Ibid.*, pp. 159–62.
11. *Ibid.*, p. 80.
12. *Ibid.*, pp. 108–11, 118–22, 159–60.
13. Tōyō Menka Co. Ltd., *Tōmen 40-nen shi* (The 40-year history of

Tōmen), 1960, p. 39.

14. Yamaguchi Kazuo, ed., *Nihon sangyōkinyū shi kenkyū: Bōseki kinyū hen* (A study of the history of Japanese industrial finance. Volume on the cotton-spinning industry), Tokyo, University of Tokyo Press, 1970, p. 234.

15. According to the records of 16 cotton-spinning companies which owned cotton-spinning machines, 96.7% of all the machines they owned in the first half of 1906 were manufactured by Platt and Co. See *Ibid.*, p. 235.

16. The composition of Japanese export and import trade in 1900 and 1914 was as follows. Figures in parentheses show the percentage of total export or import value for each commodity.

    1900 *export:* raw silk (21.8), cotton yarn (10.1), coal (9.8), silk tissue (9.1), copper (6.3)

    import: raw cotton (20.7), sugar (9.3), iron (7.6), cotton tissue (6.4), wool tissue (6.2)

    1914 *export:* raw silk (27.3), cotton yarn (13.3), cotton tissue (5.9), silk tissue (5.8) copper (4.8)

    import: raw cotton (36.8), iron (4.2), machinery (4.2), rice (4.2), sugar (3.6)

    Among these commodities, especially sharp fluctuations occurred in the prices of raw cotton, cotton yarn, cotton tissue, raw silk, silk tissue, rice, and sugar. See Tōyō Keizai Shimpō Sha, *Nihon bōeki seiran* (The foreign trade of Japan: A statistical survey), 1935.

17. The description of the development of anticipatory business in Mitsui Bussan is based on Suzuki Kunio, "A Note on Anticipatory Business—Mitsui Bussan during the Latter Half of the 1890s–1910s," *Mitsui Bunko ronsō*, Vol. 15, 1981.

18. Morikawa Hidemasa, "Meijiki Mitsui Bussan no keiei soshiki. Kyōtsū keisan seido o chūshin ni" (The management organization of Mitsui Bussan during the Meiji era: On the system for computing overall income and expenditure), *Keiei shirin*, Vol. 9, No. 1, 1972.

19. Mitsui Bussan, *op. cit.*, pp. 124–28, 176.

20. Hokkaidō Tankō Kisen, *Hokkaidō Tankō Kisen 70 nen shi* (The 70-year history of Hokkaido Colliery and Steamship Company), 1958, pp. 118, 119, 458.

21. Computed on the basis of Kōzan Konwa-kai, ed., *Nihon kōgyō hattatsushi* (The history of the development of the Japanese mining industry), Vol. 2, 1932, pp. 230, 231.

22. Kasuga Yutaka, "Mitsui zaibatsu ni okeru sekitangyō no hatten

kōzō: Nihon sangyō kakumeiki o chūshin to shite" (The developmental structure of the Mitsui zaibatsu's coal-mining industry: The period of the industrial revolution), *Mitsui Bunko ronsō*, Vol. 11, 1977, p. 176, table 29.

23. *Ibid.*, pp. 230, 235.
24. Yamaguchi, ed., *op. cit.*, pp. 456–64.
25. *Ibid.*, pp. 477–79.
26. *Ibid.*, pp. 492, 499.
27. *Ibid.*, p. 216.
28. *Ibid.*, pp. 183, 214.
29. Mitsui Bussan, *op. cit.*, pp. 270–72.
30. Nakajima Tsuneo, *Gendai Nihon sangyō hattatsushi: Shokuhin-hen* (The history of contemporary Japanese industrial development: The food-processing industry), 1967, pp. 128, 133, 136, 139.
31. Mitsui Bussan, *op. cit.*, pp. 376, 379.
32. *Ibid.*, pp. 266–70. The ratio of shares which Mitsui Hachirōjirō and Toyoda Sakichi owned to total shares of the company is computed based on *Toyoda Shiki Shokki eigyō hokoku* (Annual report of the Toyoda-Style Weaving Macine Company).
33. Ōshio Takeshi, "Zaibatsu shihon to denki kikai kōgyō" (Zaibatsu and the electrical machine-manufacturing industry), in The Institute of Industrial Management of Waseda University, *Senzenki Nihon Shihonshugi ni okeru kigyō kinyū: Jū kōgyō no bawai*, 1976, pp. 128–52.
34. Yamaguchi Kazuo, "Mitsui no seishi kinyū to kiito bōeki: Meiji kōki—Shōwa shoki o chūshin ni" (The financing of silk manufacturing and silk export by Mitsui: The latter half of the Meiji era—the early Shōwa era), in Yokohama City, *Yokohama Shi shi hokan*, Supp. Vol., 1982, pp. 289–307.
35. Morikawa Hidemasa, *Nihon zaibatsu shi* (The history of Japanese zaibatsu), Kyōiku Sha, 1978, pp. 159–61.
36. Ishiyama Kenkichi, "Kaibutsu Suzuki Shōten" (A monster Suzuki Shōten), *Kaizō*, May 1927, pp. 100, 101; Asahi Shimbun Sha, *Asahi keizai nen shi* (Asahi's annual economic history), 1928, pp. 217, 218.
37. Asahi Shimbun Sha, *op. cit.*, p. 218.
38. Mitsui Bussan, *op. cit.*, p. 218.
39. *Ōsaka Asahi Shimbun* (Osaka Asahi newspaper), April 6, 1927.
40. Katsura Yoshio, "Sangyō kigyō no ikusei to shōsha: Suzuki Shōten" (The development of an industrial enterprise and trading company: Suzuki Shōten), in Miyamoto et al., eds., *op. cit.*, p. 231.
41. Takahashi Kamekichi, *Nihon zaibatsu no kaibō* (An analysis of

Japanese zaibatsu), 1929, p. 46.

42. The description of the development process of Ōkura Gumi is based on Nakamura Seishi and Watanabe Wataru, "Okura zaibatsu no kenkyū (4)" (A study of Ōkura zaibatsu, No. 4), *Tōkyō Keizai Gakkai shi*, Vol. 102, 1977, pp. 105–7; Matsushita Denkichi, *Jinteki jigyō taikei kaiun bōeki hen* (An outline of major businesses from the standpoint of human factors: Shipping and foreign trade), 1940, pp. 111–14.

43. Although as many or more machines and china were sold as electrical machines, the machine and china categories comprised many kinds of commodities.

44. According to Shibata Nobuo, who was a director of Ōkura Shōji, "Ōkura Shōji was a sole agent for electrical machines manufactured by AEG in Germany and dealt mainly in machines." See Nakamura and Watanabe, *op. cit.*, p. 125, n. 34.

45. Kaneko Fumio and Watanabe Wataru, "Ōkura zaibatsu no kenkyū (6)" (A Study of Ōkura zaibatsu, No. 6), *Tōkyō Keidai Gakkai shi*, Vol. 107, 1978, p. 16.

46. Ōkura Gumi, *Kabushiki Kaisha Ōkura Gumi kessan meisaisho hohyō* (Detailed statement of accounts: A supplemental table), 1913.

47. The description of the development process of Iwai Shōten is based on Iwai Sangyō, *Iwai 100 nen shi* (The 100-year history of Iwai), 1964, pp. 107–281.

48. Mitsubishi Shōji, *Ritsugyō boeki roku* (A documental history of Mitsubishi Shōji), 1958, pp. 4–6.

49. *Ibid.*, pp. 629–33.

50. Ōsaka Asahi Shimbun Keizaibu, ed., *Kinyū kyōkō hiwa* (A secret story of the financial panic), pp. 6, 8.

51. Iwai Sangyō, *op. cit.*, pp. 209–14, 246, 247, 279, 280.

52. *Ibid.*, p. 362.

Comment

John R. Killick
Leeds University

Professor Yamazaki has provided a concise and lucid account of the business of the leading Japanese trading companies in the late 19th and early 20th centuries. It is very useful for a Westerner like myself with only a very generalized view of Japanese business to be given the standing of each company in the tables which occupy the first part of his paper. The interesting point about the export tables (Tables 2 and 4) is that only Mitsui Bussan and to a much lesser extent Mitsubishi Shōji seem to have been exporters of multiple commodities in the 1920s, the rest being the concern of the more specialized textile merchants such as Itō Chū Shōji. Lancashire and Yorkshire textile exports were at times also handled by large Manchester or Bradford wholesale houses which similarly marketed the products of many mills which were too specialized to have export competence. But these firms were relatively much less powerful than the Japanese exporters and did not also import and provide finance. The more complex industrial exports of European and American firms were of course increasingly handled by the manufacturers themselves. On the other hand, the import table (Table 3) does clearly show the Japanese firms acting as general traders in a way that had quite disappeared in the West. Professor Yamazaki follows the standard Japanese classification in calling the textile importers and exporters specialists, but the major commodity importers from the Americas into Britain by then were specialists in just one staple such as cotton or grain and would never have dreamed of also handling manufactured exports, even of textiles.

In the second part of his paper Professor Yamazaki suggests some reasons why Mitsui Bussan became the most important general trading company. The key factors can be conveniently summarized as below:

	Leader-Ship	Date founded	Government aid	Risk control	Zaibatsu aid
Mitsui Bussan	√	1876	√	√	√
Mitsubishi Shōji	—	1918	—	x	√
Ōkura Shōji	—	1873	√	—	√
Iwai Shōten	—	1896	—	—	√
Suzuki Shōten	—	1894[a]	√	x	√

[a] The year Kaneko Naokichi took over the management.

Given that these factors explain the dominance of Mitsui Bussan, do they also give clues to the contrast with the West? The first factor—leadership—is obviously important. Of the early Japanese merchants, apparently only Masuda Takashi really knew the West, and therefore Mitsui Bussan gained a substantial head start over its competitors. Generally, Japanese companies initially found it difficult to operate in the West—so the few that could had great advantages. By contrast, British, European, and American merchants had far less difficulty operating overseas, and the leading houses always faced serious competition from "interlopers." In fact overseas commerce, like industry, formed a natural outlet for the energies of the quite large groups that were to varying degrees excluded from European social life—and in the 19th century many of the leading commercial groups were Scottish, Scotch-Irish, Quakers, German Jews, Greeks, and the like. Their clannishness and their cosmopolitanism were of great help in operating overseas, especially before the telegraph and before limited liability, but there was no shortage of sons and cousins ready to form new competing firms, so few European firms had the field so much to themselves as Mitsui Bussan did in the late 19th century.

With regard to government assistance, Professor Yamazaki lists the privileges particular Japanese general trading companies gained from their government, partly as a matter of development policy, partly because of close social relations. By contrast, it was much more difficult for merchant firms in the Atlantic trade that might have developed into general trading companies to gain such privileges.

In the early 19th century there was generalized help for commerce—for instance, through the Navigation Acts—but the tendency after 1830 was to attempt to open up the market by reducing chartered privileges, making incorporation easier, and in the British case by introducing free trade. In the 1850s the British and American governments subsidized the Cunard and Collins mail steamers, but by then shipowning was becoming a separate specialization and these subsidies were soon ended in the United States and whittled down by Britain. Government therefore gave little help to particular firms in the Atlantic trade. On the other hand, in the Eastern and colonial trades—which I have not studied—one might suspect British firms did gain all sorts of preferences. It would be interesting to know more about these from the other specialists here—and just how important they were in assisting the large British investment groups that operated in the East.

Professor Yamazaki shows how Mitsui Bussan was the first Japanese firm to develop a carefully organized policy for controlling risk. In the 1880s it purchased and sold as an agent for others on commission, but increasingly in the 1890s, it undertook anticipatory transactions, i.e., traded on its own account, but within centrally controlled and well-defined limits. This is interesting because just about that time future sales were becoming very widespread in the Atlantic staple trades, and as a consequence the last general merchants were being forced out of Atlantic commerce. The extra security provided by hedging allowed relatively small firms to raise the capital to deal in very large volumes with very small margins. I believe that Osaka had a cotton futures exchange from 1894, and it would be interesting to know if these large firms used it or if they relied on their own commercial judgment and on offsetting transactions in several different commodities. Some firms such as Suzuki Shōten did suffer because of presumably unhedged speculation in the boom and crash of 1919–21, but prior to that were Japanese firms just lucky in that from 1896 to 1918 there were few crises? It would be interesting, for instance, to know how Mitsui coped with the cotton crisis in the autumn of 1914. It is also surprising that Suzuki found it could not control its employees, who apparently went ahead regardless and speculated on the firm's account. This would have been less easy with the small partnership firms in the Atlantic trade, where responsibility for transactions was clearly fixed.

Finally, Professor Yamazaki emphasizes the importance of the zaibatsu groups in supporting the general trading companies by directing all their foreign trade through one house. Obviously this would be an important source of strength, but it is interesting to speculate why Japanese firms chose to keep their own trading internal in this way. Surely there must have been times when it would have paid companies to conduct additional transactions through third parties rather than through their own people. Presumably even if management preferred to ignore this, the owners might have argued for the most profitable direction of additional transactions in the short run. Leaving aside the economics of this, I think in the West it was expected that big companies would not always trade internally—for instance, McFaddens and Anderson Clayton, the cotton firms I have studied, became unpopular and even sometimes broke the law when they kept all their ginning and compressing facilities for their own use. Similarly banks had to deal in a reasonably even-handed way with merchants. At the same time it was often risky to take on the responsibility of acquiring extra facilities. Bitter experience taught London and Liverpool merchants and bankers to define and limit their role in the market in order to preserve their credit-worthiness, and a major theme in British economic history is the gradual separation of functions of merchants, manufacturers, and bankers. I wonder therefore if Professor Yamazaki could discuss a little more the social and economic forces that so firmly welded the Japanese zaibatsu and their general trading companies together.

Response

Hiroaki Yamazaki

It is true that Osaka had a cotton futures exchange from 1894, but the quantity of raw cotton traded there was very small and Japanese cotton-spinning companies could hedge only a small part of their trading risks there.

As for Mitsui Bussan's response to economic crisis, the company's headquarters prohibited anticipatory transactions in the 1900 and 1908 crises, but allowed branches and departments to resume futures trading after the crises had passed. I have no data which show Mitsui Bussan adopting a specific policy to respond to the cotton crisis in the autumn of 1914.

Finally, concerning the relationship between the general trading company and the zaibatsu, I would like to consider the case of raw cotton imports. Mitsui Bussan was wholly owned by Mitsui Gōmei, the headquarters of the Mitsui zaibatsu. On the other hand, Kanegafuchi Bōseki (Kanebō), the largest cotton-spinning company in Japan before World War I, was partly owned by Mitsui Gōmei. Mitsui Bussan wanted a 100% share of the transactions of raw cotton with Kanebō, but in reality it had no more than 61%–85% in 1903–4. Kanebō imported the remainder of its raw cotton from other cotton merchants, while Mitsui Bussan imported raw cotton not only for Kanebō but also for many other cotton-spinning companies for 44 in 1902. The raw cotton imported by Mitsui Bussan for other cotton-spinning companies besides Kanebō accounted for about 40% of Mitsui Bussan's total raw cotton imports in 1902–4. Mitsui Bussan's raw cotton business was mainly represented by the transactions with Kanebō, but at the same time it handled transactions with many other cotton-spinning companies.

Development of Overseas Operations by General Trading Companies, 1868–1945

Nobuo Kawabe
Hiroshima University

I. Introduction

By *general trading companies* (*sōgō shōsha*) we ordinarily mean business corporations which deal in a broad range of commodities on a global scale and perform multifarious functions; they are considered to be uniquely Japanese. There are various definitions of the general trading company. Togai Yoshio, for example, defines the general trading company as an economic institution that has the following characteristics:

1. It has a wide variety of product lines.
2. It has many domestic and overseas branches and engages in domestic trade, export, import, and trade between countries other than Japan.
3. It transacts a large volume of business.
4. It plays the role of organizer of industry, on the one hand, supplying machinery, technology, and materials, and on the other hand, developing markets for its final products.
5. It has the nature of a holding company, with many subsidiary and affiliated companies.[1]

There are no comparable economic institutions in the Western world. By World War II some of the Japanese trading companies had already assumed the characteristics of general trading companies.

Recently, several scholars have studied general trading companies, stressing the importance of the overseas activities of these companies, but no systematic study of the activities and roles of their foreign operations has been done. There are several questions related to the activities of overseas branches of general trading companies: (1) What specific forms do these overseas operations take—i.e., do general trading companies establish branch offices, overseas affiliated firms, or subsidiaries—and why, how, and when are the forms adopted? (2) How are the opening of overseas branch offices and the establishment of local affiliated firms related to the growth strategies of general trading companies, such as diversification of business and merchandise handled? (3) What are the functions and activities of the overseas operational arms of these trading companies? (4) How are these overseas operational arms related to the corporate headquarters and how are they managed and controlled? And (5) what problems do these overseas operations arms face and how are they countered?

The objective of this paper is to answer these and related questions. We will review the development of overseas operations as one of the most important fields of activity of trading companies, from the days of the Meiji Restoration to the end of World War II, and examine the roles and functions of overseas operational arms (such as branch offices and local affiliated firms) as the nucleus of their overseas operations and their relation to the development and expansion of general trading companies as a whole. In doing so, we will base our analysis on data obtained mainly from the cases of Mitsubishi Shōji, Mitsui Bussan, and other predecessors of general trading companies.

II. The First Period (1868–1913)

Even before the Meiji Restoration of 1868, foreign trade had begun. After trade agreements were concluded with some foreign powers in 1858, Japanese ports such as Kanagawa, Nagasaki, Hakodate, and others were opened up. But foreign trade at that time was carried out only through trading houses located in foreign concessions, with actual trading business completely monopolized by foreign merchants who had trading houses in these concessions. Japanese merchants merely brought in and sold merchandise to be exported to these trading houses or bought imports from them.[2]

Because the country had been isolated for a long period, Japanese merchants had neither experience nor knowledge of foreign trade.

Nor were they rich in capital. All of this resulted in their depending on foreign merchants for the actual execution of foreign trade. For instance, in January 1872, when the first lot of Japanese rice (which had been purchased by the government) was to be exported, the government had to entrust the rice merchant Walsh, Hall & Co. with the task of handling it. The second batch of rice was exported through the domestic product department of Mitsui Bussan in 1876, but Mitsui Bussan in turn had to ask a British merchant, E. B. Watson, to actually handle it. The same applied to the export of Miike coal by the government. Senshū Kaisha was established in March 1874, but it entrusted E. Fisher & Co. and other Yokohama trading houses to execute the trading business at its initial stages. Japanese companies used not only the knowledge of foreign trading learned in this manner but also foreign merchants' capital resources.[3]

Foreign trading houses made these contributions, but many of them seem merely to have charged exorbitant commissions or abused privileges under the unequal treaties. For example, before the Sino-Japanese War (1894–95), sugar merchants in Osaka bought sugar through Chinese trading companies, which took a 5% commission. As the Japanese merchants opposed this high commission, they established the Sato Gōshi Kaisha (Sugar Co. Ltd.) to import sugar directly. This company entrusted Yasham Yoko with a 1.2% commission rate, the same rate for which the founder of Ataka Shōkai, Ataka Yukichi, worked.[4] Thus, there arose a movement among Japanese merchants to protest the unjust practices of their foreign counterparts, culminating in the incident involving the Joint Freight Office for Raw Silk at Yokohama.[5]

It was under such circumstances that some merchants came to aspire to deal with foreign markets directly. Two such merchants were Itō Chūbei and Kanematsu Fusajiro, who embarked on making direct contacts with foreign markets without much experience but emphasizing the need to protect national interests.[6] In 1874 Ōkura Gumi opened a London office, the first of a number of Japanese trading companies to do so. When in 1873 Japanese-made silk was put on sale for export for the first time, the government allowed a silk-exporting company, Dōshin Kaisha, to be established. When Japanese merchants saw many Americans coming to this country to engage in the export business, they too came to participate in this business. By 1881, as many as 10 Japanese trading companies had opened New York offices, staffed by a total of 31 Japanese employees. Itō Chūbei established Itō Sotoumi Gumi in Kobe in 1885, and opened a San Francisco office in December 1889. By this time, Mitsui Gumi, Morimura Gumi, and Yokohama Kiito, among others, had started exporting silk to the United States.[7]

The move to trade directly with foreign markets to eliminate the abusive practices of foreign merchants was mounted with the development of the spinning industry as the first modern industry in Japan. Trading companies like Mitsui Bussan, which was formed in 1876, established and organized the Japanese cotton textile industry by providing machinery and raw cotton, by developing markets for the products, and by establishing domestic spinning and weaving textile-machinery companies.[8] Osakamen, the predecessor for Naigaimen, was established in 1877, followed by Nihon Menka in 1892. Both were started to avoid dealing with foreign merchants in acquiring needed foreign materials and equipment. Other industries also required the development of trading companies. For example, Kanematsu Shōten was established in 1889 in order to import wool from Australia for the developing Japanese wool industry.[9]

In the initial phases of direct dealing, Japanese merchants seem to have first designated local agents, with whom they did business. Mitsui Bussan sent its adviser Robert Walker Irwin to London to open an agency there. When Nichimen started trading in 1894, it imported Indian cotton through Gadam Bytel & Co., Egyptian cotton through the House of André, and American cotton through McPharden Brothers. In all of these transactions the Japanese merchants used sole and exclusive agents. But gradually they began changing their policy by sending their own employees to cotton-producing areas and opening their own branch offices, rather than relying on agents.[10]

Direct trading was given impetus by the Sino-Japanese and the Russo-Japanese wars, and was given further encouragement by the expansion of Japan's foreign markets and by ongoing industrialization at home. Victory in the Sino-Japanese War gave Japan hegemony over Korea, and victory in the Russo-Japanese War (1904–5) opened up Manchuria and China as lucrative markets for Japanese industries. These victories also enhanced Japan's international standing, resulting in the abolition of extraterritorial rights and trading concessions in 1899 and in the full right to set its own tarriff rates in 1911.[11] In 1911, trade by foreign merchants accounted for 48% of exports and 36% of imports. Direct trading had thus received a further boost. Besides, as the Japanese cotton-spinning industry continued its growth, cotton cloth and products as well as yarn became export items.

Responding to such favorable conditions, many trading companies made bold attempts to go beyond the surrounding seas, particularly after the Sino-Japanese War. Not only Mitsui Bussan but also Kanematsu Shōten and others with offices theretofore only in certain regions opened branch offices and dispatched personnel to China and Korea to expand their sales network. Nihon Menka opened its Shanghai branch in May 1903, and its Hankow branch in July 1904 in order to export Japanese cotton yarn to its Chinese markets. Itō Chū Shōji (C. Itoh & Co.) and Iwai Shōten reached out to southern areas like the Philippines. Because of the phenomenal overseas expansion of traders' activities,[12] Takashimaya Iida had four divisions, dealing in traditional Japanese apparel, export, import, and the China market, as well as 10 offices in Japan, 5 abroad, and 700 employees (of whom 88 were posted abroad).[13]

What supported these expanding activities abroad by Japan's trading companies was the rising export of cotton yarn and cotton cloth produced by the ever-growing spinning industry, especially after the Sino-Japanese and the Russo-Japanese wars. In Oriental markets particularly, Japanese merchants gradually replaced Chinese merchants and compradors, and began managing their trade on their own. For example, C. Itoh created an export department in July 1906 to handle exports to Korea and then opened an office in Pyongyang the following year. In those days, Japanese merchants were able to have access to the Korean cotton yarn and cotton cloth merchants primarily through Chinese merchants with offices in Korea, which afforded the Chinese merchants a considerable amount of profit. At times, contact was possible through Korean

TABLE 1   The Opening of Mitsui Bussan Branch Offices Abroad, 1893–1910.

Year	Asia	Europe, the U.S., and others
1893	Bombay	
1896	Yingkou (Niuzhuang), Taipei	New York (reopened)
1898		San Francisco
1899	Jinsen, Xiamen (Amoy), Zhifu	Hamburg
1900	Hankow, Seoul, Guandongzhou, Manila	
1901	Java	Sydney
1902	Beijing, Guangdong	
1903	Tainan	
1904	Dalny (Dairen)	
1905	Fuzhou	
1906	Shantou, Dagou (Gaoxiong), Andong Xian, Tieling, Calcutta, Shenyang, Bangkok, Qingdao	Oklahoma City
1907	Rangoon, Jilin, Kuanchengzi (Changchun), Saigon, Harbin	Portland, Vladivostok
1908	Pusan, Zhanghua (Taizhong)	Lyon
1910	Akou	

Source: Nihon Keiei Shi Kenkyūsho, ed., *Kohon Mitsui Bussan Kabushiki Kaisha 100-nen shi* (Draft of a1 00-year history of Mitsui Bussan), Nihon Keiei Shi Kenkyūsho, 1978, p. 207.

intermediaries. C. Itoh started direct trade based on its ties with Changsin-sa and in December 1906 dispatched its own employees to develop new markets for Japan's cotton yarn and cloth. Mitsui Yōkō (of Mitsui Bussan) and Nisshin Yōkō (of Nihon Menka) were also keen on market development.[14]

In purchasing Chinese products in China, Japanese trading companies stopped going through knowledgeable Chinese compradors, and Mitsui Bussan, for one, started to pay for soybeans before harvest, while they were still standing in the field (the practice often referred to as *aota-gai*, which literally means "green field purchasing"). It expanded and improved its purchasing network while contributing to production increases in various parts of China. In 1905 Mitsui had the same number of overseas branches as its domestic branches. After that year, its overseas business became much more important, and it had more overseas branches than branches in Japan.[15] Ataka's Hong Kong branch played an important role in the expansion of its product lines.[16]

Penetration of the Chinese market did not merely mean foreign trade for these trading companies. After the Sino-Japanese War, it offered them a chance to start production activities, such as operating spinning factories. In 1902 Mitsui Bussan's Shanghai branch absorbed the Xingtai Cotton Mill, a spinning factory in Yangshupu, and operated and expanded it under the name Shanghai Cotton Manufacturing Ltd. Mitsui Bussan started a joint venture called Santai Oil Mills Ltd. in Talien in May 1907 to promote increased production of soybean cake. Nihon Menka on its part adopted the policy of simultaneously promoting commerce and industry in China by operating ginning and spinning factories. It changed the business objective in its articles of incorporation by adding product lines and operations, including bean cake and cottonseed-oil factories. Ōkura Gumi went into a joint venture with the government of Shenyang (Mukden) to establish Benxihu Coal and Iron Co.[17]

It was also during this period that some companies with extensive sales and information networks, such as Mitsui Bussan, started to do business between and among their own branch offices abroad, or between and among third countries. Table 1 describes the case of Mitsui Bussan, which had rapidly expanded its network of offices. In the fall of 1895 it started to export Chinese goods, such as silk, to Europe and the United States, and to purchase such goods as railway equipment and Oregon spruce from the United States and to export other goods from Europe to China. Its Shanghai branch, in particular, played an important role in this trade between China and the West. Nihon Menka also started vigorous trading with third countries. For this purpose, it established Menka Gesellschaft in Bremen, Germany, and sent employees to, or opened branch offices in, Liverpool, London, and Milan.[18]

By the end of this period, Japanese trading companies were operating in Asia, Europe, and the United States. In Asia they were engaged in manufacturing as well as in importing Japanese manufactured goods and exporting raw materials. In Europe and the United States they exported raw materials and semifinished goods and imported manufactured goods. This dual structure of operations

TABLE 2   Mitsubishi Shōji's Investment in Other Companies (as of June 1939).

Company	Capital (1,000 Yen)	Percentage of capital from MS	Number of executives from MS
Shanghai Mitsubishi Soko	1,000	25	1
Mitsubishi Sekiyu	10,000	10	1
Kiyosumi Seizaisho	400	100	4
Kokuyo Shōkai	400	100	4
Mango Shokusan	500	10	1
Daito Shokuhin	450	50	3
Chiyoda Sekiyu	500	28	
Daitō Bōshoku	10,000	1.2	1
Nichiro Gyogyō	53,800	2.8	1
Ōsaka Seihan	5,000	7.5	1
Morimura Arai	1,000	100	4
Sanwa Jidōsha	35	25.7	
Nittō Seifun	12,300	3.3	1
Manchurian Sekiyu	20,000	2	1
Nichiman Seifun	10,000	3	1
Tekkan Keishu Hanbai	500	2	1
Manshū Kiki	10,000	12.5	3
Mitsubishi Kakō	5,000	23.5	2
Nippon Kentetsu Kōgyō	1,000	70	6
Hōnan Unyu	200	25	
Sekiyu Rengō	300	7.7	3
Gōdō Match	30	36.7	
Kyōdo Kigyō	10,000	12.65	1
Nippon Ryūan	10,000	5	1
Nanyō Shinjyu	300	33.3	2
Shiryō Haigō	3,000	8.3	1
Santō Engyō	10,000	14.9	1
Tanaka Kikai Seisakusho	7,000	7.1	1
Becchin Kōruten Yushutsu Shinkō	500	2	1
Nippon Kōzai Hanbai	30,000	5	1
Showa Tsūsho	15,000	30	
Taiwan Kansho	480	18.6	1
Taiwan Rinsan Haigō	50	10	1
Taiwan Ryūan	60	16.7	1
Nanking Mato Kōjin	200	10	1
Teikoku Kōgyō Kaihatsu	30,000	1.7	1
Seibu Yushutsu Kōgyō	1,000	0.5	1

by trading companies promoted the diversification of product lines,, areas, and function. As a result, sōgō shōsha appeared. For example, in 1907 Mitsui Bussan handled 120 main products in domestic trade, export, import, and trade between countries other than Japan through more than 30 overseas branches and representative offices. However, most trading companies remained specialized trading companies whose activities were limited to certain areas and product lines.[19]

III. The Second Period (1914–1930)

Overseas operations by Japan's trading companies expanded during the years of the Sino-Japanese and Russo-Japanese wars. When World War I broke out in 1914, these companies were profoundly impacted. Not only did European countries stop their export, calling for a rapid development of Japan's own industries, but there was also a rising demand for Japanese products overseas. This produced a good number of new entrants to the trading business, and expanded both the range of merchandise handled and the geographical areas served, all of which created a firm foundation for Japanese traders to develop as genuine general trading companies.

Particular note should be taken of the move by the zaibatsu to establish trading companies. Mitsubishi established Mitsubishi Shōji in 1918; Furukawa established Furukawa Shōji in 1817; Asano established Asano Bussan with R. W. Grace in 1917; and Kuhara established Kuhara Shōji in 1919. As is clearly indicated by the case of Mitsubishi Shōji, whose predecessor had only been in charge of purchases and marketing, these trading companies were the purchasing and marketing divisions of their parent or affiliated companies, which were engaged in a variety of business activities.[20]

The expansionism of these trading companies involved two strategies: diversifying product lines by strengthening the relation-

Note: The companies in this table were chosen from among companies in which Mitsu-
       bishi Shōji (MS) invested according to the following rules:
       1.   MS held more than 25% of the stocks of the company.
       2.   MS supplied at least one member of the top management even if it had less
            than 25% of the company stocks.
Source: Mitsubishi Shōji, Department of Development, *Waga sha no tōshi yoran*, 1939.

ship with manufacturers and developing a worldwide network by
opening overseas offices. The first strategy played an important
part in the development of sōgō shōsha. For example, Mitsubishi
Shōji signed sole-agency contracts with manufacturers to sell their
products and buy raw materials. After the war, it developed contracts
with such Mitsubishi-related companies as Nisshin Flour Mills,
Iwaki Cement, and Nichiro Fishery Co., as well as Mitsubishi's main
companies. It also contracted with small and medium-sized companies outside of the Mitsubishi zaibatsu.

This strategy was not limited to Japanese firms. Mitsubishi Shōji
signed sole-agency contracts with well-known foreign companies,
including Goodyear Tire, Associated Oil, and Saco-Lowell. By
increasing relations with foreign companies, Mitsubishi Shōji was
able to introduce advanced Western technology and production
knowledge to Japan, particularly to the members of the Mitsubishi
zaibatsu. Overseas branches, especially those in Europe and the
United States (mostly the New York branch), made contracts,
ordered products, and paid for them.

After achieving independence from its parent company, Mitsubishi Shōji's Iwasaki Koyata developed the policy of establishing
subsidiaries to handle products and raw materials.[21] By doing this,
Mitsubishi Shōji wanted to control the distribution function of these
companies, leaving production to the independent manufacturers
(see Table 2).

Then there were others, such as Suzuki Shōten, which formed its
own group of enterprises by nurturing them through such means
as the introduction of foreign technologies. Other non-zaibatsu
trading companies, such as Iwai Shōten, also invested in subsidiary
companies.[22]

Because of the disruption of trade with Europe and the growing
foreign trade of Japan (both export and import), Japanese trading
companies expanded their areas of operation beyond China,
Manchuria, and South Asia to America and Africa. For example,
Nihon Menka had an interest in the transaction of South American
wool during World War I, and in 1919 began buying wool in
Argentina and Uruguay. As a result, it opened an office in Buenos
Aires. Kanematsu Shōten also turned its attention to the South

American market when the British government closed the Australian wool market.[23]

Nihon Menka opened a representative office in Burma for the transaction of cotton, rice, and other cereals. In March 1918 it began silk transactions through the Shanghai Bōeki. After acquiring the necessary skills in the silk trade, the Burma office began direct transactions in October 1919. Nihon Menka also developed its African market. In 1916 it sent a representative from the Bombay branch to Mombasa to transact in raw cotton and cotton cloth. The Mombasa office became independent in 1926, purchased six ginning factories in Uganda, and then sent employees to the interior of Africa to buy cotton and to sell cotton cloth. It also bought lots of land to grow cotton, beginning in 1928. However, it failed in this project for two reasons: the low price of raw cotton and the impoverished condition of the soil. In 1917 Nihon Menka opened an office in Slabaya to import and whole-sale cotton cloth, cement, veneers, and other products, and it opened other offices in the South Seas in 1924.[24]

The importance of the United States as a trade partner began to grow, and some specialty trading firms (such as C. Itoh and Iwai) started to take part in the growing American trade by diversifying the range of merchandise they handled. Iwai established a branch office in the United States in 1915, and C. Itoh and Ataka opened branch offices in 1918 and established overseas subsidiary companies in 1923.[25]

To trade in raw cotton, some Japanese trading companies established subsidiary companies, which allowed them to enjoy privileges comparable to those received by American competitors. Mitsui Bussan established its Southern Products Co. in Houston in 1911 (it was moved to Dallas in 1912). Nihon Menka established its Japan Cotton Co. in Fort Worth in 1910. Gōshō established its Crawford Gōshō Co. in San Antonio in 1913, and it also established its Gōshō Corp. in New York in 1918 for the silk business.[26]

Transactions in North America did not always develop smoothly. For example, in 1914 the San Francisco office of Mitsui Bussan opened a Vancouver office to handle wheat and wheat flour, pine trees, salt herring, and salmon. However, due to a space shortage

and the demands of war, the office could not develop transactions
and had to close in 1920. In the same year, Mitsui Bussan opened
an office in Havana to handle rice, but had to close this office three
years later.[27] In 1918 Mitsubishi Gōshi opened its Seattle office
mainly to supply Japan with iron and steel for the construction of
cargo vessels for the United States Shipping Board. After the creation
of Mitsubishi Shōji, the Seattle office became the representative
office of the New York branch in March 1921. Transactions in wheat,
flour, and lumber became an important business following the 1918
armistice. The business of these offices was not limited to transactions
in products. They also did some trade subsidiary functions. They
acted as agents for the Steamship Department and received commissions from the department as well. They attended to transshipment and other shipping details for the New York branch and
subdepartments in the United States for import and export through
Pacific Coast ports.[28]

In the early 1920s both Mitsui and Mitsubishi undertook a new
strategy which influenced the development of their San Francisco
offices. This strategy was due to technological changes and to the
military and civilian demand for petroleum as fuel usage increased
rapidly. Japanese merchants and government planners thought
mostly in terms of acquiring fuel oil for ocean steamships. Mitsui,
which had entered the oil business in 1877, attempted to get into the
competitive oil market by importing foreign oil products. In September 1921 the San Francisco office succeeded in making a contract
with General Petroleum Corp. in California. A year later, in September 1922, the headquarters set up a diesel oil section in its Coal
Department. Mitsubishi also set up a fuel department in 1923, and
consummated a sole-agent contract with Associated Oil Co. of
California. Both companies chose California oil companies as their
suppliers because it was less costly to transport oil to Japan from the
West Coast than from elsewhere and because the transfer from coal
to oil as fuel was most advanced in California. Moreover, Mitsubishi
established Mitsubishi Sekiyu Kaisha in 1932 as a joint venture with
Mitsubishi Gōshi, Mitsubishi Mining, and Associated Oil. Imports
were changing from final products to materials, and the joint venture
was a move to accommodate to the change, to become competitive

with Shell and Socony, and to get higher profits in refining. Mitsui tried to create a new refining company with the Standard Vacuum Oil Co. However, since both parties insisted on 51% ownership, this project did not materialize.[29]

In the China market, Japanese trading companies were also actively developing their operations. Nihon Menka began selling cotton yarn and cloth to the local market and exporting Manchurian soybeans and other crops. However, due to an increase in the tariff and the development of Japanese textile companies in China, the import of Japanese cotton cloth to the Chinese market decreased, Nihon Menka worked as the buying department for the affiliated Nikka Oil Co. and became the sole agent for Shanghai Toa Hemp Co.

In India, Nihon Menka began to operate ginning and compressing factories because it became necessary to do continuous operations from buying through shipping of cotton bales. However, since direct buying in the interior was disadvantageous, it bought hemp through the Calcutta market. In Burma, although meeting severe competition from British trading companies, Nihon Menka increased transactions in such miscellaneous goods as machinery belts, spinning machines, electric fans, chemicals, tiles, beer, and canned goods and operated rice-cleaning, cotton-ginning, and oil-manufacturing factories. Nihon Menka referred to itself in the following way: "Mitsui was simply a commission merchant, but Nihon Menka was the only Japanese trading company which invested in manufacturing in Burma."[30]

Mitsui Bussan also adopted a policy of vigorous investment around 1926, and started to invest not only in Japan but also in colonies and underdeveloped areas to acquire concessions or to develop natural resources. By the beginning of the Shōwa era (1926–) it had (1) invested in the joint development of anthracite coal in Korea, (2) started managing manganese mines in Portugese Goa, and (3) established an overseas affiliated firm in the Philippines, Tagun Trading Co., to sell lumber and Borneo Oil Field Association with Nippon Oil. It had also invested in the International Syndicate, an investment firm to generate electricity in Shanghai.[31]

The trade departments of Gōshō Kaisha and, later, Mitsubishi

Shōji laid the groundwork for their becoming sōgō shōsha by diversifying product lines and functions and developing a system of overseas branches. During World War I, the world market was open to Japanese companies. Mitsui opened new offices in the United States, Europe, and Asia. It exported miscellaneous Japanese goods through branches in those areas where imports from Europe had stopped. At the time Mitsubishi Shōji was established in 1918, it was handling many product lines—coal, metal, machinery, produce, oils and fats, marine products, textiles, chemicals, and miscellaneous goods in Europe, the United States, and Asia. Mitsui, which had started its operations earlier, led this diversification, while simultaneously increasing the number of its branch offices.[32]

This rapid, uncontrolled development caused problems in the recession after World War I. For example, the value of products handled by Mitsui in San Francisco decreased from ¥20 million in 1919 to ¥10 million in the 1920s. (It did not again reach ¥20 million until 1934.) It became necessary for both Mitsui and Mitsubishi to attain orderly development of the company as a whole, avoiding competition among departments and branches. Each had to develop an efficient control system. Mitsubishi established a system whereby, except in special cases, all profits and losses were to be calculated only by the *motoatsukaiten*, or original acting office, which played the central role in the transaction of a given item. For example, the New York office was an original acting office for transactions in canned crabmeat. The San Francisco and Seattle branches were *atsukaiten*, or acting office, which meant they were selling offices for certain merchandise for which the original acting office was not provided, and the other acting office attended to transactions without any profit or commission. Under this system the branches did not compete with one another in transactions.[33]

In Mitsui, the conflict between department and branch appeared earlier. In 1897 the Cotton Department introduced a common accounting system with which the headquarters controlled the branches' profits and losses in a particular item. In 1911 Mitsui developed a departmental system along product lines by which departments and main branches were entrusted with particular products. In order to control the company as a whole, Mitsui developed the main department-subdepartment system around 1914. Under this system, the Cotton Department, for example, was able to create its own subdepartment in the New York branch of the company.[34]

Another means of control was to set limits on credit. The amounts allowed for credit and transactions were not so large, and headquarters carefully controlled the branches, who had to follow the rules strictly.

Although some trading companies, such as Mitsubishi Shōji, developed into general trading companies, most of them, although they expanded during World War I, later had to reduce their operations or else went bankrupt, like Suzuki Shōten in 1927. They failed to develop further, partly because of their lack of experience and partly because of their inefficient managerial systems.

IV. The Third Period (1931–1940)

The world depression and the Manchurian Incident (1931) influenced the activities of Japanese trading companies and changed the Japanese trade structure drastically. Japan flooded the world market with its products, and the transactions of Japanese trading companies increased. This situation continued even after the outbreak of the Sino-Japanese War in 1937, in spite of worsening international relations. The Japanese government encouraged export to obtain foreign exchange with which to buy war materials.

When Manchukuo was established in March 1932, the Japanese government at once embarked on the development of heavy and other industries, including iron and steel, oil, cement, and flour. It encouraged Japanese investment of capital and technology, thus promoting the Manchurian boom, when many trading companies went into Manchuria and northern China. For example, Kanematsu opened its Sinkin office after taking over its agent, Seishin Yoko, in 1935. It opened the Tientsin and Shanghai offices in 1937 and 1938.[35] Ataka opened its Dairen office again in 1932, taking over the former office of Horn & Co. in order to enter the Manchurian market. In this venture, Kanematsu mainly handled machinery. After establishing a firm base in machinery transactions, it expanded into other product lines. Ataka also opened many offices in this area.[36]

While Ataka handled light machinery, Mitsui and Mitsubishi handled heavy machinery for heavy and power industries. This had something to do with their heavy investment not only in Japan but also in Manchuria, China, Korea, Taiwan, and other Asian countries as leading members of their respective zaibatsu groups.[37] For instance, Mitsubishi Shōji made 100 separate investments in the above area by 1945, either together with other Mitsubishi group firms or alone by absorbing existing companies, establishing joint ventures, or buying stocks. It also concluded an exclusive contract to handle West Hongay coal, consolidated its organization to purchase soybeans in Manchuria and northern China, participated in the management of Manchuria Oil and Manchuria Machinery and Equipment, and was involved in many other ventures. However, Mitsubishi Shōji is said to have invested mainly in distribution and not so much in production. Nor does it seem to have been interested in acquiring dividends of interest payments in making these investments.[38]

As in the case of Mitsubishi Shōji, the formation of international economic blocs and the military situation following the Manchurian Incident prompted Mitsui Bussan to invest in companies with joint operations, such as Manchuria Oil, Manchuria Soybean Industry, and Japan-Manchuria Flour Milling. At the same time, Mitsui Bussan also invested alone in Hoten Hemp and Japan-Manchurian Linen Spinning, and many other companies. Branch offices abroad, in addition to effecting capital participation, also supplied raw materials to Japan and marketed products from Japan. The need to acquire larger stocks of raw materials was being emphasized at this time, calling for more efforts to develop natural resources in southern Asia.[39]

In the case of Nissho, which succeeded Suzuki Shōten in 1928, the Shanghai branch aggressively invested in various kinds of manufacturing: iron and steel, spinning machinery, iron products, Japanese sake, soybean oil, cotton ginning, and weaving. "Such investment in manufacturing became useful to Nissho as trade between Shanghai and other countries stopped and self-sufficiency grew more pronounced. Financing was easier because it had factories, and such business as the acquiring of materials and the selling of products increased." The Sinkin office played a role in obtaining foreign exchange by exporting oils and fats to the American market after Japan began suffering a shortage of foreign currency. The Pyongyang office became a base for exporting Japanese textile products after economic control intensified in Japan.[40]

After the Manchurian Incident and the abandonment of the gold standard, Japanese exports increased dramatically and the American branches of both Mitsui and Mitsubishi tried to find outlets for their products in the overseas market. They began aggressively importing from Japan such goods as canned crabmeat, fertilizer, clothing, pottery, and other small wares. Japanese manufacturers had always asked Mitsui and Mitsubishi to pay attention to the possibility of export. As a result, Mitsubishi's headquarters in Japan directed branches in the United States to export products of such Japanese companies as Asahi Glass Co. (window glass), Nippon Optical Co. (optical products), and Yokogawa Electric Co. (electric meters), whose products were able to compete with Western companies.[41]

Tōyō Rubber Chemical Co., which was a joint venture of Mitsui with Nettai Sangyō, could not manufacture products for the domestic market, so it tried to secure an overseas market through Mitsui. Mitsui stressed the exploration of the foreign market for products of medium-sized and small companies. Because Mitsui's transactions were concentrated in the silk business, this accounted for 70% of all their transactions. Coal, sugar, silk clothing, flour, and camphor accounted for 15%. Since, except for these products, Mitsui's volume of exports was really small, it wanted to establish a position in the export of miscellaneous goods by using its accumulated experience and worldwide network.[42]

Branches abroad played an important role in spearheading attempts to find markets for Japanese products. They provided manufacturers with various kinds of marketing information. They did test-marketing with small consignments. When they found that Japanese products could not penetrate the market because of their questionable quality, they informed the manufacturers regarding the tastes and needs of the market, prices, and competition to enable them to overcome these problems.[43]

During this period, Japanese trading companies opened many

overseas offices. Kanematsu opened its New York and Seattle offices in November 1936. In 1931 Ataka began aggressively developing its overseas market for wool products and cotton textiles. In 1934 it began direct buying from Kishiwada Bōseki and others, and established agencies in Bombay, Baghdad, Beirut, Tehran, Istanbul, Cairo, Alexandria, Casablanca, Zanzibar, Johannesburg, and Buenos Aires.[44]

As the Japanese machinery industries developed, Ataka, in addition to importing foreign machinery, became the sole agent in the Manchurian market for Meiden Sha, Ōsaka Tekkosho, Ōkura Denki Kenkyūsho, Tōyō Kogyō, Komatsu Seisakusho, and Takachiho Seisakusho. It also opened its Bombay office in May 1938 to sell Japanese textile machinery to Indian textile companies. Further, it began to do construction-related business. Because Ataka handled moisturizing equipment for textile mills, it had to not only sell equipment but also finish the whole system (including piping), selling it ready to use. This was also the case in the installment of Takuma-made boilers and water-processing systems.[45]

Ataka continued to import machine tools. However, as imports from Germany decreased, imports from the United States increased. As a result, it became necessary for Ataka to open a subsidiary office in New York, which was named Ataka & Co. Ltd., New York. Its main business was twofold: to contact machinery manufacturers regarding shipment of machinery and to receive creosote. Later, it bought copper and steel to export to Japan and imported miscellaneous goods from their Tientsin and Dairen offices.[46]

Besides simply finding markets for Japanese manufacturers, trading companies worked to organize entire industries. Mitsui and Mitsubishi, which led in this endeavor, wanted "to lead in promoting trade, and control domestic manufacturers or cooperate with them."[47] Both companies played a particularly important role in the export of such consumer goods as cotton textile products and canned crabmeat. Companies in these industries were very small and they did not have the ability to find their own overseas markets. They competed furiously by cutting prices, though they were unable to benefit from the economies of scale in the absence of cooperative organization among the manufacturers. It was necessary for Mitsui and Mitsubishi to minimize these weak points by directing and controlling domestic manufacturers—here, export finance was important—and by encouraging shipping companies to make proper freight policies. Both Mitsubishi and Mitsui coordinated the flow of products from production to marketing. Their overseas branches played an important role in integrating these functions by giving necessary marketing information to manufacturers. For example, branches in the United States made efforts to integrate the flow of canned crabmeat from producers to consumers by developing a new distribution system and informing consumers by aggressive advertisement.[48]

From the time of the Manchurian Incident, Japan had been developing a wartime economy. After the outbreak of the Sino-Japanese War, this trend became clear, and Japan's international relationships worsened. As Japan developed a war economy, the trade patterns of the branches rapidly changed. The export of war-related materials, like oil and scrap iron, increased, while imports from Japan decreased. Some of the reasons for decreased Japanese export to the United States were shortage of materials for Japanese industries to produce export goods, continued depression in the U.S. market, and Japanese government control of the export of products like fertilizers. In response to the changing environment and the changing organization of business, Mitsui and Mitsubishi had to develop new strategies. The first strategy was to develop domestic transactions and transactions with countries other than Japan to compensate for the decrease of imports from Japan. Both Mitsui and Mitsubishi tried to develop transactions with Mexico. In 1936 Mitsui sent a representative to Mexico City, and Mitsubishi opened a representative office in 1940. After the war broke out in Europe, European trade with Mexico stopped, forcing the Mexicans to begin trade with Japan. For the Japanese, the abrogation of trade treaties between Japan and the United States increased the desirability of trade with Mexico. The primary goods handled by Japanese trading companies were rayon and mercury.[49]

The second strategy was to cooperate with other companies. This was influenced by two factors: increasing competition between Mitsui and Mitsubishi and tightening control of foreign exchange

TABLE 3 Businesses Based on Military Orders: Mitsui Bussan and Mitsubishi Shōji in Southeast Asia, 1841–1945.

Location	Category of business	Business
Philippines	factory operation	butanol factory, tobacco factory, beer brewery, cement factory, dockyard for building wooden ships, factory to make engines for wooden ships
	development	copper mine
	cultivation	jute, cotton, castor beans
Java	factory operation	oil pressing, wooden-ship building, wooden-barrel making, sulphuric acid plant
	cultivation	cotton
Sumatra	factory operation	tanning, bag manufacturing, wooden-ship building, wooden-board making
	development	coal mine
	cultivation	wheat, cotton, castor beans
North Borneo	factory operation	tanning, wooden-ship building, rice milling
	cultivation	rice, cotton
Celebes	factory operation	paint factory, brick factory
	cultivation	rubber
Malaya	factory operation	wooden-ship building, coal production, recycling of waste aircraft lubricant and automobile lubricant, coal coking, warehouses
	development	tin mine
	cultivation	mangrove

Burma	factory operation	lumbermill, lead refinery, fish refrigeration and canning, rice milling, machinery production and maintenance, shipbuilding, substitute-lubricant making, hot-bulb-engine manufacturing
	development	lead mine
	cultivation	cotton

Source: Akimoto Ikuo, "Bōeki shōsha" (Foreign trade companies), in Matsui Kiyoshi, ed., *Kindai Nihon Boeki Shi*, Vol. 3, Yuhikaku, 1963, p. 307.

and business activities by the Japanese government. For example, Mitsubishi, which had been suffering from the high cost of shipping and lack of shipping space, made a special contract with Nippon Yusen Kaisha to obtain space and a special rate. Mitsubishi also tried to build a brewery with Kirin Beer Co. in Hawaii in order to compete against the joint venture between Mitsui and Dai Nippon Beer Co. Their plan was to produce beer in Manila which they could then advantageously export to Hawaii and the West Coast. Although Mitsubishi could not realize this project due to the tight control of foreign exchange, this type of joint venture among sōgō shōsha, manufacturer, and local interest became very popular after World War II. Tight control of foreign exchange led Mitsubishi, Tōyō Steel Plate, and Tōyō Can Co. to create a new system for the settlement of accounts, whereby when Mitsubishi sold canned products using materials imported by Mitsubishi, the sales turnover was pooled at both the New York and London branches to pay for the materials.[50]

In spite of these actions, Mitsui, Mitsubishi, and other Japanese trading companies could not avoid a difficult situation. Since the outbreak of the Sino-Japanese War, anti-Japanese feeling had been increasing, particularly in the United States. In 1938 the export of weapons to Japan was banned, and in January 1940 the Japan-U.S. Commerce Treaty was abrogated, and the export of American products to Japan was placed under a license system. Finally, in July 1941, the U.S. government froze Japanese assets in the United States, placing all assets of Japanese companies under its control. Thus, Japanese companies could not operate without permission from the U.S. government, and transactions by branches of Japanese trading companies ceased. This also happened in the United Kingdom and other countries.

V. The Fourth Period (1941–1945)

After the outbreak of the Sino-Japanese War, the Japanese economy had to adjust to a new situation. In 1938 the government promulgated the National Mobilization Law to increase its control over economic activity. Various kinds of monopoly corporations were established, and the autonomy of trading companies decreased.

The government increased foreign-exchange restrictions and restricted import permissions in order to decrease imports of unnecessary products and to increase imports of materials necessary for the war. Both the Japanese and Manchukuo governments tried to promote exports to raise funds for imports.

As a result, when the Pacific War broke out in December 1941, the Japanese economy had been placed under strict wartime controls, and the trading companies had ceased to be active in Europe, Africa, and the Near East. As the war was extended from Manchuria and China to the south, the companies' areas of operations shifted toward strengthening ties with Southeast Asia, and more emphasis was laid on procuring war materials. Leading trading companies opened a great number of offices on the continent of China as well as in South and Southeast Asia.

Ataka, for instance, had as many as 39 branch offices of various sizes when the war came to an end in 1945, among which 27 had been opened since 1941. It had established branch offices in Bombay and Haiphong before the start of the Pacific War, but opened as many as 25 offices—i.e., five offices in French Indochina, two in Malaya, three in Borneo, three in Burma, eight in Sumatra, and four in the Philippines—as the Japanese army advanced to these areas during the Pacific War. These offices functioned as outposts for the eight branch offices then existing in those areas. Nissho opened 10 branches and 15 representative offices in Taiwan, Korea, Manchuria, China, and Indochina in 1943. Similar actions were taken by other trading companies, such as Mitsui Bussan, Mitsubishi Shōji, C. Itoh, Kanematsu, and Nichimen (Nihon Menka) to varying degrees.[51]

The activities of the general trading companies during the war were based on orders from the occupying Japanese military authorities. Table 3 lists typical activities of this nature carried out by Mitsui Bussan and Mitsubishi Shōji. One notes the great variety of these activities, including managing factories, developing natural resources, and planting rubber trees.

The same was true of other general trading companies. As the Japanese occupied Burma, Nihon Menka collected rice and cotton and grew cotton and hemp. The companies in China performed various kinds of operations according to the local situation. They managed flour, match, and starch mills and factories. In the domestic market, they imported miscellaneous goods and distributed them.[52]

In this period offices and shops in Japan were assigned to carry out the daily business of rationing and controls, trading in the yen areas and managing production activities in the affiliated firms. Branch offices were in charge of communication relating to the sending and receipt of military goods. Offices in Korea, Taiwan, and Manchuria were to cooperate in the physical distribution and in the military administration of their respective areas. Offices in the southern areas were directed to cooperate directly with the Army authorities in each locality. Thus Nihon Menka as a specialized trading house (its specialty was raw cotton and cotton yarn) was assigned to manage factories producing wheat flour, matches, and starch and to handle a variety of commodities.

After adding product lines and functions, trading companies changed their names to show the new nature of their business. Nihon Menka (Japan Cotton Co.) changed its name to Nichimen Jitsugyō (Nichimen Enterprise), giving the following rationale:

> This company, which was originally established to import cotton, extended its transactions to encompass various kinds of goods besides cotton and undertook such duties as factory management as well as trading. Given this wide range of activities in an emergency situation, the change of name came to be a topic discussed by company executives.[53]

For the same reason, Ataka changed its name from Ataka Shōkai (Ataka & Co.) to Ataka Sangyō (Ataka Industries) in January 1943. Ataka was engaged in the lumber business in South Asia, which is what prompted the company to go into the area. Nissho and Iwai also changed their names.[54] This can be seen as constituting a foundation on which development of these companies as general trading companies during the postwar high-speed growth period would be based.

However, the end of the war in August 1945 meant the temporary stoppage of all the overseas operations of Japanese trading companies, and a complete loss of all the overseas assets as well.

VI. Conclusion

This has been a brief survey of the historical development of the overseas operations of general trading companies and an examination of some of their salient features. I have tried to demonstrate the variety of forms of operation in foreign markets before World War II.

Before the war the Japanese trade structure consisted mainly of the export of silk to the United States, the import of raw cotton from the United States, India, and Egypt, and the import of wool from Australia. Japan processed these materials and exported semi-finished or finished products to developing areas, such as India, the South Seas, Africa, and West Asia. Less important was the import of machinery from the United States and European countries, and the export of canned products, chinaware, and other goods.[55]

In this trade pattern, the general trading companies played an important role. However, there were differences in the overseas operations of general trading companies in developed countries, such as the United States and European countries, and in developing countries, including China and southern Asia. In advanced countries, general trading companies had branch offices and subsidiaries through which they imported advanced manufactured goods and technology to Japan and other countries and exported only miscellaneous Japanese goods. They were not engaged in manufacturing. In developing countries, general trading companies traded as in advanced countries, but they were also heavily engaged in manufacturing, although before the beginning of World War II most of it was limited to the processing of agricultural products.

To understand the development of the general trading companies, it is essential to keep in mind the nature of zaibatsu. Mitsubishi Shōji and Mitsui Bussan were members of families of companies, none of which developed according to the American model. Whereas American firms were rapidly developing their ability to acquire raw materials, process them into finished products, and distribute them to consumers, such was not the case with Japanese companies before 1941. Instead, the general trading company performed these integrative functions.

Each large integrated American enterprise tried to procure raw materials and sell its products. But Mitsubishi Shōji and Mitsui Bussan worked as the procurement and sales departments of industrial companies in the zaibatsu. Whenever a member company needed a new material or manufactured a new product, Mitsubishi Shōji and Mitsui Bussan had to add it to its product lines. Why didn't they integrate these functions in the same way that most American big business firms did? The answer probably lies in their development within one company group. They had interests in common with members of the same zaibatsu. This is clearly shown in the limits on transactions and credit; for example, in transactions with member companies Mitsubishi Shōji did not impose limits. Their fate was Mitsubishi Shōji's fate. With this consciousness, member companies could leave procurement and sales functions to another member company, not needing to control the flow of products on their own.

However, not all the general trading companies grew as members of a zaibatsu. Today there are some general trading companies that started, not as member companies of zaibatsu, but as independent specialized trading companies. As in the case of Iwai and others, some specialized trading companies had assumed some of the characteristics of general trading companies before World War II, but most of them began diversifying their business activities during the war and after the Korean War started in 1950. There were several reasons why they became general trading companies. First, they had to compensate for the decrease of trade in, or the unstable market for, their main items. Second, they had a strong sense of their competition with established zaibatsu-type general trading companies. Thinking they should follow the same pattern in order to compete successfully, most large specialized trading companies became general trading companies in the 1950s. They also played an important role in forming business groups.

Because of the scarcity of raw materials and the limited Japanese market, Japanese general trading companies had to find overseas supply sources and markets for member companies. The diversification of product lines was closely related to the development of overseas branches. For example, Mitsubishi opened its Seattle branch to sell iron to Japanese shipbuilding companies, particularly Mitsubishi Shipbuilding Co. It also opened a San Francisco branch to handle oil products for the Japanese navy, which was a large and secure market in Japan. Mitsui opened its Vancouver office to procure wheat for Nippon Flour Co.

By increasing the number of overseas branches while increasing diversification, Mitsui and Mitsubishi internalized some functions of international trade that importers and exporters of host countries had traditionally performed. By internalizing international trade, both companies were able to do business without the difficulties caused by communication and cultural gaps. International transactions became those between headquarters and branches (export and import) or between overseas branches (trade between countries other than Japan). Mitsui and Mitsubishi could decrease risk in international transactions by leaving daily operations to *yoin* (employees hired locally) and Japanese *seiin* (employees), who controlled the activities of the yoin.

Once this internalized transaction system was established, trading companies could theoretically increase their product lines and overseas branches without any limitation. They could find the cheapest raw materials and the most profitable markets anywhere in the world. Actually, however, many problems prevented their further development. For example, there was the possibility that these branches and departments might compete with one another as independent operating units, with Mitsui and Mitsubishi experiencing diseconomies of scale. They had to overcome these problems to continue to grow. They developed a new organizational structure and management system. They developed a decentralized divisional structure along product lines (line departments) and geographical areas (overseas branches). With this organization top management could concentrate its effort on long-range strategic problems, while department and branch managers had responsibility for daily operations. To avoid competition among departments and branches, Mitsubishi allocated profits and commissions to certain acting offices—the motoatsukaiten and atsukaiten system—and Mitsui created a common accounting system as well as other systems.

In order to control overseas branches and firms effectively, Mitsui and Mitsubishi set limits on transactions and credit. Each branch could transact only within these limits. They also continually improved the communication and reporting system by which head-quarters could know and coordinate the activities of branches. One of the most important things for a trading company was to collect the right information as soon as possible to coordinate the activities of its branches.

A stable and regular flow of products was necessary for effective internalized transactions. It is said that these trading companies handled everything "from noodles to missiles." Though we have the impression that they handled an unlimited variety of products, careful study shows that the products they handled were limited to those for which they could effectively control the flow from suppliers to customers. In order to attain a stable and regular flow of products, the general trading companies had to perform various subsidiary functions.

The main products Mitsui and Mitsubish handled were (1) raw materials sent from large suppliers to large customers, (2) highly mechanized, expensive products, particularly machinery, and (3) undifferentiated, imperishable miscellaneous goods that were sold through many channels. In the first category, oil, the main item handled by the San Francisco branches, is a good example. In order to secure the supply of oil they had to make a sole-agency contract with Associated Oil Co. and General Petroleum Corp. In this kind of business, there were few marketing problems because of the nature of the products and the market.

In the second category of products, Mitsui and Mitsubishi mainly handled advanced Western machinery and technology for the member companies of their zaibatsu. In these transactions, trading companies seem to have given supplementary services, including financing and trade practice know-how, and to have conducted preliminary negotiations, collecting information on both products and export business affairs.

The third category of products, undifferentiated, imperishable miscellaneous goods, comprised a large variety of items exported to the Western market. Canned crabmeat was one of them. The canned crabmeat industry was very competitive and unstable, with many small canneries. Mitsubishi in particular tried to secure the supply of products in several ways. By supplying them with funds for fishing or export financing, they could control the suppliers. Mitsui and Mitsubishi played the role of promoter in the consolidation of small manufacturers into a large company. They integrated the small number of products of small producers into large transaction units and sold them to American brokers and Japanese importers through various channels. This decreased transaction cost and risk. It was necessary to control distribution in the United States in order to increase the efficiency of the internalized transactions and stabilize the flow of products, so Mitsubishi aggressively developed advertising. By appealing to consumers directly, it could keep its supremacy over distributors and control the flow of products from production to consumption.

In the process of adding product lines and overseas branches, general trading companies internalized international transactions into their own organizations. Since the management of Mitsubishi and Mitsui had to coordinate and control their departments and branches effectively in order to have efficient transactions, they developed a new decentralized organization with strong centralized control over the flow of the products they handled. They exercised control by supplying funds, making sole-agency contracts, and investing in suppliers. They also had to perform other functions, such as scheduling shipping, collecting market information, and hosting visitors from Japan. Once an effective transaction system was established, Mitsubishi did not want this disturbed by competitors—and competition among trading companies, particularly with Mitsui, was intense—because it wanted to keep its established flow of products and its transaction system intact. By means of this effective system of internalized transactions, large Japanese trading companies controlled American-Japanese trade before World War II, in spite of the fact that they faced restrictions by the U.S. government and strong competition from established American and European business interests.

NOTES

1. Togai Yoshio, "Saisho ni shutsugen shita sōgō shōsha: Mitsui Bussan" (The first general trading company: Mitsui Bussan), in Miyamoto Mataji et al., eds., *Sōgō shōsha no keiei shi*, Tōyō Keizai Shimpō Sha, 1976, pp. 81–82.
2. On foreign trade practices in those days see Tatsuki Mariko, "Bōeki to shōsha no hatten: jōyaku kaisei to shuken kaifuku (Foreign trade and the development of trading companies: Treaty revisions and recovery trade rights)," in Kobayashi Masaki et al., eds., *Nihon keiei shi wo manabu 1. Meiji keiei shi*, Yuhikaku, 1976.
3. Nihon Keiei Shi Kenkyūsho, *Kohon Mitsui Bussan 100 nen shi* (Draft of a 100-year history of Mitsui Bussan), Vol. 1, Nihon Keiei Shi Kenkyūsho, 1978, pp. 105–107.
4. Ataka Sangyō Kabushiki Kaisha, *Ataka sangyō 60 nen shi* (A 60-year history of Ataka Sangyō), Ataka Sangyō, 1968, p. 25.
5. Tatsuki, *op. cit.*, p. 154.
6. C. Itoh Shōji Kabushiki Kaisha, *C. Itoh Shōji 100 nen shi* (A 100-year history of C. Itoh Shōji), C. Itoh Shōji, 1970, p. 19; Kanematsu Kabushiki Kaisha, *Kanematsu 60 nen no ayumi* (A 60-year history of Kanematsu), Kanematsu, 1961, p. 14.
7. Tatsuki, *op. cit.*, p. 151; C. Itoh Shōji, *op. cit.*, p. 17.
8. On the role of Mitsui Bussan as an organizer of industry see Nakagawa Keiichiro, "Senzen wagakuni kōgyōka katei ni okeru 'soshikika sareta kigyōsha katsudō' " ("Organized entrepreneurial activities" in the prewar industrialization process of Japan), *Japan Business History Review*, Vol. 2, No. 2, November 1967.
9. Sakudo Yotaro, "Nihon kindaika to Kansai sen'i shōsha no seiritsu" (The modernization of Japan and the development of textile traders in the Kansai area), *Ōsaka Daigaku keizaigaku*, Vol. 23, Nos. 2–3, 1973, p. 183; Nichimen Jitsugyō Kabushiki Kaisha, *Nihon Menka Kabushiki Kaisha 30 nen shi* (A 30-year history of Nihon Menka Kabushiki Kaisha), Nichimen Jitsugyo, 1943, p. 11; Kanematsu, *op. cit.*, pp. 18–19.
10. Nihon Keiei Shi Kenkyūsho, *op. cit.*, p. 106; Nichimen Jitsugyō, *op. cit.*, pp. 14–17, 30–31.
11. Tatsuki, *op. cit.*, pp. 159–162.
12. Kanematsu, *op. cit.*, p. 55.

13. Marubeni Kabushiki Kaisha, *Kohon Marubeni sha shi: Honshihen dai 3 sho sōgō shōsha no shinten* (A draft corporate history of Marubeni: Chapter 3, on becoming a general trading company), Marubeni, 1974, p. 3.

14. C. Itoh Shōji, *op. cit.*, p. 40.

15. Nihon Keiei Shi Kenkyusho, *op. cit.*, p. 299.

16. Ataka Sangyō, *op. cit.*, pp. 34–42.

17. Nihon Keiei Shi Kenkyūsho, *op. cit.*, p. 259; Nichimen Jitsugyō, *op. cit.*, p. 19.

18. Nihon Keiei Shi Kenkyūsho, *op. cit.*, p. 296; Nichimen Jitsugyō, *op. cit.*, p. 42.

19. Maeda Kazutoshi, "Sōgō shōsha: Sono rekishiteki kento" (General trading companies: A historical overview), 1982, pp. 8–9, 13–14.

20. Nihon Keiei Shi Kenkyūsho, *op. cit.*, p. 296.

21. Mitsubishi Shōji Kaisha, *Ritugyo boekiroku* (A history of Mitsubishi Shōji Kaisha), Mitsubishi Shōji, 1958, p. 4; Mishima Yasuo, "Sekitan yushutsu shōsha kara sōgō shōsha e: Mitsubishi Shōji" (From coal-exporting company to general trading company: Mitsubishi Shōji), in Miyamoto et al., eds., *op. cit.*, pp. 137–140.

22. For Suzuki Shōten see Katsura Yoshio, "Sangyō kigyō no ikusei to shōsha: Suzuki Shōten" (The development of industrial companies and general trading companies: The Case of Suzuki Shōten), in Miyamoto et al., eds., *op. cit.*, pp. 175–271. For Iwai Shōten see Sakudo Yotarō, "Senmon shōsha kara sōgō shōsha e no michi" (From specialized trading company to general trading company), in Miyamoto et al., eds., *op. cit.*, pp. 293–295.

23. Nichimen Jitsugyō, *op. cit.*, pp. 38, 40; Kanematsu, *op. cit.*, p. 89.

24. Nichimen Jitsugyō, *op. cit.*, pp. 53–55.

25. C. Itoh Shōji, *op. cit.*, pp. 65–66.

26. Akimoto Ikuo, "Bōeki shōsha" (The trading company), in Matsui Kiyoshi, ed., *Nihon kindai bōeki shi* (The history of modern Japanese trade), Yuhikaku, 1961, p. 171; Umezu Kazuo, *Nippon shōsha shi* (The history of Japanese trading companies), Nihon Hyōron Sha, 1976, p. 127.

27. The discussion of the activities of Mitsui Bussan in the United States is based on the Mitsui materials at the National Record Center in Suitland, Maryland.

28. On the operations of Mitsubishi Shōji in the United States, see Kawabe Nobuo, *Sōgō shōsha no kenkyū* (A study of general trading companies), Jikkyō Shuppan Kabushiki Kaisha, 1982.

29. *Ibid.*, Chap. 2; Nihon Keiei Shi Kenkyūsho, *op. cit.*, pp. 598–602.
30. Nichimen Jitsugyō, *op. cit.*, p. 131.
31. Nihon Keiei Shi Kenkyūsho, *op. cit.*, p. 515.
32. Mishima, *op. cit.*, pp. 131–132.
33. Kawabe, *op. cit.*, pp. 88–100.
34. For details of the common calculation system see Morikawa Hide-masa, "Meiji ki Mitsui Bussan no keiei soshiki: kyōtsū keisan seido wo chūshin ni" (The management organization of Mitsui Bussan during the Meiji era: On the system for computing overall income and expenditure), *Keiei shirin*, Vol. 9, No. 1, 1972. *idem.* "Taishoki Mitsui Bussan no keieishi" (The business history of Mitsui Bussan during the Taishō era), *Keiei shirin*, 1973, Vol. 10, No. 1.
35. Kanematsu, *op. cit.*, p. 107.
36. Ataka Sangyō, *op. cit.*, p. 100.
37. *Ibid.*, p. 363.
38. Nakase Jūichi, "Senzen ni okeru Mitsubishi zaibatsu no kaigai shinshutsu" (Overseas investment by Mitsubishi zaibatsu before World War II), in Fujii Mitsuo et al., eds., *Nihon takokuseki kigyō no shiteki tenkai* (The historical development of Japanese multinationals), Vol. 1, Otsuki Shoten, 1980, p. 161.
39. Nihon Keiei Shi Kenkyūsho, *op. cit.*, pp. 632–633.
40. Nissho Kabushiki Kaisha, *Nissho 40 nen no ayumi* (A 40-year history of Nissho), Nissho, 1968, p. 302.
41. Kawabe, *op. cit.*, p. 109.
42. The Mitsui materials at the National Record Center.
43. Kawabe, *op. cit.*, p. 109.
44. Kanematsu, *op. cit.*, p. 107; Ataka Sangyō, *op. cit.*, pp. 242–43.
45. Ataka Sangyō, *op. cit.*, pp. 217–222.
46. *Ibid.*, p. 360.
47. The Mitsui materials at the National Record Center.
48. See Kawabe, *op. cit.*, Chap. 5.
49. *Ibid.*, pp. 185–188; the Mitsui materials at the National Record Center.
50. Kawabe, *ibid.*, pp. 188–194.
51. Ataka Sangyō, *op. cit.*, p. 436; Nissho, *op. cit.*, pp. 297–298.
52. Nichimen Jitsugyō, *op. cit.*, pp. 74–75, 82.
53. *Ibid.*, pp. 82–83.
54. Imamura Hideo, "Sen'i shōsha no sōgōka no katei" (The generalizing process of textile trading companies), Fukushima University, *Shogaku ronshu*, 1977, Vol. 45, No. 4, pp. 196–197.

55. Bureau of Administration, Ministry of Finance, *Nippon no kaigai katsudo ni kansuru rekishiteki chosa* (A historical survey of overseas activities by Japanese), Vol. 35, Tokyo, 1948, pp. 3–4.

Comment

Etsuo Abe
Meiji University

After reading Professor Kawabe's paper, I have decided to raise three points regarding which greater clarification would be appreciated. The first point concerns the relationship between general trading companies and specialized trading companies in Japan. Admittedly, in the pre-World War II period there were only two general trading companies—Mitsui Bussan and Mitsubishi Shōji—at least in a full-fledged form. Still, one of them, Mitsui Bussan, which had an unparalleled position, spun off Tōyō Menka in 1920. This signifies that a general trading company was not always the most profitable form and suggests a tendency away from the dominance of the general trading company.

Two functions of a trading company are to be distinguished. The first function is the augmentation of the number of products handled and the expansion of operating areas. Either one is closely connected to *diversification*, which is a crucial characteristic of general trading companies. Another function which Professor Kawabe underlines is vertical integration, which includes the function of organizing a variety of industries through financing. Vertical integration, i.e., *internalization*, took place not only in general trading companies but also in specialized trading companies in Japan. I was intrigued by Professor Kawabe's description of the new kinds of business Nihon Menka undertook during World War II and would like to know if it was a typical case. Internalization in both general and specialized trading companies was instrumental in developing Japanese trade and industry, and both types of trading company were of consequence in the economic scene.

In other words, internalization has to do with economies of speed, and diversification has to do with economies of scope. Specialized trading companies had economies of speed only; general trading companies had both. It seems to me, however, that economies of speed are as important as economies of scope, or in some cases even more important. The effectiveness of economies of scope might have been limited in comparison with that of economies of speed. If we assume this to be so, it seems possible to say that large specialized trading companies remained important and that Tōyō Menka was spun off from Mitsui Bussan for this reason. The effectiveness of diversification in general trading companies notwithstanding, some large specialized trading companies' persistence proves the significance of internalization.

Regarding the relationship between general trading companies and zaibatsu, I can raise a second question: whether or not it was possible for non-zaibatsu trading companies to become general trading companies in the prewar period. Professor Kawabe points out that in contrast to the integration of U.S. manufacturing firms, zaibatsu member companies entrusted functions of purchasing and selling to general trading companies in their zaibatsu because it was profitable in terms of cost and reduction of risk. I agree with this view with one condition: if the zaibatsu had a tight holding-company form, they functioned well. Alfred Chandler makes a distinction between a tight cartel and a loose cartel. Following him, we can differentiate a tight H-form from a loose H-form, where H stands for holding company. Because the zaibatsu had a tight H-form, member companies could leave purchasing and selling functions in the hands of the general trading companies.

On the other hand, general trading companies might have had very large transactions with nonmember companies. If so, I would like to know the ratio of transactions with nonmember companies to total transactions. Considering the credit limitation that was imposed on nonmember companies, if the volume of transactions with nonmember companies was substantial, wasn't there the possibility that non-zaibatsu trading companies could become general trading companies?

Finally, Professor Kawabe criticizes the impression that general trading companies handled an unlimited variety of products. He stresses that general trading companies dealt only in products which they could control. However, his categories 1, 2, and 3 are so broad in themselves that they could be considered to include almost everything of key products. Accordingly, it is likely that the range of products handled by general trading companies is quite broad.

Response

Nobuo Kawabe

In response to the first point raised by Professor Abe, I think the growth of general trading companies is based upon both economy of scope (diversification) and economy of scale (internalization). However, some specialized trading companies began adding product lines and services after attaining economy in one product line. Multiple and diverse forces drove specialized trading companies to diversify product lines and areas: entrepreneurship, the need to handle related products, and other factors.

In terms of management efficiency, it is difficult to say whether general trading companies or specialized trading companies are more significant, but we surely have to consider the strong influence of the general trading company's management style in explaining the development of the Japanese economy.

Regarding the second question discussed by Professor Abe, the development of general trading companies had a close relationship to the formation and operation of the zaibatsu. Characterized by a tight H-form, a general trading company provided essential management resources needed for overseas trade. Therefore, both zaibatsu and non-zaibatsu members relied upon the general trading company for their overseas trade. Similarly, after World War II, the transmutation of some specialized trading companies into general trading companies was closely related to the formation of business groups.

General trading companies before World War II seemed to handle almost all kinds of key products. This appearance of diversification was, in fact, misleading given the stage of development of the Japanese economy. However, when we consider the development of new industries after World War II, we find many product lines which general trading companies have not been able to handle efficiently. Therefore, we can say that the variety of product lines handled by general trading companies may be limited.

Economics, Politics, and Culture: Roots of the Decentralized Organization of Foreign Trade in American Industrialization

Glenn Porter
Hagley Museum and Library

In analyzing the place of foreign trade in the history of American industrialization, it is essential first to define the time period in which industrialization came to the United States. It is clear that the United States entered into the process of industrialization and modern economic growth[1] somewhat earlier than Japan, and earlier than most of the European countries. Most scholars believe that Great Britain was the world pioneer in that process, though this is not a universally held view.[2] The United States, in any case, followed very closely on Britain's heels and probably did so before the continental European nations. In the case of Japan, the prevailing view appears to be that approximately 1850–1950 was the period of industrialization. In this paper, it will be assumed that the United States had begun to industrialize by about 1815 and that the process had clearly been completed by about 1940. If anything, this definition may push the closing date to a later time than many American historians would, in part to accommodate more of the story of the 20th century, when the export of manufactures at last became an important part of the history of the American business community.

I. Foreign Trade and U.S. Industrialization

It is vital to understand at the outset that foreign trade was perhaps less significant in the coming of industrialization to the United States than it was in the case of Japan and Western Europe. Not until quite late in the creation of a modern industrial economy in America did the overseas market loom very large; indeed it has never been so important to the U.S. economy as to those of Great Britain and Japan. Despite the relatively large size of the 19th century American economy, for example, American exports of manufactured goods never exceeded about 7% of the world market.[3] Overall, it can be said that the United States achieved industrialization via development of its huge domestic (not foreign) market. Further, to the extent that exports were important to America, it was primarily exports of the agricultural and resource-based sectors of the economy, rather than the manufacturing sector. Manufactured goods were more important to 19th-century America as imports, though finished manufactures accounted for only half the value of imports as early as 1850, declining thereafter to about 25% of the value of imports by the end of the century.[4]

Whether one considers imports or exports, however, a fundamental fact of American economic history during the period of industrialization is the overwhelming primacy of the domestic market. As Morton Rothstein has noted, "The development of the home market in the 1840's and 1850's, when the United States was entering a period of sustained economic growth, was less and less dependent on export earnings." Indeed, "foreign trade had fallen to less than 10% of the gross national product (GNP) by 1850, and to less than 6% 10 years later."[5] This pattern of the decline of the ratio of exports to GNP was perpetuated throughout the century after 1850. The ratio did not rise above 7% in any decade between 1830 and 1900. After 1900 it "mainly fluctuated around 6–7% until the 1930's and 4–5% after World War II."[6] The economist Robert Lipsey points out that "export trade was not a major force in stimulating [U.S.] economic growth after 1830." It is clear, as he asserts, that "by any method of measurement . . . the role of exports appears to have been a fairly minor one, relative to total American output, throughout [the] century and a half [from 1820–1970]."[7] Only in the colonial era and the late 18th century were imports very significant relative to overall output. Furthermore, until very late in the transition to an industrialized society in America, manufacturing played only a small part in exports.

For many decades, then, it was not manufacturing but agriculture and the extractive industries that had the lion's share of the rather small export market. For example, Rothstein estimates that between 1820 and 1860 approximately 85% of the total value of American exports were connected with agriculture and the extractive sector.[8] Throughout the era of industrialization, foreign trade was much more critical to American farmers than to industrialists. It is striking, for example, that despite the great expansion of industry in the United States from 1850 to the 1890s, "the share of agricultural products in exports, considerably larger than the share in the domestic economy, remained almost unchanged, until the late 1890s, when it began to decline."[9] For all the attention paid to manufacturing, it was cotton, tobacco, wheat, corn, forest products, and other agricultural and extractive goods that mostly flowed through the channels of foreign trade in the 19th century. As late as 1870 or so, even "the few manufactured products that were exported reflected the richness of American resources, rather than American capabilities in processing them."[10] Ultimately this did begin to change, but not in a dramatic fashion. For the 19th century as a whole, the judgment of Irving Kravis is sound: "In their direct impact ... trade and capital movements were supplementary factors; they were handmaidens, not engines, of growth. The mainsprings of growth were internal; they must be sought in the land and the people and in the system of social and economic organization."[11]

An increasing proportion of manufactured goods were exported after the 1880s. In the 1960s some industries in the manufacturing sector had become so dependent on foreign markets that they were selling 25% or more of their output abroad. Even in those industries, however, it was almost always the experience of the successful development of the home market that was the critical factor in leading American firms to sell some of their output abroad. The development of these industries, Lipsey argues, "clearly did not depend heavily on the foreign market. Rather, these industries were based on the domestic market of the United States and reached such an advanced level in catering to that market that they became strong exporters."[12]

This brief review of the secular pattern of foreign trade in the history of the American economy leads to the conclusions that such trade, however pursued, was never of more than marginal importance to the bulk of American businesses, and that it unfolded largely in the shadow of the development of the huge domestic market. Paradoxically, then, in order to understand the evolution of the methods and structures used in foreign trade, one must first understand the history of marketing in the home market. Because trade with other nations was not so important in American history as in the pasts of some other nations, it received perhaps less attention, less creative energy, than in those nations. For most of the American past, overseas commerce was approached in an essentially passive manner. In those manufacturing industries in which such trade was pursued vigorously at the end of the 19th century and in the first few decades of the 20th century, the firms involved usually did so on the basis of their prior success in the domestic setting. In those cases the American firms were often among the most competitive in the world, but their competitive edge was gained first on home ground, and was then brought into play abroad when the growth curve began to flatten at home or when foreign markets were seen to be equal to or more lucrative than domestic ones.

The historical American indifference to cultures and markets abroad was in large part the result of long experience in which the rewards of serving the large and fast-growing domestic market were greater than those offered by distant opportunities. Economic historians have long known that the American record of per capita economic growth was not particularly remarkable in a comparative context. What was extraordinary, however, was the expansion of the size of the overall economy (that is, without regard to the per capita record). Because industrialization began at a time when the level of per capita income in America was already high by world standards, and because much of the 19th century in the United States was taken up with the task of filling up a resource-rich but underpopulated continent, the aggregate weight of the U.S. economy in the overall world economy increased at a breathtaking rate. In 1840, for example, "the American economy was smaller than either the British or the French economy, while 110 years later it was four or five times as large as the British economy and seven or eight times as large as the French."[13] Toward the end of that 110-

year period (that is, by the 1950s) the American economy, with only 6% of the world's population, was producing about a third of the world's output, the astonishing "legacy of some 300 years of extraordinary growth," as Gallman has written.[14]

In addition to the remarkable overall growth of the domestic economy, there were other reasons why it made sense for Americans in business to concentrate for so long on the home front. That huge and expanding market was, on the whole, relatively free of the entanglements and uncertainties of dealing with different cultures, different languages, different rules of the economic game, the risks of shifting exchange rates, the problems of securing foreign exchange, and the myriad other challenges of cross-national trade. Not the least important attraction of the domestic setting was the prevalence of a predictably high degree of political stability, shattered only briefly in the Civil War of 1861–65.

The results of the size and desirability of the domestic market were that Americans learned their marketing mostly at home, and that foreign trade was distinctly a sideline for most firms, at least until very late in the development of an industrialized economy. Before the middle decades of this century, for many large American businesses, including many in manufacturing, this description of the 1910–50 era in the American cigarette industry was a reasonably accurate summary: "The singular characteristic of the industry . . . is its incredible domestic development, and almost total disregard for foreign markets, overseas expansion, and investment."[15] Certainly that was not true of all firms, and it definitely describes a leitmotif of the 19th century better than it describes a leitmotif of the 20th.

The picture should not be overdrawn. Even though foreign trade accounted for a very small portion of national product, and the domestic market held the attention of most manufacturers, there was nevertheless a noteworthy degree of overseas trade. Although it is important to understand the lesser role of such trade in the U.S., it is also important to review, for the comparative purposes of this international conference on business history, the patterns and structures of such trade. How was foreign business done, particularly in the manufacturing sector, as industrialization came to the United States?

II. Patterns in Marketing

In any relatively complex and sophisticated commercial system, manufacturers can choose from a spectrum of marketing activities for manufactured goods, from the highly passive to the highly active. In the American context from 1815 to 1940, a wide variety of organizational means were utilized to pursue foreign trade. In no case, however, was there a clear American counterpart of the *sōgō shōsha*, the general trading company of Japan. Nothing in the U.S. story seems even to approach having the vast, integrated, diversified nature of such global traders as Mitsui or Mitsubishi. A few institutions in the American past had some of the characteristics of the sōgō shōsha; the general merchants of the colonial era, the 19th century private banking houses such as J.P. Morgan and Co. and Brown Brothers, and (particularly) the modern-day diversified multinational manufacturers all come to mind as partial analogues. But there was really nothing on the American scene quite like them.

As I understand them (and I apologize for my extremely limited knowledge of the Japanese case), the sōgō shōsha were the general trading companies of the great zaibatsu—Mitsui Bussan for Mitsui, Mitsubishi Shōji for Mitsubishi, Sumitomo Shōji for Sumitomo, and so on. They handled foreign trade for the zaibatsu, meeting the export and import needs of the great financial and industrial combines that pioneered the industrialization begun with the Meiji Restoration of 1868 and that were broken up at the end of World War II.[16] Such trading companies, in addition to handling exports and imports, also played other roles, notably in investing in new manufacturing enterprises and even in recruiting and promoting "capable young college graduates into key positions" in the zaibatsu.[17] This kind of general trading company, Johannes Hirschmeier and Tsunehiko Yui have argued, is "unparalleled" in Western development.[18] Certainly it is unparalleled in the case of the United States.

It is very difficult for an American to understand the sōgō shōsha without at the same time seeing them in the wider context of the few great zaibatsu, which controlled the great majority of Japanese industries before 1945. The zaibatsu are also unlike anything in the

U.S. case. Such institutions are culturally foreign to the American spirit of individualism and to American political ideals of democracy and economic competition. The absence of sōgō shōsha in the United States was in part due to the relatively lesser American interest in foreign trade, but it was also due to cultural and political barriers to such enterprises in the American setting.

Although there have been many ways in which government in America aided businesses, favored some businesses, and cooperated with companies for political and economic reasons, it nevertheless seems clear that there was always a much closer relationship between government and business in Japan than in the United States. Most accounts of the rise of the zaibatsu emphasize the close ties between them and those in power in the political system. Because industrialization and faster economic growth were very high, officially sanctioned priorities in the Meiji era, there came to be in the minds of many an identification of the interests of the zaibatsu with the national interest. This made business-government cooperation and even favoritism both logical and legitimate.

It is easy to overestimate the differences here between Japan and America, but the differences were real and important. With occasional exceptions, government in the United States played a less active role in the economy, and there was always a strong political tradition of opposition to official favoritism, state-granted monopolies, and the like. Even when there was a consensus on government action to assist some particular industry Americans were generally unwilling to subordinate their individual or group interests to those of another individual or group, if that also meant less wealth and power for themselves, as it usually did. The widely shared values of individualism and materialism in America made the encouragement or even toleration of such economic institutions as the zaibatsu or the sōgō shōsha unlikely.

Along with industrialization and the rise of big business in America came a powerful emphasis on the regulation of business by the state and on antitrust, the prohibition of some forms and practices of large-scale business. As Ellis Hawley had pointed out, the American anti-monopoly sentiments (opposition to government intervention in the economy, opposition to officially sanctioned special economic privilege, and opposition to private combinations in restraint of trade) originated in English common law but grew much stronger in the United States than in Great Britain in the 19th century.[19] This led to the creation of a set of government units designed to regulate business (at the national level the first one was the Interstate Commerce Commission, established in 1887) and a set of federal antitrust laws (beginning with the Sherman Act of 1890).

Despite the strength of that tradition in American life, there has also been a tendency to encourage business cooperation for more exports when the nation has been worried about its ability to sell goods overseas. In 1918, for example, the Congress passed the Webb-Pomerene Export Trade Act, allowing businesses to combine into associations to unite their resources and efforts aimed at foreign markets. This wish to exempt those producing exports from antitrust laws surfaces periodically. Recent concerns over America's poor performance in world markets led, for example, to the Export Trading Company Act of 1982 and the National Cooperative Research Act of 1984 to encourage joint ventures for research and development.[20] These occasional countertendencies, however, should not obscure the persistence and power of the antimonopoly tradition in America.

The Japanese, of course, have no need to be told of this American preference for antimonopoly because they learned it firsthand when the occupation government broke up the zaibatsu after the close of World War II. In the last 40 years the effects of American ideas about bigness in business have been felt in a culture much less hostile to cooperation between government and business and cooperation between businesses.

The results of antimonopoly in America, in terms of its effects on the structure of business, are much less clear than its political staying power. Clearly it discouraged cartels and overt attempts to fix prices or divide markets. As a consequence, it probably hastened the rise of the large, vertically integrated firm in manufacturing. In any case it is certain that even if economic conditions had been favorable for the coming of zaibatsu or sōgō shōsha, the political system would not have tolerated them in America. Americans have sometimes tried to exempt foreign trade from constraints placed on the domestic economy by, in effect, legally encouraging sōgō shōsha but prohibiting zaibatsu. The link between the two, however, is not an easy one to break. In opposing an activist government role in the economy and in discouraging domestic cooperation between firms either within a single industry or across industries, American cultural and political traditions encouraged very different ways of organizing foreign trade than was the case in Japan.

The types of functional equivalents to general trading companies in U.S. history have been numerous, but most belonged to two of the broad categories suggested by Professor Yoshihara in his opening paper at this conference: the specialty trading company (independent mercantile firm) or the trading department of the manufacturer. This was not true, however, of the era just before industrialization, when general, all-purpose merchants did in fact organize foreign trade.

In considering the entire period of industrialization in America, one is struck by the variety, within the overall concept of the independent mercantile firm, of organizational means for importing and exporting. Until the closing decades of the 19th century in the United States, that century belonged to the independent merchant (independent in the sense that the mercantile firms were legally separate from the manufacturing companies). Further, the great bulk of the merchants derived their economic strength mainly from wholesaling, not retailing. The overriding marketing challenge was to tie together a far-flung patchwork of producers and consumers. The American market was spread across vast spaces, and much of the nation's energies went to the task of improving the transportation and communications systems.

Because markets were diffuse and unconcentrated, and because few goods in the early industrial period carried any special marketing requirements (that is, most goods were generic ones), it was normally neither necessary nor economical for manufacturers to integrate forward into marketing. Producers were, furthermore, reluctant to subject themselves (any more than they had to) to the uncertainties of transport and slow communications, and the risk of extending credit to a mass of scattered and often unfamiliar customers. Because they had better information about changing consumer tastes, because they had better knowledge of the market and how best to reach it, and because they were willing and able to run the risks of extending credit in a still-developing economy, independent merchants were the ones who handled trade in the 19th century American economy. The power of their superior information and stronger credit was the foundation of their long reign in the industrializing United States. When large-scale change did come and manufacturers rose to dominance, it was because they chose to integrate forward. The merchant firms seldom chose to move directly into manufacturing, though they quite often provided critical financing for the manufacturers.

Throughout the colonial era (before 1776) and until the early decades of the 19th century, general merchants organized both domestic and foreign trade. They imported and exported, engaged in both wholesaling and retailing, arranged shipping and insurance, and dealt in a wide variety of goods. They were very small and simple organizations and they functioned much as merchants in the Western world had done for hundreds of years. When industrialization began in America around 1815, if any group could have evolved, under different economic, cultural, and political conditions, into sōgō shōsha or zaibatsu, it was they. Instead they either disappeared or evolved into specialized traders as the flow of commerce grew large enough to permit profitable specialization.

Although we may call them specialty traders, the mercantilists who followed in the wake of the general merchants were in fact very versatile. They often acted as financiers for new enterprises, and they were often active in politics and social life. It is true that they usually concentrated on a single line of goods (such as hardware or drugs), that they concentrated more on wholesaling than on retailing, and that they often concentrated on importing or exporting. Within the overall category of specialty trader a number of different mercantile types existed: brokers, factors, forwarding merchants, commission merchants, jobbers, manufacturers' agents, and others. Still, they were independent merchants, not employees of manufacturers. As the century went on, however, some manufacturers moved into marketing and began to eclipse the role and power of the merchants.

When manufacturers did integrate forward, they usually did so either because they had to (because their products did not fit well into the old mercantile network) or because concentrated markets made it economical and appealing for them to do their own marketing. As in the case in the independent merchants, manufacturers could choose from a variety of ways to organize their foreign trade once they decided to do so. They could employ traveling sales representatives, and they could choose to open branch offices abroad, sometimes consisting of a single person and sometimes consisting of a network of offices, each employing a large staff. If their products were ones that required expert servicing, repairs, and inventories of spare parts, they could choose to locate service facilities overseas, sometimes alone and sometimes jointly with foreign firms. The final step was to create a manufacturing subsidiary abroad, occasionally to leapfrog tariff barriers but most often to gain profits overseas by extending the manufacturing and marketing expertise they had acquired in serving the huge domestic American market.[21]

Beginning in the 1880s, many of the American firms that pioneered in the creation of modern, large-scale corporations at home by achieving massive increases in output and far-flung marketing and purchasing networks turned more attention to overseas markets. Makers of machinery and consumer goods were particularly successful at home and they were highly active overseas. By the time of the Second World War, many such American companies had worldwide operations, though of course none was fully comparable to the giant Japanese zaibatsu with their general trading companies.

Alfred Chandler has given us an excellent understanding of how and why some of the major corporations in the United States expanded overseas beginning in the 1880s. For makers of both consumer's and producers' goods, the key to the creation of integrated, modern organizations was either peculiar marketing requirements (for perishable products or specialized machinery) or "the massive increase in output made possible by the new continuous-process capital-intensive machinery that caused . . . manufacturers to build large marketing and purchasing networks."[22] Food processors and makers of specialized machinery pioneered, and by the time of

World War I the new integrated firms had also come to dominate the oil, synthetic rubber, glass, fabricated-metals, and paper industries.[23]

It was this group of leading firms that turned more attention to foreign markets as time passed. They usually did so by applying overseas the structures and techniques that had worked so well at home. They integrated manufacturing with marketing and purchasing, and generally they operated within the confines of a single industry. Customarily they used the centralized, departmentally functionalized organizational structure, often creating a foreign or international or overseas department to handle nondomestic business. Their foreign operations functioned much as their domestic counterparts did, fashioning a network of sales outlets supplied by factories either at home or abroad. Usually the marketing organization was created first, followed by the location of manufacturing facilities overseas if tariffs or the cost of transport or labor made that economical. Some also integrated into the purchasing of raw materials. This expansion continued through the 1920s and 1930s.[24]

III. The Case of Baldwin

One of the major American firms that was highly active in world markets was the Baldwin Locomotive Co., and an examination of its means of exporting will illustrate some of the general patterns.[25] The Hagley Museum and Library recently received a collection of manuscripts that tells us much about Baldwin's worldwide marketing in the late 19th and early 20th centuries.[26] This firm is one of the most dramatic examples of a maker of special industrial machinery achieving overseas expansion via a sophisticated sales and maintenance organization, though without taking the final step of locating production facilities abroad. For much of its heyday the Baldwin company was the largest producer of locomotives in the world.

The enterprise was founded at the beginning of the 19th century by Matthias W. Baldwin in Philadelphia, originally as a jewelry establishment. The decline of that trade led Baldwin into a career in the 1820s as a machinist and a manufacturer of engraving tools, printing machinery, and stationary steam engines. When the railroad business began in America around 1830 Baldwin turned to the design and production of locomotives. As early as 1838 the firm was building locomotives for overseas customers, especially in central Europe and Latin America. As the U.S. railroad industry experienced explosive growth, Baldwin expanded. By the end of the century the company's production facilities occupied 26 acres; in 1906 it built a much larger works near Chester, outside Philadelphia. By the time of the outbreak of the First World War, almost 20,000 workers turned out coal-fired, gasoline, electric, and compressed air locomotives for use throughout the world. Building on their base of strength in superior technology, large-scale manufacturing works, and a highly sophisticated sales-and-repair organization, Baldwin was the global leader in its industry in the 1920s. The firm's success in large part depended by then upon its foreign sales, which accounted for 43% of the value of the orders on hand in 1919.[27]

Like most other American firms that were very much involved with exports, Baldwin chose to make its overseas marketing effort consonant with the size of the potential market and the company's comparative advantage in that market. When the railroad industry was just beginning in the 1830s, the railway supply business was not yet large enough to encourage very active approaches to marketing by the manufacturers. Only in those initial two decades or so did independent railway supply merchants really flourish in the United States. Some early independent mercantile houses such as A. and G. Ralston of Philadelphia stocked a full line of rails, boilers, iron, and car and locomotive wheels; the Ralston firm promised that it could import "at the shortest notice . . . every description of railroad iron and locomotive engines . . . under the direction of one of our partners who resides in England for this purpose."[28]

Locomotives, however, did not long remain distributed through the network of independent merchants. Because they were expensive, technologically complex producers' goods, and because the pool of customers fairly quickly came to be a dense one dominated by relatively few firms, producers of locomotives turned rapidly to more direct and active involvement in their marketing.[29] In situations where there was a necessity for supplying spare parts and expert repair services, manufacturers also found themselves compelled to integrate forward. Although most domestic railroads soon come to have their own knowledgeable, in-house repair staff, this was not always true of railroads in less developed economies, which continued to make it necessary for locomotive producers to establish maintenance, repair, and parts facilities overseas. Often these were joint ventures between the producing firm and the local railroad.

Usually Baldwin would enter overseas markets first via traveling representatives and then through the creation of a regional office responsible for several nations. If the company's sales potential in one of those countries came to seem promising enough, then Baldwin would open a branch office there. Sales in Brazil, for example, were handled from the company's Cuban office prior to 1919, when the firm's board decided to create a sales subsidiary in Rio de Janeiro, capitalized at $10,000 and staffed initially by a full-time "representative of the Company appointed with full authority to act for it."[30]

A review of Baldwin's sales in Cuba will demonstrate the workings of an effective foreign sales operation. Cuba was among the first destinations for Baldwin-made locomotives, the firm's business there having begun with the export of two locomotives in 1838. From its very passive early approach to marketing in Cuba, Baldwin moved to a more and more active strategy because the volume of its business had "steadily kept up at an increasing rate ever since [1838]." In 1913 the company decided to establish a permanent office in Havana, under the guidance of Wallace R. Lee, later the manager of its Buenos Aires office. A decade later the company noted with satisfaction that "Mr. Lee laid the foundations on the present basis and left many friends in Cuba." Foreign business often depended on the social and political skills of the representatives of the exporting firm; it was probably not an accident, for example, that in the 1920s Cuban sugar paid 20% less duty than other sugar on entering the United States, while American locomotives enjoyed a similar tariff break on entering the Cuban market.[31]

Baldwin's sales in the post-World War I locomotive market in Cuba were strong. During the nine years 1915 to 1923, annual sales averaged about $315,000. By 1924 the company's Havana office was run by a full-time staff of four people, which, an internal report noted, "it will now be necessary to enlarge on account of increasing business." Further, matters had progressed to the point that a "joint operation" was planned with the Cuba Northern Railway for shop operations. Although the Cuba Northern supposedly was to own and manage the shops, in fact Baldwin had much influence. The Philadelphia company was to send "a competent mechanical adviser" to help with the management of the shops. In addition, Baldwin was "to act as Sales Agent for repair work"; that is, the Havana office, with its sugar plantation and railway contacts, would negotiate to have repairs done at the shops.

The locomotive market in Cuba, however, was certainly not large enough to tempt Baldwin into building a production facility there. The entire population of locomotives on the island in 1924 was less than 1,900, about a third of which consisted of narrow-gauge engines. The firm saw this market as essentially two different markets, the nearly 600 locomotives on mainline roads (of which about 45% were Baldwin-made) and the more than 1,200 locomotives operated by the sugar mills (of which more than 70% were Baldwin-made).

What accounted for this success? The 1924 Baldwin report on Cuba argued that "the strength of our position results from the superiority of our product and the superiority of our service, especially in connection with spare parts." This judgment seems very likely to have been correct; producing good machines cheaply and in volume at its centralized, capital-intensive works on the Delaware River, Baldwin secured its foreign successes via the experience and skill of its Foreign Sales Department's worldwide network of offices, parts suppliers, and repair staff and facilities. During the decade that followed World War I the Baldwin Locomotive Co. enjoyed export markets all over the world, and especially in Europe, India, the Far East, and South America.[32]

Baldwin was, in the American context, a relatively sophisticated and effective manufacturer and global trader at the height of the period of industrialization in the United States. It did not, however, have many dealings with firms outside its own specialty, and it did not funnel investments into new manufacturing lines or work so closely with the U.S. government to promote American interests abroad as did the sōgō shōsha in Japan. It was merely one example of a company carrying out foreign trade via the trading department (or foreign sales department) of a large manufacturer. Some American firms came closer to the Mitsui or Mitsubishi pattern than did Baldwin, but none really came very close in the 1815–1940 period of industrialization.

IV. Summary and Conclusions

It is always more difficult for a historian to explain why something did not happen than to explain what did in fact happen. As we have seen, the general trading company did not appear in America, nor did the zaibatsu; different conditions produced a different outcome. Foreign trade was always handled in a much less concentrated, de-centralized fashion in the United States than in Japan, and it appears to have been perhaps less important to the nation's economic growth than it was in Japan or Britain. The attraction of the home mar-ket led manufacturers to concentrate their early efforts there. Neither the specialized merchants nor the specialized manufac-turers in the United States showed any very great tendency to expand into many industries, as the Japanese zaibatsu did. Overseas trade in the period of industrialization was handled either by independent, specialized merchants or by the trading departments of single-industry manufacturers until the industrial process was well matured.

The reasons for this American pattern of foreign trade were eco-nomic, cultural, and political. The huge domestic market probably encouraged concentration on the home front and may have account-ed for the long reluctance of American merchants and manufacturers to diversify into several different industries. Strong traditions of individualism, a minimal role for government in the economy, and antimonopoly also served to make unlikely the emergence on American soil of institutions like the zaibatsu and the sōgō shōsha.

NOTES

1. For the purposes of this paper I will use the terms *modern economic growth*, *industrialization*, and *economic modernization* interchangeably. Obviously this oversimplifies matters somewhat, and it should be

noted that sustained rates of real per capita economic growth had already been in excess of 1% per annum (the customary definition of modern growth) for some time before the U.S. economy was significantly based on industry. Similarly, the socioeconomic characteristics and arrangements usually thought of in connection with modernization were also in place before industry accounted for a large portion of American economic output. (For that matter, it should be noted that employment in manufacturing never accounted for a majority of the American work force.) Nevertheless, for the purposes of this conference, it is useful to consider industrialization, modern economic growth, and economic modernization as virtually synonymous terms.

2. For the standard view see Phyllis Deane, *The First Industrial Revolution*, Cambridge, 1965, and Peter Mathias, *The First Industrial Nation: An Economic History of Britain, 1700–1914*, London, 1969. Thomas C. Cochran, in *Frontiers of Change: Early Industrialism in America*, New York, 1981, sees Britain and the United States as co-pioneers.

3. See Folke Hilgerdt, *Industrialization and Foreign Trade*, Geneva, 1945, pp. 157–58.

4. Morton Rothstein, "Foreign Trade," in Glenn Porter, ed., *Encyclopedia of American Economic History*, New York, 1980, Vol. 1, p. 257.

5. *Ibid.*, p. 256.

6. Robert E. Lipsey, "Foreign Trade," in Lance E. Davis et al., *American Economic Growth: An Economist's History of the United States*, New York, 1972, pp. 554–55.

7. *Ibid.*

8. Rothstein, "Foreign Trade," p. 255.

9. Lipsey, "Foreign Trade," p. 561.

10. *Ibid.*, p. 560.

11. Irving B. Kravis, "The Role of Exports in Nineteenth-Century United States Growth," *Economic Development and Cultural Change*, April 1972, p. 405.

12. Lipsey, "Foreign Trade," p. 561.

13. Robert E. Gallman, "The Pace and Pattern of American Economic Grown," in Lance E. Davis et al., *American Economic Growth, op. cit.*, p. 36.

14. *Ibid.*, p. 58.

15. Philip Lynn Shepherd, "Soold American! A Study of the Foreign Operations of the American Cigarette Industry," Ph. D. diss., Vanderbilt University, 1983, p. 688. Prior to the 1911 antitrust

suit that broke up the American Tobacco Co., of course, Americans were extremely active in overseas markets, dividing virtually the entire world with their British counterparts.

16. My understanding of the zaibatsu and their trading companies is based on such sources as Johannes Hirschmeier and Tsunehiko Yui, *The Development of Japanese Business, 1600–1973*, Cambridge, Mass., 1975; Kozo Yamamura, "The Founding of Mitsubishi: A Case Study in Japanese Business History," *Business History Review*, Vol. 41, Summer 1967, pp. 141–50; and the special issue of the *Business History Review*, Spring 1970, on Japanese entrepreneurship.

17. Hirschmeier and Yui, *Development of Japanese Business*, p. 215.

18. *Ibid.*, p. 182.

19. Ellis W. Hawley, "Antitrust," in Porter, ed., *Encyclopedia of American Economic History*, Vol. 2, p. 772. See also Thomas K. McCraw, "Regulatory Agencies," in the same *Encyclopedia*, Vol. 2, pp. 788–807.

20. Along the same lines, Malcolm Baldrige, the Reagan administration's secretary of commerce, has called for additional changes in antitrust laws; see his piece entitled "Rx for Export Woes: Antitrust Relief," *Wall Street Journal*, October 15, 1985.

21. The standard works are by Alfred D. Chandler, Jr., and Mira Wilkins. See Chandler, *The Visible Hand: The Managerial Revolution in American Business*, Cambridge, Mass., 1977, and Wilkins, *The Emergence of Multinational Enterprise*, Cambridge, Mass., 1970.

22. Chandler, *Visible Hand*, p. 298.

23. *Ibid.*, p. 402.

24. *Ibid.*, p. 369.

25. Baldwin is, for example, among the "giant firms" that William H. Becker says "easily gained entrance to markets abroad." See p. 177 of his essay "1899–1920: American Adjusts to World Power," in William H. Becker and Samuel F. Wells, Jr., eds., *Economic and World Power: An Assessment of American Diplomacy since 1789*, New York, 1984.

26. The collection consists of the papers of William Liseter Austin, who was closely involved with the Baldwin firm for more than half a century (1870–1932). He began as a draftsman and subsequently worked as an engineer and then as a manager. He eventually became president and chairman of the board. See manuscripts accession 1879 (hereafter cited as Austin Papers) Hagley Museum and Library, Wilmington, Delaware. (There are also some Baldwin materials in the collection of the Historical Society of Pennsylvania, in Philadelphia.)

27. See President's Report to the Board, July 17, 1919, Box 6, Austin Papers.

28. See Glenn Porter and Harold C. Livesay, *Merchants and Manufacturers: Studies in the Changing Structure of Nineteenth-Century Marketing*, Baltimore, 1971, p. 101. The Ralston advertising circular is in the collection at Hagley.

29. Although locomotives were the first element in the complex of railway supplies to move away from the control of middlemen, most of the railway supply business eventually moved out of the hands of independent merchants as railroads and manufacturing companies established direct contact. See Porter and Livesay, *Merchants and Manufacturers*, Chap. 6.

30. Synopsis of Board minutes, June 27, 1919, Box 6, Austin Papers.

31. The quotes and the information on the Cuban operations of Baldwin here and below are from the Cuba Report to S. M. Vauclain, February 24, 1924, Box 6, Austin Papers.

32. See the foreign market reports to S. M. Vauclain or N. W. Sample (the manager of the Foreign Sales Department) in Box 6, Austin Papers.

Comment

Mariko Tatsuki
Teikyo University

I was deeply impressed by Dr. Porter's report because he presented very clearly the reasons American foreign trade developed with no aid or dependency. I learned that the United States has had a very wide market since the beginning of its industrialization, and that that's why American traders came to specialize. This pattern of development was very different from that of Japan and that of Europe. The case of Baldwin & Co. is also very interesting because Mitsui & Co. imported from the United States locomotives made by the American Locomotive Works. The company was, in 1915, more capitalized than Baldwin, as Alfred Chandler's Largest Industries List shows.

Here I would like to set forth two arguments for the sake of comparing circumstances in Japan.

1. The Role of Government in Industrial Development

While it is true that the Meiji government played a very important part at the beginning of Japan's industrialization, I am afraid that Dr. Porter attaches too much importance to the role of the government. The government abolished various feudalistic systems and established new ones after the model of advanced European countries. An exception was the banking system, which was first introduced from the United States. The government also established state-run modern industrial establishments, such as a silk-reeling mill, cotton-spinning mills, armories, shipyards, a sugar refinery, and gold and silver mines, with the aid of foreign technicians. Japanese industrialization developed so rapidly and Japanese technicians learned so quickly that most of these foreign technicians returned home in 1877–78, and several years later nearly all state-run mills and mines were sold to private enterprises. Mitsui & Co. was a government protegé in its infant days, but it was not one any more when it became a *sōgō shōsha* (general trading company).

The role of the government faded in 1890s, and private enterprises were developing in all fields. The cotton-spinning industry can be taken as an example. Osaka Cotton Spinning Co. was established in 1883 without any governmental aid, and without the aid of foreign technicians except in installing machinery. After the success of this company, many other spinning mills were established, and the cotton-spinning industry developed to become the largest sector of modern industry in Japan. On the other hand, governmental aid still played an important role in heavy industries such as ship-building and iron until the early 20th century. The role of government in industrial development was not uniform, but in fact varied over time and with each industrial sector.

Countries late in industrializing had many difficulties which Britain never experienced. In such countries, governmental aid was more or less indispensable until modern industry could sustain itself. Germany solved the problem mainly by introducing protective tariffs and developing monopolies. Japan, however, could not resort to the same measures because of the restrictions imposed by unequal treaties and its small amount of accumulated capital.

2. *Sōgō Shōsha and the Infrastructure*

Whether a sōgō shōsha has more advantages than a specialized trader or vice versa is determined in part by the economic infrastructure. Many trading companies active in Asia were, so to speak, sōgō shōsha, and I can list many besides Japanese ones, such as Jardine, Matheson & Co., Butterfield & Swire, and Russell & Co., American traders at Hong Kong. They were general merchants and invested in sectors outside trade, like shipping, sugar refining, cotton spinning, and so on. It is not the spirit of individualism, the political ideals of democracy, or antitrust laws but a well-developed infrastructure that prevents the growth of sōgō shōsha. Trading companies in Asia could not conduct their business smoothly without having their own ships, and could not supply commodities of good quality without operating their own processing factories. Moreover, export business needs a somewhat centralized system, as in the United States, where infrastructure has been well developed and the Webb-Pomerene Export Trade Act exempted the Exporters' Conference from the Antitrust Law.

Mitsui & Co. was a sole agent of Platt Brothers, a famous spinning-machine maker in England. It is very interesting to compare this with Dr. Porter's Baldwin case. Mitsui & Co. conducted repairs and maintenance in its early days, which was the main reason why the business succeeded. It is not clear how Mitsui & Co. secured engineers, since at that time engineers were few and chief engineers often worked at two mills. In the late 19th or early 20th century, many engineers were trained and employed in spinning mills. Platt Brothers had neither the opportunity nor the desire to send representatives to Japan.

Besides the infrastructure, the size of the market is another consideration. Japan's import of raw cotton became so large in the 1890s that many specialized trading companies were established. Mitsui & Co., too, abolished its Cotton Department and established Tōyō Menka Co. in 1920.

Additionally, sōgō shōsha were not always members of zaibatsu. For instance, Sumitomo Shōji was established in 1952 after a zaibatsu was dismantled. Suzuki Shōten, which was the largest sōgō shōsha in Japan during World War I, was not a member of a big zaibatsu, but it formed a conglomerate itself.

The Overseas Trading Company in Britain:
The Case of the Inchcape Group

Stephanie Jones
Inchcape PLC

The *sōgō shōsha*, or general trading firm, has been regarded as a uniquely Japanese phenomenon. In other countries, foreign trade has been conducted by the specialty or colonial trading business, or by the trading department of the manufacturer concerned.[1] This paper, although with certain important reservations, argues the contrary. It discusses the origins and growth of the most important members of the Inchcape Group, which either joined Inchcape when it was formally launched on the London Stock Exchange in 1958 (principally firms in which the first Lord Inchcape had invested, often associated with the British India Steam Navigation Co. Ltd. [BI]), or joined Inchcape since then, during its spectacular expansion.[2]

In most cases the primary object of these businesses was general trading. Especially in their early days they handled the import of predominantly British goods into trading posts established all over the world. The range of goods, geographical spread, and scale of operations all grew, so that Inchcape today may be regarded, like Mitsui or Mitsubishi, as "a firm that trades all kinds of products with all nations of the world."[3] Again, like the Japanese sōgō shōsha, but unlike Unilever and ICI, discussed by Dr. Reader in his paper for this conference, Inchcape's trading business has never been concentrated heavily in Europe and the Americas. The products of the 2,300 principals which the group now represents are distributed in over 60 different countries, and from the mid-19th century, these concerns were to be found competing outside Britain's traditional trading and colonial markets as well as within them.

An analysis of the group's most recent profit figures, by business

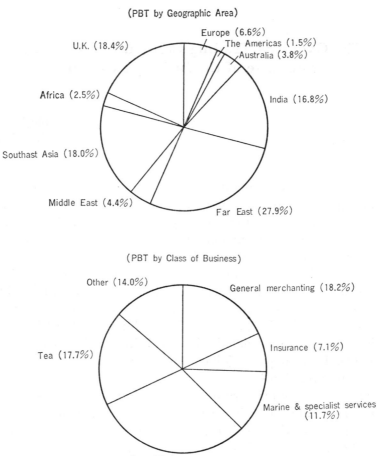

(PBT by Geographic Area)

Europe (6.6%)
The Americas (1.5%)
Australia (3.8%)
U.K. (18.4%)
Africa (2.5%)
India (16.8%)
Southast Asia (18.0%)
Middle East (4.4%)
Far East (27.9%)

(PBT by Class of Business)

Other (14.0%)
General merchanting (18.2%)
Insurance (7.1%)
Tea (17.7%)
Marine & specialist services (11.7%)
Motor (31.3%)

FIG. 1   Profits of the Inchcape Group, 1984.

Source: The Inchcape Group Report and Accounts, 1984, p. 25.   PBT refers to profit before tax.

activity and geographical spread, shows distinct similarities with the sōgō shōsha (Fig. 1), notably in its interest in merchanting and in the global nature of its activities.

Yet, in many ways, Inchcape differs significantly from its Japanese functional equivalent. Like the sōgō shōsha, it has shown, and continues to show, interest in developing local trades in the countries

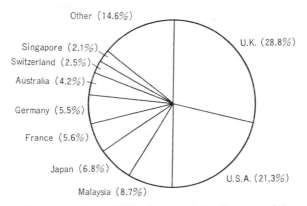

Other (14.6%)
Singapore (2.1%)
Switzerland (2.5%)
Australia (4.2%)
Germany (5.5%)
France (5.6%)
Japan (6.8%)
Malaysia (8.7%)
U.K. (28.8%)
U.S.A. (21.3%)

Fɪɢ. 2   Inchcape Group, 1984: Principals by Country of Ownership.
Source: Inchcape PLC Merchandise Agency List, July 1985.

in which it operates, and it represents and provides services such as shipping, travel agency services, and insurance; but, on the other hand, it has rarely ventured into large-scale manufacturing or into the ownership of large fleets of merchant ships. At most it has been involved in textile production, as in the case of Binny in India, and teak extraction in Thailand. It has owned lighters, tugs, and inland craft, in the case of Gray Mackenzie and Smith Mackenzie in the Gulf and East Africa respectively, and small sailing ship fleets, especially in the China tea trade. An exception was its interest in a company which owned steamers in the Australian coastal trade until 1960. And, unlike the sōgō shōsha, to which banking is an important associated activity, Inchcape's one venture into this activity was small-scale and short-lived: Gray Dawes Bank was granted authorized bank status only as late as 1971 and was sold by the group in 1982. Banking was clearly not in the mainstream of its activities. Inchcape is formally seen as "a professional distributor, marketer and seller of other people's products and technologies and a provider of skilled specialist services."

Another vital difference between a typical sōgō shōsha and Inchcape is the relationship with the home country. The general trading company of Japan imports products of foreign manufacturers and raw materials, while exporting Japan's industrial products.

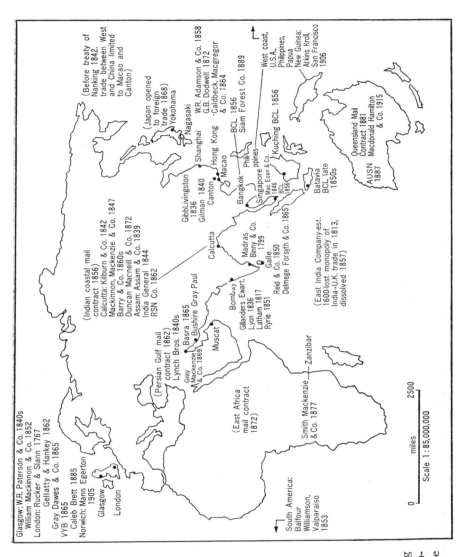

FIG. 3 Early trading posts and the Establishment of Inchcape companies.

TABLE 1 British Trade with Five Asian Countries, 1840–75 (imports from and exports to Britain shown as percentages of the countries' total trade).

Year	INDIA (millions rupees)		CEYLON (thousand pounds)		CHINA (millions taels)		JAPAN (millions yen)		SINGAPORE (million straits dollars)	
	Imp.	Exp.	Imp.	Exp.	Imp.	Exp.	Imp.	Exp.	Imp.	Exp.
1840	61 (77%)	71 (74%)	127 (19%)	298 (74%)	—	—	—	—	—	—
1845	65 (72%)	66 (49%)	306 (22%)	439 (78%)	—	—	—	—	—	—
1850	88 (74%)	81 (54%)	267 (20%)	730 (78%)	—	—	—	—	—	—
1855	147 (74%)	103 (54%)	448 (20%)	1015 (64%)	—	—	—	—	—	—
1860	217 (83%)	142 (56%)	1043 (20%)	1639 (59%)	—	—	—	—	—	—
1865	249 (85%)	434 (49%)	904 (38%)	2420 (70%)	22 (56%)	38* (72%)	—	—	8.8 (45%)	4.7 (29%)
1870	259 (67%)	313 (77%)	1531 (21%)	2907 (71%)	24 (55%)	29 (59%)	12 (44%)	5.2 (29%)	12 (49%)	8.3 (37%)
1875	345 (84%)	284 (67%)	1417 (37%)	3709 (80%)	21 (40%)	29 (59%)	15 (50%)	2.5 (15%)	10 (33%)	10.0 (32%)

* 1868 figures.

Source: Adapted from B. R. Mitchell, *International Historical Statistics: Africa and Asia*, London, 1982.

Yet Inchcape fulfills these trading requirements neither exclusively nor mainly for, or in, Britain. It buys and sells on behalf of many countries and imports goods into markets all over the world. Although originally acting principally for British manufacturers, selling their products and ensuring their raw-material supplies, Inchcape's trading expertise is now serving the needs of many others. Figure 2 analyzes Inchcape's principals by their country of ownership. The percentages are based on the number of companies of each country represented. This reveals that British or even European goods no longer loom as large in Inchcape's trading business as Japanese products do for the sōgō shosha.

My aim here is to look at the nature of the origins of these businesses, their functions, their activities, the profits they earned, their relationships with manufacturers of imports and exports, their business structure, and the impact of the changing economic climate. I have concentrated, like Dr. Reader, primarily on the period up to 1939.

The foundation of the earliest of these businesses may be seen against a background of the steady expansion in the mid to late 18th century of world trade, which was gradually developing its own infrastructure: cosmopolitan communities of merchants grew in number; credit and banking systems became established, with the international use of bills of exchange; shipping tonnage increased, and the first commercial newspapers listed the movements of vessels and their cargoes.

This encouraged and sustained the increased production of industrial goods in the towns and the concomitant need for greater supplies of raw materials and foodstuffs. The export of industrial goods overseas was vital to ensure a constant supply of bullion into Britain, necessary to pay for the costly foreign wars of the 18th century. The value of exports from Britain rose from £6.5 million in 1700 to over £40 million a century later, while imports grew from £6 million to £28 million.

The enormous level of production of cotton piece-goods from British mills, especially in Manchester, is one of the most significant features in the expansion of British overseas trading in the later

18th and in the 19th centuries. By 1829 cotton exports were valued at nearly £30 million per year; by 1870, at £70 million.[4] In seeking a market to sustain this output, and to ensure a constant source of supply of raw materials, Britain looked increasingly overseas, especially to its newly acquired territories and spheres of influence in the East (see Figure 3). Table 1 shows the development of British trade with these countries by 1875.

I

The modern Inchcape group has been built upon the enterprise of a number of British merchants who ventured overseas to these early trading posts. Besides the entrepreneurs in the East were those who stayed at home or returned there to run the equally important London end of the business. Who were these enterprising merchants? Why did they seek to set up businesses in remote parts of the world? How successful were they?

Appendix A lists over 50 of these entre-preneurs. An outstanding feature is the high incidence of Scots. No quantification of this tendency has previously been attempted. This present study shows that in a sample of 58 merchants based overseas in the period up to the beginning of the 20th century, at least 34 (about 60%) were were born in Scotland. Attention has already been drawn to this phenomenom by Sydney Checkland, who singled out F. M. Gillanders, one of these early expatriate traders, and commented: "A tall, well-built young Highlander, an obvious Scotsman in manner and speech, Gillanders did well in a trade in which Scots connections were strong."[5] Of the 11 trading houses which founded the Bombay Chamber of Commerce in 1836, at least 9 were Scot-owned.

The importance of kinship in the establishment of these trading communities is also shown in Appendix A. Nine obvious cases of direct family links in a business may be discerned, and there may be other, more distant, ties concealed by the absence of a common surname. This factor was typical of many overseas enterprises. Maggie Keswick, describing Jardine and Matheson, wrote: "Family solidarity runs strong in Scotland, and both Jardine and Matheson wanted to ensure continuity of control and the continuing influence of their families in the business. This principle carried the firm through a vital period of growth. . . . Before long James Matheson produced his nephew Alexander as an assistant in the office.''[6]

Appendix A also summarizes the timing of these first overseas ventures. In India, they were founded in the late 18th and early 19th centuries; in the Far East, in the middle decades of the 19th century; and in present-day Malaysia, in the subsequent half-century. The Persian Gulf and East Africa were settled the most recently, during the last quarter of the 19th century.

The oldest companies were usually involved in the most varied work. Before the establishment of a sophisticated commercial infrastructure, each company had to concern itself with all aspects of business: not just importing and exporting together with general agency work but providing its own banking, exchange, and insurance facilities. By the late 19th century, it had become possible for these businesses to specialize in particular trades and services. Before 1900, however, they still acted primarily as general traders, handling any commodity or providing any service for which there was a demand. In all the regions, the import of British goods, the export of local products, and the organization of the necessary transport arrangements acted as a common link between these concerns.

II

Appendix A serves as an introduction to a more detailed appraisal of the formation of the firms under review. John Binny, aged 27, sailed from London aboard an East Indiaman, for a six-month voyage which took him to Madeira, the Cape of Good Hope, and Ceylon. His ordinary cabin, with simple canvas screen, cost him, in 1796, the sizable sum of £350, which suggests that he had already made a significant profit from a previous venture, or had inherited some money. At all events, he saw better prospects in the East than in Scotland. Although he did not join an existing family firm, ties of kinship helped attract him to the early English trading post of Madras, where peace and prosperity were now enjoyed after the constant wars and political unrest of the mid-18th century.

From its early days, private banking became an important part of Binny's business. East India Co. (EIC) employees were not allowed to trade on their own account after 1800, so that private banks provided a much needed service in investing this surplus capital. The EIC's monopoly, although coming increasingly under attack, was such that when Binny founded his firm, he could act only as an agent rather than as a free merchant, selling merchandise on consignment only. After 1813, Binny sold piece goods imported directly from Britain locally.

In the period up to 1870, Binny's enterprise grew dramatically. Having started an initial capital outlay of just over £3,500 (a sum based on the contemporary exchange rate of the rupee) and an original staff of six (himself and his partner Robert Dennison with four local employees) in 1799, Binny & Co. was described by the late 19th century as "perhaps the largest general merchant in the City of Madras." In all, the number of houses of agency had increased from 10 in 1802 to 20 by 1858, and Binny's is the only name to continue over the whole period. As early as 1804, Binny and Dennison had purchased a house and grounds on the prestigious Armenian Street for £2,500, and in 1811, a surviving ledger records an overall profit for that year of £10,000. When the senior Binny, the founder, returned to Britain to retire in 1816, his prosperity was such that he was able to afford £1,000 for the best cabin available. In the mid-19th century, Binny diversified into sugar refining and indigo cultivation. It also assisted in the flotation of the Manjunhalla Coffee Co. Ltd., contributing substantially toward its capital of £17,000.

Binny went on to obtain important insurance agencies, manage the government lottery and the Carnatic Debt, and act as auctioneer and executor. Its first steamship agency, the Austrian Lloyd Steam Navigation Co., was gained in the last quarter of the 19th century at the same time that it was making its first ventures into textile production. It owned and managed three important textile mills and also invested in coal mines. Although it continued importing British goods and exporting local products, it became more heavily involved in textiles: its Buckingham Mill Co. Ltd., formed in 1876 with a paid-up capital equivalent of £35,000, was producing over 6,000 pounds of yarn per day by 1880 and paying an annual dividend of 10% to its shareholders.

The closing of the China market with the Boxer Rebellion (1900) and heavy competition with the United States, combined with the failure of a closely associated banking and agency house, shook Binny severely. It was forced into voluntary liquidation in 1906. James Lyle Mackay (who became the first Lord Inchcape in 1911) then acquired the business for the equivalent of £50,000, and launched Binny and Co. Ltd. He then used his influence to secure the BI Madras agency for Binny and developed its port facilities work. The company was able to pay a 10% dividend in the second half of 1906 by its representation of four important banks in Madras (including Barings of London) and 14 insurance companies and textile manufacturers in Glasgow and Manchester.

Binny received a great boost during the First World War, when its textile business provided over a million yards of khaki drill per month. In the 1930s it diversified into engineering, but it always maintained its trading agencies. In this respect, it resembled the sōgō shōsha. In recent times, however, the Inchcape group has increasingly concentrated on its marketing functions, and with falling profits from its mills, Binny was sold in the early 1980s.

The Anglo-Thai Corp. originally began as six separate merchant houses trading in Bombay, Calcutta, and Karachi. John Gladstone, prominent Liverpool merchant, father of the future prime minister and pioneer of free trade to India and China against the London-based EIC's monopoly, provided the impetus to this enterprise. Deciding to investigate the trading possibilities in Bengal as an adjunct to his existing West Indian business, in 1818 he employed his wife's cousin, F. M. Gillanders, as a supercargo for six vessels in the India trade owned by himself and his brother Robert.

Gillanders soon became dissatisfied with his 1% commission on purchases and sales and one-eighth share in the net profits of the voyages, and with his early sponsor losing interest in the India trade, Gillanders set up there on his own account in the early 1820s. Encouraged by further attacks on the EIC's monopoly after the Napoleonic Wars and by a loan of £5,000 from Gladstone to himself and his partner Thomas Ogilvy, their business grew. It comprised the consigning of vessels, receipt and disposal of goods dispatched by others for sale on commission, and agency business generally. An early partner was Robert Byrne, who, from 1851, expanded the firm's activities by dealing in the wool of Northwest India, by undertaking adventures in rice, sugar, and cotton, and by importing British goods wholesale on behalf of the bazaar traders.

Details of these partnerships' profits and turnover have not survived, but the partners' prominence is seen in the fact that a further partner, Edward Lyon, was a member of the Bombay Chamber of Commerce Committee. In Bombay and in Calcutta, by 1852 these firms represented the Oriental Insurance Society, the London Assurance Corp., the Victoria Insurance Society, and the Albion Life Insurance Co.

By the 1870s, these partnerships became increasingly involved in the import of Burmese teak, but were dissatisfied with the high prices, poor quality, and inadequate quantity supplied by the Bombay Burmah Trading Co. They investigated Siam as an alternative source of teak, and set up the Siam Forest Co. Profits from this business rose to over £120,000 in 1903 and reached as high as £280,000 in the postwar boom of 1920. By then timber extraction was not their sole concern, for in 1908 the Siam Forest Co. had acquired Clarke and Co., their Bangkok agent, which also ran a thriving general trading business. It held agencies for mines, insurance companies, and banks; supplied gunny bags for Chinese millers, for whom it also chartered steamers; and shipped Japanese coal on behalf of Mitsui, opium for the Siamese government, and consignments of sapphires and rubies to Europe. It marketed Siamese rice, pepper, and hides, and imported redwood sleepers for the Siamese railways. Clarke and Co.'s earnings helped maintain profits when income from the timber trade fell during the First World War and again in the early 1930s.

In Singapore the company (which changed its name to Anglo-Siam Corp. in 1918 and to Anglo-Thai in 1940) handled British imports and the export of timber and rubber. Meanwhile, the original partnerships in India continued their trading business augmented by the acquisition, in 1936, of Herbertsons of Karachi, which marketed consumer goods, many imported from Britain: income from this area exceeded that from either Siam or British Malaya in the first half of the 1930s. When the Anglo-Thai Corp. was acquired by Inchcape in 1978 it was regarded, with its long experience in marketing, as an especially suitable addition to the Group.

The most significant early entrepreneur listed in Appendix A, in terms of his role in the formation of partnerships which were subsequently to join the Inchcape Group, was William Mackinnon. He joined a fellow Campbeltown man in Calcutta who already managed a successful general mercantile business, dealing in the import of British piece goods and the export of local tea, sugar, hides, saltpet, indigo, shellac, and rice. After only four years' trading, dividends more than repaid the initial investment.

The company's assets, valued at over £11,300 in 1850, grew dramatically to nearly £50,000 by 1852, when it was reorganized into two complementary firms: Mackinnon, Mackenzie & Co. (MM & Co.) at Calcutta, and Wm. Mackinnon & Co., at Glasgow. It specialized in three principal activities: shipping cotton goods from Glasgow and Manchester for sale in Calcutta; trading general goods between Calcutta and Australia; and running a few sailing ships on the Glasgow-Sydney-Melbourne routes. Details of each adventure have survived from these early years; a total of 63 shiploads, mainly destined for Britain, were handled by the firm in 1852 alone.

The first step by which MM & Co. was transformed into the base of a worldwide network of companies was by winning the contract to carry mail from Calcutta to the Burmese ports, put out to tender by the Bengal government. Mackinnon's Calcutta and Burma Steam Navigation Co. was then established in 1856, and its early success enabled its founder to obtain further funds in Britain to increase its paid-up capital from £39,800 in 1857 to £342,685 by 1865. Then bearing the much more familiar name of the BI, the company gained further contracts enabling it to operate lines from Calcutta eastward to Burma and Singapore, from Calcutta round the coasts of India to Bombay, and from Bombay to the Persian Gulf.

MM & Co. was to become the core firm of the future Group, mainly because it was the vehicle for the extraordinarily successful business career of the first Lord Inchcape, and enabled him to develop a portfolio of investments which ultimately formed the basis for the launch of the Group in 1958. He was typical of the early entrepreneurs considered here, yet another Scotsman looking overseas for greater opportunities, with previous experience of trading from his work in Arbroath and London and with an income—a patrimony of £2,000 invested in three East Indian barques—which brought in £100 a year. Joining MM & Co. in 1874, he worked as a shipping assistant in the Calcutta office, exporting indigo, tea, jute, coal, wrought iron, and cotton.

The Indian coastal trade in the 1870s was the BI's greatest source of profit, its 60 ships of nearly 59,000 gross tons carrying at least half of the entire traffic of the Burma ports as well as those of Bombay, Karachi, and the Gulf. MM & Co.'s founders held a financial stake of nearly 30% in the BI and the firm received a 5% commission on the shipping line's gross annual earnings. Mackay's first big break occurred when he took over the BI's Bombay agency.

As in the case of Binny, Mackay and his fellow partners made substantial investments in various local enterprises. These included Macneill and Co., formed by two of Mackinnon's nephews from his Glasgow firm in 1872, who gained valuable trading agencies, for the Rivers Steam Navigation Co., the Equitable Coal Co., the Assam Railways and Trading Co., and the Kalline Tea Co. Kilburn & Co. had originated in Calcutta in 1842 importing cotton goods and yarn, and exporting local silk, hides, jute, indigo, and shellac. It acquired two important insurance company agencies in the early 1860s, that of the Assam Co. (the oldest tea business in India) in 1865, and the India General Steam Navigation Co. agency 10 years later. Barry and Co. began through the purchase of land in Chittagong for tea cultivation and investment in nearby jute-milling and gin-distilling businesses.

The First World War increased MM & Co.'s profits through the greater range of activities of BI shipping, and despite the foundation of rival local lines in the 1930s, the BI's dominant position was not significantly threatened. Thus MM & Co. maintained its successful trading business, retaining an informal partnership status.

Ceylon, as shown in Table 1, was of considerable importance as a source of imports (principally raw cotton) to the United Kingdom by the late 19th century. Combined with the products of its sugar, coffee, and cinnamon estates, its trade was such that nearly

400,000 tons of shipping, mainly from Britain and the colonies, cleared outward with cargoes in 1859. The merchant house of Reid & Co. was founded by yet another Scotsman, Alexander Reid, who was joined by an American, E. T. Delmege, after acquiring capital as a Mississippi pilot engaged in blockade running during the American Civil War (1861–65). The importance of kinship in this shipping and coaling enterprise is shown by both being soon joined by their brothers. In 1861 Reid & Co. was one of 13 European merchants based at Galle, with four British employees and six local assistants. A fortnightly service by the Peninsular and Oriental Steam Navigation Co. Ltd. linking Galle to Calcutta, Bombay, China, and London stimulated the company's business. It became officially known as Delmege, Forsyth & Co. when, after the Reids' retirement, the Delmege brothers separated. The older Delmege successfully secured the firm's agencies, specializing in the import of flour and sugar.

In the first decade of the 20th century, however, local merchants drove the firm out of this specialized market, and in 1918 it was acquired by the first Lord Inchcape, who converted it into a private limited company, in which he held 50% of the shares. It was then managed by MM & Co.'s Colombo office, which helped expand its other trading business.

III

Four companies which were subsequently to form a vital part of the Inchcape group were established in China in the middle decades of the 19th century: Gibb Livingston, Gilman, Dodwell, and Caldbeck Macgregor. First, two ex-EIC merchants founded a factory in Canton in 1836, which combined in one building the functions of office, warehouse, and residence, where they imported English cottons and woollens and exported tea, with silk and silver bullion used in payment for exports. The partners also dealt in grey shirting, velveteens, nankeens, chintz, leather, tin plate, and saltpet and acted as agents for a large number of sailing ships, organizing the payment of their port charges, consular fees, import and export duties, landing charges, and the cost of boat hire and storage of cargoes on shore.

In one month alone, March 1845, the turnover of their business exceeded £4,000, and their net profit equalled nearly £150. Despite the restrictions on the opium trade after 1842, the account book mentions several transactions involving opium, such as in May 1845: "received from Capt. Hy. Forman of the *Thomas Crisp*, schooner, demurrage and sale charges on 40 chests of Malwa opium per agreement at $16 per chest, $640." By 1863 Gibb Livingston & Co. had opened branches at Kiukiang, Hankow, Shanghai, and Woosung, as well as Hong Kong and Canton. It employed a total of 27 Europeans in China as a whole, including four members of the Gibb family.

Like Dodwell and Gilman, it was closely connected with the shipment of tea from Shanghai and Foochow, played a continuing part in the local import-export business, and acted as a shipping agent.[7] Although, as a general rule, Inchcape companies tend to act as agents rather than the owners of tonnage, Gibb Livingston briefly ventured into shipowning with its purchase of steamers to form the Gibb Line in 1899. Insurance was another continuing interest—they had been a founder member of the Union Insurance Society of Canton. An advertisement of the Imperial Hire Insurance Company of London (which mentions T.A. Gibb as a director) was undersigned by Gibb Livingston & Co., as agents for the company at Canton, Hongkong, Amoy and Shanghai, "prepared to grant . . . against *FIRE* to the extent of $40,000 on any one First Class Risk." By the end of the 19th century it had acquired agencies for no fewer than 120 marine insurance companies from all parts of the world.

A commercial guide of 1908 referred to Gibb Livingston as "one of the most important and best known merchant houses of Hong Kong." It adopted limited company status only as late as 1920, by which time it had invested in local service industries, engineering, manufacturing, and land, together with harbor facilities, in addition to its traditional activities. Like many expatriate merchant houses, it took an active part in municipal affairs and local institutions. It was acquired by Inchcape family interests in 1921 and enjoyed considerable prosperity from the trading boom in Hong Kong at that time.

A tea taster from the old established firm of Dents, Richard James

Gilman, helped form Gilman & Bowman in 1840 and also occupied a Canton factory. By 1863 the firm was also represented at Kiukiang, Hankow, and Tientsin, employing 21 staff in all, with three members of the Brand family and two Lemanns, again showing the part played by ties of kinship in these enterprises.

Heavily involved in the tea industry, Gilman was also active in the shipping trade and was appointed Lloyd's agent at Canton, Hankow, Foochow, Hong Kong, and Macao in 1862. It chartered, among many other vessels, the *Taeping*, which narrowly beat its rival the *Ariel* in the famous China Tea Race in 1866. The dependence of trading firms on the demand and supply for the products they handled was shown by the growing public preference for Indian and Ceylon rather than China teas toward the end of the 19th century. Practically bankrupt, Gilman had to close its Shanghai and Hankow branches in the 1880s, and the business was rescued only by gaining the agency for the Australian Sandalwood Co. which enabled it to respond to the enormous demand for sandalwood for joss sticks. It was taken over by an Australian firm in 1917, but suffered further financial insecurity during the depression following the First World War, when it received vital support from the Hong Kong and Shanghai Banking Corp. Relationships with local banks were crucial to many of the merchant partnerships considered here. Gilman's recovery in the 1920s was aided, like Gibb Livingston's, by the growth of Hong Kong, where it gained the Rootes agency to import cars, and retained several important shipping agencies.

Dodwell was founded as a result of the efforts of a group of Cheshire silk weavers to increase supplies of raw silk for their mills. W. R. Adamson, who arrived in Shanghai on their behalf in 1852, soon branched out into the export of tea and the import of general merchandise. He established his own company in 1858, based at Shanghai, with branches in Foochow, Hankow, and Hong Kong, with 10 European employees. Much is known of the shipping agency work and trading business of this firm in the last quarter of the 19th century through notebooks and letters kept by a young shipping clerk who joined them in 1872 and eventually took control of the whole business, George Benjamin Dodwell.

The greater part of this business was the carriage of tea to London and New York (77% of cargo shipped between May 1876 and April 1877), but straw goods, sugar, hides, and silk were also exported to Britain. Only 536 tons of cottons and piece goods were transshipped from Shanghai round the coasts of China, so Dodwell's trading interests revolved around handling Far Eastern exports to Britain, rather than vice versa. This was especially true in the case of tea. It exported between 70,000 and 150,000 chests of tea from Shanghai and Foochow per year in the mid-1870s, and in 1875 it handled more tea than any of the other 26 firms in the business, British, European, or American, including both Jardine, Matheson and Swires.

Dodwell's personal earnings from this business were remarkable. In 1881 he doubled his basic salary (equal to £1,000) by his own efforts. The business at this stage was still a private partnership, with European employees managing the branches, staffed by native assistants and clerks, and depending on the services of compradors. They acted as vital go-betweens in the local market, bringing together local buyers and sellers, settling their disputes, and securing their principals against loss.

Through expansion into Japanese trading circles, Dodwell became aware of the great demand in North America for Japanese goods, which he capitalized upon by inaugurating the first transpacific steamer line in the late 1880s on behalf of Fairfield's of the Clyde (the steamship owners) and the Canadian Pacific Railway (which provided passengers and freight for the Far East). When the Canadian Pacific Railway acquired its own fleet, Dodwell offered an alternative service, which contributed substantially to the gross profit of $20 million declared by his firm in the second half of 1891. Dodwell's business continued to expand through carrying Japanese contract labor to Hawaii, prospectors to the Klondike gold rush, and soldiers for the American government during the Spanish-American War and for the Japanese when fighting the Chinese and Russians, with brief and limited forays into shipowning.

When Dodwell became a limited liability company in 1899, the greater part of the capital was provided by the partners, their families, employees (including compradors), and local workers. This was still the case in 1972 when Dodwell & Co. Ltd. was acquired by Inchcape. Its survival in the meantime was based almost entirely on general trading and on building capital reserves in prosperous days during the First World War to cope with the subsequent depression. Just before the Second World War, it increased its agency business: for example, the Shanghai branch won representation of Glaxo products, Aspro, Kiwi polish, and Libby's canned foods. Its difficulties in this period were compounded by the decision of the Japanese to deal directly with overseas suppliers, so that Dodwell's role as a general importer and exporter declined. Like Gilman and Gibb Livingston, it recovered thanks to the great demand for motor cars in Hong Kong in the 1920s and 1930s.

Caldbeck, MacGregor and Co. differed from the other Far Eastern firms described above in that it specialized exclusively in wines and spirits, opening branches all along the China coast in the later 19th century. Before 1914 the firm enjoyed a booming trade at the ports of Hong Kong, Singapore, Kuala Lumpur, and Penang, and was regarded as "the largest and best known firm in the wine and spirit trade in the East." It supplied various expatriate and local organizations, such as clubs, hotels, military messes, and warships, manufacturing its own mineral water and soft drinks and representing an enormous range of best-quality wines and spirits. It remained a family firm, becoming a private limited company in 1920, and went public in 1929 under the Companies' Ordinance of Hong Kong. Acquired by Inchcape as part of Anglo-Thai in 1978, the group has since developed its wines and spirits distribution business dramatically.

IV

The importance of Singapore as a market for British goods has already been noted in Table 1. The Borneo Co. Ltd. was originally a Glasgow firm, W. R. Paterson & Co., which, from Singapore, opened branches in Manila, Batavia, and Bangkok. In the early 1850s the opportunity to contribute to the economic expansion of Sarawak led to the decision to float this enterprise.

Registered in London to take advantage of the limited liability status which had been introduced earlier in that same year (1856), this firm was unique among the businesses so far considered, as most preferred the less formal, more flexible style of a partnership. Merchant trading companies, in contrast with manufacturing concerns, were able to continue even until the mid-20th century as partnerships, for they required much less capital, working as well as fixed. In the commission business, shipping agency work, the representation of principals such as British manufacturers and insurance firms, those for whom they acted provided the capital: they lived by taking their percentages, usually operating from modest premises, often shared with other firms.

The Borneo Co.'s capital of £60,000 was, however, not financed by a stock exchange issue but subscribed by the partners and employees of W. R. Paterson & Co. and R. & J. Henderson, merchants of Glasgow and London, and John Charles Templar, a lifelong friend of Rajah Brooke of Sarawak. Brooke's offer of far-reaching development rights to the Borneo Co. acted as an irresistible magnet. The new firm then took over and began to develop the "mines, ores, veins or seams of all descriptions of minerals in the Island of Borneo, and to barter or sell the produce of such workings."

The Singapore branch, as the company's original base and jumping-off point, continued to thrive, especially with the prominence of British shipping at the port: nearly 70% of the total in 1871. As Lloyd's agent in Singapore, it dealt closely with these ships, including those of the Peninsular and Oriental Steam Navigation Co., which competed against French and Dutch steamers and German and American sailing ships. The Borneo Co. was one of 38 merchant houses established by 1872, 12 of them British.

Here they represented the Indo-Chinese Sugar Co. Ltd., the Norwich Fire Insurance Co., the North China Insurance Co., the Chinese Insurance Co. Ltd., the Standard Life Assurance Co., not to mention H. M. Government of Labuan, and they were founder members of the Singapore Chamber of Commerce. Despite all these activities, only nine Europeans were employed by the Borneo Co. in Singapore by 1872.

In Sarawak, the company operated antimony, gold, diamond, and cinnabar mines and played an important part in local coffee, pepper, gambier, sugar, indigo, and coconut estates and managed a small steamer. Its original paid-up capital of £60,000 had risen to

£200,000 within only four years. Its property and assets were then valued at £672,309.

Earnings rose steadily to over £100,000 per year by 1914, thanks largely to the company's gold mining activities: annual production exceeded Sarawak $1 million in value in 1901–16. Gold mining was abandoned in the early 1920s with the flooding and gradual exhaustion of the principal mines, and the company's revenue was then derived from sago, rubber, antimony, and oil exports from Sarawak and the import-export trade of Siam. One of the first foreign merchant houses in Bangkok, the Borneo Co. was joined by 10 other firms by the 1870s; but by the late 1880s it and only one French and two German firms survived. It acted for a wide range of insurance companies and ran a profitable steam rice-milling business before venturing, like the Siam Forest Co., into teak extraction. It exported timber to Europe, India, and the Far East, and sold rough-cut timber locally. It prospered with the demand for motor cars in Singapore in the mid-1920s, selling Austin, Vauxhall, Chevrolet, Oldsmobile, Cadillac, Chrysler, and Buick cars, together with several makes of trucks, trolley buses, and tractors.

V

Three other areas were explored for their commercial potential as a result of the close relationship between MM & Co. and the BI. Trusted employees and relations were installed to manage BI agencies in the Gulf, East Africa, and Australia as a result of awards of mail contracts (see Figure 3).

First, Gray Paul & Co. and Gray Mackenzie & Co. were established at prominent Gulf ports. Imports of cotton piece-goods into the Gulf were to rise dramatically as a result of the arrival of the steamers: in Bushire, for example, British goods as a proportion of total imports by value rose from 16% in 1873 to 48% by 1899, and exports to Britain, such as opium, pearls, nuts, dried fruit, and spices, rose from only 8% of Bushire's exports to 27%. Mohommerah and Basra also eagerly purchased British products, mainly for transshipment throughout this region, with the aid of another British firm which operated Tigris and Euphrates river steamers, Lynch Brothers. Over £74,000 worth of British cottons and piece goods were unloaded at Mohommerah in 1899 alone.

Gray Paul's office at Bushire, the headquarters of the BI Gulf Service, was operated by only one manager, Robert Paul, with two Persian clerks, six Persian servants and seven Indian assistants. At the Lingah office, opened in 1875, Gray Paul's branch manager was the only British resident at the port, and this was also the case at Bandar Abbas and Bahrain. British Indians enjoyed an important position among merchants and traders in the Gulf, acting as shop-keepers, clerks, and foremen of local labor. This explains the use of rupees as the official currency of the area used in statistical returns.

The partnerships benefited from the steady profits earned by the BI and other shipping lines, such as Ellerman and Bucknall: 300% over 20 years, excluding local expenses, investments, and profits plowed back in. Through their experiences in the First World War, a pooling of resources with Lynch Brothers was considered, and the Mesopotamia Persia Corp. Ltd. was formed in 1920. Lack of coop-eration and inefficient management blighted this merger, which was abandoned in 1936. Gray Mackenzie and Co. Ltd. then became a U.K.-registered limited liability company, and its trading expertise was particularly sought after with the subsequent oil boom.

Second, Smith Mackenzie & Co. established a merchant house in Zanzibar following the award of the East Africa Mail Contract. The opening of the Suez Canal in 1869, the success of the Persian Gulf Mail Contract, the need to establish a British presence in the area, and the popular clamor to fight against slavery all contributed to British interest in Zanzibar. Smith Mackenzie was actively involved in developing an existing trade: by 1867–68 imports from Britain were already valued at £153,305, and exports of local produce at £321,642. The value of the annual clove trade, for which Zanzibar became justly famous, was already approaching £100,000 per year.

The subsequent dominance of British shipping was such that a report on local trade of 1873–74 concluded that "the whole of the commerce of Zanzibar is now conveyed by English tonnage." This assured the commercial standing of the BI agents, who handled the bulk of the island's import-export trade and passenger services. They acted as Lloyd's agents, represented the Union Castle Line and many marine insurance companies, and organized the supply of coal to both British and German naval vessels (until the outbreak of the First World War).

Smith Mackenzie, representing the ill-fated Imperial British East Africa Co., arranged caravans into the interior, acted as agent for the Uganda Railway, handled news reports for Reuters, and invested in mainland coffee, sisal, and rubber estates. In 1898–99 it was appointed an agent for the Asiatic Petroleum Co., which later became Shell. The marine side of the firm's activities was so important in the First World War that it was hived off to form the African Wharfage Co., and many new branches were opened on the mainland in the 1920s. When the general produce trade declined, Smith Mackenzie sought to expand its agency business, and won contracts from BAT, ICI, BOAC, and Distillers. It assisted in the U.K. Overseas Food Corp.'s groundnuts project and acquired its own tea estate. Only as late as 1936 did this firm seek limited liability status; it was registered in Nairobi.

Third, Inchcape interests in Australia were also the result of the BI gaining the local mail contract. A merger between a local Australian steamship line and Mackinnon's Queensland Steamship Co. produced the Australasian United Steam Navigation Co. Ltd., whose shareholders were dominated by BI directors. Until 1924, when the company lost the Queensland Mail Contract with the advent of the Townsville to Cairns railway, it had enjoyed a growing business carrying passengers and freight (such as coal, sugar, flour, and general cargoes) in the Australian coastal trade. Then, with the depression in this trade, exacerbated by frequent dockside strikes, the company became more and more reliant upon its non-marine investments, so that by 1937 income from these sources exceeded that from the fleet. This continued to be largely the case until the few remaining steamers still owned in 1960 were sold when the business was acquired by the Group.

A much more typical Inchcape company in Australia was Macdonald Hamilton & Co., set up in 1915 to manage the Australasian United Steam Navigation Co. It also handled several agencies for the Peninsular and Oriental Steam Navigation Co., invested in port facilities, and was involved in wool dumping, cold storage, mining, and pastoral management.

Finally, two businesses on the American continent form part of Inchcape's past and present activities. Atkins Kroll & Co. was originally established in San Francisco in 1906, chartering ships in the Pacific trade. By 1920, it owned a fleet of 49 schooners, which carried petroleum products to Australia and New Zealand and returned to San Francisco via the Philippines, Guam, and the South Sea Islands with cargoes of copra before sail gave way to steam on this route. The firm's Guam branch, opened in 1914, was to hold one of the earliest overseas dealerships of General Motors. Its general import-export business thrived only until the Second World War, but its subsequent gain of the Guam and Micronesia Toyota agencies made it especially attractive to Inchcape when it was acquired in 1974.

Balfour Williamson & Co. began in shipping and general trading between Liverpool and South America, with capital of only £5,000. Two years later, it set up a Valparaiso branch, importing textiles, chemicals, paint, and wines from Liverpool in return for local wool, nitrates, and guano, and later opened branches in Chile and Peru. As in the case of Atkins Kroll and Inchcape firms in the Far East, Balfour Williamson briefly invested in shipping. By 1901 the firm's capital had risen to over £1 million. It continued to grow through acting as agent for oil exploration concerns, and it successfully developed its own banking facilities, which were hived off before it joined the group in 1981.

VI

These overseas merchants all required representation in London and other cities of Britain. Binny maintained trading links in Scotland and later opened a London branch; the Bombay houses set up by Gillanders, Ogilvy, and their associates kept strong ties with their Liverpool office; MM & Co. of Calcutta worked closely with William Mackinnon & Co. in Glasgow and Gray Dawes & Co. in London; the Assam Co. and the India General and Rivers Steam Navigation companies were all registered in London. Kilburn and Barry were to establish London offices soon after their formation in India, while Macneill was represented there by Duncan Macneill & Co. The companies in the Far East all had home connections: Gibb Livingston through steamers such as the Ben Line, which it represented; Gilman had formal London agents, Ashton & Co.;

Dodwell had a London branch by the 1880s; and Caldbeck Mac-
Gregor maintained an office in Glasgow, principally to supply it
with a wide range of whiskey. The Borneo Co., as we have seen, was
originally registered in London, where affairs came under close
scrutiny. Gray Dawes & Co. (founded by Archibald Gray and Edwin
Sandys Dawes, the London agents of the BI) invested in the Gulf
and Zanzibar agencies and worked closely with them. The Australasian United Steam Navigation Co. was also registered in London,
and Balfour Williamson had its Liverpool office. Of these firms,
Atkins Kroll was unusual in being a completely foreign trading company. We are concerned here only with home branches which
worked with their overseas offices: purely British-based firms of the
group are listed in Appendix B.

VII

This discussion of the origins of the Inchcape companies shows
the deep traditions of their reliance on trading. They became involved in associated activities, such as shipowning and manufacturing,
but not in the manner of typical sōgō shōsha: generally speaking
these remained ancillary, small-scale interests only. They saw their
primary role as merchants and distributors.

Why were these firms so successful at winning, and keeping,
important agencies? The prestige and commercial prominence BI
agents enjoyed was attractive to manufacturers seeking representation. Binny expanded its agency business as a direct result of gaining
the BI Madras agency in 1910. The firms made a point of cultivating
good relations with their local diplomatic representatives who could
put business their way: correspondence between Smith Mackenzie
and the British consul in Zanzibar shows that the former often imported items on the latter's behalf, and in return gained influential
support. The close relationship between the Borneo Co. and Rajah
Brooke of Sarawak and the king of Siam bestowed vital advantages.

These businesses were not afraid to open up trade in the remotest
corners of the earth. They reaped the benefits of being first in the
field, as Gray Mackenzie discovered in the Persian Gulf. Through
their success at marketing a widening range of goods over a wider
area, they were able to provide a more comprehensive service. Now,

under the Inchcape umbrella, the chairman is able to point out that "the long-standing relationships with business associates are of major importance to the Group, which offers established distribution facilities and experience of business conditions in areas in which its principals are not necessarily familiar." Thus manufacturers who would otherwise provide their own overseas outlets (by 1939 more than 200 British manufacturing firms had replaced agents) were likely to stay with the group. For example, Unilever and ICI, who, as Dr. Reader has shown, generally handle their own distribution arrangements, use Inchcape in Singapore and Malaysia.

The skill of these companies in marketing is also based on close contact with, and knowledge of the needs of, both customer and manufacturer. In Zanzibar, for example, the market for brightly colored cloth for making up into the *kangas* worn by local women was developed as a result of the agents providing Manchester cotton manufacturers with local designs. The need for railway sleepers by the London & North Eastern Railway in the 1880s prompted the Borneo Co. to import sample sleepers to Sarawak to see if they could be produced there at a competitive price.

It may be seen as a function of Japan's uniquely fast economic development in recent times that its overseas trading was conducted by large, formal organizations with strong governmental backing. Conversely, as Britain's economic development was comparatively slow and informal, the trading companies which handled its marketing needs were small partnerships which avoided limited liability status (except in the case of the Borneo Co.) and acted without direct government involvement. Overheads were low, staff numbers small, and local autonomy strong, especially with the relatively unsophisticated level of communications available during this period. A few European partners led staffs of locally recruited assistants, employing merchants on the spot (such as compradors in the Far East) to deal directly with customers. Lack of outside shareholders and the existence of strong kinship ties gave the partners a strong sense of loyalty to their businesses, and dealing with a large range of products prevented them from becoming tied to particular manufacturers, just as having a number of branches meant they were not dependent on just one market situation.

The linking into a group in 1958, necessitated by the formaliza-
tion of outside tax and legal pressures,[8] saw a change in scale rather
than structure, as the companies still largely enjoy considerable
autonomy under an informal holding company which, with only
a small head office, lacks a strong Inchcape group persona.

The continuing growth of world trade in this period was of great
benefit to these firms, especially because the dominant feature of
world trade remained the export of manufactured goods from
Europe in exchange for primary products from underdeveloped
countries. This, combined with free trade and the aim of British
politicians to encourage a British commercial presence in as many
countries as possible (shown by mail subsidies to steamship lines),
fuelled and sustained their growth. Their small individual structure,
whereby the maximum number of people was involved in the
decision-making process, encouraged innovation in products and
markets and enabled them to make the most of commercial opportunities, as shown by George Benjamin Dodwell's inauguration
of the first transpacific steamship service. Stephen Nicholas has
convincingly argued the case for the marketing success of British
overseas trading firms generally, though surprisingly he does not
cite Inchcape as an example.[9]

Despite the changes over the last two centuries, Inchcape is still
above all a general overseas trading company. Trading networks
have become more sophisticated: Inchcape companies are no longer
acting just as independent agency houses but are prepared to open
buying offices, generally in the Far East, and enter joint-trading
ventures with manufacturers (e.g., Dodwell with Pitney Bowes in
Japan, and Inchcape Berhad with Rolex in Singapore).

Yet, although the origins, the growth, and especially the present
features of the Inchcape Group show many fundamental similarities
with the sōgō shōsha, it is fair to say that Yoshihara's view of the
uniqueness of the Japanese answer to its overseas trading needs is
still largely true. The nine largest sōgō shōsha dominate Japan's
exports and have a sizable share in its imports. British general trading
companies such as Inchcape, together with Gill & Duffus, Harrison
Crosfield, Lonrho, Sime Darby, Tozer Kemsley, Yule Catto, and
James Finlay, have no such predominant role.[10] A more typical

response to the overseas trading requirements of British industry is for each firm to make its own arrangements. This pattern is discussed by Dr. Reader.[11]

Appendix A

The Original Founders of the Inchcape Group: Those Based Overseas.

	Place of birth	First place worked overseas	Date of arrival	First overseas position	Ultimate position in company
1. John Binny	Forfar, Scotland	Madras	1796	Surgeon	Founder, Binny & Co., 1799
2. Robert Dennison	Scotland	Madras	before 1796	Coffee trader, seller of army clothing	Partner, Binny & Co., 1799
3. John Binny, Jr.	Forfar, Scotland	Madras	1810	Merchant	Partner, half share in Co. 1836
4. F. M. Gillanders	Highlands, Scotland	Bombay	1818	Representative of the Gladstone family	Founder, Ewart Gillanders, Co.
5. Thomas Ogilvy	Scotland				Director, Ewart & Co. to 1842
6. William K. Ewart	Scotland	Bombay	1834	Local manager	First Bombay manager
7. Peter Ewart	Scotland	Bombay	1836	Local manager	Second Bombay manager
8. Edward Lyon	Scotland	Bombay	1836	Assistant to P. Ewart	Partner in Lyon & Co.
9. John Jackson	Liverpool, England			Merchant	Merchant for Assam Co.
10. Robert Brown	Liverpool, England	Bombay	1848	Merchant-Partner at Bombay	Third Bombay partner

No.	Name	Origin	Location	Date	Occupation	Role
11.	George Clark Arbuthnot	Scotland			Captain in East India Co.	Senior partner to 1857
12.	Arthur George Latham	Scotland	Bombay	1847	Merchant	Senior partner
13.	Robert Ryrie	Caithness, Scotland	Bombay	1851	Merchant	Senior partner to 1888
14.	William Mackinnon	Campbeltown, Scotland	Calcutta	1847	Sugar factory worker in Cossipore	Founder, Mackinnon, Mackenzie Co., 1847
15.	Robert Mackenzie	Campbeltown, Scotland	Calcutta	c. 1830s	Merchant	Founder, Mackinnon, Mackenzie & Co., 1847
16.	James McAlister Hall	Scotland	Calcutta	c. 1840s	Merchant	Partner, Mackinnon, Mackenzie & Co.
17.	James Lyle Mackay	Arbroath, Scotland	Calcutta	1874	Merchant	Partner, Mackinnon, Mackenzie & Co.
18.	Charles Alexander Bruce	Scotland	Assam	c. 1836	East India Co. Naval officer	Manager, Assam Co.
19.	J. W. Masters		Assam	1839	Local manager, Assam Co.	Manager, Assam Co.
20.	Albert de Hochepied Larpent				Merchant	Director, India General
21.	Captain A. G. Mackenzie	Scotland	India	1820s	Second officer, East India Co., shop	Founder, India General, 1844 & partner
22.	Captain J. H. Williamson		India		India General commander	Founder, India General, 1844 & partner
23.	C. E. Shoene		Calcutta	before 1842	Merchant	Founder, Schoene, Kilburn & Co., 1842

S. Jones

Appendix A (Continued)

	Place of birth	First place worked overseas	Date of arrival	First overseas position	Ultimate position in company
24. Edward Dunbar Kilburn	London, England	Calcutta	1847	Merchant	Founder, Schoene, Kilburn & Co., 1842
25. Dr. J. B. Barry	Ireland	Calcutta	1860s	Surgeon in Assam	Founder, J. B. Barry & Co., 1865
26. Duncan Macneill	Scotland	Calcutta	1858	Assistant, Begg, Dunlop & Co.	Founder, Duncan Macneill & Co., 1872
27. John Mackinnon	Scotland	Calcutta	1858	Assistant, Begg, Dunlop & Co.	Founder, Duncan Macneill & Co., 1872
28. Alexander Reid	Scotland	Galle, Ceylon	1850	Merchant, trader	Founder, Reid & Co., 1850
29. James Reid	Scotland	Galle, Ceylon	1850s	Merchant, trader	Assistant to brother
30. E. T. Delmege	United States	Galle, Ceylon	1865	Merchant, trader	Founder, Delmege Forsyth & Co., 1865
31. A. A. Delmege	United States	Galle, Ceylon	after 1865	Merchant, trader	Assistant to brother
32. Thomas Augustus Gibb	Scotland	Canton	1835	East India Co. merchant	Founder, Gibb Livingston & Co., 1836
33. William Potter Livington	Scotland	Canton	1835	East India Co. merchant	Founder, Gibb Livingston & Co., 1836
34. Abram Bowman		Canton	1830s or 1840s	Merchant	Founder, Gilman Bowman & Co., 1840
35. Richard James Gilman		Canton	1840	Tea taster	Founder, Gilman Bowman & Co., 1840
36. Jack Calbeck	Scotland	Hong Kong	1850s	Army, Crimean War	Founder, Caldbeck MacGregor & Co.,

	Name	Origin	Location	Date	Occupation	Position
37.	John MacGregor	Scotland	Hong Kong	1850s	Navy, Crimean War	1864 Founder, Caldbeck MacGregor & Co., 1864
38.	W. R. Adamson	Macclesfield(?) England	Shanghai	early 1850s	Representative of silk manufacturer in Cheshire	Founder, W. R. Adamson & Co., 1858
39.	George Benjamin Dodwell	Derby, England	Shanghai	1872	Shipping agent, trader	Founder, Dodwell & Co. Ltd., 1899
40.	A. J. H. Carlill		Foochow	1870s	Tea taster	Partner, Dodwell, Carlill & Co.
41.	Ludvig Verner Helms	Denmark	Bali	1846	Explorer, pioneer	BCL manager
42.	Robert MacEwan	West Coast, Scotland	Singapore	1846	Trader, merchant	Manager, Singapore branch, Paterson & Co.
43.	John Harvey	Renfrewshire, England	Singapore	1840s or 1850s	Merchant	Manager, Singapore branch, Paterson & Co.; succeeded Robert MacEwan, his brother
44.	Robert Harvey	Renfrewshire, England	Singapore	1840s or 1850s	Clerk, assistant	Assistant to John Harvey
45.	John Charles Templar	England			Merchant	Friend of Rajah Brooke, vice chairman, BCL
46.	Francis Richardson		Manila		Local manager, Manila merchant	Partner, MacEwan & Co.
47.	Samuel Gilfillan		Bangkok		Merchant, trader	BCL Manager, Siam

Appendix A (Continued)

	Place of birth	First place worked overseas	Date of arrival	First overseas position	Ultimate position in company
48. William Adamson		Singapore	1862	Merchant, trader	BCL Manager, Singapore
49. Louis T. Leonowens		Bangkok		Merchant, originally with BCL	Founder, Leonowens & Co.
50. John & Henry Lynch		Basra	1840s	Traders, shippers	Formed Euphrates & Tigris S. N. & Co.
51. Robert Paul	Scotland	Bushire	1865	Merchant, trader	Partner, Gray Paul & Co.
52. George S. Mackenzie	India, of Scottish parentage	Bushire	1865	Merchant, trader	Partner, Gray Mackenzie & Co. Manager, Basra, 1869
53. Captain H. A. Fraser		Zanzibar	1860s?	Merchant, shipping agent	First British India Steam Navigation Co. agent, Zanzibar
54. Edmund N. Mackenzie	Scotland?	Zanzibar	1872–73	Merchant, shipping agent	Partner, Smith Mackenzie & Co.
55. Archibald Smith	Scotland	Zanzibar	1873–74	Merchant, shipping agent	Partner, Smith Mackenzie & Co.
56. Stephen Williamson	Scotland	Valparaiso	1853	Merchant, shipping agent	Founder, Balfour Williamson & Co., 1851
57. G. H. Atkins	United States?	San Fransisco	1906	Merchant, shipping agent	Founder, Atkins Kroll, 1908

| 58. | Clifton H. Kroll | United States? | San Francisco | 1906 | Merchant, shipping agent | Founder, Atkins Kroll, 1906 |

Sources: See footnotes to Inchcape Archives and secondary sources in the author's *Two Centuries of Overseas Trading*.

Appendix B

The Original Founders of the Inchcape Group: Those remaining in Britain.

	Place of birth	First position	Ultimate position in Inchcape Co.
1. Archibald Gray	Scotland	Merchant in India	Director, GD & Co, GP & Co., GM & Co., SM & Co.
2. Edwin Sandys Dawes	Staffordshire, England	Merchant in India	Director, GD & Co, GP & Co., GM & Co., SM & Co.
3. George de Hochepied Larpent		Merchant in the tea trade, London	Director, Assam Co.
4. W. R. Paterson	Glasgow, Scotland	Merchant, trader	Founder, W. R. Paterson & Co., 1840s
5. William Morgan	Glasgow, Scotland	Merchant, trader	Director, Borneo Co. Ltd.
6. Robert Henderson	Scotland	Merchant, trader	Director, Borneo Co. Ltd.
7. Edward Younger	London, England	Worker in a London non-smelting firm	Founder Vivian, Younger & Bond, a Metal-broking firm in London, 1865
8. James Edward Vivian	London, England	Member of family smelting business	Founder, Vivian, Younger & Bond, Metal broking firm in London, 1865
9. Frank Walters Bond	London, England	Metal broker, tin maker	Founder, Vivian Younger & Bond, Metal broking firm in London, 1865
10. Duncan Dunbar	Moray, Scotland	Brewer, shipper	Founder, Duncan Dunbar & Co., 1765

	Name	Location	Occupation	Role
11.	Duncan Dunbar, Jr.	Limehouse, London, England	Shipowner	Chairman, Duncan Dunbar & Co. (succeeded Duncan Dunbar, his father)
12.	Edward Gellatly	London, England	Shipbroker & manager, originally for Duncan Dunbar	Founder, Gellatly, Hankey & Sewell, 1862
13.	Jameson Alers Hankey	London, England	Merchant banker	Founder, Gellatly, Hankey & Sewell, 1862
14.	Frederic Sewell	London, England	Brewer, Taylor Walker	Founder, Gellatly, Hankey & Sewell, 1862
15.	John Arthur Rucker	London, England	Merchant	Founder, Rucker Brothers, 1767
16.	Jonathan Rucker	London, England	Merchant	Founder, Rucker Brothers, 1767
17.	(?) Bencraft	London, England	Merchant & brother of Jonathan Rucker	Partner, Rucker & Bencraft
18.	G. N. C. Mann	Cornwall, England	Electrical engineer in Norwich	Founder, Mann Egerton, Co., 1898–1905
19.	Hubert Egerton		Early Motoring	Founder, Mann Egerton, Co., 1898–1905
20.	Alexander Balform	Scotland	Pioneer, merchant	Founder, Balfour Williamson, Co. 1851
21.	Caleb Brett	London?	Shipping agent, cargo inspector	Founder, Caleb Brett, 1885

Sources: See Appendix A.

NOTES

1. Yoshihara Hideki, "Some Questions on Japan's Sōgō Shōsha," in this volume; and see Yonekawa Shin'ichi, *General Trading Companies: A Comparative and Historical Study*, United Nations University, 1983.
2. This paper is primarily based upon the author's *Two Centruries of Overseas Trading: The Origins and Growth of the Inchcape Group*, published by Macmillan in 1986. Footnotes to secondary sources relating to particular subsidiaries and to the Inchcape Archives are thus omitted here. I would like to thank Professor Theo Barker of the London School of Economics, who, in addition to acting as an adviser and consultant in the preparation of *Two Centuries of Overseas Trading*, read and commented most usefully on this paper.
3. The Inchcape Group, Report and Accounts, 1984, p. 4.
4. See D. A. Farnie, *The English Cotton Industry and the World Market, 1815–1896*, Oxford, 1979; and P. J. Cain, *Economic Foundations of British Overseas Trade, 1815–1914*, London, 1980.
5. S. G. Checkland, *The Gladstones: A Family Biography, 1764–1851*, Cambridge, 1971, pp. 121–23, 181, 318, 341. See also R. A. Cage, ed., *The Scots Abroad*, London, 1985. No such quantitative analysis of overseas entrepreneurs appears in D. H. Aldcroft, "The Entrepreneur and The British Economy, 1800–1914," *Economic History Review*, 2d ser., Vol. 12, 1964; or Peter Payne, *British Entrepreneurship in the Nineteenth Century*, London, 1974.
6. Maggie Keswick, ed., *The Thistle and the Jade: A Celebration of Jardine, Matheson & Co.*, London, 1982, pp. 18–19.
7. Gibb Livingston was also prepared to lend money, as shown by Sugiyama Shinya in his article "Thomas B. Glover: A British Merchant in Japan, 1861–70," *Business History*, Vol. 26, No. 2, July 1984, pp. 115–38.
8. In this way the Group followed the example of many in the waves of mergers in the 1950s. See Leslie Hannah, *The Rise of the Corporate Economy*, 2d ed., London, 1983, Chap. 9, pp. 123–42.
9. Stephen J. Nicholas, "The Overseas Marketing Performance of British Industry, 1870–1914," *Economic History Review*, 2d ser., Vol. 37, 1984.
10. Daily Stock Exchange Prices and List of "International Traders," *The Financial Times*, London. When Inchcape was launched in 1958,

it was regarded as unique as a general trading company, and it is arguable that the others listed here (in many cases commodity traders only) do not have Inchcape's range of trading interests and geographical spread of markets.

11. Another example of a largely British manufacturer handling the bulk of its own overseas trading through its subsidiaries, associated companies, and overseas affiliates and using agents in smaller and more remote markets is Glaxo.

Comment

Nobuo Kawabe
Hiroshima University

I am happy to comment on the very interesting paper by Dr. Jones. In it we learn much about the development and characteristics of British trading companies. In comparing them with Japanese general trading companies, Dr. Jones deals with the constituent companies of the Inchcape Group, which handles the products of 2,300 principals which are distributed in over 60 different countries. She looks at the nature of the origins of the constituent companies, their functions, their activities, and the profits they earned, their relationships with manufacturers of import and export goods, their business structure, and the impact changing economic conditions have upon them.

First, Dr. Jones outlines a general framework for discussion. She examines the similarities and differences between the Inchcape group and the Japanese trading companies. Similarities are seen in the broad range of product lines and areas. Differences are seen in the degree of involvement in such subsidiary activities as banking and manufacturing and in the relationship of their activities with their home country. Doctor Jones also describes the general background of the development of trading companies, particularly emphasizing the development of commercial infrastructure and the development of production and export of cotton goods and the acquisition of raw materials for that trade. She also examines the characteristics of enterprising merchants, clarifying the importance of their Scottish background and kinship.

Second, Dr. Jones traces the development of constituent companies of the Inchcape Group, area by area. She deals with the development of Binny, the Anglo-Thai Corp., and William Mackinnon (Mackinnon Mackenzie & Co.) in India and Reid & Co. in

Ceylon, and then with the development of trading companies in China, such as Gibb Livingston, Gilman, Dodwell, and Caldbeck MacGregor. She continues by describing the development of the Borneo Co. Ltd. in Singapore and of trading companies which developed in three other areas in the close relationship between Mackinnon, Mackenzie & Co. and the British India Steam Navigation Co. Ltd.; Gray Paul & Co. and Gray Mackenzie and Co. in the Persian Gulf area; Smith Mackenzie & Co. in East Africa, and the Australasian United Steam Navigation Co. Ltd., and Macdonald Hamilton & Co. in Australia. She concludes with a discussion of Atkins Kroll & Co. and Balfour Williamson & Co. in North and South America.

Third, Dr. Jones explains British overseas merchants' representation in London and other cities of Britain as the way that merchants managed their import and export business and agency work most effectively. On this point, in spite of her insistence on the weak ties of British merchants with their home country, we can see their close relationship with it.

In her summary, Dr. Jones emphasizes the importance of trading functions rather than banking and manufacturing functions in the development of trading companies in Britain, functions different from those of Japanese trading companies. In this context she refers to the formation of the Group in 1958 and its development since then.

We can learn a lot about the development of British trading companies from this paper. Several questions arise, however, about the comparison with Japanese general trading companies. First, constituent British companies seem to have been specialty companies or colonial merchants. I would like to know more about the reason for the formation of the Group, which is most similar to Japanese general trading companies. Second, in Japan general trading companies played a big role as promoters of industry by providing capital and other services. So I would like to know why Binny and some other British companies were involved in manufacturing and engineering. Third, what was Dodwell's reaction when it faced competition from the Japanese as Japanese companies began direct transactions with foreign suppliers? Fourth, most companies diversified their product lines, some as they developed. Why, however, did Caldbeck MacGregor & Co. specialize in wines and spirits? Fifth, how are the constituent companies and the group as a whole managed today?

Response

Stephanie Jones

Professor Kawabe has most perceptively pointed out that the Inchcape companies before the formation of the Group were, like other British trading firms, specialty companies or colonial merchants; but with the launching of the Group in 1958, the Inchcape organization took on many features similar to Japanese trading companies'. The reasons for this reorganization were, unlike in the Japanese case, largely due to tax problems: Inchcape needed to raise public capital, to protect the salaries and pensions of expatriates, and to avoid death duties when partners of these previously unlimited companies died.

Binny is an exception among Inchcape companies in its concentration on manufacturing, which developed initially due to a decline in its trading activities. Dodwell indeed suffered when the Japanese began dealing directly with foreign suppliers; its diminished profits were offset by developing its other Far Eastern branches, like the one in Hong Kong. Caldbeck MacGregor remained exclusively a wines and spirits merchant principally because the large range of products within this sector and the healthy profits earned made diversification unnecessary. Finally, the Group is still run on a decentralized basis, but with sector directors heading each "strategic business unit" and regularly touring overseas branches and subsidiaries. I am most grateful to Professor Kawabe for his searching and useful comments.

A British Trading Firm in the Far East: John Swire & Sons, 1867–1914

Shinya Sugiyama
Keio University

I. Introduction

I intend to approach the subject of this conference by examining the British trading firm of John Swire & Sons and its role in the Far East in the period up until the First World War. John Swire & Sons began as a family concern based in England, with headquarters originally in Liverpool and then in London from 1870. According to Professor Yoshihara's definition,[1] it should be seen as a colonial trading firm, and it played an important role, partly positive and partly negative, in the economic development of the Far East.

The history of the firm has been skillfully described in *The Senior John Samuel Swire, 1825–98: Management in Far Eastern Shipping Trades* by S. Marriner and F. E. Hyde.[2] This is based on the archives of John Swire & Sons,[3] and the main focus is on the history of the firm as seen through the eyes of John Samuel Swire until his death in 1898. Events after this, including significant changes in the nature of the firm's activities, are only given brief mention.

I will examine, first, the functioning and financing of the firm and its organization in terms of policy making in both the firm and its affiliates; and, second, the changing character and policy of the firm and its affiliates against the background of the rapidly changing political and economic situation of the Far East in the decades prior to the First World War. I will pay special reference to Swires' rivalry with Jardine, Matheson & Co., the other giant British trading firm in the East, and to the effects on the firm's activities of the Japanese economic advance into China.

I have confined this paper to the period before the First World War for the following reasons: first, as I shall discuss later, John

Swire & Sons gradually changed the focus of its interests from produce trade to commission, shipping, and other agency business, and already by the late 19th century the export and import of products had lost its importance; and second, although John Swire & Sons became a private limited company in 1914, this did not necessarily bring about any great changes in its overall policy. The main changes of policy with regard to their activities in China and Japan took place prior to the First World War, at least partly in response to rapid Japanese industrialization.

II. John Swire & Sons in London

John Swire & Sons was established in 1832 by John Swire (1793–1847), a Liverpool merchant, and his sons John Samuel Swire (1825–98) and William Hudson Swire (1830–84). After their father's death in 1847, the two brothers continued the business, exporting and importing on a small capital base, and it was John Samuel who laid the foundations of the firm's subsequent prosperity in the late 19th and the 20th centuries.

The real turning point for the firm came in the 1860s. Imports of American cotton being severely restricted by the American Civil War, Swires turned to shipping British-made textiles to China and Japan, probably in order "to compensate for the loss of the cotton trade".[4] It continued dealings with America and Australia, but from then on its major business interests lay in the Far East. In 1866, dissatisfied with the financial standing in Shanghai of Preston, Bruell & Co., which handled the sale of its textiles in China, Swires entered into partnership with Richard Shackleton Butterfield to create Butterfield & Swire, and opened a Shanghai office in the following year. This partnership was short-lived, however, and Swires took total control of Butterfield & Swire, paying Butterfield for his share plus 5% interest.[5] After this, Swires gradually expanded its business in the Far East to include shipping, a sugar refinery, and a dockyard.

The 1870s were a crucial period for the growth of the firm. J. S. Swire changed the focus of its activities from traditional produce operations in British textiles and Chinese teas to the more promising areas of commission and shipping interests.[6] In 1870 the head office

TABLE 1 Capital Supplied by the Partners of John Swire & Sons, 1886–1910.

Partner/Year	1886 £	1890 £	1895 £	1900 £	1905 £	1910 £
J. S. Swire	199,745	246,451	204,934	—	—	—
F. R. Gamwell	16,435	45,518	92,395	—	—	—
W. Lang	34,990	—	—			
J. H. Scott	30,965	74,655	129,769	219,880	276, 356	274,819
E. H. Mackintosh	23,448	62,378	110,669	200,132	157,468[3]	129,709[3]
John Swire		28,377	122,647	313,612	445,926	487,023
G. W. Swire			99,791[2]	209,230[2]	345,050	488,237
C. C. Scott						49,535
Total[1]	305,582	457,378	760,204	942,854	1,224,800	1,429,323

Notes: 1. Totals are not consistent due to rounding of figures. 2. "F. R. Gamwell and others in trust G. W. Swire." 3. "E. H. Mackintosh Trustees."

Sources: John Swire & Sons, Balance Sheet, JSSI 7/26; Balance Sheets No. 1, JSS, No. 166.

of the firm moved from Liverpool to London, and in the following years various related companies were set up: the China Navigation Co. in 1872; Swire Brothers, New York, in 1873; the Coast Boats Ownery in 1874; and, in 1881, the Taikoo Sugar Refining Co.

After William's retirement in 1876, new partners were gradually drawn into the business. These were Frederick R. Gamwell (1835–1902), William Lang (dates unknown), James Henry Scott (1845–1912), and Edwin H. Mackintosh (1841–1904). In fact, however, "[t]hese partners did not supply capital in the 1870s. Under the partnership agreements, they were to receive specified shares of the profits that remained after the houses' capital had been remunerated by a payment of five per cent. interest."[7]

Table 1 shows the capital supplied to the firm by each partner from 1886 to 1910. William Lang, the senior Eastern partner, retired in 1888 and John Swire (born in 1861), John Samuel Swire's elder son, joined the partnership in that same year. J. S. Swire credited his remaining share of the profits to his younger son, George Warren Swire (born in 1883), and in 1894 G. W. Swire's name appeared on the firm's balance sheet under the trusteeship of F. R. Gamwell and others. In 1886 and 1890 J. S. Swire supplied 65.4% and 52.9% respectively of the firm's capital. In 1895 there is evidence of the decentralization of capital: J. S. Swire's share decreased to 27.0%, while F. R. Gamwell held 12.2%, J. H. Scott 17.1%, E. H. Mackintosh 14.6%, John Swire 16.1%, and G. W. Swire 13.1%. However, 56% of the capital was still held by J. S. Swire and his sons together.

In the early 20th century there were further changes in the partners of the firm. J. S. Swire died in 1898, and E. H. Mackintosh and J. H. Scott in 1904 and 1912 respectively; G. W. Swire became a substantial partner in 1905, and Colin Cunningham Scott, J. H. Scott's elder son, became a partner in 1910. In the first decade of the 20th century, taken as a whole, the firm's capital came from John Swire (about 35%), G. W. Swire (about 30%), J. H. Scott (about 20%), and E. H. Mackintosh Trustees (about 10%). When the partnership came to an end on December 31, 1913, there were three partners, all of the second generation: John Swire, G. W. Swire and C. C. Scott.

TABLE 2   Profit and Loss Accounts of John Swire & Sons, London, 1868–1913.

Period	1868–80	1881–90	1891–1900	1901–13
	£	£	£	£
Trading	*222,482	*131,156	* 17,450	* 1,117
Commissions				
Refinery profit-sharing	—	42,365	45,958	202,709
Other	123,937	41,248	33,871	132,184
Insurance	21,806	* 7,526	823	698
Butterfield & Swire	299,490	256,679	520,197	680,077
Interest	* 478	* 10,082	56,056	* 183,530
Porter store	16,788	18,836	* 5,441	—
Office expenses	* 59,749	* 48,067	* 72,575	* 240,723
Exchange	—	* 19,017	* 20,959	* 1,999
Special items	* 26,150	4,609	* 3,214	* 223,605
Sundries	* 5,119	* 198	128	* 1,597
Profit as in				
London account	148,043	147,691	537,394	363,097
Plus				
Partners' profits				
debited in Butterfield &				
Swire accounts	95,186	114,840	—	—
Adjustments	* 4,001	—	—	—
London partners'				
interest on capital	126,796	150,021	211,167	505,660
Taikoo Dockyard expenses				
debited to the firm				197,855
Estimated true				
profit	366,024	412,552	748,561	1,066,612
Average profit p.a.	28,156	41,255	74,856	82,047

Note: * Loss.
Source: Notes supplied by A. Dean to S. Marriner and F. E. Hyde, JSSXII 1 /9.

During his lifetime the organization and the business of John Swire & Sons were under the strong managerial control of "The Senior" John Samuel Swire.[8] He was a deliberate businessman, wary of speculation, but not at all conservative. He enjoyed a challenge. This is particularly evident in his decisions to enter into shipping, through the establishment of the China Navigation Co., and sugar refining, by forming the Taikoo Sugar Refining Co.

"He was a man of considerable drive and energy, retaining the direction of all the companies within his own hands[,] and on several occasions visited the East to settle important matters for himself."[9] The situation changed somewhat after his death: "Whereas John [Samuel] Swire had retained control of all concerns himself[,] later Directors divided the responsibilities between them, each specializing in certain aspects such as shipping, insurance, raw sugar purchases, staff, Dockyard. These were varied from time to time and weekly meetings were held to discuss major decisions."[10]

Table 2 shows the profit-loss accounts of John Swire & Sons in abbreviated and aggregate terms from 1868 to 1913.[11] Trading losses were a main factor in reducing profits up until the period 1881–90. For instance, the loss on exported goods amounted to approximately £97,000, that on imported silk to £78,000, and that on Chinese tea exported to the United States to £44,000.[12] The gradual decrease in such losses was in line with the shift in policy of the firm, from the unprofitable trade in produce to commission and shipping business. Even so, profits from commissions on buying and selling and on agency business did not show a corresponding increase up until the early 20th century.[13] Refinery profit-sharing commissions were an important source of profit; other commissions came from the firm's agency business for the Ocean Steam Ship Co. (Blue Funnel Line) and from the China Mutual Steam Navigation Co. In any case, any losses in trading in the 19th century were more than compensated for by the transfer of profits from Butterfield & Swire.

The rapid depreciation of the value of silver to gold in the 1880s and 1890s affected business to a great extent and reduced the gains when transferring the working profits of Butterfield & Swire from China to London. Without this, figures would have been even higher than those in Table 2. The amount transferred considerably increased from 1890–1900 onward, and was a major source of profit for John Swire & Sons. The other main source of profit was increasing investment dividends and loan interest on advances to affiliated Taikoo companies, such as the China Navigation Co. and the Taikoo Sugar Refinery. Apart from this interest, in the early 20th century commissions and the transfer of profits from Butterfield & Swire were main sources of income for John Swire & Sons.

Profits gradually decreased gradually throughout the 1900s and then recovered after recording a loss of £146,000 in 1911. Total profits for the period from 1915 to 1920 amounted to £2,445,000. In 1920, the total assets of the firm amounted to £2,415,000, 46% of which was held in government securities and 28% in business investments, mainly the various Taikoo concerns. In 1930, of the total assets of £1,486,000, 38% was invested in government securities, 17% in Taikoo concerns, 5% in public bodies and utility companies, 4% in banks, 3% in insurance companies, 2% in investment trust companies, and 6% in commercial and industrial concerns.[14]

III. Butterfield & Swire in China and Japan

Butterfield & Swire acted as the trading house of John Swire & Sons in the Far East. Since the business accounts of Butterfield & Swire in China and Japan for the period under consideration are not available, its activities in the Far East can only be traced through its correspondence with London and through the accounts of John Swire & Sons.

The Shanghai office of Butterfield & Swire opened in January 1867 with William Lang, R. N. Newby, and J. H. Scott. The Yokohama branch was also opened in 1867, and the Hong Kong office, with status equal to that of the Shanghai office, in 1870. The firm continued to grow, opening branches at Foochow in 1872, at Swatow in 1882, at Kiukiang and Tientsin in 1886, at Hankow in 1887, at Kobe in 1888, at Canton in 1892, and at Amoy in 1896.[15]

Butterfield & Swire was primarily involved in the handling of cotton, woolen, and worsted goods and other textiles for sale in China. Once it became the agency for Alfred Holt's Ocean Steam Ship Co., however, its interests extended to shipping, insurance, and other agency business. It also engaged in the produce trade of flour, rice, sugar, beans and beancakes, peas, and salt.[16] Butterfield & Swire earned commission as general agents for both the China Navigation Co. and the Taikoo Sugar Refinery, and this was very important for their Hong Kong and Shanghai offices. In addition, Butterfield & Swire played a crucial role as a channel of finance between John Swire & Sons and the other Taikoo companies during the financial difficulties of the early 20th century. This point will be discussed later.

All of Butterfield & Swire's business activities in the East were

TABLE 3   Annual Balances Transferred from Butterfield & Swire to John
Swire & Sons, London (Total Aggregate Profits).

Branch/Period	1890–1900	1904–14
China	£	£
Hong Kong	198,201	43,751
Shanghai	248,870	337,896
Foochow	15,556	* 468
Swatow	34,310	48,760
Tientsin	17,505	46,577
Hankow	13,570	66,643
Amoy	4,110	8,138
Canton	* 416	—
Tsingtao		135
Japan		
Yokohama	26,920	* 4
Kobe	31,968	11,311
Total	591,300	562,736

Notes: 1. The figures for 1890–1900 do not yield consistent totals. The figures for
1904–14 have been rounded.
2. * Loss.
Source: For 1890–1900, Marriner and Hyde, *The Senior John Samuel Swire, 1825–98*,
Liverpool, 1967, pp. 194–95; for 1904–14, J. Swire & Sons, Balance Sheets
No. 1, JSS, No. 166.

conducted by managers in Hong Kong or Shanghai in accordance
with policy and finance instructions and decisions issued by the
directors in London. "Under normal conditions the Hong Kong
and Shanghai Head Offices divided the various B&S responsibilities
between them, although maintaining consultation on issues involving both. Shanghai controlled B&S and CNCo [China Navigation Co.] branches, business and property in Shanghai, along
the Yangtze River and in coastal ports north of Ningpo, as well
as ... the Tientsin Lighter Co. Hong Kong dealt with B&S and
CNCo branches and agencies on the South China coast, in Indo-
China, Siam, the Philippines and the Straits, and with the management of the Dockyard and Refinery."[17]

As we have seen in Table 2, Butterfield & Swire was a major source
of profit for John Swire & Sons. Table 3 shows the aggregated
annual balances transferred from each branch of Butterfield &
Swire to John Swire & Sons during the period 1890–1900 and

1904–14. These figures do not represent the net profit of each branch since the Hong Kong and Shanghai offices always kept certain reserves. For 1890–1900 Shanghai and Hong Kong were the two main sources of profit. For 1904–14 transfers of profit from Shanghai increased by 36%, while those from Hong Kong decreased by 78%. The profits gained at the branches in Swatow, Tientsin, and Hankow increased, but those in Foochow and the Japanese branches of Yokohama and Kobe decreased. The large fall in profits at Hong Kong is probably due to the decrease in commission from the China Navigation Co. and the heavy burden of the Taikoo Dockyard. Again, this will be discussed in later sections of the paper.

IV. The China Navigation Co.

The China Navigation Co. was formed in 1872 in London with a nominal capital of £360,000, £300,000 of which was paid up, to serve Swires' expanding shipping interests on the Yangtze River in cooperation with Holt's Blue Funnel Line. Butterfield & Swire was appointed general agent with a 5% management commission. The China Navigation Co. ordered three new ships and also purchased two ships and some shore properties, both from the Union Steam Navigation Co. In 1874 the Coast Boats Ownery was established to handle local coastal trade, such as the transport of beans and beancakes from Newchwang to Swatow and Amoy. Ten years later it was absorbed by the China Navigation Co. During its first decade the China Navigation Co. faced severe competition from the Shanghai Steam Navigation Co. of the American firm of Russell & Co., the Hong Kong, Canton & Macao Steamboat Co., the China Coast Steam Navigation Co. of Jardine, Matheson & Co., and the Chinese government-sponsored China Merchants Steam Navigation Co.[18]

When the 10-year agreement on shipping routes on the Yangtze drawn up between the shipping companies terminated in 1877, Russell & Co. withdrew from the Yangtze trade and sold the Shanghai Steam Navigation Co. to the China Merchants Steam Navigation Co. This greatly changed the state of the Yangtze shipping trade, and Swires reached an agreement with the latter over its division. Understandably, Jardines did not react favorably

TABLE 4   Annual Accounts of the China Navigation Co., 1873–1914.

Year	Paid-up capital	Net profit	Dividend rate	Balance of reserve fund at the end of the year
	£	£	%	£
1873	360,000	—	4	
1874	360,000	47,348	5	
1875	360,000	55,802	5	
1876	360,000	44,832	5	
1877	360,000	3,002	5	
1878	360,000	69,560	10	
1879	360,000	86,958	10	
1880	360,000	76,847	15	
1881	360,000	56,962	15	
1882	360,000	56,958	15	
1883	500,000	64,619	10	
1884	500,000	74,536	5	
1885	500,000	110,690	12½	
1886	500,000	119,991	12½	
1887	500,000	96,801	10	
1888	500,000	154,967	15	
1889	500,000	158,030	15	
1890	500,000	67,680	10	256,688
1891	500,000	95,110	10	249,674
1892	500,000	87,029	10	247,313
1893	500,000	98,023	12	247,313
1894	500,000	219,647	15	247,313
1895	500,000	226,572	16	315,503
1896	500,000	98,140	10	364,200
1897	500,000	115,666	12	359,179
1898	500,000	186,016	16	358,647
1899	500,000	167,925	20	389,039
1900	500,000	302,730	20	392,645
1901	500,000	211,029	20	539,115
1902	500,000	62,246	10	590,193
1903	500,000	100,953	10	525,709
1904	500,000	221,297	15	529,274
1905	500,000	197,129	15	586,601
1906	500,000	90,485	5	586,601
1907	500,000	4,782	—	579,933
1908	500,000	43,967	—	483,307
1909	500,000	64,964	—	445,934

TABLE 4 (Continued)

Year	Paid-up capital	Net profit	Divident rate	Balance of reserve fund at the end of the year
	£	£	%	£
1910	500,000	78,106	2½	429,465
1911	500,000	143,868	6	429,465
1912	500,000	226,411	10	459,465
1913	500,000	250,226	10	509,465
1914	500,000	127,539	10	609,465

Note: Net profit means profit after paying insurance, income tax, and other outgoings.
Source: China Navigation Co., Accounts, JSS III 6/1–6/6.

to this two-party agreement, and bitter conflicts were triggered between the two Western firms over both the Yangtze and other shipping routes.[19] In 1882 the China Merchants Steam Navigation Co., the China Navigation Co., and Jardines' newly established Indo-China Steam Navigation Co. reached pooling agreements on the division of the Yangtze and Shanghai-Tientsin lines: on the former, the China Merchants took 42%, Swires 38%, and Jardines 20%; on the latter, the China Merchants had 44%, and Swires and Jardines 28% each.[20]

Table 4 shows the annual accounts of the China Navigation Co. from 1873 up to 1914. With the exception of 1877, net profits remained stable until the early 1880s. Then the amalgamation of the Coast Boats Ownery and the pooling agreements on the Yangtze and Shanghai-Tientsin lines guaranteed that its business would expand. The initial capital of £360,000 was increased to £500,000 in 1883. At the end of 1884 the China Navigation Co. held 19 steamers, with a total estimated value of £634,661, and additional properties such as hulks, godowns, wharves, and land with a total estimated value of £179,928.[21] Table 5 shows the profits on specific assets of the China Navigation Co. that were transferred to John Swire & Sons. In the 1870s the Yangtze trade was the main source of revenue, but by the mid-1890s the North China coastal trade had replaced it in importance.

Swires' position in shipping was reinforced by the expansion of

TABLE 5   Profits on Specific Routes and Property Transferred from the

Line/Year	1875	1880	1885
Shanghai Office			
Yangtze	72,839	69,595	52,896
Lower (Shanghai-Hankow)			
Upper (Hankow-Ichang etc.)			
Coast (Shanghai-Tientsin)		17,440	55,363
Shanghai-Ningpo			
Shanghai-Ichang			
Hankow-Lake Tungting			
Kiukiang-Lake Poyang			
Hong Kong Office			
Hong Kong-Canton		12,812	16,916
Hong Kong-Australia			15,480
Hong Kong-Philippines			
Hong Kong-Canton-Tientsin			
Hong Kong-Haiphong			
West River			
Swatow godowns			5,685
Shore properties			
Total (with others)	72,839	101,423	146,339

Notes: 1. * Loss 2. Distribution figures for 1880 are calculated from those in Shanghai taels and Hong Kong dollars on the basis of the sterling-Shanghai tael and sterling-Hong Kong dollar exchange rates.

pooling agreements in the 1890s.[22] From the mid-1890s the China Navigation Co. experienced increasing prosperity and high rates of profit, dividend rates reaching 20% for the three years from 1899. The number of steamers increased from 28 in 1890 to 37 in 1895 and 47 in 1900.[23] In 1900 profits in the North China coastal trade were over double those in 1895. During this period, in addition to the Hong Kong–Australia line, which had started in 1884, the company opened new shipping routes to cover not only the China coasts but also the Philippines. The Hong Kong–Manila line started in 1894, the Canton–Hong Kong–Tientsin line in 1895, and the West River (Canton–Wuchow and then Hong Kong–Wuchow) in 1897.

J. C. Bois, a Shanghai manager of Butterfield & Swire, made the following comment on the China Navigation Co.'s policy:

China Navigation Co. to John Swire & Sons, 1875–1910.

(in £)

1890	1895	1900	1905	1910
30,021	58,259	51,957	36,100	13,612
		(45,801)	(33,100)	(12,496)
		(6,156)	(3,000)	(1,116)
52,695	115,576	250,833	203,956	57,769
3,137	12,990	14,557	15,646	*6,227
	2,439			
			*1,716	1,234
			*1,481	* 703
4,504	6,517	10,984	2,063	8,963
16,120	41,991	17,644	5,584	4,989
	5,693	17,779	19,899	12,598
	9,622	11,635	9,307	10,079
				2,193
		* 869	* 9	1,320
9,795	8,607	11,214		
		2,808	24,301	28,243
116,272	262,618	388,544	313,853	134,070

Source: China Navigation Co., Accounts, JSSIII 6/1–6/5.

I carefully note all you write on this subject but if I understand you rightly I think our views do not altogether coincide. I think we should follow the "open door" policy, not that of the "sphere of influence". It is no doubt easy to obtain a monopoly of any particular trade if you are prepared to run it at a loss but so long as the trade is open to others, you will never be able to reap any benefit from your sacrifice; when rates are raised outsiders will surely cut in again. We cannot reduce rates to Amoy without affecting those to Swatow. . . . in my opinion it would be a mistake for us to attempt to keep them out by cutting our rate, if we did we would bring about a general reduction & we would lose very heavily.[24]

The first decade of the 20th century found the China Navigation Co. in gradually increasing difficulties, with pressure from growing German and Japanese competition, the effects of a severe depression, and crop failures in China. The Russo-Japanese War (1904–5) also meant that trade involved the taking of considerable risks.[25] In both 1902 and 1903 the credit balance of the company's working account was too small to provide for 8% depreciation of the steamers and for a dividend. Sums of £60,725 and £19,579 respectively had therefore to be transferred from the reserve fund for this purpose.[26]

In the second half of the decade, the North China coastal trade became considerably less profitable and provided the main reason for the overall decrease in profits. The working profits for 1907 amounted to only £4,782, and £96,626 had to be transferred from the reserve fund to allow for the depreciation of the steamers.[27] For the three years up to 1909 no dividend was paid. This led to troubles between management and shareholders at the Annual General Meeting in 1911; a proposal to alter the Articles of Association in order to reduce the depreciation rate was, however, eventually defeated.[28] As Table 4 shows, the balance of the reserve fund decreased from £586,601 in 1905 and 1906 to £429,465 in 1910. The company attempted a partial solution to the difficulty by reducing the number of steamers it actually owned. This did not, however, mean that it began selling its older ships: it kept to its policy that "as a general rule we should run our steamers to a standstill and then break them up rather than sell them to those who would use them to compete against us."[29] No new coaster was built between 1905 and 1914, even though the number of routes covered by the company was increased, with the opening of the Hankow–Lake Tungting line in 1903, the Kiukiang–Lake Poyang line in 1905, and the Hong Kong–Haiphong line in 1907. The number of steamers which it owned reached a peak of 64 in 1907, but had decreased to 56 in 1912.

During this period of depression, the China Navigation Co. suffered from a continuous shortage of short-term funds for the remittance of bills on coal, porterage, and docking and for pool settlements.[30] The shortage was met through short-term loans, mainly from the Taikoo Sugar Refinery, not through short-term credit from banks such as the Hongkong and Shanghai Bank, and through long-term loans provided by John Swire & Sons. In May 1907 the China Navigation Co. owed the Taikoo Sugar Refinery HK $165,000.[31] The balance of the company which was debited to

John Swire & Sons at the end of each year increased from £182,085 in 1903 to £429,226 in 1905, £507,754 in 1907 and £576,309 in 1908, but gradually decreased again, reaching £416,264 in 1911.[32] In other words, the company was rescued from its financial difficulties through the internal help of both John Swire & Sons and the affiliated firm of the Taikoo Sugar Refinery.

Trade on both the upper and lower parts of the Yangtze was conducted according to pooling agreements between the China Merchants Steam Navigation Co., Jardines, and Swires. By 1905, however, it became apparent that "the Japanese competition in all branches of trade was growing to be a much more serious factor to deal with than that of the pushful German."[33] The members of the pool discussed ways of dealing with this competition from government-subsidized Japanese shipping companies.[34] The situation became particularly serious with the positive entry onto the Yangtze scene of the Nisshin Kisen Kaisha in 1907, at a time when established shipping companies were already suffering from a depression. The primary backers of the Nisshin Kisen Kaisha were the Ōsaka Shōsen Kaisha and the Nippon Yūsen Kaisha. It had an initial paid-up capital of ¥8,100,000 and operated seven steamers on the Yangtze River.[35] It seemed unlikely that the newcomer would either join the Yangtze Pool Agreement or be willing to reach any agreement over freight rates.[36] However, the Nisshin Kisen Kaisha was not completely opposed to the idea of a pool agreement if the conditions proposed by the member companies were satisfactory. Major discussions centered on the method of division: whether it should be based on the actual tonnages of the vessels involved, the number of trips made, or the value of the vessels.[37] The pool companies considered that they key to the Nisshin Kisen Kaisha's success lay in its ability to achieve rapid transportation of European cargo at freight rates lower than those of the other companies in connection with on-carrying ocean steamers at Shanghai. Swires and Jardines were ready to cooperate in the carriage of foreign transshipment cargo in order to drive out the Japanese, but the inefficiency of the China Merchants Steam Navigation Co. made this plan unworkable. It was therefore feared that "unless the pool lines con-jointly or individually increase their tonnage, the N.K.K's business will continue to expand out of all proportion to any expansion likely to take place in our business."[38] The Yangtze Pool Agreement had convinced both Chinese and British companies of the advantages of coexistence in removing cutthroat competition, but their association with the Chinese company handicapped the British firms in responding to the Japanese. The more delayed their response, the more their share was whittled away. The Nisshin Kisen Kaisha did not agree to the proposed terms and demanded a four-party pool instead of the suggested two-party one, between itself and an alliance of the three original member companies.[39] In 1913, however, the Nisshin Kisen Kaisha eventually reached an agreement over freight rates with the pool companies.[40]

V. The Taikoo Sugar Refining Co.

The Taikoo Sugar Refining Co. was established in June 1881 with an initial capital of £198,000. Capital was raised by J. S. Swire and close friends such as A. Holt, P. H. Holt, James Barrow, and H. J. Butterfield, who were also shareholders in the China Navigation Co. Swires' decision to establish the refinery was stimulated by the desire to compete with Jardine, Matheson & Co.'s China Sugar Refining Co. in Hong Kong, which had a monopoly of the refined sugar market in China and Japan. The Hong Kong office of Butterfield & Swire was appointed general agent and dealt with matters such as the purchase of raw sugar and the sale of the manufactured refined sugar. The Taikoo Sugar Refinery introduced up-to-date machinery and started production in 1884.[41] By the end of 1884, the refinery had spent HK $554,397 for the construction of buildings and the purchase of land.[42]

The Taikoo Sugar Refinery purchased raw sugar from Java (through Maclaines, Watson & Co.) and the Philippines and sold refined sugar to China and Japan. John Swire & Sons explained that their desire was "first fully to supply the China and Japan markets, preferentially making them concessions where necessary to stimulate consumption, before cultivating 'dumping' outlets, such as India, Australia, and the West Coast of North America".[43] In Japan the Taikoo Sugar Refinery faced strong competition from Jardine, Matheson's China Sugar Refining Co. In 1894 the latter took 54%

TABLE 6   Annual Accounts of the Taikoo Sugar Refinery, 1884–1914.

Year	Paid-up capital	Net profit (* Loss)	Dividend rate	Balance of reserve & depreciation fund at the end of year	Production of refined sugar
	£	£	%	£	thousand piculs
1884	198,000	3,637	—		n.a.
1885	198,000	25,910	5		459
1886	198,000	25,349	5		548
1887	198,000	57,337	10	35,096	772
1888	198,000	50,168	10	72,633	760
1889	198,000	88,205	15	99,667	672
1890	198,000	142,927	15	145,117	799
1891	200,000	7,513	10	198,749	812
1892	200,000	89,939	10	185,264	1,283
1893	200,000	57,208	15	206,652	1,349
1894	200,000	* 36,637	7½	261,160	1,599
1895	200,000	3,127	3	281,792	2,218
1896	200,000	61,867	10	244,933	1,830
1897	200,000	26,249	12	229,158	2,184
1898	200,000	146,294	15	296,169	2,143
1899	200,000	9,629	5	395,536	1,963
1900	200,000	128,964	10	395,165	2,139
1901	200,000	27,087	10	485,664	2,201
1902	200,000	*129,903	—	359,626	2,302
1903	200,000	124,090	10	362,849	1,664
1904	200,000	167,959	15	450,395	1,398
1905	200,000	262,988	20	557,870	1,386
1906	200,000	55,983	15	721,238	n.a.
1907	200,000	55,100	15	740,233	n.a.
1908	200,000	76,942	15	758,441	n.a.
1909	200,000	99,860	15	778,441	n.a.
1910	200,000	137,238	15	826,853	n.a.
1911	200,000	* 7,690	10	856,853	n.a.
1912	200,000	71,337	12½	843,468	n.a.
1913	200,000	27,373	10	858,468	n.a.
1914	200,000	81,536	17½	861,757	n.a.

Note: Production of refined sugar is given as a total of the actual amount of sales, stocks, and unrealized consignments.

Source: Taikoo Sugar Refining Co., Account Books, JSSV 4/1–4/4.

of the total sales in Japan, leaving the former the remaining 46%. The following year the situation was even more in favor of the China Sugar Refinery, with a 71% share as opposed to 29% for the Taikoo Sugar Refinery.[44]

The rapid depreciation of silver to gold in the late 1890s increased both the price of raw sugar in sterling in Java and the losses incurred in transferring working profits from Hong Kong to London. The Taikoo Sugar Refinery had difficulties in raising short-term loans for the purchase of raw sugar.[45] Placed in equally unfavorable circumstances, both Swires and Jardines agreed on rates for the purchase of raw sugar, and then on the supply of refined sugar to China and Japan.[46] Increasing raw sugar prices, however, inevitably led to a rise in selling prices and put them at a disadvantage in their competition with Japanese refined sugar on the China market.

Faced with a heavy cash outlay, the Taikoo Sugar Refinery was forced both to issue debentures at 6% interest and to change its previous methods of financing. John Swire & Sons made the following comment about the tight financial situation in which the refinery found itself:

> The ordinary finance of drawing on London either Bank credit or on ourselves and covering, would have been expensive, and there might have been a hitch in the renewals. . . . *the loss on the exchange would have been exactly what we have lost through the depreciation of silver.*[47] (italics in original)

Table 6 gives details of the operations of the Taikoo Sugar Refinery from 1884 to 1914. In the 1890s its performance fluctuated from year to year and a loss was recorded for 1894, although a dividend was still paid. The balance after deductions for the dividend and other expenditures was largely transferred to the reserve and depreciation fund. This created a strong financial basis for the refinery during the time of the depression, and in the long term brought it independence from any help from John Swire & Sons.

Although the Taikoo Sugar Refinery was able to overcome the strong competition from Jardines' China Sugar Refinery, it soon faced even fiercer competition from Japanese products on the China market. Japanese control of Taiwan after the Treaty of

Shimonoseki of 1895, changes in sugar tariff import rates from 1899, and the enforcement of the drawback system of imported raw sugar in 1902, all combined to oust imported refined sugar from the Japanese market. On the Chinese market, the Taikoo Sugar Refinery seems to have had two thirds of sales, and Jardines a third.[48] Quickly recovering from considerable losses in 1902, it managed to retain reasonable profits with 10–20% dividends. In 1907, in the face of aggressive Japanese competition, D. R. Law, a Hong Kong manager of Butterfield & Swire, made the following analysis of the unpredictability of the Chinese market:

> There is no official market quotation to guide operations—everyone is a law unto himself in the matter of selling prices. *We* are moreover in the unhappy position of knowing only in a certain measure the cost of our Raws. This applies every season up to the time we have taken delivery of all our raw purchases. It means that for at least 6 months we are working more or less in the dark.[49] (italics in original)

Added to this was both the irregular demand and forward or pure speculation. Law stressed the threat of Japanese competition and suggested a solution:

> It is useless to shut eyes to the fact that the Japs are a power now in Eastern commerce, and mean to be greater, and *will* be so if Europe is foolish enough to continue loading them with cheap money for the next few years . . . As far as I can judge they [the Japanese] are bound to win in the long run, backed up as they are in every way by their Government and in undisputed possession of the valuable potentialities of Formosa as a cheap Japanese sugar producing competitor. Would it not be a much wiser policy to try & engineer our future interests along the line of least resistance, which is certainly by amalgamation with the political, and . . . the future commercial conquerors of the Far East? What I should like to advise is an Eastern Sugar Trust to include the 2 H'Kong and 3 Japanese Refineries bound together for mutual protection & self interest, & committed to a policy of maintaining their present, and increasing their future hold on the Eastern sugar markets by working harmoniously on reasonable margins designed to keep away competition.[50] (italics in original)

The increasing Japanese competition forced the Taikoo Sugar Refinery to review its production and selling methods. The management wondered whether they should seek to maintain existing profit margins by preserving ordinary sales levels through a small reduction in prices or by expanding sales through a considerable reduction in prices and a big melt. Law wrote:

> I appreciate very keenly the advantage of a big melt, but think it must not come first of all as the result of a reduction in prices but from a natural increase in demand which we must endeavour to foster and secure, the lever of lower prices being only brought into play when we find any of our markets assailed to a greater extent than we are prepared to allow.[51]

The Japanese were quick to adjust their prices according to fluctuations in the foreign exchange rate.[52] They increased their sales at Shanghai and this led to the changes in the Taikoo Sugar Refinery's lowest price limits on sales at Shanghai by quality of refined sugar. These limits acted as a basis for the prices charged at all other Chinese ports.[53] The Taikoo Sugar Refinery attempted to increase turnover but maintain moderate profit margins through an immediate extension of the Manchurian system to all parts of China, which was a change in their selling policy. Instead of trying to teach the Chinese to consume refined sugar, they adjusted the grades of sugar in order to suit the Chinese demand.[54]

Japanese competition came to pose a serious threat to the market position of the Taikoo Sugar Refinery in China.[55] This led the refinery to consider price reductions as a way of stimulating consumption rather than try to "maintain rates at a level which, though giving us good margins, tends to restrict growth."[56] J. H. Scott's instructions were that "[w]e should arrange our output to meet the demand, aiming above all things at quantity and adjusting prices of the different grades so as to induce buyers to confine the bulk of their purchases to our Sugars", maintaining a good and regular color.[57] Shanghai was at the center of Japanese competition. "The Jap. policy has been one of cutting in between our marks, offering a shade better colour at the same rate and a shade lower at say a mace reduction",[58] and Shanghai dealers were in favor of Japanese sugar.[59] This forced Swires to say that "it is certain that we have to alter many things in order to successfully meet Japanese competition".[60] While admitting the need to compete with Japanese sugar through price cutting and some concessions to the Japanese in order to hold the refinery's position in the market, the firm hesitated to do so owing to the risks that this would entail.[61] By mid-1911 the Taikoo Sugar Refinery was prepared to increase the number of grades of sugar which it produced and was considering the possibility of contracts for double grades.[62] This inevitably affected their raw sugar purchasing policy:

> ... our views at present are to buy 100,000 piculs Javas if and when we get a favourable opportunity and to hold our hand for the balance until we can see the result of our refusal to sell refineds forward in quantity and are more accurately posted with regard to the prospect of obtaining Formosans.[63]

The policy changes also meant the end of the period of coexistence with Jardine, Matheson's China Sugar Refinery. As Robertson wrote:

> Japanese competition has so altered conditions that I think it is no longer to the friendly Companies' interests to wait upon each other and act together as for years has been customary. At any rate, I am convinced it does not suit T.S.R. interests to be so restricted.[64]

The challenge presented by the Japanese competition undoubtedly brought about radical changes in the refinery. Robertson wrote to J. H. Scott that "[we] have to be much more mobile nowadays than was necessary in the old times and an increased number of grades will make for this, I think. It will enable us to do more in the way of satisfying all tastes, and make it easier for us to manipulate our Refined outturn to best advantage", although they were subject to two regulating factors in sales: the prices charged by Japanese refineries and the amount of raw sugar contracted for.[65] Policies were further modified in 1914 "in order to meet changing conditions and increasing competition" by "cutting down forward sales to a minimum and judicious manipulation of prices and colours ... to foster spot business at all ports and so regulate prices that competition is met" under the direct control of the Hong Kong office on all matters concerning sugar.[66]

VI. The Taikoo Dockyard and Engineering Co.

Since the 1880s there had been people advocating the construction of a dockyard in Hong Kong to assist the operation of the
China Navigation Co. J. S. Swire was implacably opposed to this
plan, however, partly because there already existed the Hong Kong
and Whampoa Dock Co., established by Jardine, Matheson & Co.
After J. S. Swire's death, in 1898, the decision was taken to start
construction at Quarry Bay, adjoining the refinery, but it was not
until as late as 1908 that the dockyard actually started business.

The Taikoo Dockyard and Engineering Co. was registered with
a nominal capital of £800,000 and issued mortgage debentures of
up to £700,000. Capital was raised from shareholders of the China
Navigation Co., the Taikoo Sugar Refinery, and other friends and
supporters.[67] John Swire & Sons was appointed the London manager
and Butterfield & Swire the Eastern manager. The amount of
£1,405,383 was spent on land, the dry dock, patent slipways,
workshops, machinery and plant, tugs and launches, offices, and
other items, on dwelling houses for staff, and on native quarters.[68]

The Taikoo Dockyard went into operation in 1908, but competition from the Hong Kong and Whampoa Dock immediately brought
it into financial difficulties. In 1910 G. T. Edkins, a Hong Kong
manager of Butterfield & Swire, explained the situation to London
as follows:

> ... the total liability of the Dockyard has been for some time
> in excess of three million dollars, including loans from C.N.Co.
> & House [John Swire & Sons] ... the construction and working
> of the Dockyard have required expenditure overreaching present
> Bank credit, and it is inevitable to our minds that further provision
> for working capital is necessary for a business like the Dockyard. ...
> it will in our opinion still be essential to have a substantial margin
> of liquid funds to come and go on and to meet exceptionally heavy
> calls as they arise. The crux of the situation lies in the scarcity of
> Cash or Bank Credit facilities with the three interests—House,
> C.N.Co. & Dockyard.[69]

London responded with the view that "[w]hat we have to do now
is to secure the greatest possible amount of work".[70] The two dock-

TABLE 7   Annual Accounts of the Taikoo Dockyard and Engineering Co., 1908–1914.

Year	Paid-up capital	Mortgage debentures	Net profit (* Loss)	Dividend rate	Balance debited to J. Swire & Sons
	£	£	£	%	£
1908	274,600	369,100	—	—	697,403
1909	376,600	373,600	*10,271	—	669,572
1910	376,600	378,100	*21,552	—	731,600
1911	376,600	378,100	*15,294	—	651,846
1912	376,600	408,100	* 6,465	—	612,262
1913	776,600	408,100	32,571	—	252,852
1914	776,600	408,600	26,780	—	268,524

Source: Taikoo Dockyard and Engineering Co., Old London Accounts Ledger, JSS VI 3/1.

yards were engaged in cutthroat competition over docking and ship repair work, and Swires decided to continue the fight until it could bring Jardines to agree to a pooling arrangement, although public feeling in Hong Kong was against it.[71]

Table 7 shows the accounts of the dockyard. Annual losses continued through 1912, and as the balances debited to John Swire & Sons make clear, throughout this period it was kept afloat by loans from the parent company of over £600,000. The decrease in these balances in 1913 was simply a result of an increase in paid-up capital. In addition, as we have seen, a short-term loan was supplied by the China Navigation Co., by then gradually recovering from the prolonged depression, although the Taikoo Sugar Refinery was still experiencing decreasing profits.[72]

Although negotiations had broken down due to a change of policy on Swires' part in April 1910, the movement to arrange a pool with Jardines showed renewed signs of life in early 1911. According to Swires' calculations, during the half year from July to December 1910 there was not much difference in the tonnage docked and slipped, the Hong Kong and Whampoa Dock handling 282,488 tons (53%) while the Taikoo Dockyard had 252,678 tons (47%).[73] The Hong Kong and Whampoa Dock held the advantage with regard to the following: (1) greater facilities for docking and slipping,

TABLE 8   Annual Accounts of the Tientsin Lighter Co., 1904–1914.

Year	Paid-up capital	Net profit	Dividend rate	Balance of depreciation fund at the end of year
	£	£	%	£
1904	100,000	4,784	—	—
1905	100,000	9,279	—	—
1906	100,000	7,783	—	—
1907	100,000	2,153	—	—
1908	100,000	2,577	—	—
1909	100,000	6,439	—	—
1910	100,000	4,931	—	—
1911	100,000	8,812	—	—
1912	100,000	6,135	—	52,435
1913	100,000	4,002	—	52,435
1914	100,000	4,774	5¼	52,435

Source: Tientsin Lighter Co., Ledger, JSS Add. 27.

(2) good will from their long standing in the trade, and (3) support from directors and shareholders of local firms whose interests were closely connected with the dock.[74] Fearing that "at equal rates and no working agreement between the two Companies the larger share of the trade would go to the H. K. & W. Dock Co.", the Taikoo Dockyard insisted on a half as its minimum share in any pool, stating that "we must continue to compete strongly for all work: only by such tactics are we likely to make the Directors of the H. K. & W. Dock Co. realize the folly of a fight which benefits no one but the Shipowner."[75] This competition continued up until mid-1913, when they finally reached an agreement to promote and protect their respective businesses and to facilitate and economize the working of such businesses. According to this agreement, the Hong Kong and Whampoa Dock was to take 53.75% and the Taikoo Dockyard 46.25%.[76] In 1913 the dockyard recorded its first profit, but the profit rate was less than 5%.

VII.   The Tientsin Lighter Co.

Plans to establish a company to provide lighter services for the China Navigation Co. had been proposed several times since the 1880s, but again J. S. Swire was not in favor. Lighters or coasters had to be used both to load and to unload cargo for Tientsin due to the low level of the water in the Paiho River and on the Taku Bar. The China Navigation Co. had been employing a local firm, the Taku Tug and Lighter Co., which had a monopoly on these services. However, Swires found its services inadequate and its charges unnecessarily high. In 1904 it therefore established the Tientsin Lighter Co. in cooperation with Holt's Ocean Steam Ship Co.[77]

The scarcity of available materials means that little is known of the early history of the Tientsin Lighter Co. Table 8 shows its accounts. The company recorded profits from the time of its establishment, but the rate of profit was less than 10% for the first decade, and it was only in 1914 that the first dividend was paid. This was probably of little importance as long as there were no actual losses, however, since the intention was for the company to aid the operation of the China Navigation Co., rather than for it to operate on its own right. The Tientsin Lighter Co. competed with the Taku Tug and Lighter Co. until working agreements were made in 1911–12. Although details of the agreements are not known, John Swire & Sons made the following comments regarding the projected agreements in 1911:

> Having regard to the effective value of the fleets of the two Companies, we are of opinion that, in offering to accept 40% of the trade, we are amply recognising all weight that may be considered to attach the T.T.&L.Co. owing to their long standing in the trade.[78]

VIII. Conclusion

I have traced the history of John Swire & Sons and its affiliated companies (Butterfield & Swire, the China Navigation Co., the Taikoo Sugar Refining Co., the Taikoo Dockyard and Engineering Co., and the Tientsin Lighter Co.) from the mid-1860s to 1914, when John Swire & Sons was converted into a private limited company. With the sole exception of the Taikoo Sugar Refinery, all these affiliated companies originated from Swires' shipping interests. A major external factor affecting the development of the firm was the general expansion of trade in the Far East which accompanied the establishment of a worldwide shipping network during the late 19th century. Rivalry with Jardine, Matheson & Co. was also a major factor in its entry into new ventures, but it was never Swires' intention to turn this competition into a battle unto the death.

John Swire & Sons gradually changed the focus of its interests from the unprofitable produce trade to commission, shipping, and other agency business. In this respect the creation of Butterfield & Swire in 1867 was a decisive act, since it in effect committed Swires to a future in the Far East. The first half of the 1880s was another crucial period for the growth of the firm. The China Navigation Co. expanded its scale of business by amalgamating with the Coast Boats Ownery and increasing its paid-up capital from £300,000 to £500,000; the establishment of the Taikoo Sugar Refinery was the first in a series of attempts in the industrial field. Butterfield & Swire acted as general agents for both the China Navigation Co. and the Taikoo Sugar Refinery, and the transfer of profits from Butterfield & Swire was a major source of income for John Swire & Sons. This created a strong financial basis for internal capital accumulation.

Swires expanded in anticipation of the new market opportunities which industrialization in both China and Japan would bring, and this expansion was facilitated by the small number of potential competitors, either Western or Chinese. The situation became less favorable, however, with the gradual development of indigenous industries in China and Japan.

Japan's economic advancement into China, and increasing Japanese competition from the end of the 1890s into the early 20th century, greatly changed the situation in China. The reduced profits of both the China Navigation Co. and the Taikoo Sugar Refinery can probably be traced to this increasing competition, although the long depression caused by the unstable political situation in China must also have had an effect. The emergence of the Japanese challenge was doubtless linked to Japan's rapid industrialization. In shipping the Japanese challenge endangered the long-established cooperation between Swires, Jardines, and the China Merchants Steam Navigation Co. The China Navigation Co. continued great efforts to persuade the newly founded Japanese Nisshin Kisen

Kaisha to join the pool agreements, while meeting its financial difficulties with loans from John Swire & Sons and the Taikoo Sugar Refinery. In sugar refining, the development of the industry in Japan ousted the products of the Taikoo Sugar Refinery from that country, and increasing Japanese exports of refined sugar to China weakened the position of Taikoo products there too. In order to meet Japanese competition the refinery was compelled to change its production policy through adjustments to both color and price, and to reinforce its use of up-country agencies in selling. This change of policy destroyed the agreement of coexistence between Swires and Jardines.

Building on the preceding analysis, I would like to make some general observations about Swires as a business concern. First, John Swire & Sons was a family concern; all management was under the strict control of powerful directors such as "The Senior" John Samuel Swire, J. H. Scott, and John Swire. Second, the fields of business during the period under consideration were confined to shipping-related activities and to sugar refining. This feature is particularly marked when one compares Swires with the other influential British firm in the Far East at the time, Jardine, Matheson & Co., whose interests embraced not only shipping, sugar refining, and a dockyard, but also a cotton mill, ice manufacturing, electricity, railways, land investment, and silk filatures, not to speak of finance activities though the Hongkong and Shanghai Bank. Third, the capital for the affiliated companies was not floated on the market; it was raised primarily by a limited circle of family members and other intimate friends and supporters. Fourth, John Swire & Sons rested on a strong independent financial basis built up through steady internal capital accumulation. This was a major internal factor in enabling the firm to develop and overcome financial difficulties during periods of depression.

I would like to conclude by comparing John Swire & Sons with Japanese *sōgō shōsha* in terms of the characteristics presented by Professor Yoshihara.[79] If the sōgō shōsha is to be defined as "a firm that trades all kinds of goods with all nations of the world", John Swire & Sons is clearly not eligible. However, it does share some of the features of a Japanese sōgō shōsha. If we take Professor Yoshihara's first characteristic, it seems reasonable to assume that, taken together, John Swire & Sons and its affiliate, Butterfield & Swire, dealt in a variety of products, but the focus of their business gradually shifted from trade in produce to commission and shipping business. As for his second characteristic, Swires' initial trading area was nearly global, covering America and Australia, but became confined to the Far East in the late 19th century. There is much similarity as regards the third characteristic, since Swires too became involved in other industrial areas, comprising not only sugar refining and a dockyard but also local Chinese trade and shipping. As for the final characteristic, it would be difficult to deny that Swires' scale of operation was vast, despite its being within an area limited to the Far East. Perhaps one might say that Swires falls halfway between a *semmon shōsha* (specialized trading company) and sōgō shōsha.

NOTES

I am grateful to Mr. J. H. Scott of John Swire & Sons for permission to use the Swire Papers, and to Mrs. R. Seton of the Library of the School of Oriental and African Studies (SOAS), University of London, and Dr. H. J. Ballhatchet (SOAS) for their help and advice.

1. H. Yoshihara, "Some Questions on Japan's *Sōgō Shōsha*," Paper presented at the Fuji Conference, 1986.
2. S. Marriner and F. E. Hyde, *The Senior John Samuel Swire, 1825–98: Management in Far Eastern Shipping Trades*, Liverpool, 1967.
3. The archives of the firm are now deposited in the SOAS Library. See the extremely useful introduction to the archives by E. Hook, *A Guide to the Papers of John Swire and Sons Ltd.*, London, 1977.
4. Marriner and Hyde, *op. cit.*, pp. 11–2, 17.
5. *Ibid.*, pp. 20–1. It was only in 1974 that the name of Butterfield was dropped from that of the parent companies in Hong Kong and Japan.
6. *Ibid.*, pp. 29, 34 ff.
7. *Ibid.*, p. 23.
8. *Ibid.*, p. 197.
9. Hook, *op. cit.*, Introduction.

10. *Ibid.*, p. 1.
11. See also Marriner and Hyde, *op. cit.*, Chap. 10.
12. *Ibid.*, p. 191.
13. It should be noted that profits from commissions are also included in the figures for Butterfield & Swire in Table 2.
14. John Swire & Sons, Balance Sheets No. 1, JSS No. 166.
15. See Marriner and Hyde, *op. cit.*, pp. 194–95; C. Drage, *Taikoo*, London, 1970, pp. 19–20.
16. Marriner and Hyde, *ibid.*, pp. 34–57, 114–29.
17. Hook *op. cit.*, pp. 34–5.
18. See Marriner and Hyde, *op. cit.*, Chap. 4. For the Ocean Steam Ship Co. see F. E. Hyde, *Blue Funnel*, Liverpool, 1957; and for shipping rivalry on the Yangtze River and the China coasts see Kwang-Ching Liu, *Anglo-American Steamship Rivalry in China, 1862–1874*, Cambridge, Mass., 1961, Chap. 4.; and *idem*, "British-Chinese Steamship Rivalry in China, 1873–85", in C. D. Cowan, ed., *The Economic Development of China and Japan*, London, 1964, pp. 49–78.
19. Marriner and Hyde, *ibid.*, pp. 69–70.
20. Marriner and Hyde, *ibid.*, p. 73; Liu, "British-Chinese Steamship Rivalry in China", p. 68.
21. China Navigation Co., Accounts, f. 215, JSSIII 6/1.
22. Marriner and Hyde, *op. cit.*, p. 89.
23. China Navigation Co., Accounts, JSSIII 6/2–6/4.
24. J. C. Bois to J. H. Scott, Shanghai, March 6, 1899, JSSI 2/21.
25. See China Navigation Co., Minute Book No. 2, Annual General Meetings in 1900, 1903, 1904, and 1906, JSS Add. 2; see also Marriner and Hyde, *op. cit.*, pp. 198–99, 201.
26. China Navigation Co., Minute Book No. 2, Annual General Meetings in 1903 and 1904, JSS Add. 2.
27. China Navigation Co., Minute Book No. 2, Annual General Meeting in 1908, JSS Add. 2.
28. China Navigation Co., Minute Book No. 2, Annual General Meeting in 1911, JSS Add. 2.
29. J. H. Scott to H. W. Robertson, London, July 18, 1910, JSSI 1/15.
30. For instance, see Butterfield & Swire to J. Swire & Sons, Shanghai, April 30, 1909, and May 8, 1909, JSSI 2/22.
31. Butterfield & Swire to J. Swire & Sons, Shanghai, May 13, 1907, JSSI 2/22.
32. J. Swire & Sons, Balance Sheets, JSS No. 166.
33. A Wright to J. Swire & Sons, Shanghai, February 2, 1905, JSSI 2/22.

34. For instance, see Butterfield & Swire to J. Swire & Sons, Shanghai, March 22, 1902, JSSI 2/22.

35. On Nisshin Kisen Kaisha, see *Nisshin kisen kabushiki kaisha 30 nen shi oyobi tsuiho* (A thirty-year history of the Nisshin Steamship Co. Ltd., with additions), Tokyo, 1941.

36. H. W. Robertson to J. Swire & Sons, Shanghai, August 30, 1907; A. Wright to J. Swire & Sons, Shanghai, September 20, 1907; A. Wright to J. H. Scott, Shanghai, November 1, 1907, JSSI 2/22.

37. H. W. Robertson to E. F. Mackay, Hong Kong, July 8, 1910, JSSI 2/23.

38. N. S. Brown to Butterfield & Swire (Shanghai), Hankow, November 19, 1910, JSSI 2/23.

39. E. F. Mackay to J. Swire & Sons, Shanghai, July 12, 1912, JSSI 2/23.

40. Hidemasa Kokaze, "Teikokushugi keisei-ki ni okeru Nihon kaiun-gyō" (Japan's shipping business during the formative period of Japanese imperialism), *Shigaku zasshi*, Vol. 92, No. 10, October 1983, p. 10.

41. For the activities of the refinery in the late 19th century see Marriner and Hyde, *op. cit.*, Chap. 6.

42. "Memorandum of Hongkong Expenditure on Building A/c to 31st December 1884," JSSV 4/1.

43. J. Swire & Sons to Butterfield & Swire (Hong Kong), London, February 11, 1896, JSSI 1/12.

44. *Ibid.*

45. For instance, see J. S. Swire to E. Mackintosh, London, May 1, 1890, and July 17, 1890, JSSI 1/9.

46. J. Swire & Sons to Butterfield & Swire (Hong Kong), London, May 16, 1894, and October 19, 1894, JSSI 1/11.

47. John Swire & Sons, "A Retrospect of T. K. [Taikoo] Finance and Considerations for its F'ure [Future] Working," May 13, 1898, JSSI 1/12.

48. H. Smith to J. H. Scott, Hong Kong, March 9, 1900, JSSI 2/9.

49. D. R. Law to J. H. Scott, Hong Kong, May 31, 1907, JSSI 2/10.

50. *Ibid.* For figures for Japanese refineries see the Report on Sugar, Hong Kong, 1909, JSSI 2/11.

51. D. R. Law to J. H. Scott, Hong Kong, September 3, 1909, JSSI 2/11.

52. H. W. Robertson to J. H. Scott, Hong Kong, October 21, 1910, JSSI 2/11.

53. Butterfield & Swire to J. Swire & Sons, Hong Kong, November 11,

1910, JSSI 2/11.

54. J. H. Scott to H. W. Robertson, London, December 2, 1910, JSSI 1/15; H. W. Robertson to J. H. Scott, Hong Kong, January 6, 1911, JSSI 2/11. The Manchurian system was a selling method which involved the control of business operations in local markets either through local agents or by regular inspection, so that dependence on cliques of Chinese dealers could be avoided.

55. E. F. Mackay to J. Swire & Sons, Shanghai, April 12, 1911, JSSI 2/23.

56. J. Swire & Sons to H. W. Robertson, London, January 6, 1911, JSSI 1/15.

57. J. H. Scott to H. W. Robertson, London, February 2, 1911, JSSI 1/15.

58. Butterfield & Swire to Butterfield & Swire (Shanghai), Hong Kong, July 11, 1911, JSSI 2/11.

59. Butterfield & Swire to J. Swire & Sons, Hong Kong, March 24, 1911, JSSI 2/11.

60. J. H. Scott to H. W. Robertson, London, June 16, 1911, JSSI 1/15.

61. H. W. Robertson to J. H. Scott, Hong Kong, May 12, 1911, JSSI 2/11.

62. Butterfield & Swire to Butterfield & Swire (Shanghai), Hong Kong, July, 11, 1911, JSSI 2/11.

63. J. Swire & Sons to Butterfield & Swire (Hong Kong), London, July 28, 1911, JSSI 1/15.

64. H. W. Robertson to J. H. Scott, Hong Kong July 14, 1911, JSSI 2/11.

65. *Ibid.*

66. J. Swire & Sons to Butterfield & Swire (Hong Kong), London, July 3, 1914, JSSI 1/15.

67. See "Names of Gentlemen attending a Meeting re the Taikoo Dockyard and Engineering Company of Hong Kong Limited held 28th May 1908" and "The Taikoo Dockyard and Engineering Company of Hong Kong Limited", May 28, 1908, JSSVI 5/1.

68. Taikoo Dockyard and Engineering Co., Old London Accounts Ledger, JSSVI 3/1.

69. G. T. Edkins to J. Swire & Sons, Hong Kong, March 6, 1910, JSSI 2/11.

70. J. H. Scott to H. W. Robertson, London, April 21, 1910, JSSI 1/15.

71. J. H. Scott to H. W. Robertson, London, December 22, 1910, and J. Swire & Sons to H. W. Robertson, London, December 30, 1910,

JSSI 1/15.

72. For instance, see J. Swire & Sons to H. W. Robertson, London, May 6, 1910, JSSI 1/15.

73. J. H. Scott to H. W. Robertson, London, February 9, 1911, JSSI 1/15. See also Drage, *op. cit.*, pp. 167–68.

74. J. H. Scott to H. W. Robertson, London, March 31, 1911, JSSI 1/15. See also W. D. Taylor, "Report on the Hong Kong and Whampoa Dock Co.'s Position," September 14, 1911, JSSI 1/15.

75. J. H. Scott to H. W. Robertson, London, March 31, 1911, JSSI 1/15.

76. Memorandum of Agreement, May 2, 1913, JSSVI 5/10.

77. Marriner and Hyde, *op. cit.*, p. 131; Hook, *op. cit.*, p. 142.

78. J. Swire & Sons to R. Thomson, London, February 3, 1911, JSSI 1/15.

79. H. Yoshihara, "Some Questions on Japan's *Sōgō Shosha*".

Comment

Kanji Ishii
University of Tokyo

The emergence of *sōgō shōsha* in world trade history dates only after submarine cables had joined the markets of Europe, America, and Asia in the 1860s, for the telegraph changed the mode of international trade dramatically. The introduction of the telegraph enabled so many small specialized merchants to transact on commission that the big general merchants who had dominated international trade by transacting on their own account were forced by competition with these small merchants to change their mode of transaction. When Mitsui Bussan characterized itself as a commission merchant in Article 8 of the Bylaws of the Company in 1876, it went with the stream of change. But Mitsui Bussan did not develop into a sōgō shōsha simply by trading on commission. By trading frequently on their own account, general trading companies, such as Mitsui Bussan and Mitsubishi Shōji, could overcome other commission merchants and become worldwide trading companies —sōgō shōsha.

In order to perform such business, it is necessary for branch managers of the trading company to have the power to make decisions without consulting with the headquarters each time. It is said that in Japanese companies middle management has played a very important role; similarly, in Japanese trading companies branch managers who were promoted from employee positions played an important role. Of course there were many limits imposed on their activities by the headquarters. But what is important is that their loyalty to the company was very strong and the top executives esteemed their proposals concerning company strategy. It seems to me that such a principle of organization has been so much peculiar to Japanese trading companies until quite recently that sōgō shōsha have been a uniquely Japanese phenomenon.

TABLE 1   Profit and Loss Accounts of Jardine, Matheson & Co., 1855–1885.

(Mexican Dollars)

Year	1855	1861	1865	1870	1875	1880	1885
Commodity account	1,043,513	973,490	385,862	125,103	−27,042	−74,158	81,180
Opium	168,411	54,488	302,186	20,991	2,160	−1,609	—
Piece goods	11,607	231,228	−20,869	−16,431	−57,338	−37,054	−601
Tea	75,360	377,200	91,295	238,148	−43,753	−18,942	25,340
Raw silk	765,429	189,238	224,088	−53,803	39,027	−31,731	8,286
Adventure	17,577	72,256	−99,811	552	−2,945	−4,304	−159
Others	5,129	49,080	−111,027	−64,354	35,807	19,482	48,314
Ships	−80,275	231,357	−194,087	112,229	−6,739	77,416	9,597
Shares	7,212	35,444	42,411	46,577	53,555	175,127	208,291
Properties	−24,426	—	—	—	329	43,403	21,522
Bullion	16,048	24,928	2,450	—	—	—	—
Exchange	159,235	148,853	44,350	57,360	14,860	10,232	−1,100
Underwriting	−157,455	58,134	64,955	31,540	—	—	—
Premiums	15,709	20,827	34,261	14,327	24,910	7,153	27,365
Commissions	314,616	386,394	613,552	382,561	534,057	472,339	438,096
Charges	−70,721	−218,052	−240,529	−154,860	−178,891	−163,662	−165,052
Telegraph	—	—	—	—	−13,817	−18,917	−12,669
Interest	−282,773	−515,934	−610,896	−519,397	−159,749	−113,893	−115,694
Others	−20,680	−65,443	−83,656	−95,438	−39,873	−8,640	180,463
Net profit	920,003	1,080,000	58,673	2	201,600	406,400	671,999

Source: Mayako Ishii, "Activities of the British Enterprise in China in the Latter Half of the Nineteenth Century as Found in the Documents of Jardine, Matheson and Co.," *Shakaikeizaishigaku*, Vol. 45, No. 4, 1979.

1. From this point of view, could John Swire & Sons have possibly become a kind of sōgō shōsha? This is my first question to Professor Sugiyama. I think it was impossible for it to become a sōgō shōsha. Although it tried to change its mode of transaction to that of a commission merchant, it failed in the transformation, and losses in trading on its own account accumulated until it abandoned trading. The strong managerial control of John Samuel Swire in London must have deprived the branch managers from using a free hand in East Asia and prevented them from overcoming other commission merchants.

Jardine, Matheson & Co., the strongest rival of Swires, made the transformation to commission merchant in the 1870s and 1880s (see Table 1). But it could not become a sōgō shōsha later either because it strictly adhered to its chosen mode of transaction and was defeated in the competition with Japanese sōgō shōsha.

2. The second question concerns the reason the affiliated Taikoo companies, such as the China Navigation Co. and the Taikoo Sugar Refinery, were defeated in the competition with Japanese companies. Professor Sugiyama's analysis of these affiliates is very interesting for historians of the modern history of East Asia. But it seems to me that he overestimates the role of the Japanese government in the competition. It is true that Japanese steamship companies were subsidized by the Japanese government, but we should also pay attention to the endeavors of these companies to cut into the Yangtze River trade. For example, Ōsaka Shosen Kaisha made a careful investigation beforehand and constructed not only steamers of a special type fitted for the river but also their own port facilities at each port on the river. In order to raise capital, they issued a large number of debentures in Japan.

It is also doubtful that the Japanese government support of the Japanese sugar-manufacturing companies and the supply of cheap Taiwan raw sugar to them were main factors which "weakened the market position of the Taikoo Sugar Refinery in China." First, the main raw material of Japanese refined sugar exported to China was not Taiwan sugar but Java sugar, and second, the drawback system for imported raw sugar contributed only to equalizing competition between Japanese refined sugar and Hong Kong refined sugar in China. In order to find the reason that Japanese sugar was better in quality and cheaper in price than Hong Kong sugar, we should analyze not only the process of sugar distribution but also the process of sugar production in Japan.

When we consult the letters of British businessmen, we should be careful about the bias they had against Japanese people, for most of the British businessmen at that time were inclined to overestimate the role of the Japanese government and underestimate the strength of Japanese enterprises.

Response

Shinya Sugiyama

1.   I think that John Swire & Sons could possibly have become a *sōgō shōsha* (general trading company). The fact that it did not do so was governed more by external factors concerned with the overall economic and political environment of the Far East than by the internal constraints induced by J. S. Swire's strong managerial control.

In its initial period, Swires dealt in a limited number of items, such as American cotton, Chinese tea, and British-made textiles, and in this sense it could be thought of as equivalent to a *semmon shōsha* (specialized trading company). With its shift to the Far East, however, Swires found itself in an economic environment which encouraged diversification rather than the specialized trading in which it had theretofore been engaged. Swires now became a colonial trading firm, but an atypical one, because its main trading partners, China and Japan, were not colonies. Swires remained an external factor in the industrialization of China and Japan, and made no attempt to play a positive role in the process. Thus, it soon steered clear of exporting, since articles such as raw silk and tea fluctuated greatly in price and seemed speculative, while, on the other hand, imports of textiles did not increase as expected. It seemed more in its interest to enter other areas in which it could operate under more promising conditions. There was therefore no call for it to develop into a trading firm with the wide-ranging functions of a Japanese sōgō shōsha. Later on, the opportunity to expand in this direction was blocked by Japanese competition. After 1919, therefore, Swires used the profits which it had gained during the First World War to invest in bonds and securities rather than to expand its own manufacturing and shipping business.

2. My intention in the paper was to reconstruct a picture of Swires' business activities as seen through the eyes of the firm itself rather than provide an objective analysis. Since the firm itself acknowledged, and tried to learn from, the superior methods of Japanese firms on the China market, I am doubtful of the extent to which it really believed in the role of the Japanese government in aiding Japanese competition, although it provided a useful weapon with which to attack Japan. Analysis of the Japanese sugar industry is, of course, a prerequisite for understanding the competition over sugar in the China market, which is a topic I intend to work on in the future.

Merchants or Manufacturers? British Methods in Foreign Trade, 1870–1939

W. J. Reader
Business History Unit,
London School of Economics

I. Patterns of Trade

With mingled admiration and alarm, during the years between 1870 and 1939 the nations of the West watched Japan becoming a first-class industrial power and a serious competitor in world markets: the first nation outside Europe and the United States to do so. For their success in selling and marketing, as the theme of this conference makes clear, the Japanese relied heavily on a commercial organization which had no exact parallel in the West: the sōgō shōsha, or general trading company. How, over the same period, were the functions of the sōgō shōsha carried out in Western overseas business? This is the question I have been asked to discuss, with reference to certain large British firms which I have had the opportunity of studying.

First, let me show you the present geographical pattern of trade done by two of the largest of these firms: Unilever and Imperial Chemicals Industries (ICI). Each, in its annual report for 1984, shows its worldwide turnover, and the figures look like this:

Unilever Turnover by Value, 1984.

	£m	%
Western Europe, including the U.K.	9,817	61
North & South America	3,548	22
Asia & Australasia	1,791	11
Africa	1,016	6
Total	16,172	100

209

ICI Turnover by Value, 1984.

	£m	%
Western Europe, including the U.K. (27%)	4,237	48
North & South America	2,111	24
Far East & Australasia	1,613	18
India & other markets	859	10
Total*	8,820	100

* Chemicals only. The total for chemicals plus oil was £9,909 million.

These figures emphasize the very great importance of foreign trade to each of these businesses. Much the greater part of their turnover arises outside their home countries. Unilever is an Anglo-Dutch business, and its home countries are the United Kingdom and the Netherlands. ICI's home country is the United Kingdom. In the case of ICI, foreign sales account for nearly 75% of total turnover. The home trade sales for Unilever are not given, but it is evident that they too are very much smaller than sales in world markets.

Next, consider the distribution of sales around the world. In each company sales are heavily concentrated in Europe and in the industrially advanced countries of the world, where economic activity is vigorous and spending power is high. Europe (including the home markets) accounts for 61% of Unilever's turnover and for 48% of ICI's. North America accounts for £3,109 million (19%) of Unilever's turnover and an undisclosed share, undoubtedly large, of ICI's. Notice also the comparatively high figure in each table for Australasia, which includes Australia and New Zealand, and the very low figures for the rest of the world, where in many countries either poverty or ideology—in some places both—blight the possibility of profitable trade. For quite a different reason, sales in Japan do not figure prominently. That is not because Japan is not a market worth entering, but because of the difficulty of entering it.

The overseas trade of these groups is chiefly handled by subsidiaries and associated companies, not by agents. ICI's annual report shows 21 companies in 15 countries throughout the world in which ICI holds 50% or more of the capital and 5 companies in which ICI holds less than 50%. There are 205 companies in 56 countries in which Unilever holds 50% or more of the capital, 10 companies in which it holds less than 50%. In each group, that part of the capital which ICI or Unilever does not own is usually held by investors in the country where the company is in business. The following tables give a breakdown by geographical distribution.

ICI Companies, 1984.	
Principal subsidiaries	
(owned 50% to 100% by ICI)	
Europe	8
North & South America	3
Asia,[1] Australia, & New Zealand	9
Africa	1
Total	21

[1]   Including ICI Japan Ltd. and ICI-Pharma Ltd., also in Japan.

Principal associated companies	
(less than 50% owned by ICI)	
U.K.	2
U.S.A.	1
Australia	1
South Africa	1
Total	5

Unilever Companies, 1984.	
Principal subsidiaries	
(owned 50% to 100% by Unilever)	
EEC	113
Other European countries	26
North America	13
Central & South America	9
Asia,[1] Australia, & New Zealand	17
Africa	28
Total	206

[1]   Including Nippon Lever K.K.

Principal associated companies (less than 50% owned by Unilever)	
EEC	2
Other European countries	1
Central & South America	2
Asia, Australia, & New Zealand	1
Africa	4
Total	10

The pattern of trade shown in the present-day figures of these two groups has long historical roots in the pattern of British export trade as a whole. As long ago as 1870, 14% of the total value of the country's exports were going to the United States and 10% to Germany—much more than to any other country except India, which took almost 10%, mostly, I suppose, in cotton goods.[1] In 1870 Germany and the United States were the two main industrial countries in the world after Great Britain, so about a quarter of British export trade was already set in the pattern so noticeable in the Unilever and ICI figures: that is, toward the areas of greatest economic activity and spending power.

The British Empire in 1870, which included India, took slightly more of the value of British exports—26%—than the United States and Germany, but considerably less than Europe. The countries of Europe, including Germany, took a considerably greater share of the value of British exports than any other part of the world: again, part of the pattern of trade which is conspicuous today in the business of Unilever and of ICI. Summarized, the national figures are as follows:[2]

Principal British Export Markets by Value, 1870.

	£m	%
British Empire	52	26
U.S.A.	28	14
Europe	75	37
South America	16	8
Other regions	29	15
Total	200	100

During the 1870s two groups of companies were developing which in 1926 were to have an important bearing on the foundation of

ICI. They were the Nobel group in the explosives industry and the Solvay group in heavy chemicals, especially soda ash. Bearing in mind all the figures I have commented upon—both the figures for ICI and Unilever and the figures for British exports in 1870—let us look at the early history of Nobel's Explosives Co. and Brunner, Mond & Co. Ltd.

II. Two Early Multinationals: The Nobel and Solvay Groups, 1870–1914

The 1860s and 1870s saw the beginnings of German synthetic dyestuffs; the invention by Alfred Nobel (1833–96) of dynamite and the means of detonating it safely; and the development by the Solvay brothers of their process for making soda ash.[3] These products were all aimed at world markets. The firms which produced them were organized with world markets in mind and are therefore particularly suitable for comparison with the sōgō shōsha. We shall only glance sidelong at the German dyestuffs makers, who fall outside the scope of this paper. Nobel and the Solvays fall directly within it. Let us start with Nobel and dynamite.

The Nobel Group: Until Nobel discovered how to package nitro-glycerin in *kieselguhr*, and then how to detonate it without much likelihood of blowing himself up, the only explosive which was reasonably safe to use was black powder. Dynamite and its later developments, blasting gelatin and gelignite—both also originated by Nobel—were far more efficient. Civil engineers and mining engineers rapidly found that out, and between them Nobel's inventions brought about a revolution in the high-explosives industry.

Nobel was a Swede. Mid-19th century Sweden, although it had mines, was too small a market for his very large ambitions. Nobel therefore set up dynamite factories in countries which gave access to promising markets either on their own doorstep or by way of export trade. He had little capital of his own and he had always to persuade local investors to back him. He took shares in the companies thus set up, sat on their boards and advised them, but did not control them. The result was a group—eventually two groups—of Nobel companies in various countries which had no links with each other except through the person of Nobel. To start with, much to Nobel's displeasure, they competed furiously.

First of all, in the late 1860s, Nobel established himself in Germany, where there was a large market for mining explosives. Then he went to Great Britain, and having failed to interest the moneyed men of the City of London, he went to Glasgow in Scotland, where they knew about mining and civil engineering. He explained his marketing objectives:

> Great Britain is in my opinion by far the most important of all for this branch of the business, not only on account of the vast internal trade but also the great facility for export to the colonies. . . . Think of all the Indian railways, Australian mining and so forth.[4]

Nobel's imperial vision was shared in his time and later by a great many businesspersons in Great Britain and elsewhere. The British Empire was for many years one of the central facts of British overseas trade. We must pause to explore it.

The empire at its greatest extent is said to have included about a quarter of the land surface of the globe and one third of its population. How this is calculated I don't quite know and it doesn't matter very much. It simply means that the empire was very large indeed and very complex. It consisted of three main groups of territories:
a.   the colonies, later the Dominions, with a settled white population,
b.   India, with a government maintained by British power but increasingly conscious of Indian interests, and
c.   numerous widely scattered territories, some very large, others very small, some comparatively advanced, many very primitive, under the direct rule of the Colonial Office.
Of these three groups the third, the "dependent empire," was of little interest to British manufacturers. India, on the other hand, was a long-established market for cotton goods, the most important of Victorian England's exports.

In India and the dependent empire before 1914 the doctrine of free trade prevailed, it being the creed of the imperial authorities in London. Exporters from Great Britain and other countries therefore competed on even terms.[5] One result was that German makers of dyestuffs came to dominate the lucrative trade with Indian cotton manufacturers. Another was that India long remained a profitable field for merchant firms and managing agencies—indeed, for the type of firm, discussed at this conference by Professor Jones, which is most closely comparable with sōgō shōsha. With no protective tariff there was no compelling reason for manufacturers to put up works in India. The Lancashire cotton manufacturers never did.

Nobel was principally interested in the mining enterprises of Australia, Canada, and South Africa. He was interested, that is to say, in the colonies, and, generally speaking, it was the colonies which, of all the imperial territories, chiefly attracted British manufacturers. The colonists, for the most part, were only one or two generations out from the old country, they spoke the English language, they were subject to English law, and in most other ways they were English people living abroad, thinking and behaving like the English, not foreigners. For all these reasons British industrialists looked upon the colonies as their natural market, and a very promising one, too, because although the colonists were not numerous, their rising standard of living fostered a lively demand for manufactured goods.

They were a natural market, perhaps, but by no means a captive one. The colonists, by 1870, had long been effectively self-governing, and in the conduct of their own affairs they never let free-trade principles stand in their way. On the contrary, they set out to found and protect their own industries. Exporters, therefore, increasingly found themselves faced with colonial tariff barriers. There was some sentimental preference for British goods—the natural market—and there might be a reduction for them in the rates of import duty, but in general, exporting firms, both British and foreign, found that if their products did well in a colony, local competitors would come into the market and would be protected, so that there would be strong pressure to set up a local factory rather than persist with an export trade.

Nobel's Explosives Co.—the business set up by Nobel in Scotland—ran into tariff barriers in the Australian colonies in the early 1870s. The conventional response would have been to set up an Australian factory. Nobel's German competitors, Krebs & Co., similarly hindered, set up a company later known as the Australian Explosives & Chemical Co. Ltd., but Nobel's Explosives Co. did nothing of the sort. Nobel as an individual, with his partner Paul Emile Barbe, set up six factories in Europe between 1871 and 1873, but Nobel's Explosives Co., founded specifically to sell dynamite within the British Empire, continued for more than 20 years to rely entirely on the export trade in Australia and elsewhere. When eventually they went in for manufacturing overseas—in the Transvaal in 1895—their motive was not to avoid tariffs but to end tiresome competition from another Nobel company, which joined them in the ownership of the new venture.

Nobel seems to have been far more concerned with competition, first among the companies in which he had an interest, and then between them and other explosives makers, than with tariff barriers. Between 1886 and 1897 Nobel and his successors made arrangements with all the main explosives companies of the world, both in Europe and the United States, for defining markets and, in the case of the British and German explosives companies, for sharing profits. Nobel distanced himself after 1886 from the companies which he had founded, and he died in 1896, but the policy of regulating the world's explosives industry by agreements, meticulously drafted and for the most part scrupulously observed, was carried on by his successors. Their arrangements covered both high explosives for peaceful uses and the new smokeless powders for military ammunition, much in demand as the nations of Europe built up and modernized their armed forces, particularly their navies, during the last 25 years or so before 1914.

In drawing up these agreements Nobel and his English partners were strongly influenced by German law and practice, which was sympathetic to the idea of profit-pooling cartels and to the regulation of competition generally. In Great Britain, by contrast, such agreements as the explosives companies made would have been held to be "in restraint of trade," and although they would not have been illegal, the courts would not have enforced them. In the United States "combinations . . . in restraint of trade" became illegal after the passing of the Sherman Act in 1890, though the terms of the act allowed legal argument about its precise interpretation which has kept American lawyers busy ever since. The consequence of the differences between German, English, and American law was that outside Germany the agreements could not, for the most part, be enforced at law and depended for their effect entirely on the good faith of the parties.

The centerpiece of these arrangements, on the Nobel side, was the Nobel-Dynamite Trust, an English company set up in 1886 to hold the shares of Nobel's Explosives Co. of Glasgow, of Dynamite Aktien Gesellschaft (DAG—the German Nobel company) of Hamburg, and of other explosives companies in Germany and Great Britain. It was an extremely advanced form of commercial organization for its day, based on American models[6] which were unfamiliar in England and widely disliked for their association with ruthless monopoly practices. The trust was linked by agreement not only with explosives companies in Germany and elsewhere but also, since ammunition and guns were sold as a package, with the British armaments firms and, after 1905, with the Japanese Explosives Co., which, in partnership with Armstrong Whitworth, the trust set up and controlled.

Between 1886 and 1914 three main groups of companies came to divide the world's explosives industries between them. In Europe there was the Nobel-Dynamite Trust, allied with German companies, mainly in military explosives, with whom markets were shared and profits pooled. There was also a separate group of Nobel companies—the "Latin group"—smaller but strong in nuisance value and not overnice in keeping to its agreements. Across the Atlantic there was E. I. du Pont de Nemours & Co., Inc.

The division of markets between these three groups reserved Europe for the Europeans and the United States for the Americans. Nobel's Explosives Co.'s main interests lay in Canada, Australia, and South Africa. In Canada it developed very close relations with du Pont, based on a joint company set up in 1911. Nobel's Explosives Co. held 55% of the capital in Canadian Explosives Ltd., a recognition that Canada, as part of the British Empire, lay within Nobel's Explosives Co.'s natural market, and du Pont held the rest. There were two other important firms in the Canadian explosives market, one American, one British, but they maintained prices at the same level as Canadian Explosives, and demand was growing fast enough to provide trade for all without the crudities of unrestrained competition. In South Africa, the most lucrative of all markets for mining explosives, competition could not so readily be neutralized, largely because after the Boer War (1899–1902), neither the authorities nor the mine owners, meaning principally De Beers, would allow anything like a monopoly to emerge. The trust and the Latin group, which jointly owned works originally set up in 1895, were faced by the Cape Explosives Works set up by De Beers in 1903 to prevent the trust from dominating the explosives trade, and by another English company, Kynoch Ltd., which set up a South African factory in 1909. In Australia the trust bought the Australian Explosives & Chemical Co. Ltd. from Krebs in 1897. Nobel's Explosives Co., which had no share in the Australian company, went on exporting in competition with it. Presumably they could manufacture cheaply enough at their large works in Scotland to offset not only transport costs but Australian tariffs as well.

The largest firm in the British explosives industry before the Great War—Nobel's Explosives Co.—thus appears as the largest member of a multinational group—the Nobel-Dynamite Trust and its allies—which relied heavily, for its prosperity, on trade in world markets. For Nobel's Explosives Co., that meant in particular trade in Australia, Canada, and South Africa, which were all within the British Empire, Nobel's Explosives Co.'s natural market. Its position in these countries was regulated and reinforced by elaborate agreements for profit pooling and market sharing, and although direct competition could not be entirely eliminated, it was suppressed as far as possible. In effect a system of private protection emerged alongside the protective tariffs imposed by governments. In each of the most important markets for explosives private arrangements between manufacturers did more than government policy to determine whether Nobel's Explosives Co. should carry on business by export or by local manufacture, or in some cases, notably the United States and continental Europe, whether it should trade there at all.

The Solvay Group: I want now to glance at another system of regulated competition: the Solvay group.

About 1870 two Belgian brothers, Ernest and Alfred Solvay, were bringing to the point of commercial production a new process for making soda ash (sodium carbonate), a form of alkali used in a wide range of industrial processes. The rate at which soda ash is used, indeed, is a good index of the industrialization of a nation's economy, and in the 1870s there were not many countries where it was extensively used.

In developing their business the Solvays, like Nobel, sought access to promising markets by setting up manufacturing companies in countries outside their own, which was Belgium. The Solvays invested in the companies which they set up, but, again like Nobel, they did not control them, though they could exert powerful influence. The management and much of the finance was found locally, but the whole group worked on a uniform system of cost control, which was advanced and sophisticated, and had access to technical knowledge which was protected by secrecy in preference to patent law.

The three most important countries for the Solvay group were the three most advanced industrial countries of the day: Great Britain, Germany, and the United States. Solvay's British company was Brunner, Mond & Co. at Winnington in Northwest England, where the essential materials for alkali manufacture—salt, limestone, coal—were easily available and transport facilities were good. As a consequence, soda ash could be made cheaply enough to compete in any market in the world, provided tariff barriers were not too high.

By agreements made in 1885 and 1887 the Solvay companies, like the Nobel companies, divided the trading areas of the world among themselves, and by the second of these agreements the whole of the world outside Europe and the Russian Empire was granted to Brunner, Mond. This division was not quite so generous as perhaps it sounds. In 1887 by far the largest market for alkali—probably already the largest in the world outside the United Kingdom and Europe—was in the United States, and there, by the mid-eighties, Brunner, Mond, through their export trade, was selling more soda ash than any other maker, domestic or foreign. This was not likely to last. In the first place, tariff protection in the United States, already high, was expected to rise. In the second place, the Solvay Process Co. had been established there and was competing strongly against Brunner, Mond.

Why did the Solvay group thus deliberately set up one of their own companies to compete against another?

The answer appears to be that Ernest Solvay, John Brunner, and Ludwig Mond foresaw that American protective duties would eventually kill the export trade in alkali from England, as indeed they did in the Dingley Tariff of 1897. By that time, however, the Solvay Process Co. was well established and by 1905 had the largest soda factory in the world. In the Solvay Process Co., Brunner, Mond had a financial interest. It was thereby reconciled to withdrawing, by agreement, from the American alkali trade, and between 1889 and 1905 it did so, leaving the Solvay Process Co. master of the field. Whereas Brunner, Mond had once sold more alkali in the United States than at home, after 1905 it sold none there at all.

Withdrawal from the United States left a gap in Brunner, Mond's export trade which was difficult to fill. The markets of continental Europe were closed by the regulations of the Solvay group, and in the rest of the world there was no large industrialized economy, though exports to Australia rose from 8,000 tons in 1901 to 20,000 tons in 1914 and Brunner, Mond's man in China, in 1899, wrote: "There *is* a market in . . . Japan which might perhaps keep a little works going during the gradual development of the Chinese market."[7]

The mention of Australia, China, and Japan raises matters which I shall return to in discussing ICI in the years between the wars. Meanwhile I would like to point out that the whole shape and direction of Brunner, Mond's overseas trade, on which to a large extent the company relied for growth and prosperity, was regulated by agreements with other members of the Solvay group, just as the overseas trade of Nobel's Explosives Co. was regulated by agreements with other explosives companies. This does not mean that either company was the helpless tool of foreign masters. On the contrary, those who managed Brunner, Mond and those who managed Nobel's Explosives Co. took a very active part in formulating the policy of the groups to which they belonged. It does demonstrate, however, that each of these companies, powerful as it was and independent as it appeared to be, belonged nevertheless to a multi-national group in which the members' interests were subordinate to the interest of the group as a whole. It was that, as much as market forces or government policy, which determined how their overseas activities were organized and conducted.

III.   The World of Sunlight: Lever Brothers 1885–1930

Between the businesses which I have just discussed and the business which I now propose to discuss there is a world of difference. The Nobel-Dynamite Trust and the Solvay group were suppliers of industrial materials—on the one hand explosives, on the other, alkali—and they never came near the ordinary housewife. Lever Brothers Ltd. was a soap maker, and its prosperity was founded on the rising standard of living of working-class households in late Victorian England.[8]

The marketing policy of the trust and the Solvay companies depended on careful regulations for sharing markets and restraining competition. Levers' method of dealing with their competitors was either to fight them with the weapons of mass marketing—national advertising, coupon schemes, price manipulation—or to take them over, so that by 1914 Lever Brothers Ltd. controlled in Great Britain a group of subsidiaries which included nearly all the firms of any importance which had formerly been competitors. Many were much older than Lever Brothers, which was founded in 1885 and became a public company 10 years later. In this organization there was nothing like the sophistication of the Nobel-Dynamite Trust or the Solvay group. Sir William Lever owned nearly all the ordinary capital of Lever Brothers, and the associated companies were his private collection, rather like the pictures and furniture which he was acquiring at the same time. It was not a tidy system—it was hardly a system at all—and in the end it did not make for the highest efficiency; but by 1914 Lever Brothers probably controlled about 37% of the total quantity of soap produced for the home market in Great Britain, and in later years its share of national soap production rose as high as 60%.[9]

Lever was never content with the home market alone. Quite early in his career as a soap maker—during the 1890s—he was visiting export markets as far afield as New Zealand, and he had a short way with agents if he did not consider they were putting enough effort into sales of Lever products. Agencies, and in important markets local branches of his own company, were his channels for export sales, but already by 1900 Lever Brothers had bought or built soap factories in Australia, Canada, the United States, Germany, and Switzerland, and that was only the beginning. Lever turned very early toward those countries which in his day had the highest standard of living: Western Europe, the United States, and the British colonies.

Lever was quite clear about his main motive for replacing export sales with local manufactures. In 1902 he said:

> "The question of erecting works in another country is dependent upon the tariff or duty. . . . When the duty exceeds the cost of separate managers and separate plant, then it will be an economy to erect works in the country so that our customers can be more cheaply supplied from them."[10]

He might have added that jumping over the tariff wall in this manner made it much easier for him to deal with local competitors whom the tariff was intended to protect. He might either put up his own works or buy works already established, or do both. Before 1914, in Canada, South Africa, and Australia, Lever had built up groups of companies which, on a smaller scale, reproduced the Lever group in Great Britain. He saw the possibilities inherent in Japanese economic growth, and in 1913 he opened a factory at Tori-Shindon near Kobe. It was not very successful, and after Lord Leverhulme (William Lever) died, his successors sold the business.

In some countries factories could use local raw materials to make products more suited to local demand than those exported by Lever companies from Great Britain. "More suited" usually meant "inferior," and in the years between the world wars the term applied to the output of factories set up in India, Nigeria, and the Belgian Congo (Zaire). The results, perhaps deservedly, were not uniformly excellent.[11]

Alongside the widespread foundation of overseas manufacturing companies Lever Brothers' export trade remained very important. The main problem, and here there is a parallel with the activities of Nobel's Explosives Co. and the Solvay companies, was to regulate competition between companies of the Lever group. Two in particular, Joseph Crosfield & Sons and William Gossage & Sons, had been large enterprises long before Lever Brothers came into existence. Before they passed under Lever Brothers' control in 1919, efforts were made to moderate the bitter rivalry between the three firms, and in 1928 a new body, United Exporters Ltd. (later Unilever Export Ltd.) was set up to run the export business of Lever Brothers as a whole.

Propelled by the wide-ranging force of William Lever's personality, the business which he founded to make and market soap spread into West African trading, coconut plantations in the Solomon Islands, and oil palm plantations in the Congo; it spread into shipping, oil milling, cattle foods, margarine, retail fishmongering, sausages and pies, ice cream, and a great deal else besides. By the time Lord Leverhulme died in 1925, Lever Brothers Ltd. was the central company in a sprawling multinational enterprise of highly idiosyncratic diversity which I shall not attempt to explore.

IV. Unilever, 1930–1939

In 1930, largely to avoid competition for world supplies of edible oils and fats, Lever Brothers joined the Margarine Union in a merger which produced Unilever, which still exists, much altered and enlarged, at the present day. The Margarine Union was itself a multinational group formed in 1927 by merging two Dutch margarine firms founded in the 1870s: Van den Berghs and Jurgens. Margarine was a cheaper substitute for butter and there was a demand for it, as there was for Lever Brothers' Sunlight Soap, from working-class households where the standard of living was rising.

The margarine business, like Nobel's business in explosives and the Solvays' business in alkali, had begun in a country too small for its founders' ambitions: the Netherlands. Like Nobel and the Solvays, Van den Berghs and Jurgens set out to make their fortunes in Great Britain and in Germany, but not for the same reason.

Nobel went to Germany and Great Britain because they gave access to industrial markets, chiefly in mining and civil engineering. The Dutch margarine makers went in search of working-class housewives. Because there was no protective tariff, they could export to Great Britain from the Netherlands, and neither firm had a British factory before wartime difficulties forced each to acquire one, Van den Berghs by purchase, Jurgens by building, in 1917. In Germany the case was otherwise, and protective duties forced both the Dutch firms to build factories in 1888.[12]

Round the Dutch core of their businesses Van den Berghs and Jurgens each assembled an impressive array of subsidiaries engaged in margarine manufacture, oilseed crushing, cattle feed, meat products, and other activities. The Margarine Union's collection was not quite so spectacular as Lever Brothers', and it was more heavily concentrated in Europe, but at the time of the merger with Lever Brothers the Margarine Union was the stronger party of the two.[13]

Unilever had only been in existence for about nine years when the Second World War broke out: barely long enough to set its affairs in order. Its major growth and development has come in the last 40 years or so, well outside the period I am dealing with. Nevertheless we can see the pattern of its present activities taking shape. It is heavily committed to products for the household, particularly food, detergents, and toiletries. One arm of its foreign trade, mainly inherited from the Margarine Union, is in Europe, and the other, largely a legacy from Lever Brothers, is in the wider world, especially in territories that used to belong to the British Empire.

The foreign trade of the groups I have discussed so far—the Nobel-Dynamite Trust and the Solvay companies on the one hand, Lever Brothers and Unilever on the other—developed in very different ways. The explosives makers and the alkali makers always operated within a tight framework of regulated competition, market sharing, profit pooling. Lever had no use for such arrangements, and although from 1908 onward there was a rather ill-tempered partnership between the Dutch margarine makers, there was never anything like the intricate, elegant diplomacy of the explosives industry or the smooth-running cooperative machinery of the Solvay group.

Why this difference? The only explanation I can suggest, and I have no solid evidence for it, is that the explosives makers and the alkali makers, serving other industries, could do little or nothing directly to increase the demand for their products. It depended on how many railways were being constructed, how many mines were being opened, how many battleships were being built, and more generally on the progress of industrialization throughout the world. Their best hope of prosperity was to share such demand as existed between themselves, which was what they proceeded to do. The Lever companies and the margarine makers, however, could reach the final users of their products directly by advertising and other devices and thereby increase the demand for the goods they sold. It was not in their interest to regulate their output and limit their freedom of action by entering into restrictive agreements with their competitors. They preferred, instead, to sell their products as hard as they could and deal with competition by taking over the weak or merging with the strong.

V. "Imperial in Aspect and Imperial in Name": ICI, 1926–1939

The empire was even more important to British industrialists after the Great War than before. It offered a haven of political stability and relatively low protective duties in a world troubled by economic nationalism and by wars and rumors of wars. Never had the natural market seemed more natural. It also offered attractive markets both for manufacturers' supplies and equipment and for consumer goods in the increasingly industrialized economies of the Dominions, especially Australia.

In these circumstances there were sound business arguments for expanding in the empire rather than in foreign countries, though as Ian Drummond points out, foreign countries still took a greater proportion of British exports, which casts some doubt on the opinion frequently and confidently expressed that British firms went to the empire simply to avoid competition elsewhere. The cutting edge of competition might be blunted by imperial preference, but it could never be entirely avoided except by cartel agreements, which, insofar as they affected ICI, I shall discuss later. In the absence of cartels, competition came both from heavily protected local firms and from foreigners, among whom the Japanese were prominent, especially in the cotton trade, as the Germans were in the chemical industry and the Americans in motor cars.

The empire was close to the heart of British patriotism, reinforcing business considerations and uniting the majority of members of all the principal parties, and it provided a secure foundation for British self-respect. With all that red on the map, how could Great Britain be anything but a Great Power? The imposing edifice, during the twenties and thirties, was supported by a confidence trick, but that was not revealed either to friends or enemies until the events of 1941–42.

For all these reasons, practical and sentimental, British business men concentrated heavily on empire markets between the wars, with varying results.[14] Many hoped that the empire might become a self-sufficient economic system run by its member states for the benefit of all. They seemed to be moving with the current of the times, for throughout the period from 1870 to 1939 the empire was growing steadily more important as a market for British goods. In 1870, 26% of the value of British exports went to British possessions; in 1900, 32%; in 1938, 47%.[15]

In 1926 the four largest firms in the British chemical industry came together in a merger: up to that time, the largest merger ever arranged in British business. The four firms were Nobel Industries Ltd., Brunner, Mond & Co. Ltd., British Dyestuffs Corp. Ltd. and United Alkali Co. Ltd. Nobel Industries included Nobel's Explosives Co. and was the successor to the Nobel-Dynamite Trust, broken up in 1915 because of its German connections. British Dyestuffs Corp., with government backing, was trying to establish a British dyestuffs industry independent of the Germans, and United Alkali Co. represented the competitors of Brunner, Mond.

The immediate reason for the merger was defensive. It was the British response to an even larger merger, in 1925, of the leading German chemical firms. They came together in the Interessen Gemeinschaft Farbenindustrie Aktien Gesellschaft, which might be roughly translated as Dyestuffs Union, and they thoroughly frightened their British and American competitors. The new German group was the most powerful combination of its kind in the world. There was no branch of the chemical industry which it could not invade if its management chose to do so; in most of those in which it was established it was dominant; its activities were worldwide.

There was another motive for the British merger:

> [The] Company has, of deliberate purpose, been given the title of "IMPERIAL CHEMICAL INDUSTRIES LIMITED." The British Empire is the greatest single economic unit in the world, one in which every patriotic member of the British Commonwealth has a personal interest . . . and it will be the avowed intention of the new Company, without limiting its activities in foreign overseas markets, specially to extend the development and importance of the Chemical Industry throughout the Empire.[16]

Or, as Sir Harry McGowan and Sir Alfred Mond, the joint managing directors, more briefly, more grandly, and more memorably put it:

> We are "Imperial "in aspect" and "Imperial" in name.[17]

In these statements we see some of the motives for concentrating on imperial trade which I mentioned earlier. The theme of the natural market emerges; so does the mistaken assumption that the empire was a "single economic unit," and the whole package is tied up with red-white-and-blue patriotic ribbon.

In private, McGowan developed his thoughts:

> . . . the formation of ICI is only the first step in a comprehensive scheme to rationalize the chemical manufacture of the world. The . . . broad picture included working arrangements between three groups—the IG in Germany, Imperial Chemical Industries in the British Empire and Du Ponts and the Allied Chemical and Dye in America.[18]

For this ambitious plan of action ICI was well equipped, since all the founder firms, more especially Nobel's Explosives Co. and Brunner, Mond, could make contributions. Brunner, Mond, still closely connected with the Solvay group, had no factories overseas, but it was the largest exporter of alkali in the world. It had also developed a process for synthesizing nitrogen on which ICI hoped to found a very large business indeed: the export of nitrogenous fertilizers to farmers throughout the British Empire. Nobel's Explosives Co. brought with it, besides a large export trade, the joint ownership of factories in Canada, South Africa, Australia, and Chile, and a close relationship with du Pont, running back to the days of the Nobel-Dynamite Trust.

This relationship, by the time ICI was founded, was governed by the Patents and Processes Agreement, first drawn up in 1920, which reached its final form in 1929. Over a large range of products du Pont and ICI pooled their technical knowledge and cross-licensed patents, so that each was granted the exclusive right to work each other's patents in certain carefully defined areas. Broadly speaking, du Pont had the exclusive right to work ICI's patents in Central and North America, except Canada and Newfoundland, while ICI's exclusive territory was the British Empire, except Canada and Newfoundland. To Canada and Newfoundland each party considered it could make out a claim, and patent rights there were granted to the jointly owned Canadian Industries Ltd. (originally Canadian Explosives Ltd.), in which, since it was within the empire, ICI had inherited a majority holding in the capital. In the world outside the exclusive territories ICI and du Pont were free to make other arrangements, and in Argentina and Brazil, in the mid-thirties, they founded joint companies modeled on Chemical Industries Ltd.

The Patents and Processes Agreement had the effect of eliminating competition between ICI and du Pont in the territories which it covered. For this reason it was held to be illegal in 1952 under American antitrust law, but between 1926 and 1939 it ensured that neither ICI nor du Pont invaded markets reserved to the other. That the elimination of competition, rather than the exchange of technical information, was the main object of the agreement has always been strenuously denied by du Pont, but the outside observer is entitled to an independent opinion.

The effect of the Patents and Processes Agreement, keeping ICI and du Pont out of each other's way, was reinforced as time went on by a network of cartels by which markets were defined, quotas of output were allotted, and penalties were prescribed for breach of the regulations. These agreements covered every activity of any importance in the world's chemical industry—nitrogen, dyestuffs, alkali, motor fuel produced from coal, and many more—and all producers of any importance, including in some cases the Russians but excluding the Japanese, entered into them. We have seen the 19th century roots of the system in discussing the Nobel-Dynamite Trust and the Solvay group. In the 1930s it was at its height because it seemed to be the most practical way of coping with failure of demand during the Depression. Perhaps it was. Without the cartels it is fairly certain that large areas of the British chemical industry would have been devastated.

So far as ICI was concerned, the main principle underlying these cartel agreements was that ICI should be left undisturbed in its natural market in the British Empire. This was a view which foreigners were ready to accept, provided that ICI was seen to be strong enough to defend its market if need be. ICI in return, and with a similar proviso, would agree not to disturb foreigners, meaning especially du Pont and the IG, in their natural markets in North and Central America (du Pont) and in Europe (IG). The consequence was that ICI made no attempt to enter the United States and continental Europe, so important to them at the present day, until after 1945, when the current of contemporary opinion under American pressure swept cartels away.

In developing its export trade ICI inherited Brunner, Mond's methods. In any market where the prospects looked too attractive to leave alkali sales to an agent, Brunner, Mond would set up, first, a branch office and later a selling company. A selling company, from Brunner, Mond's point of view, had two main advantages over a branch office. First, those who ran it derived greater local prestige from being directors of a company than from being managers of a branch office. Second, and more important, if the authorities in England could be persuaded to believe that local boards ran their companies in their own way, accepting advice rather than taking orders from Brunner, Mond's head office, then there were tax advantages.

By the time ICI was set up, Brunner, Mond had foreign merchant companies in China, Japan, India, and Australia. The markets which they served differed sharply. In China the trade had been started before the Great War chiefly to supply alkali for household use in the enormous peasant population of that country, and it had never quite come up to expectations, which were extravagantly high. In India, as well as a large peasant demand, there was some industrial demand near Bombay and a demand from washer men and women around Calcutta and Madras. In Australia and Japan alkali was imported to meet the growing needs of industry. Japanese consumption of alkali in the early twenties was rising very fast indeed, especially for making glass, and Brunner, Mond was sending more alkali to Japan than to any other country. Protection, for many years, was not a serious obstacle in either Australia or Japan, because the authorities in both could fairly easily be persuaded that imports of alkali at a reasonable price were needed to build up their own industries.

These companies, set up to avoid the necessity of employing agents, were all encouraged to build up agency business themselves. In 1919 they became agents for the United Alkali Co. (at that time a competitor) in China and Japan and for the British Dyestuffs Corp. in China. By the time ICI was founded, Brunner, Mond's companies in China, Japan, and India were handling business for companies in glues and chemicals, in fertilizers, in steam plows and locomotives, and in various products for the consumer market.

ICI took over the existing foreign merchant companies and formed more, until by the 1930s there were about a dozen, some very small, that were active in Asia, the Middle East, and South America. They suffered from two main difficulties. First, although for tax purposes local directors were required to act independently, in practice they were reluctant to do so, which is hardly surprising, for genuinely independent action might bring them into conflict with those awesome figures of authority, the directors of ICI, upon whom their careers depended. Second, success in any export market was likely to lead to the extinction of the merchant company that achieved it and the establishment of a local manufacturing company, so the foreign merchant companies, as a group, usually consisted of those which were struggling to stay alive. Moreover, more than half of ICI's export trade in the thirties did not go through foreign merchant companies at all. A great deal of it went through the jointly owned companies in the British Dominions and in South

America. For all these reasons, the foreign merchant companies' results in the thirties, however they were measured (several ways were tried), were miserable.

It was the jointly owned manufacturing companies, in Canada, South Africa, and Australia within the British Empire and in Argentina and Brazil outside it, which led ICI's main thrust into overseas trade and which justified the group's claim to call itself Imperial. In each country where it set up factories, ICI's policy was fundamentally the same. As much as possible of the chemical industry and its future development was to be kept in the hands of ICI and its local associates. In Canada and South America ICI was in partnership with du Pont. In South Africa, in 1924, McGowan persuaded De Beers to take a half-share with Nobel's Explosives Co. in African Explosives and Industries (after 1944, African Explosives and Chemical Industries). In Australia and New Zealand various local interests joined ICI in Imperial Chemical Industries of Australia and New Zealand Ltd. (ICIANZ).

The basis of the bargains that were made in countries where joint companies were set up was that ICI made each company the main vehicle in its own country for developing ICI's manufacturing interests, with access to capital, management, and technical help, including patent licenses, and in return the local company agreed not to compete with ICI either in its home market or in the export trade. ICI's cartel agreements shielded the local company from competition from du Pont (where du Pont was not a partner) and IG, but they could not guarantee that competitors not bound by the cartels—in Australia, Japanese firms—would not come in. Only protective tariffs, in the absence of cartels, could keep other exporters out, and then, like ICI, they might build factories. To defend their own position within a tariff wall, ICI was sometimes prepared to put up an uneconomic plant—an alkali plant in Australia, for instance—in case someone else persuaded the authorities to make it worth while to do so.

The policy of the founders of ICI, in concentrating the development of overseas trade within the British Empire, seemed to be vindicated in 1937 by figures showing that the return on capital employed in empire trade, in 1936–37, was 10.3% against a return of 3.1% on capital employed in foreign trade; in the previous year the difference had been 9.7% against 1.3%.[19] In Canada, in 1936–37, CIL earned 13.5% on capital employed, and in South Africa, African Explosives and Industries earned 34.2%. In these years, about one third, by value, of ICI's total sales were made overseas. One of the directors, with some support from another, went so far as to suggest that ICI should withdraw from overseas trade outside the empire and reinvest repatriated capital at home.

In fact, ICI's results from overseas trade were not quite a matter of the British Empire versus The Rest. The joint ventures with du Pont in Argentina and Brazil were also relatively prosperous, showing a return of 6.3% on capital employed in 1936–37, when they were still in a very early stage of development, and a joint venture with Remington Small Arms (controlled by du Pont) in Brazil showed a return of 9.7%. What did not prosper was the export trade, especially in the Middle East, India, and the Far East, although India was a very large part of the empire and there were other territories in the Far East. The foreign merchant companies' return in 1936–37, based on a rather optimistic calculation of capital employed, was 4.4% in the empire, 3.8% outside, and for the export trade of home groups, 7.4% on capital employed in empire trade, 2.4% on capital employed in foreign trade.

The meaning of these figures seems to be that wherever ICI could operate along lines first laid down in the 19th century, overseas business between 1926 and 1939, apart from the worst years of the Depression, was fairly prosperous. Business was prosperous, that is to say, where it could be regulated by cartels which, broadly speaking, reserved the British Empire for ICI, North America for the Americans, and Europe for the Germans, with fairly amicable cooperation in certain other markets, especially South America. Outside the protection of the cartels, especially in India and the Far East, where Japanese competition was uninhibited, life was far less comfortable.

ICI's overseas trade in 1939, then, relied heavily on cartels and, through them, on certain parts of the British Empire. The cartel system would not last, nor would the empire. That line of thought, however, leads us beyond the limits set for this paper.

Notes*

1. Yonekawa Shin'ichi, *General Trading Companies: A Comparative and Historical Study*, United Nations University, 1983.
2. *Statesman's Year Book*, 1972, pp. 257–58.
3. See L. F. Haber, *The Chemical Industry during the Nineteenth Century*, 1958; J. J. Beer, *The Emergence of the German Dye Industry*, 1959.
4. Reader, *ICI*, Vol. 1, p. 23.
5. Ian M. Drummond, *British Economic Policy and the Empire, 1919–1939*, 1972, p. 123.
6. A. D. Chandler, Jr., *The Visible Hand: The Managerial Revolution in American Business*, 1977, pp. 319–20.
7. Reader, *ICI*, Vol. 1, p. 225.
8. For Lever Brothers, in addition to Wilson's *History of Unilever*, see D. K. Fieldhouse, *Unilever Overseas*, 1978.
9. Wilson, *History of Unilever*, Vol. 1, pp. 124, 127.
10. *Ibid.*, p. 99.
11. Fieldhouse, *Unilever Overseas*, pp. 148–74, 340–57, 379–87.
12. Wilson, *History of Unilever*, Vol. 2, pp. 45, 71, 174.
13. W. J. Reader, *Fifty Years of Unilever*, 1980, p. 5.
14. G. G. Jones, "Multinational Chocolate: Cadbury Overseas, 1918–1939," *Business History*, Vol. 26, No. 1, pp. 57–75.
15. *Statesman's Year Book*, 1872, pp. 257–58; 1902, pp. 85–86; 1941, pp. 59–62; Drummond, *British Economic Policy*, p. 18 (the comparable figure in the *Statesman's Year Book* is nearly 50%).
16. Letter to shareholders of Brunner, Mond, Nobel Industries, United Alkali Co., British Dyestuffs Corp., December 15, 1926, quoted in Reader, *ICI*, Vol. 1, p. 464.
17. Sir Alfred Mond and Sir Harry McGowan to the President of the Board of Trade, November 5, 1926, quoted in Reader, *ICI*, Vol. 2, p. 21.
18. Quoted in *Trials of War Criminals*, Vol. 7, quoted in Reader, *ICI*, Vol. 2, p. 32.
19. Reader, *ICI*, Vol. 2, p. 229.

---

*   This paper is chiefly based on my own work in *Imperial Chemical Industries: A History* (ICI), 2 vols., 1970/1974, and on Charles Wilson's *The History of Unilever*, 2 vols., 1954. I have not thought it necessary to cite every reference to these books.

Comment

Minoru Sawai
Hokusei Gakuen University

Doctor Reader's paper, through an examination of the multi-regional development of the business activities of two giant corporations, ICI and Unilever and their predecessors, clearly sets forth British methods and aims in foreign trade. I wish to make a few observations and raise a number of questions about this essay.

1. My first observation concerns the differences in corporate behavior between the Nobel-Dynamite Trust and the Solvay companies, on the one hand, and Lever Brothers and Unilever, on the other. In his paper, Dr. Reader explains the difference in the behavior of the two groups mainly in terms of the characteristics of demand each was faced with. In other words, he contends that the demand for explosives and alkali as intermediate goods would have been fixed in the short run, and that therefore the manufacturers—insofar as they wished to coexist—had to conclude mutual agreements on market sharing, profit pooling, and so forth. He asserts that manufacturers of consumer goods such as soap and margarine, on the other hand, had closer ties with final consumers of their products and were able to stimulate demand through various means. This is why the soap and margarine producers often competed fiercely with each other.

In my opinion, however, this issue ought to be raised not only from the demand side but from the supply side as well. For instance, adjustments of operation rates and inventories in response to changes in the market situation would be more time-consuming and more expensive in the production of alkali and explosives than in the production of consumer goods such as soap; and if this was indeed the case, manufacturers of the former type of products should naturally behave differently from those producing the latter type of products. Similarly, the production of intermediate goods such as alkali and explosives would involve greater economies of scale, and thus would be more liable to suffer from overproduction than the production of consumer goods would. This would oblige the manufacturers of the former type of goods to behave differently from those producing the latter type.

2. I would also like to address myself to the question of choice between export and direct overseas investment. Doctor Reader refers to customs duties and the trends of demand in overseas markets as the major factors affecting a company's choice between promoting the export of finished products and undertaking offshore production. It is, however, important to take into account that even if a company found the customs duties imposed by a foreign country prohibitively high and saw a very promising market for its products in that country, this fact alone would by no means ensure that the company could successfully start offshore production there.

I wonder how various difficulties involved in technology transfer, and the question of recruiting eligible and competent workers who could satisfy the requirements of the head office, were actually dealt with by each company in choosing between the two alternatives. Let us take, for instance, Lever Brothers' Japanese subsidiary, Japan Lever Brothers Co., which was established in 1913 as the largest soap manufacturer in Japan at the time. The subsidiary, however, underwent a series of severe labor disputes in the years 1920 and 1921, and I wonder if Lever Brothers' decision to withdraw from Japan had something to do with these labor disputes.

3. Here I would like to raise two questions about marketing activities.

a. The paper compares foreign merchant companies and jointly owned companies by taking up the Brunner, Mond and ICI cases. Yet I wonder exactly what the similarities and differences between marketing activities of the two types of companies were. Furthermore, in connection with Dr. Reader's assertion that foreign merchant companies had to expand agency activities by their own efforts, diversifying the types of items they sold, I would like to ask, was this because they found the markets available in Japan and the Far East in general too small for the commodities they were mainly dealing with?

b.   Generally speaking, consumer products such as soap and margarine are sold to a far greater number of customers than are intermediate goods such as explosives. In view of this fact, I presume that Lever Brothers and Unilever, in organizing their marketing networks, had to undertake peculiar types of activities that ICI did not have to concern itself with. I wish to inquire as to Dr. Reader's opinion on this point.

4.   Finally, I would like to ask a few questions about the adjustment of decision making within the corporations and their business horizons.

a.   ICI was established through the amalgamation of unique predecessor companies, as was Unilever. I wonder if either company's decision-making process was disturbed by conflicts between various characteristics inherited from the forerunner companies.

b.   When they diversified their business activities into various regions, how did ICI and Unilever coordinate operations in the different regions? Did they have a sizable number of experts well informed about the market situation in various regions who played an active role in such interregional coordination of operations?

c.   It is asserted in the paper that ICI's inclination toward markets within the British Empire assured the firm of earning relatively greater profits from production and sales there than in markets outside the empire. Would I be justified in saying that, somewhat paradoxically, the assured profitable business within the empire made the company less eager to make research and development efforts than otherwise?

Response

W. J. Reader

1. Yes. Avoiding overproduction was a motive for entering into market-sharing agreements in the explosives and alkali industries.
2. The decision to build a factory overseas is one of the most difficult that any board ever has to make. The risks are illustrated by the experience of Lever Brothers in Japan.
3. a. The foreign merchant companies were intended solely for marketing goods exported from Great Britain to the countries where they were established, whereas the jointly owned companies both manufactured goods themselves and sold British exports within their own territories. Both kinds of company were set up to deal in ICI's own products, but if the foreign merchant companies could conveniently and profitably undertake agency business, they were encouraged to do so, whether or not the market for ICI's own goods was "too small."

   b. Yes. Unilever's marketing methods, because of the nature of Unilever companies' products, differ greatly from ICI's methods.
4. a. In all mergers there are conflicts of interest which must be dealt with by the holding company.

   b. Coordination must take account of both product diversity and geographical diversity, and as Professor Sawai suggests, it requires expert knowledge.

   c. No. ICI was specifically established for research and development in the chemical industry in the British Empire.

Specialized and General Trading Firms in the Atlantic Cotton Trade, 1820-1980

John R. Killick
Leeds University

I. Introduction

The well-known contrast between contemporary Anglo-American and Japanese organization of foreign trade—the former with its many relatively small commodity and financial specialists and the latter with its huge general trading companies—raises interesting questions of comparative institutional evolution. Most surprising to Western eyes is the undoubted importance in Japan of the formidable general trading companies, such as Mitsui and Mitsubishi, which seem to have grown directly from their mercantile past. In contrast, in the West the great general merchants of the pre-industrial era generally succumbed to specialized competition in the 19th century in what seems almost a law of development. However, the contrasting Japanese experience, and the recent increasing consolidation of trading and financial firms in the West suggest that possibly more particular factors may have been at work.[1]

These developments can be studied effectively in the raw cotton trade. Cotton was the principal export of the United States in the 19th century, and Britain's largest import. It was also the largest import of Japan and many other industrializing nations in the late 19th century. Furthermore, the cotton trade developed in the supposedly archetypal way. In the early 19th century it was controlled by the leading general merchants, but after 1870, with the development of cotton futures, the merchant houses left the trade to specialized dealers. In the 20th century it become more concentrated, with a few very large, but still specialized, firms dominating the trade. Recently, however, these firms too have declined, and cotton is increasingly being traded by branches of large firms with interests

239

TABLE 1   Characteristics of Selected Liverpool Merchants, 1827–30 and 1850.

Firm	Cotton imports (thousand bales) (1827)	Place (1827)	Other imports[1] (1830)	Ships[2] (1830)
1827/30				
W & J Brown	65	1st	G, NS	O, A
Cropper Benson	50	2d	G, NS	O, A
Rathbone Brothers	50	3d	G, NS	A
Bolton Ogden	30	4th	G, NS	A
Alston Finlay	20	5th	G, NS	A
Wright Taylor	15	6th	G	O, A
Maury Latham	14	7th	G	A
1850				
A. Dennistoun	48[3]	1st	G	A
W. Jackson	30	2nd	NS	A
Rankin Gilmour	19	5th	G, T	O, A
Brown Shipley	14	7th	G, NS	A
Gibbs Bright	14	8th	NS, T	O, A
Baring Brothers	10	12th	G	A
Rathbone Brothers	6	17th	G	O, A

Notes: 1.   G=Grain, NS=Naval Stores, T=Timber.   2.   O=Shipowning, A= Shipping agents.   3.   The 1850 figures are understated because the consignees of an increasing proportion of the cotton arranged for their shipments to be consigned "to order" rather than to themselves to conceal their identity. '—'=Not available.

in several commodities. In Japan, by contrast, the cotton import trade was usually controlled by more diversified trading companies, and there was not the same disintegration of functions in the late 19th century; in fact, cotton was one of the leading commodities on which these companies grew.[2]

Economists have suggested some general ideas about why diverse functions are sometimes internalized within firms and why they are sometimes controlled by specialists. Firms will obviously seek economies of scale, but scale can often be achieved either by undertaking diverse but mutually supporting activities or by undertaking large operations in one line. Firms also will seek to reduce the transaction costs of trading by absorbing, if they can manage them, activities that are costly to buy in the market outside; but both specialized and general firms had opportunities to reduce these

Manufactured exports	Exchange dealing	Agencies & branches U.S.A.	Elsewhere
Yes	Yes	N. Y., Philadelphia, Baltimore	None
Yes	—	None	None
Yes	—	None	None
Yes	Yes	N. Y.	None
—	—	N. Y., Charleston, New Orleans	None
—	—	N. Y.	None
—	—	None	None
—	Yes	N. Y., New Orleans	—
—	Yes	N. Y., New Orleans	None
Yes	—	New Orleans, Mobile	Canada
No	Yes	N. Y., Philadelphia, Baltimore Mobile., New Orleans etc.	None
Yes	—	—	South America
Yes	Yes	Boston, N. Y., Mobile	Far East
Yes	Yes	N. Y.	Far East

Source: Liverpool Branch of Bank of England to Head Office, December 1 1827; David M. Williams, "The Function of the Merchant in Specific Liverpool Import Trades," M. A. thesis, Liverpool University, 1963; Dun and Bradstreet Credit Registers, Harvard; Miscellaneous merchant papers.

costs. Similarly the structure of both specialized and general firms can be seen as a basis for the growth of modern organization. There are limits, then, to the practical explanatory power of these theories as overall systematic explanations, but they often give useful insights into particular periods or episodes. What is needed is a study—which has to be brief in the confines of this essay—of the particular factors which held the old mercantile firms together, why they lost their power in the late 19th century, and why there has been some renewed concentration since then.[3]

II. The Cotton Trade in the Late 18th and Early 19th Centuries

By 1800 the United States was becoming the largest source of cotton for the rapidly expanding textile industry in Lancashire. An increasing proportion of this cotton was handled by the leading

Liverpool merchants, who by the 1830s had become some of the largest firms in the Atlantic economy. A summary of their interests is presented in Table 1. The leading firms generally received more than 30,000 bales of cotton annually in the 1830s, whereas before 1815 the leaders had only received about 4,000. Unfortunately after about 1840 the customs receipts do not give details of all cotton consignments, but the largest firms do not appear to have increased their receipts much above 50,000 bales before 1860. These figures represent very large sums for the economy of the time—65,000 bales in 1827 would have been worth about $3.0 million when U.S. exports to Britain were worth about $26 million—and they impressed contemporaries. Thus in 1827 the Bank of England reported on W. & J. Brown: "Their concerns are very large indeed. They have already this year had 70 ships from America consigned to them, and expect 30 more, and they hold about 30,000 bags of cotton unsold."[4]

The Liverpool receipts, and the history of the firms whose records have survived, show that although there was some specialization, the larger Liverpool merchants were mostly active general traders and received large amounts of grain, tobacco, naval stores, and timber, as well as cotton, and in the 1820s were the principal exporters of many British manufactured goods. In many of these transactions they operated as commission merchants giving advances to manufacturers, factors, or planters on goods consigned to them, but they also quite frequently bought and sold on their own account. They were often shipowners either in their own right or through their partnership houses in America. There was a definite trend toward specialization in the early 19th century and they dropped many ancillary activities, such as cotton, ship and passenger broking, and manufactured goods exporting, but they still imported several commodities from America and seemed to be increasing their geographical range in the 1840s. Finally, most of these firms were international houses, as it was necessary to have trusted partners or employees overseas because of the huge risks of price fluctuation in the long period between the transmission and receipt of orders across the Atlantic. Of course firms could be entirely safe by framing their orders in a cautious way but then they would do little business, so the agents or partners in the eastern or southern United States ports had to be given considerable discretion to act on their own initiative. Therefore the size of the trade, combined with the distance involved, created the necessity for delegation of authority in what were effectively multidivisional structures.[5]

The problem for these houses was that the cotton trade rapidly become very competitive in the early 19th century. "The cotton trade is no doubt a pleasant one," wrote George Brown to William Brown in Liverpool in 1834, "but the competition for it being so great we understand that people will go to almost any lengths to get the consignments. We understand many houses will advance the whole cost." Competition was especially sharp when cheap credit was available in the 1830s and 1850s and smaller firms were able to enter the trade and offer very large advances in return for consignments. The trade was easy to understand, and it was not difficult for small Liverpool or northern American firms to make the necessary arrangements in the Southern ports. At these times the receipts of the larger, more respectable houses fell, but after the financial crises of 1825–26, 1837–39, and 1857, when many of the smaller houses were weakened, they recovered their position again. The ease with which smaller houses and speculators could enter and debase the trade was therefore a threat to the larger merchants.[6]

The traditional strategy merchants used to limit their liabilities in the face of lack of information and fast-moving prices was to endeavor to make other parties in the trade take the major risk of holding the cotton during its passage across the Atlantic and during marketing in Lancashire. In the very early years of the trade some of the largest manufacturers, and some Manchester dealers, had purchased cotton directly in order to secure the exact staple they required. However, the spinners, not generally large firms, naturally wished to reduce their exposure, and by 1815 the trade had become large enough to support a specialized class of brokers who could provide them with the required grades. After 1815 these brokers were sometimes willing to finance cotton imports in order to secure the exact cotton staples they required. Since they were usually able to obtain what they wanted in Liverpool, it was normally the planters who held the cotton until its sale, and in return for consigning the cotton to particular merchants and paying them commissions, they received large advances. Under severe competition, as illustrated in Brown's complaint above, advances could reach nearly 100%, thus destroying the merchants' strategy.

This left two alternatives open to the leading merchants. The one adopted by the Browns was to specialize in the finance of the trade rather than in trade itself, and taking advantage of the collapse of the Bank of the United States in 1839–42, they used their branches in New York, the American South, and Liverpool to negotiate the exchange of smaller British houses buying or making advances on cotton in the Southern ports. Accordingly they conducted an enormous exchange business in the 1840s and 1850s. However, in time, in this specialization too, competition increased and by 1860 the Browns calculated that they only earned £11,422 on sterling remittances of £9,299,833 from the United States, or less than one eighth of 1%. After the Civil War (1861–65) this competition stabilized, but only firms which had the necessary reputation and which were prepared to undertake a very large business on small margins found it profitable. The development in other financial specializations was similar. Other merchants copied the Browns, and although they retained some general merchant interests, the necessity for liquidity and reputation in finance made extensive commodity trading difficult.[7]

The alternative strategy undertaken by many prominent merchants was to maintain or even increase their range of activities. They still sought cotton consignments, or purchased substantial amounts outright, but they also conducted many other interlocking activities. The Rathbones, for instance, had been American specialists and major receivers of cotton since 1800. The increasing competition of the 1830s and harsh times from 1837–42, however, disenchanted them with cotton and they opened branches in China and imported tea and other Chinese produce to New York while exporting American cotton and grain to Liverpool. Rankin Gilmour, on the other hand, a branch of a leading Glasgow house with traditional interests in eastern Canada, probably entered the cotton trade to find seasonal employment for its large fleet of timber ships. At the same time Barings, while purchasing substantial quantities of cotton, also began to show increasing interest in the East as the direction of British trade changed in the 1850s. There were obvious economies of scale in using capital, personnel, ships, and information in several trades simultaneously. There was also often increased security in holding a portfolio of commodities, and offering a full range of services, including shipping and exchange negotiation, might often attract consignments. Similarly, operating ships was often a good hedge in large-cotton-crop or bad-European-harvest years, when freights were forced up, and vice versa.[8]

These basic strategies were modified by the close personal and trading relations within the mercantile community of the time. For instance, although the Browns' Liverpool house owned no ships, they had a long-standing arrangement with Thomas Cope of Philadelphia, who organized the leading Philadelphia packet line. The Browns' Baltimore house provided two ships for the line from 1822–42 and shared profits. The Copes carried the Browns' British exports to Philadelphia and the Browns handled the Copes' ships and sold their cargoes of grain, cotton, and turpentine in Liverpool. When the Copes sent their ships on a southern passage the Browns' southern agents arranged cargoes. The Copes' shipping interests therefore fitted tightly into the Browns' mercantile organization. This closeness of personal and trading relationships was characteristic of the cotton trade. For another instance, the Rathbones used Rathbone Duckworth and Co., which included close family, as a cotton broker. Very often children from the large families of the time were dispersed among the various specializations, thus preserving close cooperation. At the same time, there were extremely close relations between the leading planters, factors, and merchants. Thus R. G. Dun's New Orleans agent reported in 1847–48 that Washington Jackson, the second largest Liverpool cotton importer in 1850 "has sev. monied friends in Louisiana and Miss. and is very much respected here. . . . Dr Duncan of Natchez said to be worth two million $ is a particular friend of J's and gives him assistance whenever needed." Duncan was one of the richest planters in the United States but also had family relations in banking in New York. Similarly, the leading merchant houses at first dominated many of the new specialized commercial institutions and public utilities that were established in the early 19th century. Thus the large New Orleans factors controlled the banks in upstream ports like Natchez in order to enhance their trade. In Philadelphia both Thomas Cope and J. A. Brown were directors of the Bank of the United States, and Nicholas Biddle complained that the Browns used their position to assist their own operations.[9]

III. The Decline of the General Merchant in the Atlantic Cotton Trade

The merchants in the Atlantic cotton trade were therefore under pressure in the period before the Civil War, but survived increasing competition and easy entry levels by a combination of specialization and horizontal diversification that delivered economies of scale while minimizing risk. These policies worked as long as there were no other means of reducing the risk of holding cotton for long periods. However, with the introduction of the telegraph and futures markets, risk became less important than technical efficiency in moving the crop in determining the structure of the trade, and vertically integrated traders with the appropriate organization and location to reduce transactions costs to the minimum triumphed.[10]

The Civil War itself was a serious blow to traditional merchants in the cotton trade, and some houses like Washington Jackson, which in 1861 was doing "a large and safe business," never reopened. Still, the immediate effects of the war on trade were mitigated by the huge growth in grain consignments from the North, and by opportunities in the fluctuating exchange and produce markets. Rankin Gilmour and Rathbones, for instance, made good profits from cotton sales at very high prices. However, after the war Browns, Rankin Gilmour, A. Dennistoun, and other large Liverpool houses lost interest in the South. The remains of the plantation system were being destroyed and replaced by a system of small sharecropping tenants, landlords, and small interior stores. Initially the coastal factorage system recovered after the war, but cotton was increasingly marketed by local merchants at small towns in the interior. Accordingly, Liverpool merchants still interested in the trade no longer had solid parties to deal with who could deliver large volumes of cotton and whose credit was backed by land and slaves. In the future the only really effective way to buy large volumes of cotton of desired grades was to have agents in at least the major railroad concentration and compressing points in the South, and preferably in many of the smaller markets as well. The South was also a very dangerous market in which to buy cotton. Observers repeatedly miscalculated the speed of southern recovery and the strength of Lancashire demand and there frequently were disastrous speculations on the new futures markets. It was easy in these conditions for merchants to make ruinous purchases or advances. Browns in fact did well from cotton consignments immediately after the war before less prestigious competitors recovered, but Rathbones lost continuously from 1864 to 1874, including £50,000 to £60,000 in one month in 1867, and Rankin Gilmour had some good, but mostly bad years from 1866 to 1873.[11]

Barings is a good example of one house which did temporarily retain its interest in cotton. In the late 1860s and early 1870s they were importing heavily on their own account and received large consigments from Duncan Sherman & Co. of New York. In December 1873 they took advantage of the financial panic to increase their business and noted that "the whole of Duncan Sherman & Co's Liverpool business is now being conducted as it should be and is very large and valuable to us." However, during the 1870s competition increased and it became increasingly difficult to attract consignments without making commission rebates, offering large advances, or incurring dangerous risks. They constantly had to watch Duncan Sherman's methods. In January 1874 Duncan Sherman invited their to join in burying in Liverpool 5,000 bales for May, June, and July delivery, but Barings "strongly opposed such distant operations" and was "disinclined to have much to do with the arrival market which is chiefly manipulated by unsound buyers and sellers." Nevertheless they calculated in May 1874 that they held about 40,000 bales in Liverpool, mostly consigned to their by Duncan Sherman. Duncan Sherman collapsed in 1876, and although Barings endeavored to attract consignments from southern factors, they found it impossible to find reliable substitutes. Of course one solution would have been to go into futures itself and to have purchased large volumes of hedged cotton, but despite recognizable improvements in bargaining rules that had been introduced in Liverpool, their correspondence from New York rightly demonstrated how dangerous that market was for legitimate traders. The Ranger failure of October 1883, for instance, which was watched closely by Barings, destroyed or embarrassed many well-established Liverpool firms.[12]

By the middle 1880s the trade was becoming controlled by smaller houses, usually with a partner in the Liverpool Cotton Exchange and relations or agents who purchased from local markets in the South. In 1885 Barings explained that there was no chance of receiving consignments from the few American houses left in the trade. "Neither we nor our neighbors can. The whole trade is changed in character, everything is done on the basis of 'firm offers' covered by 'future delivery' contracts, and the business is conducted mainly by English houses." A typical firm which applied to Barings for credit in 1878 was A. B. Paton of St. Louis, Memphis, and Liverpool. One brother, Alexander Allan Paton, who had emigrated to the United States from Scotland just before the war, purchased cotton in Memphis and St. Louis, and consigned it to two other brothers for sale in Liverpool. The firms' collective capital in 1878 was about £30,000, and on this they transacted about 30,000 bales. In 1883, according to R. G. Dun & Co.'s St. Louis reporter, their business was over 77,000 bales, "the largest doubtless in this section," and Alexander Allan Paton was worth over $200,000. Such firms, buying their cotton skillfully in the South and paying only brokers' commissions for hedging, or being cotton brokers themselves, could undercut traditional firms like Barings. Even when in 1881 Barings offered George McFadden and Brothers of Philadelphia a cut in commissions to 1%, it could not win consignments. Instead in the same year McFaddens, whose operations are discussed in detail below, established its own Liverpool agency. It was cheaper for such firms to pay an agent's salary or open a branch in Liverpool on the large volume of business that the introduction of futures allowed than to pay even small commissions. Accordingly Barings' commissions, which in the early 1870s were regularly worth £30,000 per annum, had by 1884 sunk to £8,000, and their correspondence shows that they were despairing of finding traditional mercantile work.[13]

The other Atlantic trades that had integrated with cotton before 1860 also became more competitive during and after the war. The structure of the grain trade had been changing since the 1840s as futures trading became an accepted practice in the Midwest. Although as a result, consignments became far more difficult to obtain after the middle 1850s, Copes, Barings, Browns, and Rathbones were still purchasing grain in the early 1860s. The system of buying grain cargoes "to arrive" appeared in the Atlantic trade before the Civil War, but the futures system proper was not completely accepted in Liverpool until 1883. As a result, margins in the grain trade became gradually smaller, and the efficient selection and transportation of grain to market, rather than timing, became essential for success. This was best done by firms on the east coast with "the inside track" with the trunk line railroads or at strategic locations in the West. Barings realized they could not compete with such specialists when in 1877 they were asked if they would accept the drafts of Gill and Fischer of Baltimore against documents for cargoes of grain sold by them to British country millers direct for a 0.5% commission. They commented: "The chief objection to the business . . . is that it is another step towards doing away with the merchant in foreign trade. If millers in England will trust foreign buyers and these men will work for 1% and a broker on this side for 1/2% no 'decent trader' can compete." Similarly, in the timber trade traditional merchants gave way to local processors, timber being exported as deal planks rather than as rough square timber. As a result, Rankin Gilmour's Canadian branches closed in the 1870s and it deserted the cotton trade at the same time.[14]

Many Liverpool merchants, like Rankin Gilmour, became successful shipowners, often in the Far Eastern and Latin American trades, but the Atlantic trade was especially challenging for shipowners. Before 1860 the novelty and expense of steamships deterred merchants. After the war the rapid advances in technology and size of ships on the New York run, combined with fluctuations in freight rates, made shipowning a business for specialists like Cunard. Although the huge grain shipments during the war and the recovery of the cotton trade after the war kept freight rates relatively high until 1873, this prolonged the life of many sailing ships without increasing their long-run attractiveness. Many merchants, like Copes and Rankin Gilmour, kept their old vessels, built in the late 1840s, in the cotton trade until they wore out during the 1870s. Copes' records show that as a result, there were always so many ships waiting in the cotton ports that cotton shippers could never have had any difficulty finding space. By the late 1870s, steamships with regular arrangements with the railroads were taking the best cargoes on the New Orleans run. Simultaneously at the bottom end of the market lightly manned Canadian and Scandinavian schooners were freighting cotton at very low rates, and the last merchant-owned sailing ships were forced out of the trade. None of these parties, or the new operators in the cotton trade, like the Patons, had the available liquidity or managerial skills and interest to combine shipping with cotton operation.[15]

IV. The Reorganization of the Cotton Industry after 1880

By 1880 it was obvious that while the old merchant firms could still prosper by offering specialized financial services, the horizontal strategy of general trading in the Atlantic economy had failed. What mattered now was being able to shave fractions of a cent off the costs at each stage of distribution by effective physical management of the crop. It was therefore the growth of relatively small firms like A. B. Paton with good connections in the South and Liverpool which undermined the position of the large Liverpool merchants. Patons were able to undertake a large business on a relatively small capital base because they carefully hedged their cotton on the futures exchanges and were thus able to convince Barings and other bankers of their credit-worthiness. However, with the major risk of fluctuations in price greatly reduced, it became important for firms to develop a network of local agencies, compresses, and warehouses in the South, to establish good relations with railroads and shipping lines, and if possible, to have direct connections with spinners. At first, as contemporary directories show, cotton marketing was very disorganized, with hundreds of firms in the small interior markets scattered over the South. However, by 1914 a few large firms had developed the necessary organization to control cotton marketing over quite wide areas, and by 1930 they dominated the trade. The most important of these were Anderson Clayton of Houston, Texas, George McFadden and Brothers of Philadelphia, and Alexander Sprunt and Son of Wilmington, North Carolina.

The first of these to emerge was McFaddens. George H. McFadden was born in Ireland in 1816 and emigrated to Philadelphia as a young man. By 1858 he was established in Memphis as a wholesale dealer in notions, varieties, and possibly cotton. He returned to Philadelphia in 1862, opened another store, and died in 1868. His three sons continued the business, but specialized in cotton, and by the early seventies, were sufficiently successful to form an agency relationship with Louis Reinhart of Le Havre, a prominent French cotton importer. This implied hedging the cotton as it crossed the Atlantic, and in 1881 the eldest son, George H. McFadden, joined the New York Cotton Exchange. The same year they established an agency with Frederic Zerega & Co. of Liverpool, which in 1886 was converted into a partnership with John H. McFadden, the second brother, stationed in Liverpool. In 1892 this firm established a branch in Bremen, McFadden Zerega and Co. Finally in 1899 the McFaddens formed a joint agency with Louis Reinhart, with whom they had done an increasing business on joint account—the Société d'Importation et de Commission—and this with the other firms gave McFaddens access to all the major spinning areas of Europe. From 1900 the Le Havre firm imported about 100,000 bales a year and the Bremen firm about 200,000 bales, out of about 6 million bales exported from the United States.

The extension of McFaddens' connections in Europe meant that they had to improve their sources of cotton in the United States. Prior to 1885 they purchased cotton from factors in the leading ports and river railroad centers like Memphis. In 1888 they visited Texas, then growing rapidly as a cotton state, and realized the potential of developing presses at concentration points at small interior railroad towns where cotton could easily be assembled by purchases from local storekeepers. Once pressed, cotton could be shipped more cheaply on the railroads, and if heavy duty presses were used, the second pressing at the ports before shipment could be eliminated. From the late 1880s they purchased or built many cotton compresses in the interior of Texas and other cotton states and thus began to bypass the traditional marketing by port factors. In 1890 they chartered a subsidiary, the National Compress Co. of New Jersey, to control these presses, and in 1894–95 they shipped 400,000 bales from Galveston alone. So successful were these and similar presses at transferring the marketing of cotton from the ports to the interior of the cotton belt that they were attacked by port interests and small interior farmers. Accordingly, the Texas Railroad Commission began to control their rates (which were customarily incorporated with railroad freight rates) and in the late 1890s forced McFaddens to partly divest control of the company to other shippers, as the presses, like the elevators in the grain states, were considered public utilities. McFaddens' interest in them remained sufficiently large, however, to ensure that it was still able to direct large volumes of cotton to the European agencies of the firm for marketing. During the next few years the firm claimed "to pioneer better methods of getting cotton from the fields to the mill on a large scale and more economically."[16]

The second firm to achieve market prominence was Alexander Sprunt and Son of Wilmington, North Carolina. The development of this firm was broadly similar to that of McFaddens, but whereas the latter was originally a northern firm that came South to purchase cotton, but maintained its head office in Philadelphia, the Sprunts were southern based. The founder of the firm, Alexander Sprunt, was Scottish and arrived in North Carolina in 1852. James Sprunt, his son, the real founder of the firm, served as a blockade runner in the Civil War, and developed strong southern sympathies. Later in life he saw his major business achievement as creating the direct cotton trade with Europe that the South needed to avoid dependence on the North.

The progress of the Sprunts' firm can conveniently be described by quoting from a letter James Sprunt wrote to the Interstate Commerce Commission in 1908. "Up to the year 1875 the movement of the cotton crop in North Carolina, South Carolina and Georgia (from which we draw our business) depended largely and almost entirely upon factors. . . . The factor received and stored the farmers' consignments of cotton and sought at his convenience a buyer at the port. The factor's charges, including his commission, aggregated at least $1.50 per bale, often more than that. The port buyer, in turn, shipped the cotton north at a profit to himself of about $2.00 a bale in margin plus commission. The receiver in the North made his profit, sometimes amounting to as much as $5.00 a bale, by selling it to a northern mill or by exporting it to a foreign market. By this process, the farmer paid three intermediaries $6.00 to $8.00 per bale—a burdensome tax on his well earned product."

Sprunt then went on to describe his firm's part in changing this situation. "In 1879, after a thorough study of the problem of better facilities for direct cotton trade, we became the pioneers of the present system which has brought the producer and consumer together without an excessive number of intermediaries! We chartered the first steamer that ever sailed from the port of Wilmington for a port abroad. The result of this experiment . . . was disastrous. We repeated the experiment again and again and ultimately established upon its present foundation, the system which has saved our farmers millions of dollars since 1875, and which has been accepted at all cotton ports from Norfolk to New Orleans."

In the development of the business Sprunt claimed that he "crossed the Atlantic twenty one times, and travelled yearly from the Mediterranean to the Gulf of Finland and established more than one hundred agencies abroad in seventeen different countries." At the same time, like the McFaddens, the Sprunts developed interior contacts with the storekeepers and farmers through a network of agencies and branches in the southeastern states, and thus cut out the traditional coastal intermediaries. In this case, all the compressing continued to be done at Wilmington on the coast, as it was the most convenient concentration point for its area. As a result, James Sprunt boasted in 1908 that "we have brought the farmer and foreign spinner into practically direct personal relations . . . we charter fifty steamers at our own risk every year to complete the connection . . . last year we shipped to foreign ports 501,000 bales out of Wilmington."[17]

The third large firm, which ultimately came to dominate the international cotton trade, was Anderson Clayton and Co. Before 1914, although the two partners, Will Clayton and Frank Anderson, had

TABLE 2   Location and Number of Agencies and Branches of Selected Leading Cotton Firms, 1911, 1929–30, and 1962.

Firm	North America					Eu.	St.Am.	Nr.Et.	Far.Et.[1]
	S.A.	E.S.C.	W.S.C.	N.Et.	Wt.				
1911									
Anderson Clayton	—	—	5	1	—	—	—	—	—
McFaddens	15	15	19	5	—	3	—	—	—
Sprunts	22	—	—	—	—	3	—	—	—
Weil Brothers	4	14	—	1	—	—	—	—	—
1929–30									
Anderson Clayton	12	4	11	5	1	3	—	—	—
Weil Brothers	4	12	1	1	—	—	—	—	—
McFaddens	7	9	9	5	2	2	—	—	—
Sprunts	7	1	4	2	—	2	—	—	—
Cook	—	10	4	—	—	—	—	—	—
Bunge and Born	—	—	—	—	—	1	1	—	—
Ralli Brothers	—	—	—	—	—	3	—	3	—
Volkart	—	—	—	—	—	3	—	7	3
Japan Cotton Co.	1	1	11	1	1	1	—	7	12
1962									
Anderson Clayton	5	1	4	2	2	4	8	2	—
McFaddens	5	2	3	3	1	2	8	—	1
Cook	3	1	1	2	2	3	8	1	1
Weil Brothers	2	3	3	1	3	—	—	—	—

Bunge	—	—	—	1	1	12	6	7	9
Ralli Brothers	—	—	—	—	2	4	—	9	3
Volkart	2	1	2	2	1	2	5	4	—

Source: The Standard International Cotton Shippers' Book Comprising a Directory in the American South of Cotton Buyers, Cotton Shippers ..., Savannah, Ga., 1911; Skinner's Cotton Trade Directory of the World, Oldham, 1929–30, 1962.

(1) The regional divisions are S. A.—South Atlantic United States; E.S.C.—East South Central United States; WSC—West South Central United States; N. Et.—Northeastern United States and Canada; Wt.—Western United States and Canada; Eu—Europe; St. Am—South America; Nr. Et.—Near East, India, South Africa; Far Et.—Southeast Asia, Japan, China, Australia.

gained wide experience in the cotton trade, their firm based in Oklahoma City was very small and they were limited by their lack of capital. They bought cotton in local markets and graded and sorted it ready for export, but then sold it almost immediately to European merchants who had the capital to hold it while it crossed the Atlantic and was distributed to spinners. During the First World War, however, and immediately afterward, the firm grew very rapidly, taking advantage of the discomfiture of the European firms and the cheaper capital now available in New York. They very quickly established a network of buying agencies all over the South, and selling agencies in the spinning areas of the eastern United States, Europe, and Japan. The cotton was carefully organized for the most efficient transit from cotton field to spinner. They operated their own interior gins and presses, moved the cotton where possible in their own trucks and river barges, and stored, sorted, and compressed it for export in large modern coastal compress warehouses for overseas shipment to particular customers. In the 1920s Anderson Clayton went further toward an integrated cotton-shipping company than either Sprunts or McFaddens. They owned their own machine shops in Houston to make and repair presses, operated a small textile mill to make use of unwanted cotton, produced several oilseed products from surplus cottonseed, and in the pest-free irrigated areas of California even offered credit to farmers. As a result, in the 1920s the firm dominated the cotton trade, handling about 2 million bales a year.[18]

These American cotton companies, and a few other cotton firms like them, had by the 1920s gone far toward eliminating the intermediaries in the cotton trade and offering an integrated service from the farmer to the mills. Although they were family firms, their total sales were very large indeed. Sprunts' 500,000 bales of cotton in 1907 were worth about $30 million, which is a surprising amount when set against, for instance, the total value of American exports to France—about $110 million—or Germany—$250 million—that year. McFaddens was dealing in equal amounts. In 1928 Anderson Clayton's far larger 2.4 million bales were worth about $240 million when U.S. exports to France were $240 million and to Germany, $470 million.

V. The Cotton-Shipping Industry in the Twentieth Century

The particular strength of these specialized firms was their efficiency at collecting and distributing cotton from small markets in the South. However, since the 1920s their local advantages have been dissipated with the modernization of the South and increasing government intervention in the cotton trade. Consequently many of the specialist firms have left the trade and recently there has been some return to general trading. Some evidence for this development is suggested by Table 2, which is based on cotton trade directories and analyzes the structure of the trade in 1911, 1929–30, and 1962. These directories are impressive books indicating with lists of thousands of locations and firms all over the world the geographical range of the cotton trade at its height. Only the leading American firms are included in 1911, but in 1929–30 the Japan Cotton Co. (Nihon Menka) and in 1929 and 1962 the branches of the Swiss and English firms Volkart and Rallis and the Argentinian cotton and grain firm Bunge have been added to demonstrate the growth of multinational firms in the trade.

The most striking feature of the 1911 directories is the dense network of agencies that the major companies established in each locality. Sprunts, for instance, was the leading firm in North Carolina and resented intrusion by outside firms. Similarly, Weil Brothers, which was based in Montgomery, Alabama, had established agencies in the nearby small towns. Each firm employed local buyers to fill in the gaps, and through the cotton season the whole firm worked extremely hard to collect the cotton from small towns, and even from individual planters and farmers in their territory, and to class, sort, and dispatch it to the ports. Clearly only local specialists could provide this service, and when European or Japanese companies wished to buy cotton they had to work through local dealers. After the First World War the most successful firms continued to develop their markets in depth and ignored local interests at their peril. For instance, when in 1921 McFaddens, which was the only firm to develop a branching system over the whole South before the war, found itself falling behind Anderson Clayton, they blamed the independence of their southern agents, who bought cotton well in their respective territories, but were allowed to sell it to McFaddens at near market prices. In theory competition between agencies kept prices down, but in practice McFaddens never knew the exact cost of cotton in the various markets and the agents made large profits at their expense. "The only way we can win today," they claimed "is by our experience in handling futures, making forward sales etc. . . . How can we compete with Anderson Clayton when Clayton sits in Houston and knows exactly what cotton costs in the interior and then offers this cotton direct to Europe," and the firm recommended much tighter control of their southern agencies.[19]

At the same time the larger firms attempted to open branches in the major centers throughout the whole cotton belt. One reason for this was the relative decline of the Southeast and the continued westward displacement of the cotton belt into Texas. Thus in 1908 Anderson Clayton opened an agency in Houston, and in 1916 moved their headquarters there. In 1916 Sprunts opened a large compress and warehouse in Houston, and by 1929 Weils had a branch there. There is no evidence from the directories, however, that Sprunts or Weils developed local agencies as assiduously as they had earlier in the East. Anderson Clayton, clearly the largest firm by the middle 1920s, established branches in Memphis to serve the delta region, in Los Angeles in 1920 to serve the new, irrigated cotton-growing areas developing in Califonia in the 1920s, and in New Orleans and Savannah during the First World War. It was also necessary for the large cotton firms to have agencies in the spinning areas, like Atlanta, Boston and Fall River, Massachusetts, and Montreal. Finally, most of the larger firms were members of several cotton exchanges. For instance, Weils was a member of the New York, New Orleans, Dallas, and Memphis cotton exchanges and a member of the Atlantic and Texas cotton associations, and an associate member of the Liverpool Cotton Exchange.

The Depression and the New Deal were severe tests for these firms and Sprunts, for instance, who lost $1 million on cotton futures in 1930, never really recovered. More important than particular losses, from 1929 government intervention began to prevent the natural operation of the futures market and raise American prices above international levels. Hoover's Federal Farm Board was relatively ineffective at maintaining prices, but the New Deal restrictions on output and the Commondity Credit Corporation, which purchased huge stocks of cotton, increasingly gained control. This, in principle, made the traditional shipper's policy of carrying large stocks hedged against futures unworkable because the fluctuation of futures in reasonable parallel with commercial values could no longer be relied upon. From 1930 to 1935, however, Anderson Clayton was able to acquire very large stocks—reaching a peak of 2.5 million bales in 1933—at such low prices that as the government slowly succeeded in reducing output and prices rose, it was able to make substantial profits. These were not speculative purchases, as no firm could have risked such large amounts and the spot purchases were hedged against future sales. However, by 1935 spot prices were so high in relation to futures that it was no longer practical to hedge in the traditional way except for occasional short periods, and Anderson Clayton calculated that they would have to change their whole policy. At the same time the artificial raising of American prices, combined with switching from crops such as coffee even more disastrously hit by the Depression, rapidly increased foreign competition in the European and Japanese markets, and reduced American exports.[20]

As a result, smaller firms like Sprunts and Weils found their exports from Wilmington and Savannah diminishing and were restricted to a domestic mill business, which involved buying cotton in Georgia and Tennessee and running it to the nearby mills. This was safe, as it required firms to hold the cotton for very short periods during which prices could not change much, but it was also easy to enter and extremely competitive, involving a great deal of work for small returns. Anderson Clayton and McFaddens, however, chose the more adventurous course of developing alternative sources of cotton by establishing agencies in Latin America and Egypt, and thus maintaining their foreign selling agencies in business. Anderson Clayton had established a subsidiary in Mexico in 1921 to sell cotton to the Mexican mills, and in 1930 it purchased a firm in Alexandria. But its major expansion in Latin America came in the middle 1930s when it opened branches in Argentina, Brazil, Mexico, Paraguay, Peru, and Upper Egypt. Similarly, McFaddens opened branches in

Brazil, the most rapidly growing cotton area, in 1936. As a result, Anderson Clayton purchased 1.9 million bales in the United States in 1937–38, 118,000 in Mexico, 387,000 in Brazil, 71,000 in Argentina and Paraguay, 136,000 in Peru, and 149,000 in Egypt and the Sudan.

The American companies found their new sources of supply had far fewer basic facilities for cotton marketing than the United States. Thus Anderson Clayton in particular, even more than in the United States, built its own gins, seed-crushing plants, compresses, and warehouses. For instance, in Peru there were no heavy compresses, so Peruvian cotton was expensively shipped in large bales. Accordingly Anderson Clayton developed a special steam press that did not damage the delicate long Peruvian staple. In Mexico there were few gins and oil mills and inadequate facilities for financing and supervising cotton growing, so Anderson Clayton built its own facilities, organized crop financing and supervision, and chartered a bank in the principal cotton center. It also found to a greater extent than in the United States that there were opportunities to use all the byproducts of cotton in profitable local manufactures. Thus Anderson Clayton first became a food producer when it bought a Mexican mill in 1930 which manufactured refined oil, shortening, and soap from cottonseed. Later on, it made a wider variety of processed foodstuffs based on vegetable oils, first in Latin America, then in the United States, and introduced soft margarine there.

Most cotton firms remained small specialized partnerships, but gradually the largest became corporations. Small-scale partnership was initially a great advantage since successful cotton trading required swift decisions throughout the season and personal responsibility, while unlimited liability helped to raise the very large working capital needed. It was necessary for firms to have access to compresses and warehouses and other facilities on fair terms, but this was possible through leasing, and public opinion opposed firms using their own facilities exclusively. Nevertheless, most of the large firms, such as Sprunts, did have compress interests, but if possible they hived these off into separate companies. Anderson Clayton most determinedly acquired fixed facilities all over the cotton belt, but it too formed these into subsidiary companies, sometimes only partly owned, leaving the central trading organization a partnership.

The Achilles' heel of partnerships was the retirement and death of leading members, necessitating paying estates and attracting adequate substitutes, and family events were important in persuading Sprunts, McFaddens, and Anderson Clayton to incorporate. The problem was to combine the flexibility of the partnership with the continuity of the corporation. Gradually, though, the need to operate over a wider geographical area, to acquire more fixed facilities, and to deal with the extra risk imposed by government intervention led to full incorporation. Anderson Clayton became a Texas joint-stock company, retaining unlimited liability, in 1920. In 1935 the company became a Delaware corporation with sufficient independent assets and reputation to back its operations. However, it did not become a full corporation quoted on the stock exchange with an executive committee of the board of directors until 1962, by which time cotton marketing was only a small part of its operations. Similarly McFaddens and Weils, much less diversified firms, only slowly moved toward incorporation.[21]

After the 1920s firms reduced their local representation. Although cotton farming was at its peak, improvements in transport and communications meant that it was not necessary to have agents in every market town, and Sprunts and Weils shut their smaller agencies. During the Depression many small markets disappeared completely as cotton prices fell and the New Deal restricted output and encouraged consolidation. Government purchasing and cooperative marketing of cotton also reduced the need for local branches. The period from 1950 to 1970 was very depressing for traditional firms in the cotton trade. The decline of cotton farming in the South and government price supports continued to prevent normal marketing, and reduced American exports. Consequently there was a great reduction in the number of firms in the industry, and many of the cotton exchanges closed or were reduced to shadows of their former selves. Alexander Sprunt and Son of Wilmington stopped trading in 1956, the McFadden partnership was terminated in 1970, and Anderson Clayton followed the logic of its diversification into vegetable oil-based foodstuffs and ended its domestic cotton marketing in 1973.[22]

A consequence of these changes was that there was some return to general trading in the cotton trade. With the decline in the futures markets risk was once again an important factor in determining structure. It now helped to deal in several commodities simultaneously, and firms had to be strong enough to handle large amounts of less well hedged cotton. Cotton marketing often became one division of a multidivisional enterprise which was able to gain economies of scale across many areas and functions. The largest cotton firms also now operated on a worldwide basis, while few firms had more than a few branches in each region. Consequently the specialization which derived from family operation and local control no longer applied. Thus one listing of the largest firms in the cotton trade in 1981 included Ralli Brothers, Bunge and Born, and Cargill, originally grain traders but now multinational conglomerates; Cook Industries, a Memphis cotton firm turned grain trader; and the Japanese general trading companies, as well as a few remaining specialists.[23]

VI. Conclusion

It is difficult to draw conclusions for Asian trade from the separate history of the Atlantic cotton trade. The early 19th century merchants in the Atlantic trade were very different from the later Japanese *sōgō shōsha* (general trading companies), but the bonds which held such diversified firms together were similar—the economies of scale of interlocking operations, the attempts to reduce risk by holding a portfolio of commodities, the dominant credit and marketing position over manufacturers and suppliers, the connections with finance, the carefully organized international branching, etc. What seems different, apart from the scale of modern compared with 19th century commerce, is the openness of Atlantic society, and the easy challenge that small firms were able to mount against the great merchants. It is remarkable in fact how slowly the leading British merchant banks acquired wealth in the 19th century—only just maintaining their position while accepting an increasingly specialized role.[24]

The decline of the great Liverpool merchants was partly due to the particular development of the Atlantic economy, as well as to the growth of volume trade and the evolution of futures. As early as the 1850s the position of merchants in the American ports was being undermined by the success of manufacturers in marketing their increasingly complex products. The stagnation of British manufactured exports to America after the Civil War, and the gradual location of the control of staples marketing nearer the source of production in the South and West meant there was less opportunity for Liverpool firms to combine several different trades. By contrast, British merchants interested in *Asian* trade enjoyed rising manu- factured exports, far less competition to control the staple trades, and consequently continued opportunities for successful diversifica- tion in the late 19th century. The success of the Japanese firms in the early 20th century seems an extension of this progression.[25]

It is interesting to speculate why the specialist American cotton firms did not undercut the Japanese general trading companies in the same way they undercut the Liverpool merchants. In the early 20th century firms like Sprunts and McFaddens were absorbed in establishing their contacts with the European mills. Meanwhile the Japanese firms enjoyed extraordinary opportunities for growth due to Japan's industrialization, 1890–1914, and its de facto neutral- ity during the First World War. Between the wars American ship- pers like Anderson Clayton and McFaddens established themselves in Osaka and won a proportion of the import business. However, they always dealt through Japanese firms rather than making direct contact with the mills, while the Japanese firms established their own comprehensive network in the American South and elsewhere. Possibly the closeness of Japanese society, and the dependence of the Japanese spinners on the trading companies for finance, prevented this direct contact from occurring. Even the Liverpool market maintained a degree of independence, and it would have been far more difficult for the American firms in Japan. The Japanese trading companies dealing in cotton also became more specialized after 1921, presumably partly in response to foreign competition, partly because of the risk of dealing in large volumes of cotton in this period, and increasing sophistication in handling these risks. After the Second World War the specialist firms in the Atlantic cotton trade faced increasing problems, and as described above, there was some return to diversification. As the Japanese firms recovered from the war and the Occupation antitrust regime, they returned to their diversified trading strategy, and in contemporary conditions were in no danger from specialized competition.

NOTES

1. For the special history of Japanese trading companies see Yama-mura Kōzō, "General Trading Companies in Japan—Their Origins and Growth," in Hugh Patrick, ed., *Japanese Industrialization and Its Social Consequences*, Berkeley, 1976; Yoshihara Kunio, *Sogo Shosha: The Vanguard of the Japanese Economy*, Tokyo, 1982; Yonekawa Shin'ichi, "The Formation of General Trading Companies: A Comparative Study," *Japanese Year Book on Business History: 1985*. For standard views of specialization in the West see Glenn Porter and Harold C. Livesay, *Merchants and Manufacturers; Studies in the Changing Structure of Nineteenth-Century Marketing*, Baltimore, 1971; Alfred D. Chandler, Jr., *The Visible Hand: The Managerial Revolution in American Business*, Cambridge, Mass., 1977.

2. For the cotton trade in the 19th century see Thomas Ellison, *The Cotton Trade of Great Britain*, London, 1886; for the cotton trade in the 1930s see Alston H. Garside, *Cotton Goes to Market*, New York, 1935.

3. R. H. Coase, "The Nature of the Firm," *Economica*, 1937; Oliver E. Williamson, "The Modern Corporation: Origins, Evolution, Attributes," *Journal of Economic Literature*, 1981; G. B. Richardson, "The Organization of Industry," *Economic Journal*, 1972.

4. Liverpool agent of Bank of England to Bank of England, September 8, 1827, Bank of England Records, Bank of England, London.

5. Stanley Chapman, *The Rise of Merchant Banking*, London, 1984; Sheila Marriner, *Rathbones of Liverpool, 1845–73*, Liverpool, 1961; Ralph W. Hidy, *The House of Baring in American Trade and Finance, 1763–1861*, Cambridge, Mass., 1949; John R. Killick, "Bolton Ogden & Co.: A Case Study in Anglo-American Trade," *The Business History Review*, 1974.

6. J. R. Killick, "The Cotton Operations of Alexander Brown in the Deep South, 1820–1860," *The Journal of Southern History*, 1977.

7. Edwin J. Perkins, *Financing Anglo-American Trade: The House of Brown, 1800–1880*, Cambridge, Mass., 1975; J. R. Killick, "Risk, Specialisation and Profit in the Mercantile Sector of the Nineteenth Century Cotton Trade: Alexander Brown and Sons, 1820–1880," *Business History Review*, 1974.

8. Marriner, *Rathbones of Liverpool*; John Rankin, *A History of Our Firm*, Liverpool, 1921; Hidy, *The House of Baring*.

9. See Copes' letterbooks, 1822–1880, in the Historical Society of Pennsylvania. Marriner, *Rathbones of Liverpool*; Robert E. Roeder, "New Orleans Merchants—1790–1837," Ph. D. diss., Harvard University, 1959; R. G. Dun & Co. Credit Registers, R. G. Dun & Co. Collection, Baker Library, Harvard University Graduate School of Business Administration. Nicholas Biddle to Dr. John Campbell White, February 26, 1828, John Campbell White Papers, Maryland Historical Society.

10. Ellison's *Cotton Trade of Great Britain* is a standard account of the effect of the introduction of futures on commerce.

11. Perkins, *Financing Anglo-American Trade*; Marriner, *Rathbones of Liverpool*; Rankin, *History of Our Firm*; Woodman, *King Cotton*.

12. Baring Brothers, Liverpool, to Baring Brothers, London, at dates indicated, 1873–1883, File MC3.35, Baring Brothers Archives, London; For a description of the Ranger failure see Thomas Ellison, *Gleanings and Reminiscences*, Liverpool, 1905.

13. Baring Brothers, Liverpool, to Baring Brothers, London, August 4, 1885, and November 27, 1878, Baring Brothers Archives, File MC3.35; R. G. Dun & Co., Credit Registers, St. Louis, Mo., Vol. 8, p. 307, Baker Library, Harvard; Thomas Baring, New York, to George H. McFadden, Philadelphia, June 2, 1881, Liverpool Correspondence, Vol. 18.

14. Morton Rothstein, "American Wheat and the British Market, 1860–1905," Ph. D. diss., Cornell University, 1960; Baring Brothers, Liverpool, to Baring Brothers, London, October 10, 1877, Baring Brothers Archives, File HC3.35; Marriner, *Rathbones of Liverpool*, Rankin, *History of Our Firm*; Arthur Lower, *Great Britain's Woodyard: British America and the Canadian Timber Trade, 1763–1867*, Montreal, 1973.

15. Rankin, *History of Our Firm*; Cope Records, Pennsylvania Historical Society; Francis E. Hyde, *Harrisons of Liverpool: Shipping Enterprise and Management, 1830–1939*, Liverpool, 1967.

16. This account of the McFaddens is based on several undated typescript memorandums in the historical file of the firm's offices in Memphis, Tenn.

17. Alexander Sprunt and Son to the Hon. Judson Clements, Interstate Commerce Commission, Washington, D. C., November 6, 1908.

Sprunts records are in the William R. Perkins Library, Duke University, Durham, N.C. See also J. R. Killick, "The Transformation of Cotton Marketing in the Late Nineteenth Century: Alexander Sprunt and Son of Wilmington, N.C., 1884–1956," *The Business History Review*, 1981.

18. For Anderson Clayton see Ellen Clayton Garwood, *Will Clayton: A Short Biography*, Austin, Tex., 1958; Lamer Fleming, "Growth of the Business of Anderson Clayton & Co.," in James A. Tinsley, ed., *Gulf Coast Historical Association Series*, 1966; and several typescript histories of the firm in their offices at Houston, Texas.

19. Benjamin S. Barnes, "My Fifty years in the Cotton Business," typescript at Weil Brothers offices, Montgomery, Ala.; Barclay McFadden, "Consideration of the Southern Agency System," typed memorandum, March 1, 1921, at McFadden Brothers' offices, Memphis, Tenn.

20. This and the following paragraphs are based on memorandas at Anderson Clayton's offices in Houston, McFaddens' offices in Memphis, and Weil Brothers' offices in Montgomery, and the records of Alexander Sprunt & Son at Duke University, Durham, N.C.

21. Fleming, "Growth of the Business of Anderson Clayton."

22. "Anderson Clayton Blossoms Out," *New York Times*, July 8, 1973.

23. Frederick Clairmonte and John Cavanagh, *The World in Their Web: Dynamics of the Textile Multinationals*, London, 1981; Dan Morgan, *Merchants of Grain*, New York, 1979.

24. Chapman, *The Rise of Merchant Banking*.

25. Chapman, *The Rise of Merchant Banking*; Porter and Livesay, *Merchants and Manufacturers*.

Comment

Tetsuya Kuwahara
Kyoto Sangyo University

I

Doctor Killick's paper focuses on the changes in the operations of trading firms in the Atlantic cotton trade since the end of the 18th century. The types of trading firms have changed from general merchant to specialized merchant, and then from specialized merchant to general merchant. To approach this theme the author analyzes the strategic behavior of these trading firms under changing external situations using the key concepts of minimizing risks and achieving economies of scale.

His findings and analyses are summarized in four major points. The first concerns the dominant position of the Liverpool general merchants in the Atlantic cotton trade in the early stages. These merchants internalized the functions of risk minimization and achieved economies of scale within their own firms. He explains that Liverpool merchants achieved these needs by holding a portfolio of commodities, by interlocking trade with financing and shipping, and by trading with a variety of distant places.

The second point is about the new external situations under which general merchants declined and specialized merchants rose after the 1870s. He insists upon the importance of the introduction of futures into the Atlantic cotton trade and the development of large-scale futures markets, along with the emergence of new means of transmission of information and the expanding demands for U.S. cotton from the cotton spinners in Europe. These situations gave good opportunities for growth to U.S. cotton merchants. They could minimize risks by hedging cotton on the futures exchanges and could therefore deal in a large volume of cotton. The position of the Liverpool general merchants was undermined by their new competitors from the United States.

The third point concerns the growth strategies of specialized merchants. Under the increasingly severe competition they had to reduce distribution costs. They integrated channels of trade for efficient distribution of the crop from local markets in the South to the spinning mills in Europe. They had to develop a network of local agencies, compresses, and warehouses in the South, and establish good connections with cotton spinners in Europe. Through these strategies they achieved the dominant position in the Atlantic cotton trade.

The fourth point is about the adaptive responses of the cotton-trading firms to the stagnation of American cotton production during and after the New Deal. To relieve cotton farmers who were suffering during the Depression, the U.S. government intervened in the cotton market. It controlled the output of cotton and supported the price. With government intervention, futures markets lost some of their functions. American cotton also decreased in international competitiveness. Facing this situation, the U.S. cotton-trading firms developed strategies of multinationalization and diversification of commodity lines.

II

An interesting comparison can be drawn between the Atlantic cotton trade and that of Japan. The Japanese cotton trade was generally dominated by specialized trading firms in the pre-World War II period. Foreign merchants located in open ports and Mitsui Bussan Kaisha of the Mitsui family traded in cotton along with other goods in the early Meiji era (1868–1912). But after the 1890s, when the cotton industry began its steady growth and demands for imported cotton greatly increased, the firms that specialized in cotton import gradually took the dominant position. These firms were Naigaiwata, Nihon Menka, Gōshō, and Tōyō Menka. Mitsui Bussan also spun off its Cotton Division (established in 1911) and incorporated it as Tōyō Menka Kaisha in 1920. The three largest cotton merchants, Nihon Menka, Tōyō Menka, and Gōshō imported as much as 55% to 70% of the total cotton imported to Japan in

TABLE 11 Japanese Import of Cotton from all Foreign Countries 1901–39.

Unit: 1,000 bales (500 lbs/bale)

	1901	1905	09	13	17	21	24	29	33	37
Mitsui Bussan	106	144	191	237	347	—	—	—	—	—
Tokyo Menka						369	429	527	658	680
Nihon Menka	62	140	109	299	283	560	508	581	513	527
Gosho	—	—	44	156	289	282	352	503	594	491
Naigaiwata	58	52	28	4	—	—	—	—	—	—
Other	229	351	330	518	523	844	582	1,116	1,613	1,810
Major foreign merchants	146	97	43	97	89	143	165	222	106	63
Total of firms listed above	601	784	745	1,311	1,631	2,198	2,036	2,949	3,484	3,571
Japan total	719	1,219	1,112	1,879	1,988	2,443	2,266	3,010	3,484	3,840

Notes: 1. The cotton volume of each firm's import does not represent the total imported to all ports of Japan. The volumes of 1901 and 1905 represent those to the port of Kobe only, 1909 and 1913 the total to the ports of Kobe and Yokohama, and 1917 to 1937 the total to the ports of Kobe, Yokohama, Osaka, Kanmon, Yokkaichi, Nagoya and Nagasaki.

2. "Other" represents 102 firms, including 28 small foreign merchants, at the end of 1926. (Nihon Menka dogyokai ed. Menka junpo (Ten Days Report of Cotton Import) Jan. 1927.

3. "Major foreign merchants" represents 8 to 5 firms.

4. "Japan total" is the total volume imported to all Japanese ports.

Source: *Nihon Menka kyokai* (Japan Cotton Association) ed., *Menka hyakunen* (One Hundred Years of Cotton), 1969, pp. 140, 143, 202, 203, 206, 207, 354–357.

the 1920s (see Table 1). Though these firms diversified and began to export cotton manufactured goods in time, their main merchandise was cotton. They achieved their growth through the cotton trade. After World War II they gradually transformed themselves into *sōgō shōsha*, or general trading companies.

The growth of Nihon Menka Kaisha presents a typical case of a specialized cotton firm before World War II. Nihon Menka was organized as an importer for cotton spinners in Osaka in 1893. It began to import cotton from China and India in 1894, and then from the United States. Faced with increasing competition, Nihon Menka embarked on local purchases of cotton in India in 1907 and in the United States in 1910. It built or bought local ginning mills, compresses, and warehouses. After 1903 it also exported cotton yarn and cloth manufactured by its Japanese customers. This contributed to its enlarged sales outlets for cotton in Japan. The ferm's import of cotton reached a peak 762 thousand bales (500 pounds per bale) in 1927. It also exported cotton from India and the United States to European countries and China after World War I. The value of raw cotton as a proportion of the total value of its merchandise account on the annual reports was more than 60% in the 1920s.

We find some common features in the history of the Japanese cotton trade and the Atlantic cotton trade. The dominant position of specialized merchants in the cotton trade on both sides of the world can be understood from the following:

1. The volume of the cotton trade was large enough for merchants to achieve economies of scale even in their own specialized trade of cotton.
2. Futures markets for cotton were developed on a large scale and on a worldwide basis.
3. Specialized merchants were able to make swift decisions in the cotton trade, and this enabled them to make timely purchases of cotton of the desired quality in local markets. They could also concentrate their efforts on building up an efficient cotton distribution system from the local markets to the customers.

Response

John R. Killick

I must thank Professor Kuwahara for his useful comments and tables. The table includes cotton imported from all areas, but initially, as he indicates in his footnotes, only the main ports reported imports by firm. However, the proportion consequently omitted is small, and the table is a good indication of the relative standing of each firm.

Professor Kuwahara emphasizes the common features of the Atlantic and Japanese cotton trade, and follows the Japanese convention of calling the pre-World War II cotton importers specialists. They were much less specialized, however, than the firms I studied, which generally handled *nothing* but cotton until after World War II, but in much greater volumes (see Table 1). Thus by comparison with Sprunts, a small family firm from a backward region, Mitsui Bussan only imported about 100,000 bales per annum in 1902–5 and 170,000 bales in 1907–10, but mixed this with many other activities in what looks like a general merchant strategy. Even in the 1920s, as the tables in Professor Yamazaki's paper for this conference show, the specialist textile firms were handling many types of fabric as well as raw cotton.

What is the explanation for the greater relative diversification of the Japanese firms? Nearly all developed from traditional mid-19th century general merchants with considerable experience in inland trade and finance. But as Japanese industrialization was based on textiles, there was less competition than in Germany or the United States from large manufacturers of advanced products. Unlike in Britain, there were no well-developed commodity and financial markets to support small specialized firms. Instead, growth was extremely fast and unsettled. Few firms under these conditions had the skills to trade overseas, leaving those that had such skills

TABLE 1   Cotton Sales for Sprunts, 1902–1910, and Anderson, Clayton, 1925–1938.

Bales of cotton purchased or sold	(annual wage)			
Alexander Sprunt and Son	1902–5	296,000	1907–10	382,000
Anderson Clayton	1925–28	2,087,000	1936–38	2,288,000

Source: Firms' Archives in Wilmington, N. C., and Houston, Tex.

with oligopolistic advantages and an incentive to internalize the supporting functions. Government and society also favored domestic firms, and it was difficult for outsiders to intrude. These special circumstances restrained the development of specialized methods, and Mitsui and other firms could often safely (until 1921) make large profits trading unhedged cotton on their own account. Of course their administrative apparatus developed as they grew in size, and as overseas companies they had a special emphasis on foreign education. Thus although initially the backbone of many of these firms was cotton, as Professor Kuwahara maintains, in my opinion, they continuously had wider interests and experience than the American specialists, and this was a good preparation for their later development into *sōgō shōsha* (general trading companies).

The Rise of International Commodity Trading Companies in Europe in the Nineteenth Century

Philippe Chalmin
Conservatoire National des Arts et Métiers

The growth of general trading companies in Japan since the end of the 19th century is well known. Nowadays one is not likely to find an equivalent to the Japanese *sōgō shōsha*, which not only dominate Japanese external trade but are deeply engaged in offshore operations. By comparison, their European counterparts are limited to postcolonial operations and lack their links with local industrial and business communities, as well as their worldwide systems of communication and logistics.[1] The only field in which European companies have maintained a certain leadership through the years is commodity trade, and as a matter of fact, the only companies that can be compared with the Japanese Mitsuis or Mitsubishis are a handful of international commodity trading companies based in Europe and in the United States. The purpose of this paper is to show the historical context of their birth and development in the 19th century. The analysis will mainly focus on Europe, and especially on Great Britain and France.

On the eve of the 19th century European international trade was still much dominated by the so-called India companies, which held monopolies in numerous parts of the world for Britain, the Low Countries, France, and many lesser countries. In the course of the centuries those monopolies were abolished, but some companies managed to survive even to this day (like Hudson's Bay Co., founded in 1670). They were replaced by a first category of actors that we'll call *colonial traders*. Meanwhile, the development of European ports and the needs of nascent industrial production

TABLE 1   Examples of Companies Operating within a Colonial Empire.

Country with a colonial empire	Company	Location of headquarters	Year of founding
France	CFAO	Marseille	1834
	SCOA		
	Niger Français		
United Kingdom	United Africa Co.	London	(merger in 1929 but parts as early as 1865)
	John Holt & Co.	London	
	Booker McConnell	Liverpool	1834
	Dalgety	Melbourne	1842
Netherlands	Internatio	Rotterdam	1863
	Curaçaoshe	Curaçao	
	Borsumij	Batavia	1883
	Wehry	Batavia	1867
Belgium	Société Anversoise du commerce du Congo	Anvers	1891

induced the development of *harbor traders*, who had direct relationships with overseas counterparts and specialized in export or import. As relations grew more direct between producers and consumers, a need was felt for an intermediary who could handle information and quickly link demand to offer or vice versa. This was the age of the *brokers*, who from 1850 to 1950 were indeed the main participants in international trade. Finally, for some specific products like grains or metals, for which the size of the market was truly international, there have appeared, since the beginning of this century, *trading companies*, which are generally specialized in one category of product or another and which have known a tremendous growth since the 1960s.

Colonial traders, harbor or import-export traders, brokers, trading companies—such are the four categories of operators that we'll try now to analyze in their historical context.

I. The Colonial Traders

The French Revolution marked an end to the era of the India companies. Some managed to survive, but on a fairly diminished scale.[2] Their place was taken by trading companies operating within the limits of colonial empires or competing on certain open markets like China, Russia, or South America. Four countries were mainly concerned with colonial empires: the United Kingdom and the Netherlands and on a lesser scale France and Belgium (See Table 1). In the British Empire emerged a number of companies that specialized in colonial trade and often monopolized trade between Britain and a particular colony. Such was the case for the United Africa Co. and for John Holt and Co. in British Africa. In 1929 the United Africa Co., which resulted from the merger of the Royal Niger Co. and the African and Eastern Trading Co., accounted for 60% of the palm oil, 45% of the palm kernel, 60% of the groundnuts, and 50% of the cocoa exports of the British West African colonies (Nigeria, Gold Coast, Sierra Leone).[3]

In exchange for buying primary commodities from the colonies, these companies exported British manufactured products. But they almost never had direct links with British industrial firms. When Unilever formed UAC in 1929, it was more with a logic of diversification from its more traditional plantation activity than with an intention of integrating colonial markets for its British-made products.[4] The same could be said when John Holt was bought in 1969 by Lonrho. In fact, colonial traders generally emanated from business circles in ports like London or Liverpool. They acquired trading points along the coasts and often indulged in commodity production: sugar in the West Indies (Booker MacConnell, for example), rubber in Malaysia (Guthrie), and so on.

One can say almost the same in the case of the French colonial empire, where trade was dominated by companies like SCOA, CFAO, and Maurel et Prom originating from such ports as Bordeaux or Marseille. (For more details on French trade organization see Appendix A.) For the Low Countries the main area of expansion was the Dutch East Indies, where companies like Internatio, Borsumij, and Wehry emerged. Belgium was in some ways a particular case, as all trading interests in the Belgian Congo were linked to financial groups associated with King Leopold II.

A second category of colonial traders operated in areas which were not formally colonies but were quite open to outside interests. China was the most important of these. As early as 1834, in the wake

TABLE 2   Companies Operating in Open Markets.

Open Market	Company	Company's home country	Location of headquarters	Year of founding
Asia	C. Olivier	France	Shanghai	1888
	Melchers Co.	Germany	China	1806
	Annold Otto Meyer	Germany	Singapore	1840
	C. Illies	Germany	Nagasaki	1859
	Volkart Gebr.	Switzerland	Bombay	1851
	Jardine, Matheson & Co.	U.K.	Canton	1832
	Swire Pacific	U.K.	Shanghai	1866
	East Asiatic Co.	Denmark	Thailand	1884
Latin America	Balfour Williamson	U.K.	Liverpool	
Russia	Optorg	France		1905

of the abolishment of the East India Co.'s monopoly on the tea trade, the first British traders appeared—Jardine, Matheson & Co., founded in Canton. But one can also name the French Compagnie Olivier (in Ningpo near Shanghai in 1888), the German Melchers (in China in 1806) and others (see Table 2). Here again these companies had few industrial links with their mother countries but were mostly engaged in commodity trade and transport activity. Some were also engaged in industrial activities: Jardine, Matheson owned two sugar refineries in China and Butterfield & Swire owned one in Hong Kong (Taikoo Sugar Refinery). Apart from Asia, Russia was, before 1917, a good "hunting ground": in 1905 the French company Optorg was founded in order to develop trade with that country. One could give numerous other examples for Latin America, the Middle East, and Africa.

So the general characteristic of European colonial traders appears to have been a development of activities linked only tenuously to the industrial activities that would later be important. Originating from trading circles at European ports, they were more concerned with commodity production and transport. Their golden era was the period between the world wars, when they typically dominated the economies of their respective colonies. But with the decolonization that began in the 1950s, they found difficulties in adapting themselves to the new political conditions (especially the development of state trading corporations and marketing boards, which cut them from commodity trade). In Africa, French and British companies generally stayed and became more involved in the distribution of goods (even owning supermarkets). The British companies in China retreated to Hong Kong where for about 30 years they have dominated the economy. But apart from a few cases, it can be said that the era of colonial traders is definitely finished.

II. The Harbor or Import-Export Traders

That category of operators which emerged in the course of the 19th century is more difficult to define, due to its extreme heterogeneity. Each great harbor—Hamburg, Bremen, London, Liverpool, Le Havre, Bordeaux, Marseille—generated a good number of traders more or less specialized by category of products. On the import side one found numerous firms dealing in tropical products, metals, or other primary commodities and playing the role of wholesale distributors. In Britain, Joseph Travers and Sons, a very old established company going back at least to the Great Fire of London in 1666, is one of the most interesting examples of such an undertaking. In 1779 it was known under the name of Smith, Nash, Kemble and Travers and was located in Cannon Street, London, at the "Sugar Loaf."

The main products handled were tea and sugar, later spices and dried fruit. The Travers firm owned and published the daily *Producer's Market Review*, which was, with the *Public Ledger*, one of the chief organs of the fiercely free-trade British commercial community. In 1899 it opened a branch in Singapore for the purpose of exporting spices and tinned pineapple. Other agencies were subsequently opened in Malaysia, Indonesia, and later in Borneo. Thus around 1930, Travers began to develop into a true international trader in spices and tropical fruits.[5] Other major firms were James Budgett of London, S. W. Berisford of Manchester, Billingtons of Liverpool, and Swiffens of Birmingham. S. W. Berisford was already one of the largest firms in domestic trade in refined sugar. In Switzerland, the firm founded by Georges André in 1877 was, in 1914, one of the major grain importers in the country. In France, one can give the names of Hecht Frères, specializing in rubber and Raoul Duval, trading in coffee in Le Havre, among others.

Germany was a case in itself: without a colonial empire it developed a very active import trade in tropical products at the Hanseatic ports of Hamburg and Bremen. On the other hand, the export side was treated by *Export Vertreters* in Hamburg, Bremen, and the Ruhr. There the trading companies were linked with the powerful industrial groups which dominated the German economy: Thyssen, Stinnes, Klöckner. It is, to my knowledge, one of the few cases where the European experience can be linked with the Japanese one.

I won't say much more on this category of operators, which, on the whole, was not so important. In fact, a lot of commodity or industrial companies preferred to act as their own traders, using brokers for their information and their knowledge of markets.

III. The Commodity Brokers

Before 1945, the international intermediaries par excellence were the brokers who received a commission for transactions which they carried out on behalf of another. Business would be conducted either on behalf of the buyer (the buying brokers) or the seller (the selling brokers). Very often it was they who organized the auctions (still on the model of those of the East India Co.). The London Commercial Sale Rooms at Mincing Lane in London opened their doors in 1881 and continued to function until 1920; today, however, eight brokerage firms are responsible for the tea auctions which are held in London.

The brokers circulated information, organized auctions, or, quite to the contrary, represented industrialists in the conduct of business with importers. But the role of the brokers can only be fully understood through a closer study of these operations.

James Man, born in 1754, started out as a wet cooper.[6] In 1792 he joined up with another cooper, William Humphrey, and became a broker. And so it was that on March 26, 1795, they were selling "by the candle" at Garraway's coffee shop in London the following merchandise:

    50 hogsheads of refined sugar for export
  250 hogsheads of refined sugar for export
  100 bags of black and white ginger
    20 goads [?] of Barbados aloes
1200 skins from the West Indies
    50 bags of cocoa

On February 11, 1796, James Man advertised for sale on his own premises:

    25 hogsheads of sugar
  205 casks and 60 bags of Jamaican coffee
  237 bags of black ginger
    84 bags of white ginger
    36 bags of cotton
    30 tonnes of bark
    30 goads [?] of Barbados aloes
     1 cask of tortoise shell
     8 casks of indigo
    50 barrels of Carolina rice

The merchandise for sale was generally recorded in a catalogue which the broker prepared and distributed on the eve of the sale. Brokers therefore acted either on behalf of the producer or the merchant-exporter, with whose assistance they established a catalogue and estimated the value of the lots. Their commission, payable by the seller, was generally 0.5%. Brokers thus played a fundamental role in the circulation of information. As a rule, each brokerage firm also published a weekly bulletin on the markets of the products which it traded. Thus for sugar there was Czarnikow in London and Lamborn and Farr in New York.

Under various company names, Man continued its brokerage activities throughout the 19th century, moving in 1808 to Mincing Lane, which was at the time—and has remained to a great extent—the center of the London commodities trade. Man remained first and foremost a colonial broker, specializing gradually in sugar, rum (in 1870 the company became a broker for the Admiralty, procuring the rum distributed daily to the sailors), cocoa, coffee, and spices. Twice monthly Man published a circular containing

TABLE 3   Some Great British Brokerage Firms.

First company name	Present name	Year of founding	Kind of trade
Allen and Woodhouse	Woodhouse Drake & Carey	1748	colonial
Robert Lewis	Lewis and Peat	1775	general
Humphrey and Man	Ed. F. Man	1792	colonial
Rucker and Bencraft		1780	general
Hale and Sons		1780	general
Paines and Read		1815	general
John Drake	Woodhouse, Drake & Carey	1825	coffee
James Carey	Woodhouse, Drake & Carey	1820	colonial
J. Rouse	R. J. Rouse (Mercantile House)	1840	general
Arthur B. Hodge	Ed. F. Man	1850	sugar
Czarnikow	Czarnikow Ltd.	1861	sugar
Golodetz	Golodetz	1908	sugar
Farr (New York)		1920	sugar

information on the market. Gradually the auctions were abandoned and the company became an intermediary operating on order both in actuals and on paper.[7]

Mark Woodhouse started out as a sugar broker around 1767. Before long he became a factor for a number of Jamaican planters, whose sugar he sold. On August 7, 1816, he organized a sale "by the candle" of pepper, ginger, coffee, and cocoa. The Woodhouse firm continued to grow, specializing, in the twenties, in the sale of coffee from Central America. In 1926, it merged with Carey and Browne (James Carey had been a coffee broker since 1825). In 1899 Carey and Browne had organized the largest auction of coffee in human memory: 13,121 bags were sold in three days. In the thirties, Woodhouse Carey and Browne became involved in trade, notably in sugar. But this brings us to the dawn of a new period.[8]

It was in 1775 that Robert Lewis began to organize auctions of colonial produce. His son Arthur pursued these activities, holding sales at the famous Garraway coffee shop. Renamed Lewis and Peat in 1846, the firm continued to expand, opening an office in Singapore in 1919. In the twenties, it was the largest produce broker in the city.

London's foremost sugar broker around 1880 was Czarnikow and Co., founded in 1861 by a German emigrant, Cesar Czarnikow, who started out as a sworn broker. Czarnikow gradually took charge of sales for a number of West Indian producers—and even those of the Colonial Co. from 1897—and before long began to publish a weekly price list which was the information authority on the market. He was the first to introduce beet-sugar trading in Great Britain and opened branches in Glasgow (1871), Liverpool (1881), and New York (1891).

Following his death in 1909, the firm continued to grow and was, in all likelihood, the world's foremost sugar broker in the thirties.[9] The sugar broker was responsible for bringing the more or less regrouped exporters into contact with one another. Thus Czarnikow was, from 1923, the exclusive agent of Colonial Sugar Refining, the company which accounted for all Australian sugar exports.

In the field of sugar and colonial produce there were also a number of particularly outstanding British firms. These are listed in Table 3.

Prominent among the French firms was Duclos et Fils, founded by Maurice Duclos in 1874, with a range of trade goods extending from nonferrous metals and colonial foodstuffs to a royal Siamese elephant and a portion of the gold from the roofs of the Kremlin churches sold to the West by the Soviets around 1920.[10]

The first French broker to enter the grain trade was J. A. Goldschmidt. Founded in 1866 in Mulhouse by Elie and Aaron Goldschmidt, the firm specialized in the brokerage of wheats and flours. Having started on the domestic market, the Goldschmidts expanded to the international market at the end of the century and opened branches in Antwerp (1908), Naples (1919), and Marseille (1920).

At that time, Goldschmidt represented some 10 American and, before 1914, Russian export firms in France selling either directly to the millers or to merchant-importers. Michel Goldschmidt describes for us an example of how a typical transaction was executed in the thirties: at 11 p.m. the Paris office would receive coded cables from Chicago. After they had been decoded, offers would be dispatched at midnight to the Mediterranean Basin for reply on the following day at 2 p.m., in time for the opening of the Chicago market at 3:30 p.m. The operations were small ones: very often

1,000 quarters, the equivalent of 217 tonnes. Until about 1930, Australian wheat was transported in 300 to 500 tonne sailboats, making it possible for the end-users—the millers—to import directly.[11] Transactions were carried out according to the standard forms of contracts established by the Grain and Feed Trade Association, which contained provisions against all possible disputes.[12]

As we can see, in view of the quantities dealt in and the general climate of commercial security, it was possible to import or export directly, a development which rendered superfluous the services of international traders. It was the brokers who acted as intermediaries, although they never appeared as principals in the transactions, their responsibility coming to an end as soon as the contract was signed.

In general the brokers were also active on the futures market and in France they were known as *commissionaires*. Most often they also had to guarantee the successful outcome of transactions in as much as produce clearinghouses were not prevalent until much later and were not necessarily obligatory to use. Although the London clearinghouses were established as early as the end of the 19th century, a clearinghouse for the Parisian market, for example, was not set up until the twenties. The brokers were therefore obliged to protect themselves by making regular margin calls on their clients. Margin calls notwithstanding, dealing in futures could be a rather risky activity. Speculation on the European sugar markets caused many a brokerage firm to go out of business, notably in 1905.[13]

On the other hand, brokers only infrequently doubled as traders. They would, however, do so on occasion, especially when precise regulations called for it, but in general the separation of the professions was rather strict, and the brokers—at least those who managed to survive over a long period of time—likewise refrained from speculating for their own accounts. But it is difficult to generalize on this level: Czarnikow, a firm mentioned above, was not only the world's foremost sugar broker, but it also possessed a produce department responsible for a number of other products and was, especially in the thirties, the world's foremost pepper merchant, with almost 55% of world exports.[14]

Brokers were, not infrequently, called upon to deal in several products at the same time, although a distinction was made in fact between the colonial brokers, who dealt in a range of products, from sugar to coffee through spices, the grain brokers (who also dealt in certain oilseeds), the metal brokers, and others who specialized in one kind of product or another. Finally, alongside the great international firms, there were numerous national, departmental, and even cantonal brokerage firms.

The brokers, whose basic capital was the possession of information and the control of the means of communication, reached the height of their development at the end of the 19th century and the beginning of the 20th century. As soon as their capital had lost its strategic value, the brokers' function was stripped of its importance. Between the 16th century, the age of the merchant, and the 19th century, the age of the broker, there was a transition from goods to services, just as in a parallel field there was a transition from goods to banking with the introduction of acceptance and bills of exchange.

With the development of communications, the importance of brokers diminished. With the rise of international risks (financial, monetary, political), their service was insufficient. Soon after the Second World War, most international brokerage firms either disappeared or adapted and became traders.[15]

IV. The International Commodity Traders

International commodity traders are companies engaged in offshore international trade without special reference to their mother country, but following the main fluxes of exchanges. Of such a type had been the great companies which dominated European trade in the 14th and 15th centuries (the Fugger, Welser, and other Ravensburger *Gesellschaft*). They vanished in the following centuries but reappeared with the free-trade era in the second half of the 19th century. The first generation of companies could be called general merchant shipping firms. As we can understand, the transport side of the business was important, as was the financial one: companies like Alexander Brown and Sons or, even better, Baring Brothers were good examples.[16] They dealt in cotton or grain or even more elaborated products during the first half of the 19th century. As time went on, most of these firms either withdrew from trading to concentrate on banking or shipping functions (Barings in banking, for example) or specialized in a narrower range of commodities. The case of grain is, in that respect, of some interest. In the 19th century, the great export centers were North America and, even greater, Russia. (Argentina and Australia came to the fore only around 1920.) Until 1913 it was Russian wheat which filled the breadbaskets of Europe. From the 18th century, the Russian wheat trade was controlled by Greek merchants who dispatched shipments from the port of Odessa: around 1850, the Baltic Exchange of London, then the nerve center of the grain trade in Europe, counted some 300 Greek members out of a total of 400.[17]

It was in 1818 that John and Eustratio Ralli set up in London and began to deal in silk and grains. The Rallis were a family of five brothers: John and Eustratio in London, Auguste in Marseille, Thomas in Constantinople, Pandia in London at first and later in Odessa. In 1850 they opened branches in Calcutta and then in Bombay.[18] They were in New York in 1870.

From 1870, the Greek firms began to encounter serious competition from the European firms. Leopold Louis Dreyfus, originally from the Upper Rhine, had started out in 1850 as a grain merchant in Basel. From 1860, he dealt with the countries along the Danube. In 1872, he settled in Marseille and began to take an interest in Russian wheat, setting up an agency in Odessa. In 1902, he had his first ship built and around the same time opened a banking department.[19]

The British were no less active: the firm Ross T. Smith and Co. of Liverpool, had branches in Trieste, New York, Odessa, Rostoff, Karachi, and Buenos Aires. In 1877, the Crédit Lyonnais, which had just set up operations in Russia, even envisaged extending its activities to wheat by shipping Ukrainian wheat through the Baltic ports. The project never materialized.[20] The main problem on the Russian end of the chain was the lack of an effective collection and storage system: in 1913, the Russian Agricultural Bank decided to finance the construction of 83 elevators (13 of which were constructed by July 1914).

Although not a major exporter before 1914, North America had already composed an elaborate grain-collection system, connecting local silos to terminals on all the major routes. The American merchants Rosenbaum, who dominated the Chicago market, and P. N. Gray, associated from 1920 with Bunge, Cargill in the Great Plains, were, nevertheless, by no means active in international trade before 1935.

Argentinian grain exports were dominated by foreign firms. In 1910, three firms accounted for 80% of exports: Bunge and Born, founded in 1884 in Buenos Aires and associated with Bunge and Co. of Antwerp (founded in Amsterdam in 1818), Louis Dreyfus et Cie, and Weil Brothers.[21] At the end of the twenties, Bunge and Born accounted for one third of all Argentinian grain exports.

All the same, the grain trade offered the only examples, before 1939, of multinational undertakings. Some firms were in fact present both on the producer markets and on certain consumer markets: Louis Dreyfus and Bunge and Born were the most interesting cases before 1939. The same can be said of the Liverpool-based Ralli Brothers, which moved from grain to cotton trading.

Apart from grain and cotton, it was in metals that one found a number of international traders. Most of them originated in Germany, which at that time was leading the European metal expansion and where the tradition of the metal trade went back to the Fugger's time. In 1881, an Englishman, Wilhelm Merton, founded the Metallgesellschaft. From trading, the company went into industry and especially metal refining (with subsidiaries like Hoboken in Belgium) and seems to have dominated the European metal trade before 1914. Other companies to be mentioned are Philipp Brothers, founded in Hamburg around the middle of the 19th century, established in England around 1900 and in New York in 1914, and Lissauer founded in Cologne at the turn of the century.

The commodity trading companies remained rather marginal apart from a few particular fields till around 1950. At that time, conditions of world trade changed dramatically—colonial empires collapsed, plantations and mines were often nationalized, vertically integrated companies had to adapt—and finally in 1973 the world monetary and financial systems exploded. Risks—of any nature— mounted and so did the importance of traders able to cover those risks. The growth of international commodity trading companies was thus extraordinary. Companies like Philipp Brothers, Cargill,

Richco, and Louis Dreyfus became in a few years the world's biggest traders, diversified into industry and services.[22] They are the only challengers that Europe and the United States can offer to the trading empires of the Japanese sōgō shōsha.

The situation described here lasted roughly from the end of the 19th century till immediately after the Second World War. Then the collapse of colonial empires, coupled with the rise of nationalism in many countries, provoked the end of the colonial traders as such. Most companies indeed survived, developing activities in real estate (in Hong Kong), plantations (in Malaysia), distribution (in Africa), but they scarcely reached their old level of power. Most harbor traders have also disappeared: with the development of efficient communications systems, the exact location of a company's headquarters is not of much importance. Apart from the firms which have developed on a national or international basis (Toppfer in Hamburg, Man Produkten in Rotterdam), most others have seen their activities reduced and eventually stopped. The contrary can be said for brokers: they have survived on a local basis (generally as one-person companies), but have been swept away on international markets, where they are not needed any more. A lot of old brokerage houses have survived by becoming commodity traders.

International commodity traders have been the category on the rise. It can be said that nowadays the biggest part of world commodity trade (worth about $1,000 billion), is handled by no more than 50 companies based in Europe and North America (the biggest are Cargill from the United States and Philipp Brothers, also from the United States). Some of these companies have invested in industry and now head industrial empires: in food, Cargill is probably the third largest company in the world, and Bunge and Born is the biggest in Latin America. Every day on world markets they are competing with the Japanese sōgō shōsha, which at the same time have emerged as truly international traders.

NOTES*

1. It is interesting to see how governments (U.S.A., Korea, Malaysia, Brazil) are keen to develop Japanese-style trading companies, with for the moment very little success.

2. In fact, at the end of the 19th century one saw a revival of the concept of charter companies within the British Empire: British North Borneo Co. (1881), Royal Niger Co. (1886), and of course the British South Africa Co. (the famous "chartered" of Cecil Rhodes).

3. Bertrand Berlan, *Unilever une multinationale discrète*, Paris, 1978, p. 87.

4. It seems that the first motivation of Lord Leverhulme's decision to buy first the Niger Co. in 1920 and then in 1929 to merge it with the African and Eastern Trade Corp. was to secure raw materials (palm oil from Nigeria) for its British factories. But quickly that aspect vanished and the companies operated quite independently. See Charles Wilson, *The History of Unilever*, London, 1951, Vol. 1, p. 252.

5. Joseph Travers and Sons, "A Few Records of an Old Firm," London, May 1924; *idem*, "Chronicles of Cannon Street," London, 1953. On the eve of World War II, Travers had 117 employees.

6. The fact that most merchandise was transported in casks explains the importance of this profession, whose members were often actively involved in trade. See Tim Dumas, "The House of Man," 1966.

7. Man is nowadays one of the biggest sugar traders in the world.

8. C. H. Woodhouse, *The Woodhouses, Drakes, and Careys of Mincing Lane*, London, 1977.

9. Hurtford Janes and H. J. Sayers, *The Story of Czarnikow*, London, 1963.

10. "Les fils et les petits-fils de Maurice Duclos: 1874–1974," Internal publication.

11. Archives of the Goldschmidt firm. The Goldschmidt code books, published in 1908, are interesting reading: on the export end we find at least 20 American shippers, but on the import end in Italy, where Goldschmidt was particularly active, we find a considerable

---

* This paper is based on material gathered for a book on the subject of international commodity traders. Most of the information comes from interviews and company histories which were never published.

number of importers and, especially, a great many millers and pasta manufacturers (no fewer than 20 for the town of Florence alone).

12. The Grain and Feed Trade Association (GAFTA) was located in London at the Baltic Exchange.

13. See Jacques Fierain, *Les Raffineries de sucre des ports de France (XIXè début du XXè)*, Lille, 1976, p. 175. Note that in those days brokerage firms were most often private firms and were therefore responsible to the extent of their own assets. In some of the articles published in the *Journal des Fabricants de sucre* (JFS) in connection with the crash of 1905 we can find scenes worthy of Balzac's "Cesar Birotteau."

14. Janes and Sayers, *op. cit.*, p. 79. Pepper was, however, perhaps a special case, given the extremely speculative nature of the market. In 1935 one of London's brokerage firms, James and Shakespeare, tried to corner the pepper market after having successfully cornered the shellac market in 1934. Its failure led to the bankruptcy of many brokerage firms, among them, one of the oldest, Rolls and Sons. See *ibid.*, p. 92, A. Dauphin Meunier, *La City de Londres*, Paris, 1940, p. 81.

15. There are still some international brokers, but of a lesser importance. For example, one can estimate that three grain brokers do account for 5%–10% of international grain trade.

16. Morton Rothstein, "Multinationals in the Grain Trade, 1850–1914," in J. Attack, ed., *Business and Economic History*, 2d ser., Vol. 12, 1983.

17. G. L. Rees, *Britain's Commodity Markets*, London, 1975, p. 130.

18. "History and Activities of the Ralli Trading Company," Internal publication, London, 1979.

19. Louis Dreyfus Co. internal publication, undated. In the interwar period, one of Leopold's sons, Louis Louis Dreyfus, was to play a prominent role in French political life.

20. Jean Bouvier, *Naissance d'une banque: le Crédit Lyonnais*, Paris, 1968, p. 227.

21. Raul H. Green, Catherine Laurent, *Bunge and Born: Histoire d'un secret bien gardé*, Paris, 1984.

22. See Philippe Chalmin, *Négociants et chargeurs*, 2d ed., Paris, 1985.

APPENDIX: Notes on the Development of French Trade Organization in the Nineteenth Century

During the 19th century, the role of France in world trade declined quite abruptly, from 12.7% in 1875 to 7.6% in 1913, taking fourth place after Britain, Germany, and the United States. This does not reflect the place of the French economy and finances on the world scene, as France ranked second only to Britain regarding the export of capital and money.

French external trade was never dominant in the French economy and was in fact looked on as a secondary matter by French politicians and industrialists. The first and foremost reason was the lack of a proper trading organization. This can be explained by French business thought and practice.

I. Trade as a Parasitic Activity

The 19th century saw in France the emancipation of industry from trading interests. Traders, who had helped initiate the first industrial revolution at the end of the 18th century, became industrialists to an ever greater degree. In fact, the whole industrial world saw the marketing of goods as a more and more ancillary activity. The following quotation from the great French politician, Louis Thiers, written in 1851, is interesting in this regard:

> In England, the manager (or owner) of a factory can't be a trader. In France, the factoryman from Roubaix or Lille comes to Paris when his workers are at work; he divides his time in two parts: he is an industrialist and a bit of a trader and there is no intermediary between him and the retailer. As in England, there are three or four traders who buy linens as wholesalers and then sell them either in England or abroad. Besides those traders, there are wholesalers who sell those linens in 300- or 400-piece lots. Then there is the retailer who sells by twos or threes. Between production and the consumer, two or three intermediaries take all the benefit.

This text illustrates very clearly the first disease of French trade: the determination of the industry to do its marketing itself. But a job half done is a job badly done, and this was particularly true for external trade. Another problem was that French products, under the protection of high tariff barriers after 1875, were expensive on world markets.

The second disease was the belief in the quality and good taste of French products. Cognac, champagne, perfumes, and fashion were almost too easily sold. Why bother to send representatives abroad or to appoint traders when it was so easy to export certain products characteristic of French *bon gout*.

Those two problems combined explain the weakness of the French trading presence abroad.

II. French Weaknesses

The first weakness was the lack of proper trading companies. The only exceptions were the companies working in colonial Africa (SCOA, CFAO), which benefited from the lack of competition. One might also mention some companies in Asia (Olivier) or Russia (Optorg), but it would be difficult to find a name in North or South America. In fact, it appears that French trading companies were far more efficient on the import side of external trade and were even selling raw materials to third countries. Such was the case for grain traders operating out of Russia and the Balkan countries (Louis Dreyfus), for silk merchants working in Asia for factories in Lyon, and even for some colonial products traders. But Paris never succeeded in becoming a world market for commodities, as Liverpool did for cotton or London for metals (and even Hamburg for sugar). The crash of the Comptoir d'Escompte in 1889 after the famous Secretan corner on the world copper market marked the end of French ambitions in that field.

But apart from traders, French manufacturers had fewer representatives abroad than manufacturers in other countries had. First, there were fewer and less important French communities: in Odessa, so important for grain trade, one counted in 1910, 12,000 Germans for only 300 French people. In fact, French interests there were represented by Greeks. At the beginning of the 20th century there was a great effort to induce young graduates to work abroad, but too few responded positively. The commercial presence was at the same level: it was only in 1908 that six diplomatic posts were given a commercial attaché (Britain, Germany, Russia, Turkey, Asia, and Latin America). Even when official inducement existed, what was lacking was the will of manufacturers. A good example is what happened in 1897. One of the biggest French successes in the field of trading was the new concept of *grands magasins* (multistores), developed in the 1840s by Boucicaut with his Le Bon Marché and soon imitated in France and abroad (with stores like Harrod's or Selfridge's in London). In 1897 the French Foreign Office proposed using multistores opened in new markets to sell French products. The idea was a good one and could benefit from the then-high reputation of French fashion. Some store developers were interested: E. Cognacq, owner of La Samaritaine, proposed opening outlets in Germany, Britain, Belgium, and the Netherlands. The Magasins du Louvre opened a successful store in St. Petersburg. But the idea eventually collapsed from lack of interest from the manufacturers.

The manufacturers were not the only ones so chary of external trade. French banks were far more interested in dealing with the budgetary problems of foreign countries and in negotiating state or city loans than in helping French exporters. Apart perhaps from the Comptoir d' Escompte in Asia, the Banque du Nord, subsidiary of the Société Generale, in Russia, French traders did not find much help in their banking institutions: to develop his own trading activities, the grain trader Louis Dreyfus had to create his own bank. Further, France lacked a really efficient system of "accepting houses" (known in Britain as discount houses): in 1913, London had an "accepting market" of 8 billion francs, when Paris had only 1 billion. In fact, there was no equivalent to the very concept of merchant bankers, exemplified by Barings (former grain and cotton merchants), Lazard, or Hambro. On that aspect, it is interesting to compare the strategies of the French and of the English sides of the Rothschild family.

To conclude this short note on French trade organization in the 19th and early 20th centuries, it can be said that trading companies were very secondary to manufacturing industries and banks and had no real opportunity nor desire to develop. In the colonies, their power was something of a myth and Jacques Marseille has clearly shown that they were less important than banks, mining companies, and even local manufacturers. No equivalent to the British or to the German models can be found.

Comment

Matao Miyamoto
Osaka University

To begin with, I would like to express my gratitude to Professor Chalmin for giving us valuable information about the history of the European trading companies. As a Japanese historian who knows little about European history, I have learned a great deal about how different types of operator have in turn taken the leadership in the international trade in Europe.

In order to understand his paper better and to achieve a better comparison between European and Japanese trading companies, I would like to raise a few questions, all of which are very simple.

1. Professor Chalmin categorized the European trading operators into four types: colonial traders, harbor traders, brokers, and international commodity traders (trading companies). This categorization is very helpful in understanding what kinds of change have occurred on the scene of international trade. Because of my lack of knowledge about the subject, however, it is hard for me to identify the functional and temporal differences in these four categories. I would like to ask Professor Chalmin for some additional explanation in this regard. For instance, to what extent does the categorization by Professor Chalmin coincide with that made by Professor Yoshihara in his opening paper here at the Fuji Conference, namely, the classification of highly specialized, area-specialized, and goods-specialized trading companies, and *sōgō shōsha* (general trading companies)?

2. The second question relates to the first. What kinds of connection did European trading operators have with domestic distributors? The Japanese sōgō shōsha have acted sometimes as brokers, sometimes as wholesalers, and sometimes as agencies. In addition, they have traditionally helped other distributors with advanced or

deferred payment plans. With these functions the sōgō shōsha have successfully systematized a domestic distribution channel of their own. I would like to know whether or not the situation in Europe differed from the one in Japan.

3. My third question concerns the European international commodity traders. Professor Chalmin argues that the international commodity traders are by now the only challenger that Europe and the United States can offer to the Japanese sōgō shōsha with their trading empires. In that case, is there any possibility that these commodity traders, who have so far specialized in some specific goods, will become sōgō shōsha in the future? I would like to know how Professor Chalmin evaluates the likelihood. The reason I want to raise this question is that it is related to the question, Under what conditions do sōgō shōsha emerge?

Response

Philippe Chalmin

On the second and third points, I would like to stress that European companies lack the backing of an industrial "group" like the *sōgō shōsha* have. I don't think that commodity traders, in particular, will ever have the opportunity of becoming *sōgō shōsha*.

The Export Organization of the German Economy

Wilfried Feldenkirchen
Universität Bonn

I

Export trade and industry, a component factor of the marketing objectives of an enterprise, comprises all efforts that have to be made in the raw materials, investment, and consumer goods markets when export goods and commodities are transferred to foreign customers. The sales-oriented economy of the domestic market is complemented by the functions and risks of the export trade and industry that result from geographical distances and linguistic barriers, as well as from differences in mentality and requirements. The term *export organization*, in this context, is understood to mean the systematic cooperation of economic institutions in the transfer of export goods and commodities into a respective market.[1]

A study of the export organization of the German economy before World War II is nonexistent. The quantitative and qualitative development of German foreign trade has been looked into fairly intensively on the basis of—not always reliable—statistical surveys,[2] which, however, correctly reflect the tendencies. But there can be no question of a comprehensive investigation of the export organization.[3]

The research papers relevant to German foreign trade emphasize the schools of thought dealing with sales-oriented export strategies. It is impossible to obtain exact data on the export-oriented branches of German industry for the pre-World War II period because the publications of individual companies (e.g., company records and histories) furnish merely scanty concrete information. Only a system-

295

atic investigation of company archives would yield comprehensive data.[4]

My study will cover the period from the middle of the 19th century until the end of the Weimar Republic (1919–33). It will deal in depth—for factual reasons—with the period between 1870 and 1933. It will start with the 1850s, when the process of industrialization in Germany entered the phase of economic takeoff and an increased world-economic integration. It will view in perspective the years between the end of World War I and the peak of the Great Depression, because the outcome of the war and the clauses of the Versailles Treaty determined the scope and the organization of the German export trade before the Nazis set the German export trade new targets together with a new organization.

Between 1850 and 1933 the export organization of the German economy underwent considerable changes in the period of necessary adaptation to the changes in production structures and in foreign markets. Within the period under investigation there were three single factors which, however, had no direct effect on the size of exports but were instrumental in changing the export organization: mergers of enterprises and the trend toward the formation of major business combines; the growing importance of the production of capital goods; and the expansion of transportation and communication services.[5]

The move toward economic concentration that had been noticeable in all branches of industry since the 1870s had inevitable consequences for the export industry, in particular for certain product divisions of individual enterprises. The horizontal and vertical growth of the enterprises made it necessary to develop new forms of sales organization in the domestic as well as in foreign markets. The major firms benefited from more favorable conditions for their independent handling of exports because they were better equipped to fund the build-up of a cost-intensive export organization of their own.[6]

Concurrent with the shift in emphasis to the secondary sector of the economy as a whole during the industrialization phase, this sector underwent a restructuring process which expressed itself in the rising importance of the capital goods industries. This shift in weight also affected the export organization. As a result of the smaller number of customers,[7] the (high) value of the contract, the professional and technical expertise expected from the producer and its sales organization, explanations and instructions required by the user for the proper handling of the goods and/or machinery, and the need for subsequent repair and maintenance services, the sale of capital goods in foreign markets required more direct contacts between producer/exporter and user than did the sale of consumer goods.[8]

The extension of transportation and communication services had similar consequences. Shipments were speeded up and transportation costs lowered. The transmission and execution of orders as well as the observation and analysis of markets were facilitated by the use of telephony and telegraphy. New markets became thus accessible to sections of the export industry that had, up to then, only been open to well-established firms. Contacts between producer/exporter and user/customer no longer required the services of intermediaries and their communication facilities.[9]

All these new factors not only exerted a favorable influence on exports as a whole but also caused a shift of priorities within the export organization. These changes will be discussed in Part III. I shall now give a short overview of the quantitative and qualitative evolution of German foreign trade during the period under investigation.

II

The beginning of railroad construction, the foundation of the Deutsche Zollverein (German Customs Union) and the setting-up of large-scale manufacturing enterprises in the textile and engineering industries, as well as considerable production hikes in the coal-mining and metal-working industries, created between 1835 and 1849 the conditions for the process of industrialization in Germany that set in suddenly after 1850.[10] The growth of the German economy proceeded without major interruptions from the middle of the 19th century until World War I. The years 1873–80 were an exception. Assisted by the favorable consequences of Germany's late entry into the take-off phase, industrialization went on at a much faster pace

TABLE 1   German Net National Product and Sector Product, 1850–1933[15]
(1913=100).

Year	GNP	Sector I	Sector II	Sector III
1850	19.5	39.0	9.0	20.1
1860	23.9	46.5	12.2	14.8
1870	29.2	50.9	18.3	18.6
1880	36.5	57.0	25.0	36.4
1890	48.7	68.6	39.5	40.9
1900	68.4	88.1	60.9	64.8
1913	100.0	100.0	100.0	100.0
1925	93.9	63.5	101.2	106.1
1929	110.6	75.0	119.3	124.2
1933	93.0	91.3	81.5	110.3

than in the established industrial nations. A central place in the development of German industry was occupied by the production and capital goods industry because those branches of German industry that produced consumer goods did not enjoy such favorable conditions for production and sales as their British competitors, who held a dominating position in world markets owing to the cheapness and good quality of their products.[11]

Growth rates in Germany between 1850 and 1913 had a tendency to rise and the net national product (NNP) grew annually by an average of 2.9% in that period, i.e., much faster than that of the established industrialized countries, Great Britain and France.[12] In 1913 the German NNP held second place, behind the U.S. NNP, because the German population increase was much faster than that of the other nations. The French NP was surpassed toward the end of the 1870s and that of Great Britain after the turn of the century. During the industrialization phase Germany substantially improved its rating according to the criterion of NP per inhabitant, as well as of NP per person employed. By 1913 the French and Belgian values had been equaled and the relative gap separating German and British values had been narrowed.[13]

This upward trend was interrupted for a long time by World War I (See Table 1). The course and the outcome of the war as well as the Versailles Treaty caused heavy losses to the German economy, so that the German GNP did not reach its 1913 level until 1929,

TABLE 2   Sectoral Employment Structure and the Contribution of the Economic Sectors toward the German Net National Product, 1850–1933.[17]
(%)

Sector	I		II		III	
Year	Employ-ment	Contri-bution	Employ-ment	Contri-bution	Employ-ment	Contri-bution
1850	56.0	46.5	23.6	20.7	20.4	32.8
1860	51.7	45.2	27.3	23.0	21.0	31.8
1870	49.3	40.5	28.9	28.2	21.8	31.3
1880	48.7	36.4	29.5	32.0	21.8	31.6
1890	42.8	32.8	34.6	36.5	22.6	30.7
1900	38.2	29.9	37.3	40.0	24.5	30.1
1910	35.8	24.7	37.4	43.1	26.8	32.3
1913	34.6	23.2	37.8	45.0	27.6	31.8
1925	31.5	15.7	40.1	48.5	28.4	35.9
1929	29.2	15.8	40.3	48.5	30.5	35.7
1933	33.9	22.8	32.6	39.5	33.5	37.7

only to decline rapidly during the worldwide economic depression.[14]

The slowing down of economic growth in the 1920s was also caused by the comparative stagnation of the process of industrialization. Up to World War I the sectoral employment structure of the economy toward the NP had shown the changes and shifts typical of the industrialization phase. (See Table 2.) These changes had, concurrently with a rise in employment and production in all spheres and areas of the economy, led to a noticeable shift to the secondary sector. After 1918 there occurred hardly any change in the ratio of persons employed in the productive sector and the overall employment figures, so that an important source of the production increase of the economy as a whole dried up.[16]

The structure of the German secondary sector during the entire period under investigation was marked by the predominance of the producing and capital goods industry. Up to the end of the 19th century the upswing was chiefly supported by the coal and the steel as well as the engineering industries. After 1895 their role was taken over by the rapidly growing use of electricity and the rising chemical industry. Both were fundamental innovations in the sense defined by Schumpeter. The growth rates of the producing and capital goods

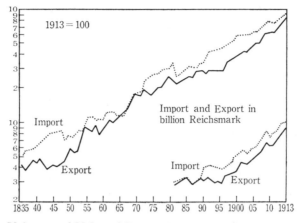

FIG. 1   Volume and Value of German Foreign Trade, 1835–80—1913.[20]

industry, which was characterized by the predominance of large-scale enterprises, and whose growth was supported and accelerated by new funding methods, were persistently higher than those of the old consumer goods industries, where former artisan-operated plants were converted into factories. Their development appears as a protracted continuous process that had begun in the 18th century.[18]

By the middle of the 19th century Germany was already one of the three greatest exporting countries. Its major export goods were raw materials and foodstuffs. In the course of industrialization the German economy was increasingly integrated into the world trade system because of the international division of labor and Germany's evolution from an agrarian into an industrial country. Between 1850 and 1913 German foreign trade increased by an annual average of 4%, i.e., more than its NP. (See Figure 1.) Germany's share of world trade rose to 13% in 1913. The favorable development of German foreign trade, which substantially contributed to the general economic boom, continued steadily up to World War I. The slightly irregular development in the 1870s and 1880s is attributable to a period of economic weakness and protectionism. In spite of the considerably rising domestic demand, German industry had, since the 1870s, become increasingly dependent on world trade.[19]

TABLE 3   The Export Quota and Germany's Share of World Trade, 1880–1933. (%)[24]

Year	Export quota	Share of world trade
1880	14.7	
1890	12.0	
1900	12.6	
1913	19.3	13.0
1925	20.4	8.1
1929	26.4	9.5
1933	10.5	9.5

TABLE 4   The Structure of German Exports, 1880–1934, by Five-Year Periods.[26]

(Distribution in %)

Period	Foodstuffs	Raw materials	Semifinished goods	Finished goods
1880–84	20.9	13.9	15.3	49.9
1885–89	16.2	15.1	13.7	55.0
1890–94	14.9	15.8	16.0	53.4
1895–99	13.7	15.6	16.4	54.4
1900–04	10.7	16.0	17.8	55.4
1905–09	9.6	15.8	19.3	55.2
1910–13	10.2	15.5	21.0	53.3
1925–29	5.3	14.7	20.6	59.1
1930–34	3.9	12.4	18.6	64.6

The export quota of German industry after 1870 rose and fell in long cycles, depending on the fluctuations of purchasing power in the agrarian and raw-materials-producing countries. (See Table 3.) This up-and-down movement reached its peak in the years 1885 and 1913, and a low in 1872 and between 1895 and 1900. In the face of growing difficulties in the domestic market, exports acted as a safety valve, yet export prices slumped structurally, owing to rising competition in foreign markets.[21]

After the end of World War I the German economy tried to resume its traditional trade relations within the framework of existing options. The depreciation of the currency, the reparation payments imposed on Germany, as well as the destruction of traditional German economic entities, adversely affected the quick recovery of

TABLE 5   Foreign Trade in Primary and Industrial Products, 1880–1934, by
          Five-Year Period.[29]

(in million Mark/Reichsmark)

Period	Import surplus of primary products	Export surplus of industrial products
1880–84	1,024.7	1,075.7
1885–89	1,294.9	1,130.1
1890–94	2,024.8	1,085.0
1895–99	2,402.9	1,366.3
1900–04	3,090.9	2,037.3
1905–09	4,431.4	2,777.9
1910–13	5,431.4	4,081.5
1925–29	7,091.9	5,581.9
1930–34	3,155.4	4,364.5

TABLE 6   The Structure of Finished Goods Exports, 1880–1934, by Five-Year
          Period.[30]

(Distribution in %)

Period	Textiles	Machines & metals	Chemicals
1880–84	43.6	14.3	16.1
1885–89	43.7	15.6	13.6
1890–94	39.6	17.2	16.9
1895–99	33.6	23.2	18.3
1900–04	31.4	28.7	16.3
1905–09	28.0	35.1	17.1
1910–13	23.2	39.6	18.6
1925–29	19.0	43.0	18.7
1930–34	15.4	47.2	18.5

the export trade, a situation that was aggravated because the internationally necessary changeover from a wartime economy to a
peacetime economy furthered growing national protectionism.[22]
By 1923 German exports had reached 50% of their prewar value.
By 1928 they had increased by a third again. Trade with countries
with whom binding customs agreements—beyond the most-favored-
nation clause—had been entered into, increased by as much as 40%.
The German share in world trade in the 1920s remained at less than
10%, i.e., distinctly below the corresponding figure for 1913.[23]
Apart from expanding foreign trade, industrialization led to a

TABLE 7 The Regional Structure of German Foreign Trade, 1890–1938.[34]
(Distribution in %)

Year	Europe	North America	Africa	Asia	Australia
1890	78.1	17.8	0.6	2.8	0.7
1900	77.8	14.7	1.5	4.9	1.1
1913	76.1	15.3	2.1	5.4	1.0
1925	74.8	15.3	2.2	7.2	0.5
1930	78.3	12.6	2.2	6.3	0.9
1938	69.7	15.4	3.9	9.9	1.4

change in the spectrum of goods and commodities imported or exported. (See Table 4.) In the 1850s raw materials and foodstuffs represented the major portion of German exports, but dropped to 25% of total exports in the last prewar year. The percentage of finished and semifinished products kept rising, but the percentage of semifinished products dropped after World War I.[25]

There were also shifts within individual categories of goods and commodities in the course of industrial development. Consumer goods constituted almost three quarters of the German export of finished goods in the 1880s. By 1913 their share had dropped to 48%.[27] The most striking phenomenon was the receding share of textile exports, which began to lose ground as early as the middle of the 19th century. (See Table 6.) The share of textiles in the export of finished goods dropped from 80% in 1855 to 50% in 1873 and fell to 25% in 1913.[28]

From early on, the industrialized countries were the most important trade outlets for German goods and commodities. (See Table 7.) European countries used to buy three-quarters of German exports because Germany was in a better geographical position than Great Britain as far as transport facilities and routes were concerned. Although prior to 1914 attempts to gain a foothold in overseas markets were successful, export drives to America and Asia encountered strong British and American competition.[31] An examination of the development of exports to individual countries reveals, as the most striking phenomenon, the receding importance of British and U.S. markets for the German export business.[32] The German colonies never played a major role as trade outlets. The geographic distribution of German investment abroad was according to the regional structure of trade.[33]

During the entire period under investigation, German imports outweighed exports, but in the pre-World War I years compensation for the negative trade balance was no problem because, particularly after 1880, the services sector showed a very positive picture.[35]

Before 1914 state intervention in foreign trade was chiefly restricted to customs regulations and trade policy measures which curtailed foreign trade in favor of the domestic market.[36] Government influence on the material promotion of exports in the form of foreign-exchange control, tax relief, assistance in funding and insurance, and so forth was of minor importance. However, institutions were set up to promote exports. We should note here the reorganization of consular services, the establishment of export-oriented chambers of commerce, and permanent trade exhibitions in the main foreign trading centers—measures which improved marketing information and communication. The permanent trade exhibitions were of no great value for the promotion of exports.[37]

During the war and in the postwar period, i.e., 1914–24, the German government massively intervened in foreign trade matters, particularly by introducing legislation meant to hamper or even prohibit exports.[38] When Germany regained sovereignty in trade policy matters on January 10, 1925, the government very quickly adopted extensive measures to assist the material promotion of exports with a view to obtaining the financial means for the payment of reparations. The government had hoped for trade surpluses, hopes which, however, did not materialize.[39]

Much more than the government did the German banks contribute to the rise of German exports. Their policy also had indirect effects on the industrial export organization, as I shall show later. The banks assumed special importance through their foreign loan transactions, which, as a rule, were connected with export orders for German industries and through the prefinancing of German exports.[40] From 1888 to 1911 the exports financed with the assistance of the German banking system rose from 11.8% to 61% of total German exports.[41] The following three banks exerted great influence in this respect: the Deutsche Überseebank, the Deutsch-Asiatische Bank, and the Deutsch-Südamerikanische Bank.[42] It should be noted, however, that for the banks, profitability calculations had a higher priority than the desire for the promotion of industrial exports by means of the export of capital. The fact that German foreign investments, estimated at 25 billion marks for 1913,[43] did not grow at the pace that could have been possible—given existing chances for investment—should not be interpreted as a general reluctance on the part of the German banks to invest abroad, as might appear from the reports submitted by German diplomatic missions.[44] On the contrary, responsible German bankers made a rational decision in first exploiting national investment options which had grown strongly because of Germany's upswing in economic activity, and they expected higher profits. With the exception of marginal pressure groups, the German Foreign Office again and again had to request bankers and industrialists to commit themselves more intensively in the field of foreign investments.[45]

III

The available relevant literature about the 19th century says little about the systematic selection of trade routes in accordance with modern criteria on decision making, although the subjects most widely discussed in Germany at the turn of the century were the pros and cons of direct versus indirect exports. Despite the complexity of the then-existing forms of business organization, a comparison of the different branches of industry reveals correspondences and parallels which suggest that chance or randomness were only partly instrumental in shaping the structure of export sales.[46]

In our survey of factors influencing the export organization, we have come to the conclusion that the decision to sell goods abroad with the help of an independent or producer-owned export organization was subject not only to general economic and political influences but also to considerations specific to the product, the enterprise, and the particular foreign market. The question of whether the product belonged to one or the other category (i.e., consumer goods or capital goods) was the most important of all product-specific criteria. The type and number of users as well as the frequency (and intensity) of use influenced the decision for or against direct or indirect exports. The growing share of capital goods in German exports required more intensive counseling of the customers. The exporting firms, it is true, were able to point out their independence from producers, but were lacking in knowledge of merchandise and technical know-how, assets that had become almost indispensable. The goods and commodities had also become technically sophisticated, so that the advisory functions had to be complemented by maintenance and repair services. That, of course, overtaxed the technical capability of the export trade.[47]

Even though it is certainly true that the hope for higher prices or more outlets also promoted the decision for direct export, the company's size and financial strength were of particular importance. The rapid growth of large-scale enterprises was a characteristic feature of the German industrialization.[48] Another phenomenon was their close link with major banks[49] which, if need be, were able to prefinance export goods. All these advantages spoke in favor of direct exports. We should not fail to mention that in building up an export organization, the particular enterprise did not follow a rigid, predetermined plan. There were substantial differences with regard to product category and foreign market peculiarities.[50]

Of all the specific influences on the export trade the most important criterion was the degree of development of the particular foreign market. During the entire period under investigation there were divergent market determinants that were also reflected in the regional structure of German foreign trade. The large-scale enterprises of the electrotechnical, chemical, metal-producing, and metal-processing industries preferred direct exports to Europe and America, but in a number of countries sales were made with the help of independent export organizations.[51] These were countries with low consumption (as a result of low purchasing power) and small populations. Among them were countries that could be described as underdeveloped in view of their limited chance of becoming promising export markets.[52] This was generally true for German colonies, but it was true also of a great many overseas countries where direct imports appeared to be either too costly or even impossible for legal, economic, cultural, and geographical reasons.[53]

Around the middle of the 19th century the export of almost all kinds of goods was affected by independent export trading organizations, if it wasn't affected at exhibitions and fairs.[54] The main agents for indirect exports were primarily export trading firms, whose chief objective was the continual and systematic exchange of goods and commodities with foreign countries. The firms established in foreign trade centers were commercial enterprises organized for the handling of imports and exports. Because of marketing methods that required a high outlay of capital, they were geared to individual countries, whose demands they tried to satisfy.[55] Their external organizational structure included various marketing agents. Apart from the commercial travelers, the pioneers of the export business, there were other representatives, as well as contractual agents, before the first trading centers were set up. With a view to better adaptation to the modern, export-oriented economy, the export trading firms, toward the end of the 19th century, added supply depots and assembly, repair, and maintenance workshops, or they hired engineers for the purpose of better countering the growing trend toward direct exports. The marketing efforts grew in intensity from one level of trade to the other, but they were dependent on the type of goods in demand and on peculiar market or local conditions.[56]

The concentration of all the necessary export functions that existed at mid-century underwent substantial changes during the period under investigation. Because of their geographical specialization, the traders' attention was directed more to their customers than to their merchandise. In this respect they acted more as purchasing agents on behalf of local clientele than as sales people for the products of German industry.[57] For various reasons the export trading companies didn't stick to one producer. Indeed, they often bought goods and sold them under their own trade name, so that the producer could not be identified and remained dependent on the trading company. The introduction of branded merchandise by the producers was thus a way to get away from their dependency.[58] The trader's broad assortment of goods, originally mainly consumer goods, his consequent concentration on their use and/or application, as well as his job of opening up new markets, combined to make his other functions recede; however, such functions as advance ordering, stockpiling, stockkeeping, looking after the exporter's interests, and counseling became more and more vital. With the growing share of exported capital goods the foreign trade organization proved less and less suitable for the handling of exports.[59]

Unlike the above-mentioned type of organization for indirect exports, often referred to as Hanseatic export trade, the so-called independent industrial export trade was not specifically geared to a country or group of countries. Functionally it was closely connected with the corresponding branch of industry, a fact reflected in the geographical concentration of production centers. That is why the development of industrial export trade had its origin in, and was closely connected with, the development of particular branches of industry, which were traditional industries originally organized like manufacturers that had been in existence prior to industrialization, e.g. the toy makers in the Nuremberg area, the jewelry makers around Gablontz and Pforzheim, the small-scale iron industry around Remscheid and Solingen, the textile and weaving industry in the Rhineland, and the leather industry in Offenbach.[60] The characteristic features of these branches of industry were, on the one hand, the production of consumer goods, geographical concentration, the high specialization of some firms, but on the other hand, a great variety in production and a high export quota.[61] Small and medium-scale enterprises were in the majority. The growing size of the enterprises diminished the chances of the independent industrial export trade for participation in the export business. As the industrial export trade was not oriented to a specific country, it did not have at its disposal local branch establishments, but had to rely on traveling salespeople and commercial representatives. It was the marketing agent of industry and, to a lesser degree, the purchasing agent for the foreign customers. Similar to the Hanseatic trade, the independent industrial export trade gradually lost its transport and credit functions as well as most of its responsibility for the opening-up of new markets.[62]

In the course of the evolution of the export economy, the export trading firms were increasingly replaced by producer-owned organizations which were able to cooperate with subsidiary export

organs. The increased direct export by industry is mainly a phenomenon of the turn of the century, but the attempts of industry to
disengage itself from trade began as early as the beginning of industrialization.[63] In the 1870s, in the midst of a phase of economic recession, doubts arose as to the ability of foreign trade to cope with
responsibility for foreign sales. These doubts, as well as the demand
for the better promotion of foreign trade, were the starting points
for intensified efforts to export directly, promoted by the hope of
increasing profitability by excluding the trading companies.[64]
Particularly the modern branches of industry, i.e., electrotechnics
and chemistry, tried to get away from foreign trade, which held
a dominant position at that time.

The engineering and the iron and steel industries took a very long
time to develop a comprehensive sales organization—comparable
to that of the electrotechnical and chemical industries—that was
not only well planned in view of foreign competition but also success
oriented and trend setting. In the 1920s the electrotechnical industry
had a well-functioning sales organization also in overseas territories,
but the enterprises of the engineering and the coal and steel industries, until 1925, carried out most of their overseas operations
with the help of exporters or, at most, relied on a few overseas bases.[65]
The trend toward direct exports, however, persisted during the entire
period under investigation. It is estimated that the share of export
agents in foreign trade had dropped to less than 50% by 1913.[66]
In 1935 direct exports probably accounted for two thirds of total
exports.[67]

The importance of world markets for the iron and steel industries
had been rising since the 1870s because production increased faster
than the domestic market. Exports grew to 6.5 million tons, i.e., by
more than 700%, in the period 1880–1913. It was an almost steady
rise, although the export quota was particularly high in periods
of declining domestic demand. Rather than cut back on production, the enterprises tried to sell abroad at or below cost products
that were unsalable on the German domestic market. In periods of
declining domestic demand, exports were boosted with the help of
export bounties granted by cartels of primary production levels.[68]

After 1873, when the economic crisis caused by German rapid in-

dustrial expansion began, the enterprises of German heavy industry
could not help devoting more attention to foreign markets because
of the decline of railroad construction orders that used to provide
regular employment.[69] Above all, the established corporations like
Krupp, Bochumer Verein, and Phoenix, intensified their efforts.
Earlier on they had—quite successfully—tried to boost exports by
attending trade fairs and exhibitions and by organizing a network
of representatives. Bochumer Verein, as early as 1873, had 11
agencies in European countries and 1 in New York. In the early
1880s it was able to sell abroad more than 50% of its production.[70]
Krupp had a similarly high export quota and exceeded Bochumer
Verein in some product categories.[71] Newer firms such as Thyssen
and Deutsch-Luxemburg often enjoyed geographical advantages
in mass-produced standardized goods. Their export quota rose
quickly after the turn of the century.[72]

In the mining and the iron and steel industries the horizontally
and vertically structured corporations organized most of their
own exports into industrialized countries. Uniformity and standard-
ization of their products contributed considerably toward the
elimination of the export trade. The products were sold via the commercial subdivisions of corporation headquarters and management
divisions, via corporation-owned or financially dependent trading
firms, via representative agents, or via cartels and syndicates.
Most transactions—e.g., purchase of railroad construction material—
were effected by the customer approaching the firm in question and
asking it to make an offer. The agents' main job in this type of
business transaction was the making, consolidation, and extension
of contacts. The actual acceptance of the order was mostly no
concern of theirs. In the case of minor deliveries, agents were
authorized to sell the products themselves. In exchange for their services they were entitled to 0.5%–1.0% of the net value of the article.
They mostly represented only one of the big iron and steel corporations because of the similarity of the production programs.[73]

Whereas most iron and steel corporations preferred working with
(authorized) agents, August Thyssen and its subcorporations preferred branch offices as the better way of opening up foreign markets.[74] Branch offices with major supply depots were considered very

profitable for business transactions in Europe and overseas, although markets differed in their rating.[75] In addition to branch offices in Nikolajeff (1908), in Algiers, Port Said, Newcastle and Naples (1913), Oran and Suez (1914), August Thyssen founded the N. V. Handels en Transpoort Maatschappij Vulcaan, of Rotterdam, in 1910.[76]

It was generally true that the iron and steel industry in particular considered exports as a sales outlet and therefore engaged in aggressive export drives in quest of world markets. All attempts to regulate exports by methods applied to domestic sales failed. The corporations stuck to their independence.[77] In 1906 Phoenix rejected a proposal of the Conference of German Iron and Steel Producers suggesting the setting-up of a Joint Bureau of Exports. Neither was Phoenix prepared in 1913 to cooperate with Thyssen.[78] Mannesmann, which had several foreign production plants in operation, flatly refused to subject its foreign sales—particularly in the Pipe Syndicate—to any controls or restrictions whatsoever. On the contrary, Mannesmann began to extend its own export organization and tried, in 1906, to found an export corporation of all Mannesmann firms operating worldwide, in order to neutralize internal competition. These attempts did not succeed before 1936.[79]

The 1870s saw the beginning of a development that reached its climax in 1926, when, through the foundation of the Vereinigte Stahlwerke, the influence of export trading firms practically ceased to exist, because Vereinigte Stahlwerke, in a drive for greater production efficiency, set up Vereinigte Stahlwerke-owned export trading companies. The export trading firms owned by the founding firms of Vereinigte Stahlwerke had worldwide interests in the form of investments in production and joint-stock corporations. These firms were now concentrated and given specific objectives. The Stahlunion-Export GmbH, which was an offspring of the Otto-Wolff GmbH, dominated foreign markets, although in the field of special products, sales were made by the producers themselves.[80] The streamlining of the organization was facilitated through the comprehensive preparatory work done by the firms that had founded Vereinigte Stahlwerke. Relatively late, but not less successfully, the Gutehoffnungshütte under Paul Reusch reorganized its export business in the 1920s. By means of capital investment in the Dutch N. V. Allgemeene Ijceren Staal-Maatschappij Ferrostaal, Den Hague, the Gutehoffnungshütte was, at last, able to establish itself internationally. Previously, the method of individual sales effected through the sales division and the employment of area-oriented representatives had prevailed, but after 1930 the Ferrostaal AG acted as Gutehoffnungshütte's sales organization that looked after the worldwide interests of the parent corporation.[81]

Because of the absence of specialized dealers and because products were only produced on order, the engineering firms were, from early on, forced to take charge of the sale of their products themselves.[82] The necessity for explanations and instructions required by the user for the proper handling of the goods and/or machinery and the resulting problems with regard to selling and maintenance very soon led to the establishment of an enterprise-owned network of agents, to the dispatch of qualified technicians, or to the setting-up of direct branch offices. To give an example: the Gasmotoren-Fabrik Deutz had numerous branch offices as well as 16 sales bureaus in 14 European countries and overseas. In the overseas countries the engineering firms tried to cope by selling via traders, but toward the end of the 19th century increasing competition forced the firms to dispatch their own qualified staff wherever the sales volume did not warrant enterprise-owned bureaus.[83]

The foreign sales organizations of the enterprises of this branch of industry developed at varying speeds and took varying shapes. Compared to other branches of industry its strategy was less far-sighted and less uniform, but there was no mistaking the fact that the German parent corporation was always in effective control, although its foreign bases operated at varying degrees of independence. This variety was conditioned by the level of demand and the degree of development, as well as on local investors' capital assets and their readiness to invest. Reactions to economic crises followed comparable patterns, and the methods applied were adequate to prevailing situations and managerial options.[84]

Within the metal-working industry, which employed 17% of the work force before World War I and, in this respect, headed all branches of industry, the electrotechnical industry was its most

modern and most growth intensive. In 1913 its exports amounted
to 290 million marks, i.e., 46% of world electro exports.[85] Almost
three quarters of these electro exports went into European countries,
but in the final prewar years overseas markets gained importance as
access to European and American markets was impeded by protective duties.[86]

Siemens & Halske, founded in 1847, and Allgemeine Elektrizitäts-
Gesellschaft (AEG), founded in 1883/1887, played a pioneering role
in the development of the German electrotechnical industry.
Owing to the importance of exports for its own development, the
electrotechnical industry was the first branch of industry to begin
with the systematic buildup of an extensive export organization,
after Siemens & Halske had already opened up foreign markets
during the first serious sales crisis in the early 1850s.[87]

Siemens & Halske first tried to exploit the experiences gained by
the big export trading houses of Hamburg and Bremen in the
service of an export organization of its own. First contacts were made
in Russia where Werner and Carl Siemens were active. Other
contacts were made later on in Austria and France, while the
British market was opened up by Wilhelm Siemens.[88] In the 1880s
numerous contracts were signed with commercial representatives
in nearly all important countries.[89] Siemens & Halske preferred
those export trading firms that had a technological division. These
firms could be assumed to possess technical expertise or the ability
to cope with technical problems.[90] Although the staff of the firms
was supplemented with technically qualified Siemens personnel,
Siemens's requirements were inadequately met. Major investments
transactions that accompanied the construction of telegraph lines,
the advent of high-voltage electrotechnology, and the building of
repair shops increasingly overtaxed their resources and capacities.
That is why those contracts served as pioneering models for the
worldwide organization which Siemens had been building up since
the end of the 19th century.[91]

For the purpose of communication with its overseas representative
agencies the parent corporation had to set up a special division in
the 1880s. It was composed of two subdivisions, the export bureau
and the transportation bureau. Their objectives were sales and

after-sales service. In the beginning of the 20th century the Berlin-centered parent corporation of Siemens proceeded to a redistribution of market shares. The British Siemens corporation, Siemens Brothers & Co. Ltd., and Siemens Brothers Dynamo Works Ltd., were made responsible for trade relations with the British Dominions and colonies, while trade with remaining overseas territories was left to Siemens's German branches.[92] At the same time the German and British negotiators of Siemens decided on the foundation of an overseas division whose administration center and headquarters were stationed in Berlin. This division had a London branch.[93]

As soon as market conditions permitted, contracts with agencies were gradually canceled and Siemens agencies were established in the form of Siemens-owned firms whose working capital was supplied by the parent corporation. The reorganization of the sales structure brought about the founding of a geographically structured division for overseas trade, which had its own accounting department and was responsible for all business transactions with Siemens's overseas branches and agencies. Organizational control was exerted by the central overseas division. The sales organization for European countries was divided in accordance with technological criteria.[94] It was a typical feature of the Siemens export organization that each individual market had but one Siemens representative for all types of business.[95]

After World War I had radically severed profitable overseas trade links with Great Britain, South America, South Africa, India, Japan, and China, foreign trade was resumed in 1919. The loss of the British Siemens firms and their subsidiaries made it necessary to set up new trade links. The reconstruction of the foreign trade network in Europe and overseas was so successful that in 1928 Siemens held at least a 40% share of total German electrotechnical exports.[96]

Similar to the Siemens firms, the AEG sold its products through representatives, corporation-owned sales bureaus, and import-export firms, as well as directly. The AEG operated successfully above all in Western Europe and Russia. It was represented in the Austro-Hungarian Empire and in Great Britain by firms where it exerted influence through its capital holdings.[97] The AEG operated overseas mostly through contractors before it proceeded in 1912 to slowly establish overseas branch offices. The firm's motive for the transition to AEG-owned branch offices was the possibility of concluding business deals at prices that were unattractive to the local independent agent, but contributed to covering the cost.[98]

The so-called Unternehmergeschäft [use of contractors] was characteristic of what were known as the *Universalfirmen* of the German electrotechnical industry, which had to adopt other marketing strategies than the established branches of industry did.[99] As the electrotechnical industries could not execute enough orders for electrical power plants, they did their own financing, i.e., by means of contractors. The electrotechnical industry was at first forced to assume the functions of power supply companies if it wanted to boost its sales. The electrotechnical industry created demand for its own products in order to set in motion the process of electrification. The basic consideration was that the electrical power plants, after an initial high capital outlay, would make high profits because the demand for electricity could be expected to rise steeply. In order to lessen its commitments in terms of time and capital, the electrotechnical industry pursued its operations through finance companies of its own.

In neighboring European countries the big electrotechnical corporations acquired franchises for the building of electrical power plants, then founded an operating company to which they then transferred the franchise, and finally made the operating company award the order for the construction to themselves. In the case of horsedrawn trams they acquired the majority of stock in a given company. Then they decided on its electrification and issued new stock, which they had to buy themselves. The AEG chiefly applied these methods of business in its sales to South America, while Siemens preferred direct sales because of the great risks connected with the South American market.[100]

The export organization of the smaller specialized electrotechnical firms, such as the cable and wire makers Felten & Guilleaume, was basically different from that of the two Universalfirmen. Unlike Siemens and the AEG, Felten & Guilleaume before World War I never seriously considered the setting up of their own sales agencies abroad, although the firm relatively early and regularly supplied overseas markets with articles developed from their wire production.[101] The goods were sold through various sales divisions organized by groups of countries and languages. Inspectors of the German Reichspost sometimes checked product quality on the firm's premises.[102] Felten & Guilleaume relied more on the receptivity of the foreign market and tried to consolidate and extend its own market position through price-fixing agreements with other producers, attendance at industrial fairs and exhibitions, and direct contacts with customers.[103] In addition, it had, since the 1880s, successfully built up a network of representatives abroad with a view to crowding out its British competitors.[104] After the turn of the century, Felten & Guilleaume's management discovered that they had failed to employ technicians for market analysis and customer advisory service. Representation by commercial agents had not been enough.[105] For this reason and because of the trend toward the construction of large-scale plants—which benefited the Universalfirmen—the export quota was only 30%, with a strong emphasis on European markets.[106]

In trying to answer the question as to who gave the strong initial impulse and who kept up the momentum—two factors that made the second German industrial take-off so dynamic—we should emphasize not only the role of the electrotechnical industry but also that of the chemical industry. Like the high-voltage technology in the electrotechnical industry, the aniline dye technology in the chemical industry produced the conditions for a quick expansion, which was supported by large-scale enterprises that carried out intensive research and were oriented toward world markets.[107]

The chemical industry usually opened up and exploited markets through country-oriented sales divisions which were assisted by commercial travelers and chemical engineers who knew their products professionally. These sales divisions, as well as the very high quality of German products, contributed substantially to a German monopoly in aniline dyes. The German chemical industry was a world leader in the field of fertilizers, medical drugs, and cosmetics as well as industrial-commercial auxiliary materials.[108] The chemical industry possessed quite a few production plants abroad but hardly any overseas. In dyes and pharmaceutical products German superiority was so great that its position could not be endangered by high protective duties introduced by some countries. In 1913 the value of German dye production was three quarters of the world output in dyes.[109]

Not unlike the Vereinigte Stahlwerke, IG Farben, which was founded after World War I, introduced joint sales organizations and centralized the control of its export operations in Frankfurt. Its development was interrupted only by World War II. The network of foreign sales branches and investments was further extended. The new joint sales organizations were product-oriented, independent, operating divisions with their own accounting, statistical, and legal subdivisions. In spite of a certain amount of decentralization, the coordination of export sales attained the highest degree possible.[110]

Quite different was the procedure of the German textile industry. Up to World War II, it sold its products through export trading firms (*Exporthandelshäuser*). An export organization comparable to that of other branches of industry was practically nonexistent. Commercial travelers employed by Rhenish textile makers were only locally successful.[111] The same is true, to some extent, of the German porcelain industry, the ironmongery industry, the toy makers, and the jewelry and leather industries. I could go on enumerating the articles whose producers were financially not strong enough as well as not organized for independent exports. Frequently articles were produced in cottage industries or by small workshops, a fact that rendered impossible the establishment of internal or external export organizations. There were seasonal, irregular exports of delicatessen and luxury foods, such as fruit cakes (*stollen*) and Nuremberg gingerbread before Christmas. Stollwerck was an exception because it owned foreign sales outlets and production plants.[112]

Business policy aiming at investments abroad and production plants of one's own in foreign countries arose from the realization that it was impossible to ignore the overseas trend—present sine the 1880s and much stronger after 1918—toward the development of national industries and the protection of domestic economy. For the export industry that meant considerable handicaps connected with import restrictions and high customs barriers. Corporation-owned factories and trading establishments appeared to offer the optimal prerequisites to the safeguarding of foreign sales. Customs tariffs were raised repeatedly, thus confronting German industrial enterprises with the question of whether, under the prevailing conditions, it was preferable to export into a certain country, or transfer production plants thereto the foreign market. Procedures were different in any given branch of industry.

The selection and dispatch of personnel from the parent corporation often led to direct investments, which, at the time, were not always considered advantageous from the point of view of strengthening of domestic economy. There were a vast variety of reasons and arguments that induced German enterprises to found subsidiaries abroad. The foremost consideration underlying all direct investments was the problem of an increasingly protectionist trade policy, except in those cases where the particular German branch of industry, if it held a monopoly position, was able to retain its market share in spite of high import duties. That was true, in any case, of the German potash industry before 1914 and of the dyestuff industry.[113] But the decision was also influenced by the size of the market, the expected growth of sales, and the consequential costs of a direct investment.

This can be illustrated by examples from all major branches of industry. Major investments in foreign enterprises were held mainly by three corporations of the iron and steel industry, i.e., Bochumer Verein, Mannesmann Röhrenwerke, and, for a short length of time, Rheinische Stahlwerke. When, through strong competition and trade barriers, German exports to some countries fell, Bochumer Verein tried through investments in an existing Spanish firm in 1887 to defend its market position, although with little success.[114] A venture in Italy resulted in considerable losses.[115] Mannesmann stepped up its production abroad following the turn of the century, after granting licenses in European countries[116] had largely been unsuccessful. Production abroad began in Komotau, Austria. In 1899 the Mannesmann Tube Co. in Landore was taken over. After the turn of the century production facilities in Austria were expanded and new plants were set up in Italy.[117] Similar ventures in the United States, however, failed.[118] After a short time Rheinische Stahlwerke abandoned its investment in a Russian steelworks.[119]

Many examples can also be cited for the German engineering industry. Many German firms were forced into taking such a step when unilateral customs tariffs were introduced by Austria-Hungary, the second biggest buyer of German engineering products at the turn of the century.[120] American customs tariffs had a similar effect on the founding of subsidiaries.[121] Since 1906 Robert Bosch had had a subsidiary corporation and numerous sales agencies and repair shops operating in the United States. Bosch wished to be represented in the U.S. automobile market through its own organizations.[122] The big electro Universalfirmen owned extensive production facilities abroad before 1914; to a lesser extent so did the chemical industry.[123] Siemens, usually very successful, had to give up its U.S. subsidiary.[124]

After World War I there was a strongly growing tendency to set up corporation-owned foreign subsidiaries or to acquire stock in foreign firms. Soon after having been founded, Osram set up foreign sales depots in the form of joint-stock companies where foreign capital was represented. Sales depots were erected in Zurich, Vienna, Oslo, Copenhagen, Milan, Stockholm, Bucharest, Helsingfors, Amsterdam, Riga, Shanghai, Brussels, London, and Rio de Janeiro. Sales companies were founded—in conjunction with other producers—in Argentina and Mexico.[125]

A special position in the export organization was held by the *Exportgemeinschaften* (joint export organizations), which were the only practicable form of export organization for numerous very small, small, and medium-sized firms, as well as for cartels, whose influence was more important in Germany than in other countries.[126] The wish for intensive cooperation in exports cannot be generally interpreted as an attempt to bridge the gap between the desire for independence from the export trade on the one hand, and the inability to find an autonomous solution to the problems inherent in export sales on the other. This was mainly true of the small enterprises which were unable to export independently and profitably because they lacked the experience and the necessary funds. As they could not offer sureties, they were not granted bank loans and could not set up export organizations of their own. Joint export organizations enabled these enterprises to set up joint-export trading exhibitions, or export divisions, or even sales depots. Scope and business volume of the joint export organizations differed a lat and were often not open to investigation by outside observers. In the economic crises in the 1870s, in the 1890s, and after World War I, joint export organizations increased in number, particularly in the field of raw materials, semifinished products, and mass-produced goods. More and more major enterprises joined them in order to boost their competition potential.

Contrary to the general development of cartels in Germany, export cartels were of minor importance.[127] It was a significant fact that cartels rarely conducted export business for their member firms.[128] Their functions were in the following fields: agreeing on sales conditions and prices, allotting market shares, gathering market-relevant information, and strengthening solidarity in the face of foreign competitors. Cartels were formed particularly in the engineering and automobile industries, and in the industries producing metal finished goods and semifinished products. The electrotechnical had one cartel; the chemical industries, two. In the raw materials sector there were five cartels. Here the Rheinisch-Westfälisches Kohlensyndikat occupied a prominent position, because through its coal sales division (*Kohlenkontor*) it played an outstanding role in exports. It had branches in Belgium, the Netherlands, France, Austria-Hungary, Switzerland, and Italy.[129] Coal exports overseas were handled by the Deutsche Kohlendepot Ltd., Hamburg.[130] The Stahlwerksverband (Steel Works Association) founded in 1904, acting on behalf of its member firms, exported semifinished products, processed steel plate, and railroad materials. For the Steel Works Association export was not an end in itself, but a means for regulating the domestic market.[131] The other cartels that had export functions were of minor importance. They had little influence on the organization of the export trade. Many enterprises believed, and not without cause, that cartels might be harmful to direct contacts between customer and producer and have an undesirable influence on market observation and the decisions resulting therefrom, i.e., regulating production volume in keeping with demand and developing sales strategies. Apart from legitimate contacts with other producers for the purpose of avoiding duplication of investments, the corporation-owned internal and external export agencies were the obvious means to increase sales, and to consolidate their own position in world markets, because the domestic market did not have the conditions indispensable to expansion of the enterprises.

IV

The result of this investigation into export organization from the middle of the 19th century until the period between the two world wars can be summarized as follows:

The export organization of German industry expanded considerably in the three decades preceding World War I and adapted itself to the needs and requirements of an industrialized nation that was dependent on world markets.

When exports shifted to production plants and capital goods, direct exports grew substantially.

Some branches of industry had developed their own type of export organization which depended on the average size of the enterprise, the type and category of goods to be sold, and the market structure of the importing countries.

NOTES

1. Cf. Dessauer, "Entwicklungstendenzen," p. 105f. The footnotes just mention the author's name, the first noun of the title, and the page referred to. For full bibliographic details see the list of books at the end of this paper.
2. Hoffmann, *Strukturwandlungen*, p. 287.
3. Cf. Schäfer, "Wandlungen," p. 201f.; Grebler, "Problem," p. 2; Wagenführ, *Bedeutung*, p. 39.
4. Cf. Blaich, "Absatzstrategien," p. 6; Kröger, "Industrieausfuhr," p. 18, Yet there is the difficulty that the trading houses were usually

sole proprietorships or limited partnerships, which didn't report on their activities.

5. Cf. Nissen, Bedeutung, p. 64ff.; Kröger, Industrieausfuhr, p. 14f.; Wagenführ, *Bedeutung*, p. 13f.

6. Cf. Becker, Absatzorganisation, p. 22; Dessauer, Entwicklungstendenzen, p. 95; Grebler, Problem, p. 7ff.; Nissen, Bedeutung, p. 84; Pohl, Konzentration.

7. This is true for the telegraph companies, the cable companies, and the railroads, which usually invited tenders for a subscription, so that a special marketing effort was not necessary. The workshops of the companies were also in charge of service and repair. Cf. Siemens archive, SAA 47/Lg 772.

8. Cf. Dessauer, Entwicklungstendenzen, p. 100.

9. Cf. Dessauer, Entwicklungstendenzen, p. 102; Schäfer, Wandlungen, p. 217; Vogt, *Überseebeziehungen*, p. 72; Predöhl, *Verkehrspolitik*, p. 18.

10. Cf. Feldenkirchen, Technologie, p. 79f.

11. Cf. Overbeck, Methoden, p. 12ff.; Harms, *Zukunft*, p. 1f.; Röpke, *Weltwirtschaft*, p. 87; Borchardt, Wachstum, p. 203ff.

12. Cf. Feldenkirchen, Rivalität, p. 82ff.; Marczewski, *Produit*, p. 81; *Historical Statistics*, p. 74ff.

13. Cf. Kindleberger, Overtaking, p. 254; Feldenkirchen, Technologie, Table 11.

14. Overbeck, Methoden, p. 17f.; Witt, Wirtschaftspolitik, p. 168.

15. Compiled according to Hoffmann et al., *Wachstum*, p. 454ff.

16. Cf. Borchardt, Wachstum, 1914–1970, p. 687f.; Feldenkirchen, Technologie, Table 20b.

17. Compiled according to Hoffman et al., *Wachstum*, pp. 204–6; p. 454f.

18. Cf. Feldenkirchen, Technologie, p. 125f.

19. Cf. Petzina, *Wirtschaft*, p. 64; Svennilson, *Growth*, p. 292ff.; League, of Nations, ed., *Memorandum*, Vol. 1, p. 590; Levy, *Grundlagen*, p. 15; Wagenfür, *Bedeutung*, p. 36f.

20. Cf. Tilly, Verkehrswesen, p. 584.

21. Cf. Tilly, Verkehrswesen, p. 584; Wagenführ, Bedeutung, p. 45ff.; Ullmann, Exportförderung, p. 170.

22. See Feldenkirchen, Zollpolitik.

23. Cf. Hoffmann, Strukturwandlungen, p. 289; Kröger, Industrieausführ, p. 49.

24. Calculated according to Hoffmann, Wachstum, p. 817f., p. 827f.; Wagemann, Struktur, p. 388f.

25. Cf. Wagenführ, *Bedeutung*, p. 42f.
26. Calculated according to Hoffmann, Wachstum, p. 153.
27. Cf. Wagenführ, *Bedeutung*, p. 42.
28. Cf. Dessauer, Entwicklungstendenzen, p. 252.
29. Cf. Hoffmann, Wachstum, p. 520f., p. 524f.
30. Cf. Hoffmann, Wachstum, p. 520ff.
31. Cf. League, Memorandum, Vol. I, p. 112f.; Levy, Grundlagen, p. 90ff.; Petzina, Wirtschaft, p. 65f.
32. Cf. Borchardt, Währung, p. 32; Jantzen, Ausfuhrhandel, p. 30; Henning, Industrialisierung, p. 258; Borchardt, Wachstum 1850–1914, p. 234.
33. Cf. Borchardt, Wachstum 1850–1914, p. 235f.; Lanz, Wesen, p. 48.
34. Cf. Bevölkerung und Wirtschaft, p. 198ff.
35. Cf. Tilly, Verkehrswesen, p. 585; Borchardt, Wachstum, p. 234f.
36. See Feldenkirchen, Zollpolitik.
37. Cf. Bancken, Bedeutung, p. 6ff.; Ullmann, Exportförderung.
38. See Feldenkirchen, Zollpolitik.
39. Cf. Grebler, Problem, p. 68ff.
40. For the relationship between banks and industry see Feldenkirchen, Banks.
41. Kellenbenz, Wirtschaftsgeschichte, p. 288ff.
42. Siemens archive SAA 12/Lm 910; Müller-Jabusch, Jahre.
43. Born, Geld, p. 263.
44. For examples see Feldenkirchen, Kapital, p. 72.
45. Cf. Krupp archive WA IX a 106.
46. Cf. Blaich, Absatzstrategien, p. 8.
47. Cf. Grebler, Problem, p. 8ff.; Schäfer, Wandlungen, p. 213ff.
48. Blaich, Absatzstrategien, p. 9.
49. Cf. Becker, Absatzorganisation, p. 222; Kühn, Ausfuhrzwischenhandel, p. 109ff.; Feldenkirchen, Industrie.
50. Cf. Aschenbrenner, Exporthandel, p. 9ff.
51. Thyssen-archive A/645/1, D21; Becker, Absatzorganisation, p. 36; Aschenbrenner, Exporthandel, p. 75.
52. Cf. Russenberger, Auswirkungen, p. 85ff.; Henzler, Außenhandel, p. 31ff.
53. Cf. Dietrich, Export, p. 31ff.; Vogt, Überseebeziehungen, p. 72.
54. FWH-archive 5 46 00.
55. Cf. Kröger, Industrieausfuhr, p. 8f.; Grebler, Problem, p. 33f.; Jantzen, Ausfuhrhandel, p. 27ff.
56. Cf. Schäfer, Wandlungen, p. 223.
57. Cf. Schäfer, Wandlungen, p. 207f.

58. Cf. Grebler, Problem, p. 13; Nissen, Bedeutung, p. 67.
59. Cf. Kühn, Ausfuhrzwischenhandel, p. 112f.; Bancken, Bedeutung, p. 19f. Cf. also: Siemens archive SAA 11/Lg 724 Franke.
60. Cf. Becker, Absatzorganisation, p. 28ff.; Bartels, Exportfrage, p. 4.
61. Cf. Grebler, Problem, p. 31; Wagenführ, Bedeutung, p. 11f.
62. Cf. Hirsch, Organisation, p. 144f.; Nissen, Bedeutung, p. 3ff.
63. Aschenbrenner, Exporthandel, p. 9; Henzler, Außenhandel, p. 39ff.
64. Cf. Grebler, Problem, p. 32; Schäfer, Wandlungen, p. 209; Ullmann, Exportförderung, p. 177f.; Dessauer, Entwicklungstendenzen, p. 196f.
65. Mannesmann-archive M 11.009; Siemens archive SAA 25/Ld 644; Grebler, Problem, p. 10.
66. Hirsch, Handel, p. 148.
67. Cf. Schäfer, Wandlungen, p. 210.
68. Cf. Feldenkirchen, Eisenindustrie, p. 221ff.
69. Cf. PA AA I A China 22, PA AA I A China 4; Krupp archive WA III 13, WA IX a 106. For that reason there was a meeting in 1885 when the Disconto-Bank and the Deutsche Bank invited representatives of Krupp, of Dortmunder Union, Bochumer Verein, van der Zypen & Charlier, Maschinenbau AG Nürnberg, Sächsische Maschinenfabrik Chemnitz, and Stettiner Vulcan to discuss railroad projects abroad. Cf. Feldenkirchen, Kapital, p. 71.
70. Bochumer Verein archive 420 01 Nr. 1, 517 00 Nr. la; Däbritz, Bochumer Verein, p. 144; Feldenkirchen, Eisenindustrie, p. 230.
71. Krupp archive WA I 1420; Feldenkirchen, Eisenindustrie, table 72.
72. Cf. Feldenkirchen, Eisenindustrie, p. 232f.
73. Cf. Feldenkirchen, Eisenindustrie, p. 233.
74. Thyssen-archive A/645/4.
75. Thyssen-archive A/650/2, A/645/1.
76. Thyssen-archive A/628/2, A/595/1.
77. Mannesmann-archive P 1 25 24 3; Feldenkirchen, Eisenindustrie, p. 221ff.
78. Mannesmann-archive P 1 25 24 3.
79. Mannesmann-archive M 11,009; cf. Koch, 75 Jahre, p. 75 ff.
80. Thyssen-archive VST CK 40, VST XXIV 1, A/608/7; Ufermann, Stahltrust, p. 76ff.
81. Gutehoffnungshütte archive HA 20211/49, 304014/0–34, 304014/37–65, 304014/71–119, 304024/13–23, 30442/5, 14, 39, 40, 4001012025/0–16.
82. Cf. Blaich, Absatzstrategien, p. 9.

83. Cf. Matschoss, Jahrhundert, p. 264; Goldbeck, Kraft, p. 226.

84. Cf. Blaich, Absatzstrategien, p. 20; Becker, Absatzorganisation, p. 222.

85. Siemens archive SAA 11/Lb 581 Lietke, 29/Lp 355; cf. Jacob-Wendler, Elektroindustrie, p. 11.

86. Siemens archive SAA 11/Lb 581 Lietke, 29/Lp 355; cf. Jacob-Wendler, Elektroindustrie, p. 11.

87. Siemens archive SAA 60/Lh 751, 47/Lg 786, 68/Ld 851.

88. Siemens archive SAA 68/Li 219, 68/Li 141, 68/Li 268, 11/Lg 816, 47/Lg 780.

89. Siemens archive SAA 60/Lh 751, 60/Lb 8.

90. Siemens archive SAA 60/Lh 751, 68/Ld 851.

91. Siemens archive SAA 11/Lg 724 Franke, 60/Lh 751, 60/Lb 8, 68/Li 177, 16/Li 296, 68/Li 312. In 1913 Siemens had 168 agencies in foreign countries, among them 104 in Europe, 7 in Africa, 4 in the United States, 31 in Central and South America, and 21 in Asia. In Australia and New Zealand Siemens was represented, too. At the same time Siemens had 17 plants in 9 European countries. Cf. Siemens archive SAA 60/Lh 303.

92. Siemens archive SAA 68/Lr 488, 68/Li 141, 68/Li 268, 30/Ls 462.

93. Siemens archive SAA 68/Lr 488, 30/Ls 462, 68/Li 219.

94. Siemens archive SAA 33/Lh 292, 60/Lh 103, 11/Lb 377 Haller, 47/Lg 742, 68/Ls 913.

95. Siemens archive SAA 12/Lm 910, 60/Lb 8.

96. Siemens archive SAA 68/Lr 488, 33/Lh 292, 12/Lm 910, 11/Lf 472 Köttgen, 11/Lf 55 Bingel, 54/Lb 2, 11/Le 577 Graupe.
    By 1936 Siemens had 16 plants in Europe and 1 in Argentina. Cf. Siemens archive SAA 50/Ld 88.

97. Cf. Jacob-Wendler, Elektroindustrie, p. 44.

98. Cf. Jacob-Wendler, Elektroindustrie, p. 220f.

99. Cf. Loewe, Industrie, p. 85; Siemens archive SAA 47/Lg 786.

100. Cf. Jacob-Wendler, Elektroindustrie, p. 221.

101. Cf. Jacob-Wendler, Elektroindustrie, p. 19; Vagt, Überseebeziehungen, p. 72.

102. F & G archive A I/g-0127; Vogt, Überseebeziehungen, p. 51.

103. Cf. Vogt, Überseebeziehungen, p. 91.

104. F & G archive A I/2c/2.

105. F & G archive A I/1b/5. A II/2 Nr. 1/14, A I/2c/1.

106. F & G archive A I/2c/1. A I/1b/5; Feldenkirchen, Fürnostgeschafte, p. 182.

107. Hohenberg, Chemicals; Beer, Emergence; Feldenkirchen, Finanzierung Großunternehmen, p. 95f.

108. Hohenberg, Chemicals, p. 38; Haber, Industry, p. 101; Feldenkirchen, Rivalität, p. 103.

109. Cf. Redlich, Bedeutung, p. 18f.

110. Cf. Blaich, Absatzstrategien, p. 20.

111. Cf. Russenberger, Auswirkungen, p. 83ff.; Blumberg, Textilindustrie, p. 214.

112. Becker, Absatzorganisation, p. 167ff.; Blaich, Absatzstrategien, p. 22f.; Kabisch, Kapital, p. 168f.

113. Cf. Kabisch, Kapital, p. 224ff.

114. Bochumer Verein archive 126 00/2, 129 00/15.

115. Bochumer Verein archive 129 00/15, 129 00/18, 142 04 Nr, 5, 163 02 Nr. 1–9.

116. Cf. Koch, 75 Jahre, p. 33.

117. Cf. Koch, 75 Jahre, p. 75ff.

118. Cf. Kabisch, Kapital, p. 246.

119. RSW archive 12300.

120. Cf. Blaich, Absatzstrategien, p. 16; Siemens archive SAA 68/Li 268.

121. Kabisch, Kapital, p. 148ff.

122. Kabisch, Kapital, p. 222.

123. Siemens archive SAA 68/Lr 488, 15/Lm 824.

124. Siemens archive SAA 33/Lh 292.

125. Siemens archive SAA 54/Li 258; Thyssen-archive D21. A/645/6, A/645/4, A/647.

126. Cf. Schäfer, Wandlungen, p. 22ff.: Eichler/Hoppmann, Exportkartell, p. 233ff.; Kleeberg. Exportkartelle, p. 16ff.; Aschenbrenner, Exporthandel, p. 10.

127. Cf. the list of all export cartels in Schäfer, Exportkartell, pp. 250–309.

128. ZSTA Merseburg, Ministerium für Handel und Gewerbe, Rep. 120 C VIII 1. Nr. 72 vol. 1; Eichler/Hoppman. Exportkartell, p. 236; Kliem, Wesen, p. 3ff.; Becker, Absatzorganisation, p. 42; Siemens archive SAA 11/Lb 313 Haller.

129. ZSTA Merseburg, Ministerium für Handel und Gewerbe, Rep. 20 C VIII 1. Nr. 65 vol. 4; Ullmann, Exportförderung, p. 170.

130. Rips, Stellung, p. 85.

131. ZSTA Merseburg, Ministerium für Handel und Gewerbe. Rep. 120 C VIII 1. Nr. 72 Adh. 53 Vols. 1–4: Grebler, Problem, p. 31.

Bibliography

Archives used

Political Archive of the Auswärtiges Amt. Bonn (PA AA); Zentrales Staatsarchiv Merseburg (ZSTA); Bochumer Verein; Gutehoffnungshütte; Hoesch; Fried, Krupp; Mannesmann; Rheinische Stahlwerke (USW); Siemens; Thyssen; Felten & Guilleaume (F & G); Friedrich-Wilhelms-Hütte (FWH).

Rudolf, Aschenbrenner: "Exporthandel und direkter Industrie-Export in der Nachkriegszeit." Ph.D. diss., Leipzig, 1929.

Ausschuss zur Untersuchung der Erzeugungs- und Absatzbedingungen der deutschen Wirtschaft: Der Bankkredit, Verhandlungen und Berichte des Unterausschusses für Geld-, Kredit- und Finanzwesen, Berlin, 1930.

Alexander Bancken: "Bedeutung der Vertriebsform für die deutsche Exportförderung," Ph. D. diss., Cologne, 1941.

Kurt Bartels: Die Exportfrage im Handwek, Diss. Köln 1934.

John Joseph Beer: *The Emergence of the German Dye Industry,* Illinois Studies in the Social Sciences, no. 44, Urbana, Ill., 1959.

Hans Herbert Becker: "Die Absatzorganisation im Export deutscher Konsumfertigwaren nach den Vereinigten Staaten von Amerika unter besonderer Berücksichtigung der Verhältnisse in der Spielwaren-, Porzellan- und Automobilindustrie," Ph. D. diss., Nuremberg, 1964.

Fritz Blaich: "Absatzstratogien deutscher Unternehmen im 19. und in der ersten Hälfte des 20. Jahrhunderts," in Hans Pohl, ed., *Abstzstrategien deutscher Unternehmen, Gestern-Heute-Morgen,* Wilhelm Treue, Zeitschrift für Unternehmens geschichte, Beiheft 23, Wiesbaden, 1983, pp. 5–48.

Horst Blumberg: *Die deutsche Textilindustrie in der industriellen Revolution,* East Berlin, 1965.

Knut Borchardt: "Wirtschaftliches Wachstum und Wechsellagen, 1800–1914," in H. Aubin and W. Zorn, eds., *Handbuch der deutschen Wirtschafts- und Sozialgeschichte,* Vol. 2, Stuttgart, 1976, pp. 198–275.

Karl Erich Born: *Geld und Banken im 19, und 20, Jahrhundert,* Stuttgart, 1976.

Statistisches Bundesamt Wiesbaden, ed., *Bevölkerung und Wirtschaft, 1872–1972: hrsg, anl. des 100 jährigen Bestehens der zentralen amtlichen Statistik,* Stuttgart, 1972.

Walter Däbritz: Bochumer Verein für Bergbau und Gußstahlfabrikation in Bochum. Neun Jahrzehnte seiner Geschichte im Rahmen der Wirtschaft des Ruhrbezirks, Düsseldorf 1934.

Marianne Dessauer: "Entwicklungstendenzen der betrieblichen Exportwirtschaft in Deutschland seit der Mitte des 19. Jahrhunderts," Ph. D. diss., Munich, 1981.

Hugo Dietrich: Der deutsche Export von Gebrauchswaren nach China, British Indien, Niederländisch Indien, Diss, Köln 1935.

Hermann Eichler, Erich Hoppmann, and Erich Schäfer: Exportkartell und Wettbewerb, Köln und Opladen 1964.

Wilfried, Feldenkirchen: The Banks and the Steel Industry in the Ruhr, in *German Yearbook on Business History*, Vol. 1, 1981, pp. 27–51.

Wilfried Feldenkirchen: Die Eisen- und Stahlindustrie des Ruhrgebietes 1879–1914 (=Beiheft 20 zur Zeitschrift für Unternehmensgeschichte), Wissbaden 1982.

Wilfried Feldenkirchen: Fernostgeschäfte der Felten & Guilleaume Carlswerk AG bis zum Beginn des Zweiten Weltkrieges. In: Zeitschrift für Unternehmensgeschichte. 22. Jahrgang, 1977, pp. 91–108, pp. 162–182.

Wilfried Feldenkirchen: Zur Finanzierung von Großunternehmen in der chemischen und elektrotechnischen Industrie Deutschlands vor dem Ersten Weltkrieg. in Richard Tilly, ed., *Beiträge zur quantitativen vergleichenden Unternehmensgeschichte*, Historischsozialwissenschaftliche Forschungen, Vol. 19, Stuttgart, 1985, pp. 94–125.

Wilfried Feldenkirchen: Deutsches Kapital in China, Erwelterte Fassung eines im April 1983 beim 2. Europaischen Bankenkolloquium in Frankfurt gehaltenen Vortrages. In: Bankhistorisches Archiv Heft 2. 1983, pp. 64–80.

Wilfried Feldenkirchen: Die wirtschaftliche Rivalität zwischen Deutschland und England im 19. Jahrhundert. In: Zeitschrift für Unternehmensgeschichte. Jg. 25, 1980, p. 77–107.

Wilfried Feldenkirchen: Technologie, Wirtschaftswachstum und Arbeitszeit im internationalen Vergleich. Deutschland, Großbritannien. Frankreich, Belgien und die USA 1835–1914. In: Technologie, Wirtschaftswachstum und Arbeitszeit im internationalen Vergleich (=Beiheft 24 der Zeitschrift für Unternehmensgeschichte), Wiesbaden 1983, pp. 75–155.

Wilfried Feldenkirchen: Die Zoll- und Handelspolitik 1914–1933, in the forthcoming *Papers*: Papers of the 11. Arbeitstagung der Gesellschaft für Sozial- und Wirtschaftsgeschichte, April 1984 in Stuttgart.

Gustav Goldbeck: Kraft für die Welt. Klöckner-Humboldt-Deutz AG

1864–1964. Düsseldorf-Wien 1964.

Leo Grebler: Das volkswirtschaftliche Problem der industriellen Absatzorganisation. Diss. Gießen 1926.

L. F. Haber: *The Chemical Industry, 1900–1930: International Growth and Technological-Change*, Oxford, 1971.

Bernhard Harms: Die Zukunft der deutschen Handelspolitik, vol. 1, Jena 1925.

Friedrich Wilhelm Henning: Die Industrialisierung in Deutschland 1800–1914, Paderborn 1984.

Reinhold Henzler: Außenhandel, Betriebswirtschaftliche Hauptfragen von Export und Import. Wiesbaden 1961.

Julius Hirsch: Organisation und Form des Handels und der staatlichen Binnenhandelspolitik. In: Grundriß der Sozialökonomik, 5. Abtailung. Vol. 1, Tübingen 1918, pp. 38–235.

Walther G. Hoffmann: Strukturwandlungen im Außenhandel der deutschen Volkswirtschaft seit der Mitte des 19. Jahrhunderts, *Kyklos*, Vol. 20, 1967, pp. 287–306.

Walther G. Hoffmann, et al.: Das Wachstum der deutschen Wirtschaft seit der Mitte des 19. Jahrhunderts, Berlin, 1965.

Paul M. Hohenberg: Chemicals in Western Europe 1850–1914. Chicago 1967.

Gerhart Jacob-Wendler: Deutsche Elektroindustrie in Lateinamerika. Siemens und AEG (1890–1914) (=Beiträge zur Wirtschaftsgeschichte 16), Diss. München 1981.

Günther Jantzen: Hamburgs Ausfuhrhandel im XX. Jahrhundert. Ein Beitrag zur Geschichte eines deutschen Kaufmannsstandes und des "Verein Hamburger Exporteure" 1903–1953, Hamburg 1953.

Thomas R. Kabisch: Deutsches Kapital in der USA. Von der Reichsgründung bis zur Sequestrierung (1917) und Freigabe, Stuttgart 1982.

Hugo Kaulen: Die internationalen Beziehungen der deutschen Kunstseidenindustrie, Diss, Köln 1929.

Hermann Kellenbenz: Deutsche Wirtschaftsgeschichte, vol. 2. Vom Ausgang des 18. Jahrhunderts bis zum Ende des Zweiten Weltkrieges. München 1981.

Charles P. Kindleberger: Germany's Overtaking England, 1806–1914. In: Weltwirtschaftliches Archiv, vol. 111, 1975, pp. 477–504.

Rudolf Kleeberg: Das Exportkartell als Absatzorgan, Köln und Opladen 1959.

Werner Kliem: Das Wesen der Ausfuhrgemeinschaft und ihre Exportaussichten. Diss. Berlin 1934.

Heinrich Koch: 75 Jahre Mannesmann. Geschichte einer Erfindung und eines Unternehmens. Düsseldorf 1965.

Otto Kröger: Direckte Industrieausfuhr nach Übersee und hanseatischer Ausfuhrhandel, Diss. Hamburg 1940.

Hans Kühn: Der Ausfuhrzwischenhandel im Übersee-Verkehr. Grundzüge seiner Technik und Organisation und seine wirtschaftliche Bedeutung. Diss. Leipzig 1907.

League of Nations (ed.): Memorandum on Balances of Payments on Foreign Trade Balances, vol. I–II, Genf 1925.

Friedrich Lenz: Wesen und Struktur des deutschen Kapitalexports vor 1914. In: Weltwirtschaftliches Archiv, vol. 18, 1922.

Hermann Levy: Die Grundlagen der Weltwirtschaft, Leipzig, 1924.

Joseph Loewe: Die elektrotechnische Industrie. In: Die Störungen im deutschen Wirtschaftsleben während der Jahre 1900ff., vol. 3.3 (=Schriften des Vereins für Social-politik 107). Leipzig 1903.

Jean Marczewski: Le Produit physique de l'économie Française de 1789 à 1913. Comparaison avec la Grande-Bretagne (=Cahiers de l'ISEA, A. F. 4), 1965, pp. VII–CLIV.

Conrad Matschoss: Ein Jahrhundert deutscher Maschinenbau von der mechanischen Werkstätte bis zur Deutschen Maschinenfabrik 1819–1919, Berlin 1919.

Brian R. Mitchell (ed.): European Historical Statistics 1750–1970, London 1975.

Maximilian Müller-Jabusch: Fünfzig Jahre Deutsch-Asiatische Bank 1890–1939, Berlin 1940.

Hans Werner Nissen: Die wirtschaftliche Bedeutung der Ausfuhrhändler deutscher Industrieerzeugnisse. Diss. Halle-Wittenberg 1931.

Anne Marie Overbeck: Die wesentlichen Methoden und Gestaltungskräfte in der deutschen Außenwirtschaft von Weltkrieg zu Weltkrieg. Diss. Heidelberg 1946.

Dietmar Petzina: Die deutsche Wirtschaft in der Zwischenkriegszeit (Wissenschaftliche Paperbacks 11, Sozial- und Wirtschaftsgeschichte), Wiesbaden 1977.

Hans Pohl: Die Konzentration in der deutschen Wirtschaft vom ausgehenden 19. Jahrhundert bis 1945. In: Die Konzentration in der deutschen Wirtschaft seit dem 19. Jahrhundert (=Beiheft 11 der Zeitschrift für Unternehmensgeschichte), Wissbaden 1978, pp. 4–44.

Andreas Predohl: Verkehrspolitik, Göttingen 1958.

Fritz Redlich: Die volkswirtschaftliche Bedeutung der deutschen Teerfarbenindustrie, München-Leipzig 1914.

Franz Rips: Die Stellung der deutschen Eisenindustrie in der Außen-handelspolitik 1870–1914. Diss, Jena 1941.

Wilhelm Röpke: Weltwirtschaft und Außenhandelspolitik, Berlin 1931.

Hans Russenberger: Die Auswirkungen der Industrialisierung von Agrarländern auf Industrie-Export-Staaten. Diss. Sankt Gallen 1948.

Erich Schäfer: "Wandlungen in der absatzwirtschaftlichen Organisation des Fertigwarenexportes," in *Deutschland und die Weltwirtschaft*, Schriften des Vereins für Socialpolitik. N.F. 10, Berlin, 1954, pp. 201–30.

Ingvar Svennilson: Growth and Stagnation in the European Economy, Genf 1954.

Richard H. Tilly: Verkehrs- und Nachrichtenwesen, Handel, Geld-, Kredit- und Versicherungswesen 1850–1914. In: Handbuch der deutschen Wirtschafts- und Sozialgeschichte. ed. by H. Aubin/W. Zorn, vol. 2, Stuttgart 1978, pp. 563–98.

Paul Ufermann: Der deutsche Stahltrust, Berlin 1927.

Hans-Peter Ullmann: Staatliche Exportförderung und private Export-initiative. Probleme des Staatsinterventionismus im Deutschen Kaiserreich am Beispiel der staatlichen Außenhandelsförderung (1880–1919). In: Vierteljahresschrift für Sozial- und Wirtschaftsge-schichte, Vol. 65, 1978, pp. 158–216.

Helmut, Vogt: Überseebeziehungen von Felten & Guilleaume (1874–1919). Eine Fallstudie zur Absatzstrategie der deutschen elektro-technischen Industrie im Kaiserreich (=Beiträge zur Wirtschafts-geschichte 11), Stuttgart 1979.

Ernst Wagemann: Struktur und Rhythmus der Weltwirtschaft, Hamburg 1931.

Rolf Wagenführ: Die Bedeutung des Außenmarktes für die deutsche Industriewirtschaft (=Sonderheft 41 des Instituts für Konjunktur-forschung), Berlin 1936.

Peter-Christian Witt: Staatliche Wirtschaftspolitik in Deutschland 1918–1923. Entwicklung und Zerstörung einer modernen wirtschafts-politischen Strategie. In: Feldman, G. D. et al. (ed.), Die deutsche Inflation. Eine Zwischenbilanz, Berlin/New York 1982, pp. 151–179.

Comment

Hisashi Watanabe
Kyoto University

The paper of Professor Feldenkirchen is very informative, and I would like at first to express my appreciation of his thoroughgoing research, including archives work, in preparing this paper, which gives us a comprehensive view of this little-explored field of German business history. Now we have a broader perspective on the basic changes in the German export institutions, especially during the period 1850–1914. Furthermore, his list of citations is also an instructive contribution to those researching the growth of, and change in, the German export trade from the middle of the 19th century.

This does not mean I have no questions. I would like to raise a few points which do not concern fact finding, but rather views expressed in the paper.

1. If I understand Professor Feldenkirchen correctly, he has emphasized relatively strong correlations among three tendencies in the period concerned, i.e., the priority of capital- or technology-intensive industries in the industrial structure, the priority of capital or technologically sophisticated goods in export goods formation, and the priority of direct export in the export channels. Generally speaking, I have an impression that he might have been a little too eager to stress the role of capital- or technology-intensive industries to clarify the factors of change; we must pay a little more respect to the unchangeable factors. He himself pointed out the share of consumer goods in the export of finished products amounted to almost 75% in 1880, and it was still approximately 50% right before World War I began. The share of textiles in the export of finished goods dropped, according to his description, from 80% in 1855 to

25% in 1913—a drastic fall. However, the share of finished goods itself rose considerably from the middle of the 19th century to the outbreak of World War I, so that the share of textiles in the total export did not decrease so dramatically as its share in the export of finished goods. In any case the value of 25% for a single category of export goods should not be underestimated. In my opinion, the formation of German export goods before World War I was characterized not only by the increasing importance of capital goods but also by the persistent, even if declining, importance of textile goods.

2. According to Professor Feldenkirchen, the role of the so-called independent industrial export trade of the industrial centers was declining steadily in the latter half of the 19th century. However, I am a little skeptical as to whether this category did not survive the changes in the German export trade. If I understand him correctly, the firms concerned refer to the chain of commission merchants for certain groups of goods, including textiles and ironmongery produced by *Manufakturisten* or *Fabrikanten* in the Lower Rhenish area, which played a decisive role in the industrialization of Germany. It is very likely that they succeeded in turning themselves gradually to one of the special trade functions, such as transportation, insurance, warehousing, and, not last, banking (*Privatbankier*). Certainly they were no longer direct executers of export trade, but they offered services indispensable to the formation of the infrastructure for expanding German export. In this sense, I do not see a contradiction in the relationship between independent export trading firms and newly emerging industrial enterprises, but rather a division of functions.

3. When we thus turn our attention to the export trading firms in the "traditional" industries I do not find it so easy to clearly distinguish between "direct" or "independent" export and "indirect" or "dependent" export. Even when "independent" export trading firms seem to have played a great role, they were often connected more or less with Fabrikanten in family and capital accounts (for instance in the case of Hasenclever in Remscheid or von der Heydt in Elberfeld). In such cases "indirect" export trade by "independent" trading firms could be considered as

"quasi-direct" trade by "quasi-dependent" firms. In my opinion the method of dichotomy is not adequate to investigating these industry groups at least.

4. As for the Hanseatic export trade, Professor Feldenkirchen generalizes that "with the growing share of exported capital goods the foreign trade organization proved less and less suitable for the handling of exports." I would like to give one case against this generalization. C. Illies & Co. was established in Nagasaki in 1859, as Professor Chalmin also mentions. After a few years Carl Illies moved the headquarters from Nagasaki to Hamburg. In the first stage of the industrialization of Japan, C. Illies supplied chemical goods, raw materials, and textile machines from Germany and Britain. After World War I, it established branch offices in China and Manchuria too and played a major role in export from Germany to East Asia until World War II, especially the export of precision machines and ship apparatus. After the War, in 1951, C. Illies again opened trade with Japan, and today it has branch offices and subsidiaries not only in East Asia but also in Africa and America. The share of the trade with Japan amounted to 27% of the total sales of the Illies group in 1983.

The most important goods C. Illies deals in now are machine tools, plastic and rubber processing machines, press machines, paper machines, foodstuff processing apparatus, and, not last, sophisticated consumer goods. It offers its services especially to small and medium-scale enterprises in Germany which are not strong in capital account but are still technologically supreme in the world market. C. Illies deals with licenses, too, and exports goods produced in Japan under the license introduced by C. Illies to other Asian countries through its own sales network. The chairman of the Illies group, Karl Heinz Illies, is now the president of the chamber of commerce in Hamburg, and C. Illies & Co. in Tokyo is the commercial representative of Free and Hanse City Hamburg. The case of C. Illies illustrated how successfully, given the right circumstances, a Hanseatic export trading firm can achieve enterprise growth under the accelerated process of the industrialization in Europe and Japan.

5. Professor Feldenkirchen did not forget to mention the role of such institutions as consulates and chambers of commerce.

However, he gave few words to the contribution of these institutions. From the viewpoint of comparative history the role of chambers of commerce should not be neglected, especially as to the functions of gathering information and organizing entrepreneurial activities, which are also indispensable functions of Japanese *sōgō shōsha* (general trading companies). In Germany, chambers of commerce have made great contributions in building up the decisively export-oriented infrastructure of the regional economy, especially through promoting export by small and medium-scale firms. In this sense I would like to see a study of the functional equivalence of the two institutions, each characteristic of its respective country, i.e., the German chamber of commerce and Japanese sōgō shōsha.

Response

Wilfried Feldenkirchen

Between 1850 and 1933 German export changed its structure due to German industrialization and developing world trade. Professor Watanabe recognizes that development too, but stresses "unchangeable factors" and attributes a lot more importance to them than they had. In reality, it was not the unchangeable factors that were important for the structural change in German foreign trade organization between 1850 and 1933, but rather the dynamics of the capital-intensive new industries, the growing concentration in industry, and the expansion of the traffic and communications system. All this provided the basis for increased direct exports. Fairs and exhibitions had a certain relevance, but the foundation of export departments and of dependent trade firms, or foreign investments, were much more important. The traditional trade companies worked more or less for small and medium-sized firms or in countries of lesser importance to German foreign trade. Consulates and chambers of commerce endorsed exports and gave advertising support, but even though their backing may have been helpful in some cases, their overall relevance should not be overestimated.

Professor Watanabe's helpful comments dealt more with the situation in the mid-19th century than with the development of German export organization in the period 1850–1933 that I was talking about.

The Business History of the Sōgō Shōsha in International Perspective

Hideki Yoshihara
Kobe University

I. Historical Perspective and Cross-national Comparison

Given that the *sōgō shōsha*—the general trading company—is a uniquely Japanese institution, is it really meaningful to hold an international business history conference devoted solely to the sōgō shōsha? It is natural for such a question to be raised, so it was decided that the conference would adopt as its central theme the question, How and through what sorts of organization were the *functions* performed in Japan by the sōgō shōsha (in particular, the export function) performed in the United States and various countries in Europe?

There are, of course, many points and issues that need to be clarified regarding this question, and I discussed them to a certain extent in my opening paper.[1] They may be summarized in the following three questions:

1. Why did the sōgō shōsha develop in Japan?
2. What kinds of foreign trade organization existed in the United States and Europe and why did they develop in the manner that they did?
3. Is there a common logic which explains the development of foreign trade organizations in Japan, Europe, and the United States?

These questions demanded that two approaches be adopted by conference participants. They were to make international comparisons, specifically, comparisons between Japan, the United States, Great Britain, Germany, and France, and they were to take a historical approach. For Japan, the period of history covered was from around 1870, when the sōgō shōsha had their start, to around 1940. A similar time span was set for the other four countries as well.

In what follows I would like to report on a number of the findings concerning the history of the sōgō shōsha which emerged from the 10 papers presented at the conference and the two-and-a-half days of discussion and half-day of concluding debate during the conference itself.

II. The Management System and Human Resources

The sōgō shōsha is unique to Japan and is not found in other countries. (Some argue that something like the Japanese sōgō shōsha existed in Britain. I will address this point below.) Why, then, did it develop in Japan?

Prior to the conference, several theories existed regarding the development of the sōgō shōsha. Nakagawa Keiichirō argued that the sōgō shōsha represented organized entrepreneurship. Morikawa Hidemasa and Daitō Eisuke posited the view that they represented a way to fully use scarce resources, human resources in particular. Yamamura Kōzō emphasized the risk-reduction and economies-of-scale aspects of the sōgō shōsha. Yoshihara Kunio pointed to market differences.[2] Three new hypotheses emerged at the conference.

Mitsui Bussan (Mitsui and Co.), the pioneer among Japan's sōgō shōsha and the epitome, some think, of that corporate form, was established in 1876 and developed into a full-fledged sōgō shōsha during the first years of the current century. In the late 19th century, as Mitsui Bussan was developing into a sōgō shōsha, three important events occurred which had a far-reaching impact on the form of foreign trade organizations. The first was the development of undersea cable communications, which made transatlantic telegraphic communication between the United States and England possible in 1866. The second was the opening of the Suez Canal in 1869, which contributed to the development of shipping between Europe and Asia. The third was the development of international commodity exchanges.

These three developments decreased the difficulties and risks of international trade and brought about great changes in the patterns of international trade organization. One such change was the transformation of general trading firms like the British colonial merchants into commission merchants. Another was the rise of the small special-ized traders.[3] It was precisely during the period that these con-trapuntal tendencies appeared in the trading firms of Europe and America that Mitsui Bussan, Mitsubishi Shōji (Mitsubishi Corp.), Suzuki Shōten (Suzuki and Co.), and other sōgō shōsha appeared and developed in Japan.

When viewed in an international context, one of the distinctive aspects of the sōgō shōsha is that they developed only in Japan, a point which has been the subject of extensive debate. A further distinctive feature of the sōgō shōsha was brought out in the con-ference discussion. This is the particularity of the *period* during which sōgō shōsha arose and developed. It was during the late 19th and early 20th centuries, when a movement away from developing into sōgō shōsha represented the dominant trend among international trade organizations, that the sōgō shōsha developed in Japan. Thus, the development of the sōgō shōsha in Japan is distinctive in two senses.

Why, then, did the sōgō shōsha develop in pre-World War II Japan? In his paper Yamazaki Hiroaki gives the following as the reasons why Mitsui Bussan developed into a sōgō shōsha: (1) the superior leadership abilities of the company's founder, Masuda Takashi; (2) business with the government during the early period; (3) the development of a risk-management system for trading on one's own account; and (4) business with the Mitsui zaibatsu. Of these, the third and fourth reasons received particularly strong atten-tion at the conference. If one interprets the third reason broadly, one could say that the company developed a modern management system. One could also include as part of this broader definition a global network for the collection, analysis, and transfer of informa-tion among domestic and overseas branches, a managerial account-ing system, and a personnel-management system covering the recruitment, training, and placement of personnel. In addition, one could label the global organizational structure which delineated the functional relationships among, and the lines of authority and communication between, the home office and domestic and foreign branch offices as a further aspect of the modern management system.[4]

Mitsubishi Shōji and the other sōgō shōsha, too, had to a considerable extent developed a modern management system.[5]

Mitsui Bussan, which started with commission-based transactions with the government as its main business, later diversified the products it handled and the geographical areas in which it transacted its business by increasing the amount of trade on its own account, eventually developing into a sōgō shōsha. As Yamazaki points out, this increase in trading on its own account depended on the development of its risk-management system. While there is a lack of information regarding the situation in other companies, it is likely that there, too, it was because a modern management system had been developed to a greater or lesser extent that they were able to deal in a wide range of products on a global scale.

The high qualifications of the personnel must also be noted with respect to this modern management system. Mitsui Bussan began regularly recruiting college graduates in the 1880s, and by 1914 had 731 such individuals in its ranks. While this figure was lower in the other sōgō shōsha, they nevertheless did employ a considerable number of college graduates. These individuals became foreign trade experts and composed the lower, middle, and top levels of management. Most did not go to other firms, but remained in their particular companies for extended periods of time. Their level of expertise was high and they also possessed a high degree of loyalty to their company.[6] The modern management system of the sōgō shōsha was able to perform its functions through these highly qualified trade specialists, supervisors, and managers.

Let us compare these characteristics with those of the trading companies of other countries. Did the colonial merchants of England, the general merchants of the United States, the Hanseatic merchants of Germany, and various other small-scale specialized trading firms develop modern management systems? Did they maintain within their ranks a large number of college graduates?

Stephanie Jones's paper on the Inchcape group is instructive on this point. This company was comprehensive with respect to products handled, regions in which business was conducted, and function, and it was large in scale. To this extent it resembled the Japanese sōgō shōsha. The present Inchcape group was established in 1958. It was a loose association of a large number of independent trading houses and was not an integrated organization based on a common business strategy, a common management system, or common management resources. The central supervisory unit of the group's head office was relatively small-scale. Given these facts, it would appear that a modern management system had not developed. If one looks at the companies which composed the group, one finds that they were primarily rather small, family-owned firms which did not for the most employ college graduates.[7] Here too, it would be difficult to find a modern management system. And the Inchcape group was not exceptional in these respects. We would probably find a similar situation in other non-Japanese trading firms. That is, in the pre-World War II period foreign trading firms had not, as a rule, developed modern management systems, nor did they possess a pool of highly educated employees.

It is sometimes said that the sōgō shōsha performed the role of a commodity exchange. It was the fact that the sōgō shōsha had developed a modern management system that made this possible. Borrowing the terminology of Alfred Chandler, we can say that a modern management system and a pool of highly qualified personnel constitute a "visible hand." We could argue that the sōgō shōsha's "visible hand" was able to perform the exchange function more efficiently than the "invisible hand" of the commodity exchange.[8] Mitsui Bussan, Mitsubishi Shōji, and other sōgō shōsha were able to counter the "invisible hand" of the market because they possessed this "visible hand" and were therefore able to grow into sōgō shōsha. By contrast, the non-Japanese trading firms had not developed "visible hands" and were thus forced to delegate their transactions to the "invisible hand" of the market. They were therefore unable to develop into sōgō shōsha. It would seem that the development of a modern management system and a pool of highly qualified personnel represent an important explanatory variable in explaining why the sōgō shōsha developed in Japan and, in particular, why they did so during the late 19th century and the early 20th century, the period when the trend away from developing into the sōgō shōsha form was apparent in Europe and the United States.

III. Business with Zaibatsu Firms

In his paper on the prewar Japanese sōgō shōsha, Yamazaki refers to Mitsui Bussan, Mitsubishi Shōji, Suzuki Shōten, Ōkura Shōji (Ōkura and Co.), and Iwai Shōten (Iwai and Co.) and states that these five firms were in each case able to develop into sōgō shōsha on the basis of their business with a specific company group (referred to hereafter as a zaibatsu). The specific form of the ties with the zaibatsu differed among the sōgō shōsha, and the manner in which the transactions with the zaibatsu served as a factor in the development of these firms into sōgō shōsha also varied. For example, in the case of Mitsubishi Shōji, which began as a trading department of the Mitsubishi zaibatsu, business with firms in the Mitsubishi zaibatsu represented a decisive factor in its development. In contrast, for Mitsui Bussan, which began as a *goyo shonin* (a merchant working for the government), the importance of transactions with the Mitsui zaibatsu was not as important a factor as it was for Mitsubishi Shōji.[9]

Nevertheless, in comparison with non-Japanese trading houses, it is not these differences of degree of linkage between sōgō shōsha and their respective zaibatsu that is most apparent, but rather the fact that each sōgō shōsha built its development into a sōgō shōsha on the basis of business with a particular group of Japanese companies. Since the activities of a Japanese zaibatsu were not limited to a particular industrial area, business with a zaibatsu meant the handling of a wide range of products and materials. Hence it is possible to see this factor as contributing to the development of the sōgō shōsha in Japan.

Although sōgō shōsha did conduct business with non-zaibatsu firms, these too were for the most part Japanese companies. The main business of the sōgō shōsha was above all with Japanese companies. With their export of Japanese goods overseas and their import of raw materials and other products into Japan, the sōgō shōsha were firmly rooted in the Japanese economy and Japanese industry, and in this sense they were truly *Japanese* sōgō shōsha.

By contrast, the growth of firms without a significant base of transactions with home-country firms is hardly unusual in the case of non-Japanese traders. Jones's paper points to the difference in linkage between the company and the home-country economy as one of the differences between the Inchcape group and the Japanese sōgō shōsha. The Inchcape group did not have strong links with the British economy and transactions with England did not represent a major proportion of its total transactions. As already mentioned, the Inchcape group still maintains its character as a loose association of a large number of trading houses. Many of these constituent firms are not based in Britain but in such overseas countries as India, Sri Lanka, Malaysia, Singapore, Thailand, China, Hong Kong, and the Philippines, and many have as their primary business domestic trade in these countries and trade between these countries and countries other than Britain. Their ties to the British economy are not, as a rule, strong, and such ties do not represent a major factor in their growth.

What is true for the Inchcape group is also true for other British trading houses and colonial merchants (Gill and Duffus, Harrisons and Crosfield, Lonrho, Sime Darby, Antony Gibbs, Guthrie, etc.). As J. R. Killick points out in his paper, the trading firms involved in the transatlantic cotton trade consisted of many firms which did not have strong roots in their home-country economy.[10] From this perspective, it is not necessarily appropriate to consider such trading companies *British* trading companies. Perhaps we could call them *expatriate* British general trading companies.

IV. Undifferentiated Commodities of Low Technology

As discussed above, the Japanese sōgō shōsha developed through the export of products and the import of raw materials and machinery on behalf of companies (particularly manufacturing firms) affiliated with a particular zaibatsu. Why did these companies not undertake the export of products directly? The experiences of Germany and the United States, discussed in two conference papers, are instructive.

According to Wilfried Feldenkirchen, the indirect export of German manufactured goods through trading companies was the norm until the mid-19th century. However, the ratio of products exported directly by manufacturing firms gradually grew. Feldenkirchen estimates that by 1913 the ratio had grown to over one half and by 1935 surpassed the two-thirds level. Why did the mode of export marketing change hands in this manner from the trading companies to the manufacturers?

Feldenkirchen cites three reasons which are grounded in the nature of the products exported, the manufacturing firms, and the export market. As industrialization proceeded capital goods of the electrical machinery and chemical industries came to constitute the core of German exports, and this gave rise to the need to provide technical assistance, repair and maintenance, and other services to the user. It was difficult for the trading firms to respond effectively to such needs, requiring the manufacturing firms to involve themselves directly in exporting. These capital-goods manufacturing firms were quite large in scale and were blessed with financial resources, and were thus able to establish their own organizations to conduct this direct exporting. The major markets for German industrial goods were found in the advanced countries of Europe and North America. The differences between these markets and the home market were not all that great, so it was not too difficult for manufacturing firms to involve themselves in these markets through direct exports.

Incidentally, not all the products of Germany's manufacturing firms were exported directly. Toys, jewelry, certain steel products, textiles and apparel, and leather goods, among others, were exported by trading companies. The scale of the firms manufacturing these goods was small and most did not possess the financial capacity to engage in direct exporting. Furthermore, these products were not advanced technologically and there was little need for the producer to provide servicing. It should be noted, however, that in markets outside Europe and the United States, even electrical machinery, chemicals, steel, and other capital goods were exported primarily through trading companies.

Next, according to Glenn Porter's report on American foreign trade organization, the general merchant was the primary medium for exports from the latter half of the 18th century through the early years of the 19th. After this, the specialized trading firm gradually replaced the general merchant. At the time, the major export products were cotton, tobacco, wheat, corn, and lumber, all of which do not require marketing related services. After the turn of the century, exports of various types of machinery and durable consumer goods gradually increased. In these product areas, one finds numerous examples of manufacturing firms exporting directly. In such instances, it was typical for the firm to utilize overseas the marketing techniques that had proven successful in the domestic market (so-called American-style marketing). This was particularly true in the case of the export markets in Europe.

The examples of the United States and Germany hint at an answer to the question of why manufacturing firms in Japanese zaibatsu did not engage in their own exporting. We can see that the characteristics of the products exported are significant. In both Germany and the United States, the products which were exported directly by manufacturing firms were primarily products involving a high level of technology or differentiation. By contrast, products which did not involve advanced technologies, which did not involve brand identification, and which did not require maintenance and other services were exported through trading companies in both the United States and Germany.

What, then, were the primary export products of pre-World War II Japan? Japan's major export products during the latter half of the 19th century and the early years of the 20th century were raw silk, silk cloth, cotton thread, cotton cloth, tea, copper, matches, and china.[11] All of these can be considered low-technology, undifferentiated products. Technically advanced goods (perhaps best exemplified by machinery) and differentiated products such as consumer durables constituted only an extremely small proportion of Japan's exports. One reason that manufacturing firms in zaibatsu did not engage in direct exporting but exported through sōgō shōsha lies in the fact that, as we have just seen, their export products were low-technology goods or undifferentiated goods for which there was little need for specialized marketing services on the part of the manufacturer.

It deserves note that even in prewar Japan some manufacturing firms exported directly. Ajinomoto and Matsushita Electric Industrial cultivated overseas markets themselves and represent two

of the few examples of direct manufacturer exporting.[12] Ajinomoto
produced artificial flavorings and Matsushita, batteries, bicycle
headlights, and electric fans. These can be considered advanced
technology and/or differentiated products. As in Germany and the
United States, advanced technology and differentiated products
were exported directly by the manufacturer in Japan.

V. Toward a Definition of the Sōgō Shōsha

While some business historians have recently begun to argue that
something which can be described as a general trading firm also
existed in England and that therefore the sōgō shōsha is not something which exists only in Japan,[13] we already found in discussing
the Inchcape group and other British general trading companies
(often referred to as colonial merchants) that on two points—whether or not they were modern business enterprises and whether or
not they were firmly rooted in the home economy—there is a basic
difference between the two. Thus, the Japanese sōgō shōsha and
the British general trading companies, in spite of their similarities
on the surface, were fundamentally different with respect to internal
organizational characteristics and external function.

The comparison of the Japanese sōgō shōsha and the British
general trading company expands the definition of the Japanese sōgō
shōsha. The most common approach in the past was to define the
sōgō shōsha as a trading company with the following two characteristics:

1. It is comprehensive in the types of products handled, in the
    geographical spread of its business activity, and in function.
2. It is very large.

We can now add the following two characteristics to that definition:

3. It takes the form of a modern business enterprise.
4. It is rooted in the home economy.

If we apply this definition to the large international commodity
traders which are sometimes said to resemble sōgō shōsha—some
examples are Anderson Clayton, McFaddens, Sprunts, Cargill,
Philipp Brothers, Richco, and Louis Dreyfus—what conclusion can
we draw? At the present conference, Killick from the United Kingdom and Philippe Chalmin from France presented papers describing

such companies. These international commodity traders had, first of all, a tendency to limit their trading activities to specific international goods, like wheat, cotton, and sugar, and in this they differ from the sōgō shōsha. In addition, they had not developed a modern management system nor did they possess a pool of highly qualified personnel. Furthermore, they engaged in a large number of offshore transactions and did not necessarily develop with the home economy as a base. Taking these points into consideration, it seems appropriate to consider the international commodity traders as something different from the sōgō shōsha.

VI. Foreign Trade Organizations in Various Countries

In preparation for this conference, I took a look at accessible published materials and spoke with specialists in Japan regarding the organization of foreign trade in Japan, the United States, Britain, Germany, and France. This preliminary investigation suggested to me that the main foreign trade organizations in each of these countries were as follows:

> Japan: sōgō shōsha
> Britain: specialized trading companies and general trading
> companies (colonial traders)
> United States: export departments of manufacturing firms
> Germany and France: not certain

What did the conference add to our knowledge about the organization of trading firms in these countries?

According to Yamazaki, the sōgō shōsha was not the only form of trading company found in prewar Japan. Particularly significant in this respect were the trading firms specializing in textiles (Nihon Menka, Tōyō Menka, Gōshō, Nihon Kiito, Itō Chū Shōji, Kanematsu Shōten et al.). In prewar Japan, then, two major forms of external trade organization existed: the sōgō shōsha and the specialized textile trading company.

Why did specialized firms develop in the area of textiles? In this regard, the comment of Kuwahara Tetsuya on Killich's paper and the discussion which followed was insightful. The textile industry was the leading Japanese industry at the time. Since the industry was large and the pace of its growth was rapid, one could specialize in textiles and still achieve economies of scale, thereby satisfying the drive for growth. These specialized textile trading companies did not simply export the products of Japan's textile companies, but often imported the raw materials. Commodities like cotton and wool were subject to severe price fluctuations. The handling of these products thus demanded a special kind of expertise as well as a quick and flexible decision-making capability.

Next, let us consider the foreign trade organizations of Great Britain. Previously, the tendency was to assume that the characteristic feature there was the development of specialized trading companies.[14] More recently, one can observe research focusing on the colonial traders, which were general trading companies. At the present conference, there was a paper on a third type, manufacturing corporations which exported directly. This was W. J. Reader's paper on Unilever and ICI, two large corporations. He points out that during the latter half of the 19th century both companies developed their own overseas marketing network and were engaged in direct export. The major products exported were chemicals (ICI), soap, and margarine (Unilever). Chemicals were an advanced-technology product, while soap and margarine were differentiated products. The primary export markets of both of these firms were the British colonies and the advanced countries of Europe and America.

What sort of division of labor was there among the specialized trading company, the colonial trader, and the direct export manufacturer, and what was the relative importance of these three types? While there were several discussions on this topic, a conclusive answer to the question must await further research. However, it does appear possible to state that among the major large corporations of Britain, those which produced goods requiring advanced technologies or differentiated products tended to engage in direct exporting.[15] On this point, the foreign trade organizations of Britain closely resemble those of Germany and the United States.

The main export goods of the United States were undifferentiated products with a low technological input, such as cotton, wheat, and lumber. They were handled primarily by general merchants and specialized trading firms. As the number of differentiated products requiring sophisticated marketing services, like sewing machines, harvesters, locomotives, and automobiles, began to expand, products began increasingly to be exported directly by manufacturers. Indeed, this meant that the change from merchant to manufacturer as the predominant marketing agent within the American domestic market, with a certain time lag, occurred in almost identical form in the overseas export market.[16]

There were no previous studies on German foreign trade organizations and Feldenkirchen's detailed report was most informative. An outline of its content has already been presented above. The major feature was that with the advance of industrialization—and in particular the advance of heavy industry—the predominant form of German export organization changed from the trading company to the manufacturer exporting directly. It can be said that Germany experienced the same sort of change as that which occurred in the United States.

Until recently, research on the French case was also virtually nonexistent. Chalmin addressed this need with the appendix to his paper. He says the most conspicuous feature of French foreign trade organization was the fact that the appropriate foreign trade organizations did not exist. There were no powerful trading companies and there were few cases of manufacturing firms engaged in exporting themselves. As a result, the growth rate of French exports was low compared with that of other European countries. The basic reason for this low growth rate, according to Chalmin, was the low level of interest in exporting on the part of the French corporations, government, and people. Exporting was viewed as a parasitic endeavor and not as an important one.

VII. Topics for Future Research

Although there have been many business history studies on the sōgō shōsha, this does not mean that the subject has been explored fully. For example, studies from a cross-national perspective were virtually nonexistent. The conference represented an attempt to explain the nature of the Japanese sōgō shōsha through comparisons with foreign trade organizations in a number of countries and is significant in that it has added a new dimension to the business history study of the sōgō shōsha. We have so far reviewed the major findings of the conference. In conclusion, I would like to touch upon the topics remaining for future study.

I stated at the outset that the conference had three basic themes. I have gone into considerable detail regarding the first and second themes. With respect to the third theme, the search for a common logic to explain the development of foreign trade organizations in various countries, including Japan, we must admit that there was not much progress. This topic remains to be explored further in future research.

One of the fruits of the conference was the characterization of the Japanese sōgō shōsha as a modern business enterprise, with a modern management system and highly qualified staff. Several research topics are suggested by this characterization. One is the source of the idea for the modern management system of the sōgō shōsha. When Mitsui Bussan established its risk-control system, did it use a foreign corporation as a model? Or did such a model exist within Japan? Was it the management and organization of the big merchant of the Edo period (1603–1868) that provided the model? The second topic is the process of the formation of the modern management system. By whom, when, for what reason, and in what way was this modern management system initiated and developed? The third is the recruitment and training of sōgō shōsha personnel. It has been stated by conference participants that it was unthinkable in Britain, Germany, France, and the United States for college graduates to find employment in trading companies prior to World War II. However, in Japan the sōgō shōsha was able to recruit a large number of college graduates. Why was this so? How did the companies train the college graduates so recruited? How did they pass on to them the specialized know-how of trade and the skills of managerial control? And how did they instill organizational loyalty? Research into the modern business enterprise character of the sōgō shōsha can be expected to greatly advance the business history study of the sōgō shōsha.

One other research topic that I would like to bring up is the clarification of the overall picture of foreign trade organization in various countries. In Great Britain, there were three types of foreign trade organization: the specialized trading company, the general trading company (the colonial merchant), and the export department of a manufacturing firm. However, we still know little about the relationships among, and the division of labor between them nor do we know much about their relative importance in the total trade picture. Just as little is known about the foreign trade organizations of Japan, the United States, Germany, and France. A major task for the future is to fill this gap in our understanding.

It would appear effective, as Feldenkirchen did in the case of Germany, to take into consideration such variables as export product, exporting company, export market, and time period. Each country developed its own pattern of foreign trade organization. If we analyze each country's development pattern in terms of its products, firms, markets, time period, and so on, perhaps we can discover a common pattern. If this should happen, we may discover the common logic which explains the development of foreign trade organizations in Japan and other countries in the world.

NOTES

1. Unless otherwise indicated, all references are to papers presented at the Fuji Conference, 1986, and published in these proceedings.
2. These hypotheses are discussed in the author's conference paper.
3. These points were touched on by Ishii Kanji in his comment on Sugiyama Shinya's conference paper. These two changes were also observed in the organizations engaged in the transatlantic cotton trade. See J. R. Killick's conference paper.
4. On the relationship between the Japanese head office and the overseas branches see Kawabe Nobuo's conference paper.
5. However, research on this matter is as yet undeveloped and conclusive comments are difficult to make.
6. On the importance of personnel in the sōgō shōsha see the following: Morikawa Hidemasa, "Sōgō shōsha no seiritsu to ronri" (The establishment and logic of the general trading company), in Miyamoto Mataji, Togai Yoshio, and Mishima Yasuo, eds., *Sōgō shōsha no keiei shi*, Tokyo, Tōyō Keizai Shimpō Sha, 1976, pp. 64–69, and Yonekawa Shin'ichi, "The Formation of General Trading

Companies," *Japanese Year Book on Business History: 1985*, Vol. 2, pp. 19–22.

7. Based on discussion which occurred during the conference.

8. The concept of the "visible hand" is used here in a somewhat broader sense than Chandler uses it. Here the visible hand is the modern management system. See Alfred D. Chandler, Jr., *The Visible Hand: The Managerial Revolution in American Business*, Cambridge, Mass., Harvard University Press, 1977.

9. Mishima Yasuo, "Sekitan yushutsu shōsha kara sōgō shōsha e: Mitsubishi Shōji" (From coal-exporting company to general trading company: Mitsubishi Shōji), in Miyamoto et al., eds., *Sōgō shōsha no keiei shi.*

10. On the British colonial traders see Sugiyama Shinya's conference paper; Yamazaki Hiroaki's conference paper; Saruwatari Keiko, "Igirisu shokuminchi shōsha no takakuteki seichō: Harrisons and Crosfield sha no jirei, 1884–1982" (The diversified development of a British colonial trading company: The case of Harrisons and Crosfield Ltd., 1884–1982), *Hitotsubashi ronsō*, Vol. 90, No. 3, *idem,* "Igirisu shōsha no keiei senryaku to soshiki: Guthrie sha no jirei, 1821–1981" (Strategy and organization in a British trading company: The case of Guthrie Company, 1821–1981), *Keiei shigaku,* Vol. 17, No. 4, 1983.

11. Matsui Kiyoshi, ed., *Kindai nihon bōeki shi* (A history of trade in modern Japan), Vol. 2, Tokyo, Yūhikaku, 1961, p. 164.

12. Outside of these two companies, there were at least six other manufacturing companies in prewar Japan which engaged in direct exporting: Dai Nippon Seitō (Dai Nippon Sugar Manufacturing), Katakura Kōgyō (Katakura Industry), Asahi Glass, Asano Cement, Shōwa Seikosho, and Kokusan Kōgyō (Kokusan Industry). The author is indebted to Suzuki Yoshitaka of Tōhoku University on this point.

13. Yonekawa, "The Formation of General Trading Companies."

14. This view is apparent, for example, in Nakagawa Keiichirō, "Nippon no kōgyōka katei ni okeru 'soshiki sareta kigyōsha katsudō' " ("Organized entrepreneurship" in the industrialization of Japan), *Keiei shigaku*, Vol. 1, No. 3.

15. See Stephen J. Nicholas, "The Overseas Marketing Performance of British Industry, 1870–1914," *Economic History Review*, 2d ser., Vol. 47, No. 4, 1984.

16. For the change in domestic marketing in the United States see

Glenn Porter and Harold C. Livesay, *Merchants and Manufacturers: Studies in the Changing Structure of Nineteenth-Century Marketing*, Baltimore: The Johns Hopkins University Press, 1971.

MEMBERS OF THE ORGANIZING COMMITTEE

Chairman:	Yonekawa Shin'ichi	(Hitotsubashi University)
	Fukuo Takeshi	(Tokyo Keizai University)
	Kobayashi Kesaji	(Ryukoku University)
	Miyamoto Matao	(Osaka University)
	Okochi Akio	(University of Tokyo)
	Yamazaki Hiroaki	(University of Tokyo)
	Yui Tsunehiko	(Meiji University)
Secretariat:	Abe Etsuo	(Meiji University)
	Kikkawa Takeo	(Aoyama Gakuin University)
	Hidaka Chikage	(University of Tokyo)
	Yoneyama Takao	(Kyoto Sangyo University)
	Carlile, Lonny	(University of Tokyo)
	Nonaka Izumi	(Aoyama Gakuin University)
	Addington, Vince	(Osaka University)

Participants in the Third Meeting of the International Conference (Third Series) on Business History

Abe Etsuo
  (Meiji University)
Chalmin, Philippe
  (Conservatoire National des
  Arts et Métiers)
Feldenkirchen, Wilfried
  (Universität Bonn)
Ishii Kanji
  (University of Tokyo)
Jones, Stephanie
  (Inchcape PLC)
Kawabe Nobuo
  (Hiroshima University)
Killick, John R.
  (Leeds University)
Kuwahara Tetsuya
  (Kyoto Sangyo University)
Livesay, Harold C.
  (Virginia Polytechnic and
  State University)

Miyamoto Matao
  (Osaka University)
Porter, Glenn
  (Hagley Museum and Library)
Reader, W. J.
  (Business History Unit,
  London School of Economics)
Sawai Minoru
  (Hokusei Gakuen University)
Sugiyama Shinya
  (Keio University)
Tatsuki Mariko
  (Teikyo University)
Watanabe Hisashi
  (Kyoto University)
Yamazaki Hiroaki
  (University of Tokyo)
Yonekawa Shin'ichi
  (Hitotsubashi University)
Yoshihara Hideki
  (Kobe University)

Index

Acting office. *See Atsukaiten*
AEG, 53
Africa: expansion to, by zaibatsu, 80
Agency business, 140–41, 148
Alexander Brown and Sons, 283
Alexander Sprunt and Son, 252–53, 256–59, 261, 263
America: expansion to, by zaibatsu, 80
Anderson Clayton and Co., 253–56, 257–61, 263
André, House of, 74
Anglo-Thai Corp., 140–42
Anticipatory transactions, and risk management, 41–44
Antimonopoly tradition, as discouraging the formation of cartels, 116
Areas of operation, expansion of (1914–30), by zaibatsu, 80–91
Asabuki Eiji, 45
Ataka & Co., Ltd, New York, 88
Ataka Shōji: opening of Dairen office, 85
Ataka Shōkai: change of name to Ataka Sangyō, 94; Hong Kong branch of, 77; imports from Tientsin and Dairen, 88; number of branch offices in 1945, 93; opening of Bombay office, 88; as sole agent in Manchurian market, 88
Ataka Yukichi, 73
Atsukaiten (acting office), 84, 97
Auditing system, internal, xi
August Thyssen: geographical advantages of, 310; opening up of foreign markets with branch offices, 310–11

Baldwin Locomotive Co.: the case of, 120–24; and trade with Cuba, 122–23; and trade with South America, 122, 123
Banking houses, private, 114
Baring Brothers, 283–84
Benxihu Coal and Iron Co., 51, 77
Binny & Co.: diversification of, 139, 140; and engineering, 140; and insurance agencies, 139; outline of history of, 138–40; and sugar refining, 139; and textile production, 139, 140
Boxer Rebellion (1900), 140
Brazil, Baldwin locomotive sales in, 122
Britain: colonial traders in, 275; harbor traders in, 277; methods in foreign trade (1870–1939), 209–32; and overseas trading, 131–57; patterns of trade, 209–13
British empire, as central fact of British trade, 214
British India Steam Navigation Co., Ltd., 131
Brokers: the age of, 274; colonial, 279; *commissionaires*, 282; commodity, 278–83
Brunner, John, 220
Brunner, Mond & Co.: and foreign merchant companies in Asia and

357